CFA Institute

CW01677911

ALTERNATIVE INVESTMENTS

CFA® Program Curriculum

2026 • LEVEL I • VOLUME 8

WILEY

ISBN 978-1-961409-90-3

May 2025

Please visit our website at www.WileyGlobalFinance.com.

WILEY

CONTENTS

How to Use the CFA Program Curriculum

The CFA® Program exams measure your mastery of the core knowledge, skills, and abilities required to succeed as an investment professional. These core competencies are the basis for the Candidate Body of Knowledge (CBOK™). The CBOK consists of four components:

A broad outline that lists the major CFA Program topic areas (www.cfainstitute.org/programs/cfa/curriculum/cbok/cbok)

Topic area weights that indicate the relative exam weightings of the top-level topic areas (www.cfainstitute.org/en/programs/cfa/curriculum)

Learning outcome statements (LOS) that tell you the specific knowledge, skills, and abilities you should gain from each curriculum topic area. You will find these statements at the start of each learning module and lesson. We encourage you to review the information about the LOS on our website (www.cfainstitute.org/programs/cfa/curriculum/study-sessions), including the descriptions of LOS "command words" on the candidate resources page at www.cfainstitute.org/-/media/documents/support/programs/cfa-and-cipm-los-command-words.ashx.

The CFA Program curriculum that candidates receive access to upon exam registration.

Therefore, the key to your success on the CFA exams is studying and understanding the CBOK. You can learn more about the CBOK on our website: www.cfainstitute.org/programs/cfa/curriculum/cbok.

The curriculum, including the practice questions, is the basis for all exam questions. The curriculum is selected/developed specifically to provide candidates with the knowledge, skills, and abilities reflected in the CBOK.

CFA INSTITUTE LEARNING ECOSYSTEM (LES)

Your exam registration fee includes access to the CFA Institute Learning Ecosystem (LES). This digital learning platform provides access to all the curriculum content and practice questions. The LES is organized as a series of learning modules consisting of short online lessons and associated practice questions. This tool is your source for all study materials, including practice questions and mock exams. The LES is the primary method by which CFA Institute delivers your curriculum experience. Here, you will find additional practice questions to test your knowledge, including some interactive questions.

DESIGNING YOUR PERSONAL STUDY PROGRAM

An orderly, systematic approach to exam preparation is critical. You should dedicate a consistent block of time every week to reading and studying. Review the LOS both before and after you study curriculum content to ensure you can demonstrate the knowledge, skills, and abilities described by the LOS and the assigned learning module. Use the LOS as a self-check to track your progress and highlight areas of weakness for later review.

Successful candidates report an average of more than 300 hours preparing for each exam. Your preparation time will vary based on your prior education and experience, and you will likely spend more time on some topics than on others.

ERRATA

The curriculum development process is rigorous and involves multiple rounds of reviews by content experts. Despite our efforts to produce a curriculum that is free of errors, we must make corrections in some instances. Curriculum errata are periodically updated and posted by exam level and test date on the Curriculum Errata webpage (www.cfainstitute.org/en/programs/submit-errata). If you believe you have found an error in the curriculum, you can submit your concerns through our curriculum errata reporting process found at the bottom of the Curriculum Errata webpage.

OTHER FEEDBACK

Please send any comments or suggestions to info@cfainstitute.org, and we will review your feedback thoughtfully.

Alternative Investments

LEARNING MODULE

1

Alternative Investment Features, Methods, and Structures

LEARNING OUTCOMES	
Mastery	***The candidate should be able to:***
☐	describe features and categories of alternative investments
☐	compare direct investment, co-investment, and fund investment methods for alternative investments
☐	describe investment ownership and compensation structures commonly used in alternative investments

INTRODUCTION

1

Alternative Investments are grouped together not because they have similar features but instead because they have characteristics distinct from traditional investments. Investing in alternatives can be done through fund investing, co-investing, or direct investing. Alternative investments typically offer investors greater diversification and higher expected returns than traditional investments but often involve longer-term, illiquid investments in less efficient markets. Investing in alternatives requires specialized knowledge. Alternative investments typically rely on more complex and richer compensation structures than traditional investments in order to better align manager and investor incentives over longer periods.

LEARNING MODULE OVERVIEW

- Alternative investments are investments other than ownership of traditional asset classes (public equity and fixed-income instruments and cash) and include private capital, real assets, and hedge funds.
- Private capital includes private equity and private debt. Real assets include real estate, infrastructure, and natural resources. Hedge funds may invest across both traditional and alternative asset classes and are distinguished by their investment approach, which often includes leverage, derivatives, or other strategies.

- Investors often consider alternative investments in pursuit of greater portfolio diversification and/or increased expected returns. In doing so, they usually face longer investment periods, reduced liquidity, and less efficient markets than for more traditional assets.
- Alternative investment fund investors fully outsource the control and management of investments in exchange for relatively high fees, while co-investment and direct investment methods involve greater investor effort and control over the selection and management of assets in exchange for relatively lower fees.
- Another common type of alternative investment structure is a limited partnership in which responsibilities are flexibly allocated between investors and managers—with managers as general partners and investors as limited partners. Limited partnerships usually have more complex compensation structures, which include both management and performance fees.
- Additional alternative investment structures include trusts and limited liability companies.

LEARNING MODULE SELF-ASSESSMENT

1. Identify which of the following choices is *most likely* an alternative investment:

   A. An investment in a hedge fund focused on traditional assets

   B. Shares in a manufacturing firm traded on the Bursa Malaysia exchange

   C. A euro foreign exchange future purchased on the Chicago Mercantile exchange

   Solution:

   The correct answer is A. An investment in a hedge fund, even one that purchases traditional exchange-traded assets, is considered an alternative investment. B is incorrect because shares traded on a public exchange, such as the Bursa Malaysia exchange, are considered traditional, not alternative, investments. C is incorrect because a euro foreign exchange future purchased on a public exchange, such as the Chicago Mercantile exchange, is considered a traditional, not an alternative, investment.

2. An advantage of investing in alternative investments *most likely* is:

   A. high liquidity.

   B. low investment fees.

   C. higher expected returns.

   Solution:

   The correct answer is C. Investors are often attracted to alternative investments seeking greater diversification and/or higher expected returns. A is incorrect because investors usually face longer investment periods, reduced liquidity, and less efficient markets with alternative investments than with more traditional assets. B is incorrect because alternative investments often carry higher fees, including performance and/or incentive fees.

3. Investors with limited experience *most likely* enter into alternative investments through:

   A. co-investing.

   B. fund investing.

   C. direct investing.

   Solution:

   The correct answer is B. Investors with limited resources and/or experience generally enter into alternative investments through fund investing, where the investor contributes capital to a fund and the fund identifies, selects, and makes investments on the investor's behalf. A is incorrect because co-investing is more appropriate for investors who already have some experience investing in funds; in co-investing, the investor invests in assets indirectly through the fund but also possesses rights (known as co-investment rights) to invest directly in the same assets. C is incorrect because direct investing, which occurs when an investor makes a direct investment in an asset without the use of an intermediary, is typically reserved for larger and more sophisticated investors.

4. When an investor invests in an asset without the use of an intermediary, it is called:

   A. co-investing.

   B. fund investing.

   C. direct investing.

   Solution:

   The correct answer is C. In direct investing, an investor makes a direct investment in an asset without the use of an intermediary. A is incorrect because in co-investing, an investor invests in assets indirectly through a fund but also possesses rights (known as co-investment rights) to invest directly in the same assets. B is incorrect because for fund investing, an investor contributes capital to a fund and the fund, not the investor, identifies, selects, and makes investments on the investor's behalf.

5. Which statement regarding alternative investment partnership structures is *most* accurate?

   A. The fund manager has limited liability for anything that goes wrong.

   B. The fund manager is a limited partner, and investors are general partners.

   C. Investors' upfront cash outflow can be a small portion of their total commitment to the partnership.

   Solution:

   The correct answer is C. Limited partners (LPs) are outside investors who own a fractional interest in the partnership based on the amount of their initial investment and the terms set out in the partnership documentation. LPs commit to future investments, and their upfront cash outflow can be a small portion of their total commitment to the fund. A is incorrect because the fund manager is the fund's general partner (GP) who runs the business and theoretically bears unlimited liability for anything that goes wrong. B is incorrect because the fund manager is the fund's general partner, not a limited partner, and the investors are the limited partners.

6. After failing to meet the hurdle rate, which of the following would a general partner still *most likely* receive as compensation?

   A. Carried interest

   B. Management fee

   C. Committed capital

   Solution:

   The correct answer is B. Alternative investment funds are usually structured with a management fee typically ranging from 1% to 2% of assets under management (e.g., for hedge funds) or 1% to 2% of committed capital (e.g., for private equity funds). (Committed capital is the total amount of money that the limited partners have committed to the fund's future investments.) A performance fee (also referred to as an incentive fee, carried interest, or carry) is applied based on excess returns. The partnership agreement usually specifies that the performance fee is earned only after the fund achieves a return known as a "hurdle rate." The hurdle rate is a minimum rate of return that the general partner must exceed in order to earn the performance fee. A is incorrect because "carried interest" is another name for a performance fee, which is earned only after the fund achieves its hurdle rate. C is incorrect because committed capital is the total amount of money that the limited partners have committed to the fund's future investments, not a fee to the general partner.

2 ALTERNATIVE INVESTMENT FEATURES

☐ describe features and categories of alternative investments

Alternative investments are investments other than ownership of public equity securities, fixed-income instruments, or cash that represent the more traditional asset classes. These investments are referred to as alternatives to traditional asset classes because of their characteristics and the way they are structured. Investors are often attracted to alternative investments when seeking greater diversification and/or higher expected returns in exchange for what are often longer-term, illiquid investments in less efficient markets. The features of these investments necessitate specific skills and information to evaluate their performance and include unique factors investors must consider if adding them to a portfolio.

Alternative Investments: Features and Categories

Some alternative investment features are shared with traditional public debt and equity securities, while others are significantly different. Features that may distinguish alternative investments include the following:

- The need for specialized knowledge to value cash flows and risks
- Typically low correlation of returns with more traditional asset classes
- Illiquidity, long investment time horizons, and large capital outlays

These features lead to the following alternative investment characteristics:

- Different investment structures due to the challenges of direct investment

- Incentive-based fees to address/minimize information asymmetry between managers and investors
- Performance appraisal challenges

For example, while many alternative investments have equity or debt characteristics, they often require a larger or longer financial commitment due to an underlying investment's extended life cycle or different investment methods and vehicles used to align the capabilities and incentives of managers and investors over time. Unlike individual securities, the size and type of some alternative investments may also be prohibitively large for certain investors. For these reasons, most investors limit alternative investments to that portion of their portfolio designated to fund obligations several years in the future. Sophisticated investors with the longest investment time horizons, such as large pension funds, sovereign wealth funds, and not-for-profit endowments, tend to allocate a larger share of their portfolio to these assets.

Alternative investment categories include private capital, real assets, and hedge funds.

Private Capital

Private Capital is a broad term for funding provided to companies that is sourced from neither the public equity nor the public debt markets. Capital that is provided in the form of equity investments is called private equity, whereas capital that is provided as a loan or other form of debt is called private debt.

Private equity and private debt are alternative investments with features similar to public equity and public debt. For example, both private and public equity investors are company owners with residual claims to future cash flows and dividends. However, while investors in private equity may have full access to company information and latitude to influence day-to-day management and strategy decisions, investors in publicly traded equity receive only publicly available information, such as annual reports and periodic financial statements, with voting rights limited to decisions requiring shareholder approval.

Private equity refers to investment in privately owned companies or in public companies with the intent to take them private. In general, private equity is used in the *mature* life cycle stage or for firms in *decline*,with leveraged buyouts being a key approach. Private equity managers often use the greater control and flexibility of private versus public ownership to make management and strategy changes, including closing, selling, or reorganizing lines of business to increase profitability over a several-year period. **Venture capital** is a specialized form of private equity whereby ownership capital is used for non-public companies in the *early* life cycle or *startup* phase, where often an idea or business plan exists with a limited operation or customer base.

EXAMPLE 1

Venture Capital vs. Private Equity

Heartfield Digital is an early-stage digital media venture established 18 months ago. Heartfield plans to convert conventional music and art collection rights to digital form for sale and distribution. Its founders are seeking early-stage investors in order to conduct market research, build partnerships, and initiate operations.

In contrast, Arguston Inc. is a mid-sized manufacturing firm in a mature industry that is experiencing a decline in profitability. Arguston's share price has stagnated, and given its high-cost structure and dwindling operating cash flow, Arguston lacks the scale to make necessary technological upgrades to maintain competitiveness. A prospective private equity investor might consider an investment plan to restructure Arguston's operations, acquire a smaller competitor, and/or create efficiencies, perhaps by updating the plant and equipment. In several years, Arguston may emerge as a more profitable independent company or as an attractive acquisition target for a competitor.

Technically, venture capital (VC) is a form of private equity. The main difference is that while private equity investors prefer stable companies, VC investors usually come in during the startup phase. Venture capital is usually given to small companies with huge growth potential, such as Heartfield Digital, while broader types of private equity financing would be more appropriate for a mature firm, such as Arguston.

For **private debt**, in addition to private loans or bonds, venture debt is extended to early-stage firms with little or no cash flow, while distressed debt (introduced in a separate fixed-income lesson) involves public or private debt of corporate issuers believed to be close to or in bankruptcy that could benefit from investors with capital restructuring skills.

Real Assets

In contrast to financial assets, **real assets** generally are tangible physical assets, such as real estate (for example, land or buildings) and natural resources, but also include such intangibles as patents, intellectual property, and goodwill. Real assets either generate current or expected future cash flows and/or are considered a store of value. **Real estate** includes borrowed or ownership capital in buildings or land. Developed land includes commercial and industrial real estate, residential real estate, and infrastructure. Commercial real estate includes land and buildings where private business activity is the primary cash flow source, whereas residential real estate's cash flows stem from rents or mortgage payments by households. Publicly traded forms of real estate include real estate investment trusts (REITS), which are issuers of equity securities, and mortgage-backed debt securities, which are introduced and discussed in a fixed-income lesson.

Infrastructure is a special type of real asset that typically involves land, buildings and other long-lived fixed assets that are intended for public use and provide essential services. Bridges and toll roads are common examples of tangible infrastructure assets. Infrastructure may be developed either solely by governments or through a **public–private partnership (PPP)**in which private investors also have a stake. For example, a public–private partnership might be used in order to attract long-term private investment for a broadband internet investment. Infrastructure assets create cash flows either *directly* in the form of fees, leases, or other compensation for access rights or *indirectly* by promoting economic growth and supporting a government's ability to generate increased tax revenue on future economic activity. When private investors are involved, a contract known as a **concession agreement** usually governs the investor's obligations to construct and maintain infrastructure as well as the exclusive right to operate and earn fees for a pre-determined period.

EXAMPLE 2

Public–Private Partnership for Infrastructure Projects in Indonesia

PT Indonesia Infrastructure Finance (IIF) is a private national company established in 2010 by the government of Indonesia to accelerate and improve private participation in infrastructure development in Indonesia. Together with the World Bank, the Asian Development Bank, and other institutions, the IIF provides infrastructure financing and advisory services for commercially viable infrastructure projects. This approach has facilitated development of PPP projects, increased equity investment in Indonesian infrastructure projects, and increased institutional awareness and capacity to implement environmental, health, and safety and social issues. Looking ahead, the IIF anticipates the need to spend USD150 billion over a five-year period to construct power plants and toll roads. While the government will be able to fund 30% of this cost, the remainder will be financed by the private sector through PPPs.

Natural resources involve either less developed land, which itself is the source of economic value, or naturally occurring standardized products that are harvested, extracted, and/or refined. Less developed land includes farmland, timberland, or land for exploration for natural resource deposits, such as minerals or energy. Sources of return for these types of less developed land include expected price appreciation over time and cash flows. For example, farmland generates crop yields or agricultural lease payments, future timber harvests generate timberland income, and mineral or drilling rights to extract and refine natural resources can provide income. In some cases, these investments may be considered for environmental, social, and governance (ESG) purposes—for example, when promoting sustainable farming practices for agriculture or creating carbon offsets for timberland, as in the following example.

EXAMPLE 3

Using Timberland to Create Carbon Offsets

Companies eager to offset emissions are paying timberland owners not to cut acres of trees. Growing trees absorb carbon in the atmosphere.

- Companies that pay timber owners not to harvest trees receive credits in the form of carbon offsets. Large companies, which inevitably generate emissions in the course of doing business, can fund carbon offsets to demonstrate to their investors, customers, and others (including regulators) that they are serious about reducing pollution and helping the environment.
- For large and small owners of timberland, choosing not to harvest makes sense, too. Their trees continue to grow, leading to higher future volumes of timber, and they earn non-timber income in the meantime.

In other cases, undeveloped land may also have future potential for commercial, residential, or infrastructure development.

Standardized, traded goods known as **commodities** include plant, animal, energy, and mineral products used in goods and services production. Commodities do not themselves generate cash flows but, rather, are ultimately sold by commodity producers to commodity consumers for economic use. Investors seek to benefit from commodity price changes based on their future economic use as well as a lower correlation of returns versus other asset classes over the economic cycle. With their lower correlation of returns with other asset classes, commodities also can serve as a countercyclical holding and as an inflation hedge.

EXAMPLE 4

Rising Demand for Lithium, an Increasingly Important Commodity

Demand for lithium is growing rapidly as demand for electric vehicles (EVs) climbs. Lithium is popular with battery manufacturers because, as the least dense metal, it stores a large proportion of energy relative to its weight.

The sales of battery electric and plug-in hybrid electric cars exceeded 2 million for the first time in 2019. China dominates this market, accounting for more than half of all current EV sales worldwide. An industry source has forecast that EV sales will grow from 2.5 million in 2020 to approximately 11 million in 2025 and will exceed 30 million by 2030, garnering approximately 32% of the total market share for new car sales at that time.

Demand for lithium will rise accordingly. The growth in lithium demand is expected to foster new lithium mining and more production in more countries worldwide.

Other real alternative assets include tangible collectible assets, such as fine art, wine, rare coins, watches, and other rare assets, as well as intangible assets, such as patents, and litigation, and so-called **digital assets**. "Digital assets" is the umbrella term covering assets that can be created, stored, and transmitted electronically and have associated ownership or use rights.

DIGITAL ASSETS

The term "digital assets" covers a wide variety of assets, such as cryptocurrencies, tokens (security and utility), and digital collectables (such as digital art). The following diagram provides a simple breakdown of digital assets.

Digital Assets diagram

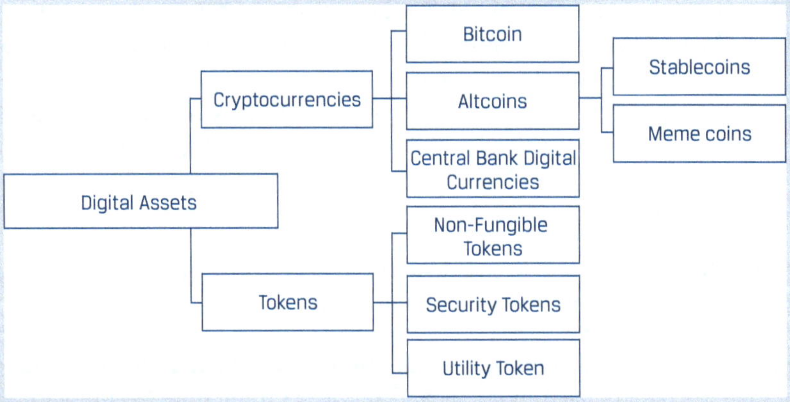

Cryptocurrency and tokens utilize cryptography, an advanced encryption technique that assures the authenticity of crypto assets. The key difference between these two classes of digital asset is that cryptocurrencies have their own blockchains, whereas crypto tokens are built on an existing blockchain.

For example, cryptocurrencies are the native asset of a blockchain—such as Bitcoin (BTC) or Ethereum (ETH). However, tokens are created as part of a platform that is built on an existing blockchain, such as the many ERC-20 tokens that make up the Ethereum ecosystem. The Ethereum ecosystem is used as a network for decentralized applications, such as non-fungible token (NFT) marketplaces and decentralized finance (DeFi) projects.

Digital assets are covered in more detail in a subsequent alternative investments learning module.

Hedge Funds

Hedge funds are private investment vehicles that may invest in public equities or publicly traded fixed-income assets, private capital, and/or real assets, but they are distinguished by their investment *approach* rather than by the investments themselves. Hedge funds make frequent use of leverage, derivatives, short selling, and other investment strategies, which often results in a substantially different risk and return profile from that of merely buying and holding the underlying assets in an investment portfolio. Investors may also invest in a portfolio of hedge funds, often referred to as a **fund of funds**.

QUESTION SET

1. Tangible physical assets that generate current or expected future cash flows and/or are considered a store of value are *best* labeled as:

   A. real assets.

   B. private equity.

   C. venture capital.

   Solution:

   The correct answer is A. In contrast to financial assets, real assets are generally tangible physical assets that generate current or expected future cash flows and/or are considered a store of value. Major categories of real assets include real estate and natural resources, as well as intangibles such as patents. B is incorrect because private equity, considered an alternative investment, is non-publicly traded capital that is invested directly in private companies (or in public companies that are being taken private). It is typically used to invest in firms in the mature life-cycle stage or in decline. C is incorrect because venture capital is ownership capital used for non-public companies in their early life cycle or startup phase.

2. Contrast private equity and venture capital.

   Solution:

   Private capital is used at different times in a company's life cycle and in different forms. Most private equity is used in the mature life cycle stage or for firms in decline. Private equity managers often use the greater control and flexibility of private versus public ownership to make management and strategy changes including closing, selling, or reorganizing lines of business to increase profitability over a several-year period. In contrast, venture capital is used for non-public companies with high growth potential in their early life cycle or startup phase. Venture capital is essentially a specialized form of private equity; it represents a small portion of the entire private equity market by value.

3. Identify which statement about a digital asset is *most* accurate. A digital asset:

   A. includes digital art but not cryptocurrencies.

B. is anything that can be stored and transmitted electronically and has associated ownership or use rights.

C. must adhere to very specific designs or requirements in order to work within the limited types of technology that support it.

Solution:

The correct answer is B. Digital assets continue to evolve and vary in terms of design and application. Digital assets can be thought of as anything that can be stored and transmitted electronically and has associated ownership or use rights. A is incorrect because digital assets include cryptocurrencies, tokens (security and utility), and digital collectables (such as digital art). C is incorrect because digital assets may take many forms (such as digital tokens and virtual currencies) and may use various underlying technologies. They are not limited to specific designs or technology.

4. Determine the correct answers to fill in the blanks: Alternative investment categories include ______________, ________________, and ______________.

Solution:

Alternative investment categories include *private capital*, *real assets*, and *hedge funds*.

3 ALTERNATIVE INVESTMENT METHODS

☐ compare direct investment, co-investment, and fund investment methods for alternative investments

Investors seeking greater diversification and higher expected returns from alternative investments must consider how best to enter into such an investment. The long-term, illiquid nature of many alternative investments along with the specialized knowledge involved in evaluating and overseeing these investments make investors more dependent on manager decisions over longer time periods. Large, sophisticated investors can address this issue by taking greater control over the investment process, while other, less sophisticated investors must outsource this process and seek to align manager incentives with investor objectives.

Alternative Investment Methods

Investors can access alternative investments in three ways:

- Fund investment (such as a in a PE fund)
- Co-investment into a portfolio company of a fund
- Direct investment into a company or project (such as infrastructure or real estate)

Institutional investors typically begin investing in alternative investments via funds. Then, as they gain experience, they may begin to invest via co-investing and direct investing. The largest and most sophisticated direct investors (such as some sovereign wealth funds) compete with fund managers for access to the best investment opportunities. Exhibit 1 shows an illustration of the three methods of investing in alternative investments. We will refer to this exhibit several times during this lesson.

Exhibit 1: Three Methods of Investing in Alternative Assets

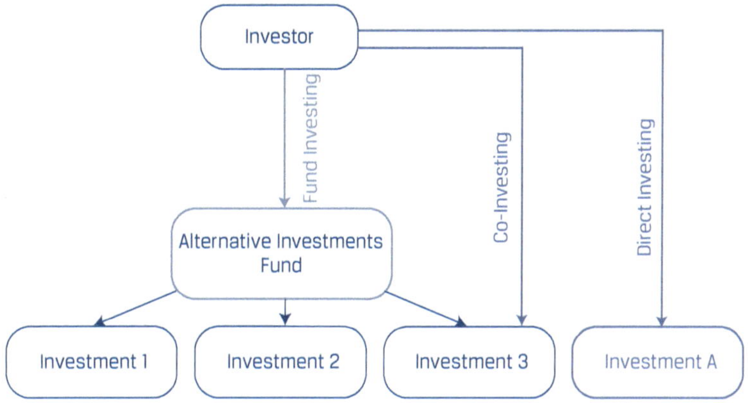

Fund Investment

Investors with limited resources and/or experience generally enter into alternative investments through **fund investing**, where the investor contributes capital to a fund and the fund identifies, selects, and makes investments on the investor's behalf. For the fund's services, the investor is charged a management fee, plus a performance fee if the fund manager delivers superior results versus a hurdle rate or benchmark. In Exhibit 1, the investor invests in the "alternative investments fund." The fund itself invests in three investments: Investments 1, 2, and 3. Fund investing can be viewed as an indirect method of investing in alternative assets.

Fund investors have little or no leeway in the sense that their investment decisions are limited to either investing in the fund or not. Fund investors typically have neither the sophistication nor the experience to invest directly on their own. Furthermore, fund investors are typically unable to affect the fund's underlying investments. Note that fund investing is available for all major alternative investment types, including hedge funds, private capital, real estate, infrastructure, and natural resources.

Allocation to alternative assets requires distinct specialized skills that many investors likely do not possess. These investors can achieve this exposure through fund investing, where one or more investors contribute capital to an investment management company that identifies, selects, manages, and monitors investments on the investors' behalf, as shown in Exhibit 2.

Exhibit 2: Alternative Investment Fund Structure

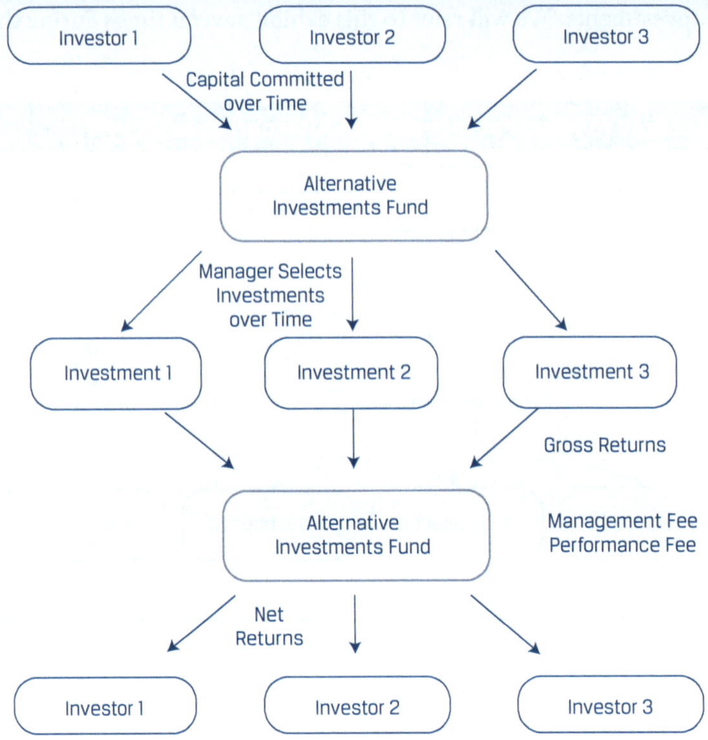

A. Investments

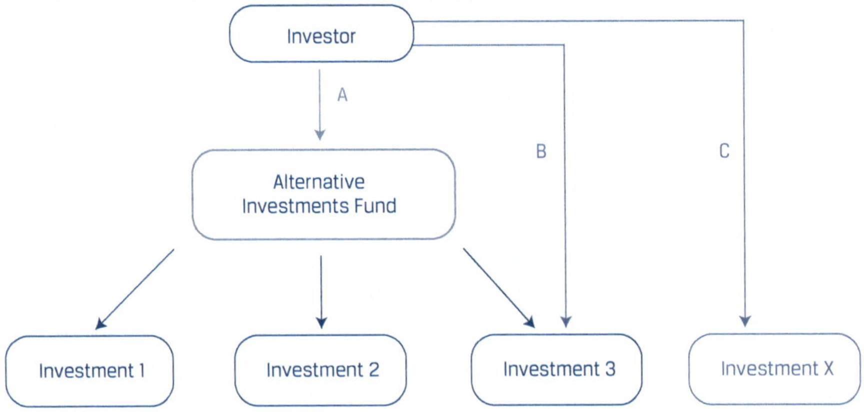

B. Returns

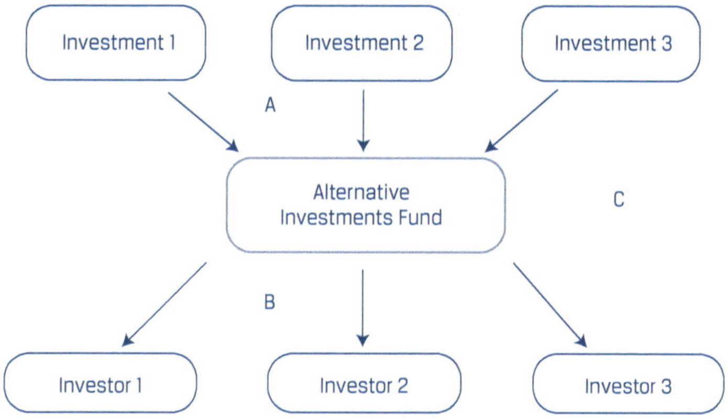

Fund investment structures for alternative investments differ substantially from traditional public equity and fixed-income fund or ETF investments. For example, alternative funds usually involve (1) the pre-commitment of funds prior to investment selection and an extended period during which the fund may not be sold, (2) higher management fees with more complex fee structures, and (3) less frequent transparency on periodic returns and fund positions versus equity or fixed-income funds. Investors in alternative funds therefore usually compensate managers using a performance-based, as opposed to flat, fee structure to better align manager and investor incentives over longer periods. Important terms are provided in a term sheet; a sample term sheet for fund investment with Tenderledge Investments LLC is provided in Exhibit 3. Further details of these terms are discussed in subsequent lessons.

Exhibit 3: Tenderledge Investment Fund VIII Limited Partner Agreement Term Sheet

Tenderledge Investment Fund VIII, L.P.
Term Sheet

Fund	Tenderledge Investment Fund VIII, L.P
General Partner	Tenderledge Investment LLC
Fund Manager	Tenderledge Investments
Maximum Size	Not to exceed USD750 million
General Partner's Commitment	Equal to at least 2% of the aggregate Commitments of the Limited Partners
Initial Closing Date	The date the General Partner determines that aggregate Commitments equal or exceed USD500 million
Final Closing Date	Twelve (12) months from the Initial Closing Date
Term of the Fund	Ten (10) years from the Initial Closing Date
Investment Policy	To provide attractive, long-term investment return from a diversified portfolio of alternative investments
ESG	In accordance with the General Partner's environmental, social, and governance policy
Management Fee	1.5% per annum of the commitment of each limited partner
Hurdle Rate	A hard hurdle rate of 10%

Tenderledge Investment Fund VIII, L.P. Term Sheet	
Performance Fee	20% of fund returns in excess of the specified hard hurdle rate
Side Letters	If any Side Letter grants more favorable rights to any Partner than those provided to other Partners, the more favorable rights will be granted to all other Partners

Co-Investment

Once investors have some experience investing in funds, prior to investing directly themselves, many investors gain direct investing experience via **co-investing**, where the investor invests in assets *indirectly* through the fund but also possesses rights (known as co-investment rights) to invest *directly* in the same assets. Through co-investing, an investor is able to make an investment *alongside* a fund when the fund identifies deals; the investor is not limited to participating in the deal solely by investing in the fund. Exhibit 1 illustrates the co-investing method: The investor invests in one deal (labeled "Investment 3") indirectly via fund investing while investing an additional amount directly via a co-investment. Co-investing allows investors to expand their investment knowledge, skills, and experience beyond what they would gain from taking a fund-only investment approach. Co-investing also provides investors access to an investment opportunity at a lower fee than they would owe as fund-only investors in the same asset. Co-investors can learn from the fund's process to eventually pursue direct investments themselves. Co-investors weigh the benefits of greater control and lower fees versus higher oversight costs.

Managers benefit from choosing one or more co-investors to

- accelerate investment timing when available funds and expected inflows are insufficient for a specific deal,
- expand the scope of available new investments, and
- increase diversification of an existing pool of fund investments.

EXAMPLE 5

Co-Investment Opportunity

Moreton Bay Pension Plan is an investor in Tenderledge LLC Alternatives Fund. Tenderledge has identified a take-private transaction in Fancy Roofing Co. that requires a USD1.5 billion capital investment. However, the fund concentration limit allows Tenderledge to invest only up to USD1 billion in any one investment. Tenderledge offers the additional USD0.5 billion to Moreton Bay Pension Plan and other investors in the fund as a co-investment on a reduced fee and no carry basis. In this case, the co-investment allows Tenderledge the ability to secure the investment without needing to bring an additional fund manager into the transaction, and the co-investors gain additional exposure to Fancy Roofing Company at a reduced management fee and zero performance fees.

Direct Investment

The largest, most sophisticated investors with sufficient skills and knowledge to manage individual alternative investments often do so via **direct investing** *without* the use of an intermediary, as previously shown in Exhibit 1 (labeled "Investment A").

Direct investors retain maximum flexibility and control when it comes to investment choice, methods of financing, and timing. In the case of private equity, this involves the purchase of a direct stake in a private company without the use of a fund managed by an external asset manager or general partner. It also requires the direct investor to have the resources to provide the specialized knowledge, skills, and oversight capabilities that direct investment requires. Although the direct investment approach usually applies to private capital and real estate, some very large investors, such as pensions and sovereign wealth funds, also invest directly in infrastructure and natural resources.

EXAMPLE 6

Direct Investment in Renewable Energy

Singapore sovereign wealth fund GIC announced in 2021 that it will directly invest USD240 million in a Singapore-based energy firm, Arctic Green Energy, becoming an equity partner in the firm. The investment will help Arctic Green Energy expand its global operations and increase its capability in geothermal energy. Geothermal energy is derived from hot underground springs and is a renewable, economically competitive, and sustainable alternative to using fossil fuels for heating and cooling. Arctic Green Energy uses geothermal resources to generate power and produce clean heat. GIC has noted that investing sustainably is one of its core long-term investment mandates.

QUESTION SET

1. Referring to the diagram below, identify the label that best corresponds to the three methods of investing in alternative assets:

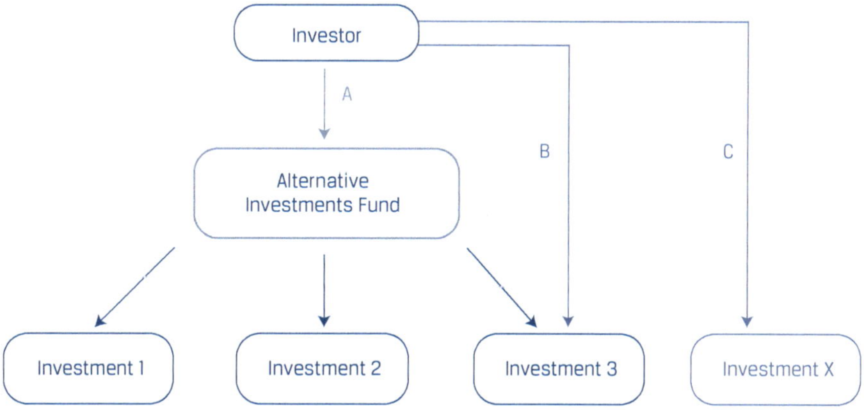

A.	1. Co-investing
B.	2. Fund investing
C.	3. Direct investing

Solution (as seen in Exhibit 1 of this lesson):

A. 2 is correct. In fund investing, the investor contributes capital to a fund and the fund identifies, selects, and makes investments on the investor's behalf.

B. 1 is correct. In co-investing, the investor invests in assets indirectly through the fund but also possesses rights (known as co-investment rights) to invest directly in the same assets.

C. 3 is correct. In direct investing, an investor makes a direct investment in an asset (labeled "Investment X" in the diagram) without the use of an intermediary.

2. Determine the correct answers to fill in the blanks:The ________ and ________ nature of many alternative investments and the ______________ required to evaluate and oversee these investments make investors more dependent on manager decisions over longer time periods.

Solution:

The *long-term*and *illiquid* nature of many alternative investments and the *specialized knowledge* required to evaluate and oversee these investments make investors more dependent on manager decisions over longer time periods.

3. Identify two reasons investment managers offer co-investment opportunities to investors. Managers might choose to add co-investors for such reasons as:

   1.

   2.

Solution:

Managers might choose to add co-investors for such reasons as:

- accelerating investment timing when available funds and expected inflows are insufficient for a specific deal.
- expanding the scope of available new investments.
- increasing diversification of an existing pool of fund investments.

4. Identify one reason an investor would elect to participate in each of the following alternative investment methods:

   1. Fund investing
   2. Co-investing
   3. Direct investing

Solution:

1. Fund investing	Fund investing gives investors with limited resources or experience an entrance into alternative investing.
2. Co-investing	Investors who have better specific skills and greater ability to allocate investments to individual assets may select a more active investment approach while retaining manager involvement. This results in lower fees for the investor than for a purely fund-based approach. Also, co-investors select and manage an investment jointly with a general fund manager, which potentially gives them greater control and higher returns than they could earn in a fund-only structure.
3. Direct investing	Direct investing offers investors flexibility and control when it comes to choosing their investments, selecting their preferred methods of financing, and planning their approach.

ALTERNATIVE INVESTMENT STRUCTURES

4

☐ describe investment ownership and compensation structures commonly used in alternative investments

Beyond the direct or indirect method of investing in alternatives, the illiquidity, complexity, and long-term nature of these investments require more complex structures to bridge potential gaps between manager and investor interests. Alternative investment structures may explicitly address both the roles and responsibilities of investors and managers to address these gaps. In addition, alternative investment structures tailor the distribution of returns between these two parties to better align the incentives (or interests) between manager and investor.

For example, managers may require investors to be responsible for future capital contributions, while investors may place restrictions on manager investment selection to avoid conflicts of interest or hostile takeovers among other investment criteria. Performance-based compensation structures, which can include minimum return requirements for investors, delayed payouts, and/or the ability to reclaim incentive compensation in the event of poor fund performance, encourage managers to maximize returns in the best interest of investors.

Alternative Investment Ownership and Compensation Structures

In this section, we discuss the ownership and compensation structures of alternative investments.

Ownership Structures

Alternative investment vehicles often take the form of partnerships in order to maximize flexibility in the investment structure to allocate business risk and return and to distribute special responsibilities between investors and managers as required. Limited partnerships, introduced in a corporate issuer lesson, involve at least one general partner (GP) with theoretically unlimited liability who is responsible for managing the fund. Limited partners (LPs) are outside investors who own a fractional interest in the partnership based on the amount of their initial investment and the terms set out in the partnership documentation. Exhibit 4 shows the basic GP/LP structure together with the various investment approaches (fund, co-investment, direct) introduced earlier.

Exhibit 4: Basic GP/LP Structure and Various Investment Approaches

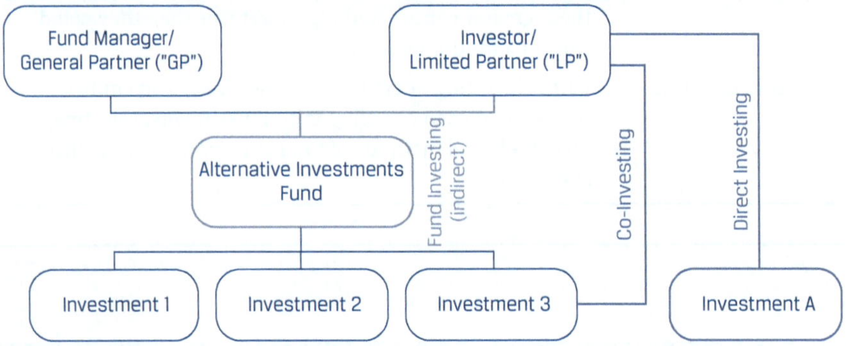

LPs commit to future investments, and the upfront cash outflow can be a small portion of their total commitment to the fund. Funds set up as limited partnerships typically have a limit on the number of LPs allowed to invest in the fund. LPs play passive roles and are not involved with the management of the fund (although co-investment rights allow for the LPs to make additional direct investments in the portfolio companies); the operations and decisions of the fund are controlled solely by the GP.

Limited partners (LPs) have their liability capped at the amount of their investment in the partnership, as shown in Exhibit 5.

Exhibit 5: Example Limited Partnership Structure

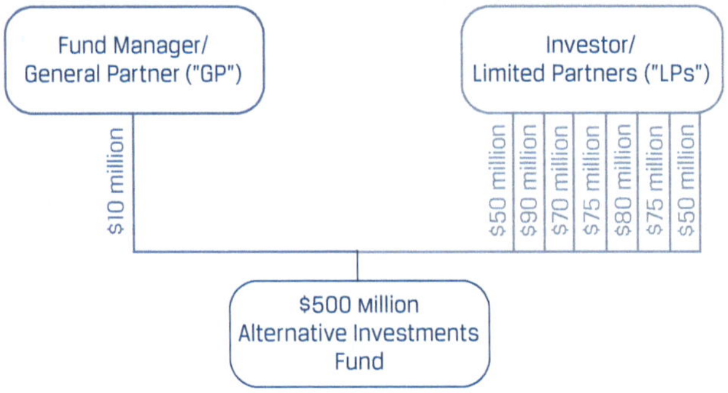

A restricted number of limited partners hold a fractional interest in the fund. LP investors must generally meet certain minimum regulatory net worth, institutional, or other requirements, as so-called **accredited investors**, to access these investments, which are less regulated than general public offerings. The GP (Tenderledge Investments LLC in Exhibit 6) agrees to manage the fund's operations under an agreed standard of care and perform such activities as buying or selling assets, borrowing funds, establishing reserves, or entering into contracts on behalf of the fund.

Exhibit 6: Limited Partnership (Tenderledge Investment Fund)

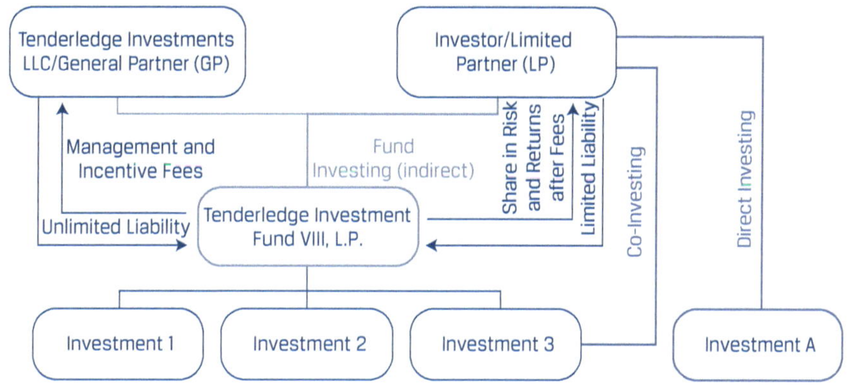

A GP may manage multiple funds at a time. A **limited partnership agreement (LPA)** establishes terms of an LP as governed by a limited partnership agreement.

Key features of an LPA include the distribution of profits and losses (covered in detail below); manager roles and responsibilities, such as investment criteria and restrictions; and terms governing transfers, withdrawals, and dissolution of the agreement.

Adjustments to LP terms are sometimes made to address the unique legal, regulatory, or reporting requirements of a specific investor. In this case, a supplemental document known as a **side letter** is issued between a GP and one or more LPs with terms that override or modify the original LPA terms. These terms might include such features as increased investor ability to transfer investments to a related or successor fund; first right of refusal and other similar clauses to outline potential treatment (regarding fees, co-investment rights, secondary sales, and potentially other matters) in comparison to other LPs; ability to forgo a contractual capital contribution (known as an excusal right); or ability to receive additional investment reporting. One feature of a side letter might include a "most favored nation" clause ensuring any more favorable or additional terms negotiated outside of the LPA with other investors will also apply to a particular LP. The customized features of the LPA and any side letters stand in contrast to a standardized indenture applicable to all bond investors in the case of public fixed-income securities.

Different specialized structures are commonly adopted for other alternative investments. For example, infrastructure investors frequently enter into public–private partnerships, which are agreements between the public sector and the private sector to finance, build, and operate public infrastructure, as shown in Exhibit 7. Exhibit 8 shows the PPP structure for PT Indonesia Infrastructure Finance (IIF), as discussed in Example 2.

Exhibit 7: Public–Private Partnership

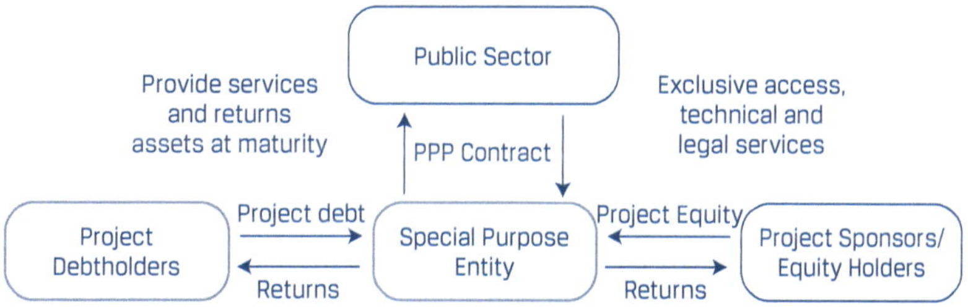

Exhibit 8: Public–Private Partnership Structure of IIF

Infrastructure projects often involve a special purpose entity that raises borrowed and ownership capital for the construction and operation of a specific road, bridge, or other long-lived asset under the terms of a concession agreement, after which the asset is sold or returned to a public sector entity.

Real estate or natural resource fund investors are often classified as unitholders in what is referred to as a **master limited partnership (MLP)**, which has similar features to the limited partnership described earlier but is usually a more liquid investment that is often publicly traded. Other forms of more liquid investments in alternative assets are real estate investment trusts (REITs), commodity funds, and various exchange-traded funds (ETFs). In the case of direct real estate investments, joint ventures are also a common partnership structure. Infrastructure and real estate will be discussed further in a subsequent alternative investment learning module.

Compensation Structures

The asymmetry in information between the general partner, with specialized knowledge and control, and the limited partners in alternative investments means that more complex compensation structures are usedto better align general and limited partner incentives. Most funds that own public equity or debt securities charge management fees as a fixed percentage of assets under management. Alternative investment funds, in contrast, usually combine a higher management fee (often 1%–2% of assets under management) with a **performance fee** (also referred to as an incentive fee or **carried interest**) based on a percentage of periodic fund returns.

While hedge funds and REITs typically charge a management fee on assets under management, private equity funds often levy this fee on **committed capital**, which consists of the total amount that LPs have promised to fund future investments. Private equity funds raise committed capital and draw down on those commitments, generally over three to five years, when they have a specific investment to make. The life of a typical private equity fund is 10 years. Note that the management fee is typically based on committed capital, *not* invested capital; the committed-capital basis for management fees is an important distinction from hedge funds, whose management fees are based on assets under management (AUM). Using committed capital as the basis for management fee calculations reduces the incentive for GPs to deploy the committed capital as quickly as possible (in order to increase near-term management fees). This allows the GPs to be selective about deploying capital into investment opportunities. In addition, since the GP has so much influence on the value of the assets, it would be inappropriate to pay management fees on the basis of the value of assets under management.

Performance fees are often subject to a minimum fund return or **hurdle rate** (also known as a "preferred return"), as well as other modifications, to align manager incentives as closely as possible with those of investors over long investment periods. Hurdle rate agreements sometimes distinguish between a **hard hurdle rate**, where the manager earns fees on annual returns in excess of the hurdle rate, or a **soft hurdle rate**, where the fee is calculated on the entire return when the hurdle is exceeded. With a soft hurdle, GPs are able to catch up performance fees once the hurdle threshold is exceeded.

If we ignore management fees and assume a single-period fund rate of return of r, a hard hurdle rate of r_h, and a GP performance fee (p) as a percentage of total return, then the GP's rate of return (r_{GP}) is as follows:

$$r_{GP} = \max[0, p(r - r_h)]. \qquad (1)$$

For example, if a fund earns r of 18% over a period and receives a performance fee of 20% (p) of returns in excess of the hurdle rate, r_h, of 8%, then r_{GP} is equal to 2%:

$$2\% = \max[0, 20\%(18\% - 8\%)].$$

Performance fee modifications include rewarding managers for exceeding the hurdle rate or generating returns on specific deals or penalizing them by limiting or requiring the return of performance fees for declining performance over time. The acceleration of performance fees once a fund exceeds the soft hurdle rate is known as a **catch-up clause**, as illustrated in Exhibit 9. Under the catch-up clause using the prior example, the GP earns an *immediate* 2% (catch-up return of r_{cu}) once the hurdle is exceeded, resulting in a 1.6% higher return than without the catch-up feature. In other words, the LP will receive 100% of all cash distributions until it earns the hurdle rate of 8%. Then, the GP will receive 100% of distributions until the split of profit is 80%/20%. The remaining distributions will be split 80%/20%. The GP's rate of return (r_{GP}) from Equation 1 with a catch-up clause becomes

$$r_{GP} = \max[0, r_{cu} + p(r - r_h - r_{cu})]. \qquad (2)$$

$$3.6\% = \max[0, 2.0\% + 20\%(18\% - 8\% - 2\%)].$$

Exhibit 9: Catch-Up Clause Illustration

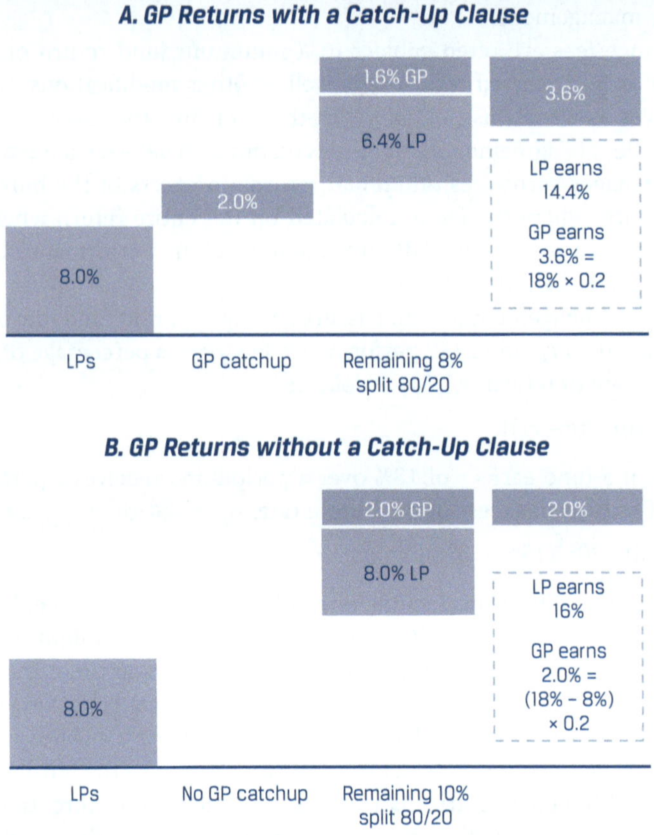

In other instances, managers are penalized with fee reductions in cases of poor or declining performance. One example of this in the case of hedge funds is the use of a so-called **high-water mark**, which reflects the fund's peak value as of a performance calculation date net of fees. If the fund's value subsequently declines below the high-water mark, the hedge fund manager may not charge performance fees until the fund value exceeds the previous high-water mark. The use of high-water marks seeks to reward managers for sustained performance and protect LPs from paying twice for the same returns.

A **clawback** provision, in contrast, actually grants LPs the right to reclaim a portion of the GP's performance fee. Clawback provisions are usually activated when a GP exits successful deals early on but incurs losses on deals later in the fund's life. For most alternative investments, investor high-water marks carry over into new calendar years, but in the case of hedge funds, an investor may no longer claw back incentive fees paid for a prior calendar year if portfolio losses are incurred later. Given the generally more illiquid and longer-term nature of their holdings, private equity and real estate investments are more likely to contain clawback clauses for the entire life of the portfolio.

Finally, as in the case of asset-backed securities described in fixed-income lessons, alternative investments often use a waterfall structure to determine the distribution of cash flows to GPs and LPs. In alternative investments, GPs usually receive a disproportionately larger share of the total profits relative to their initial investment, which incentivizes them to maximize profitability.

There are two types of waterfalls: *deal-by-deal* (or *American*) waterfalls and *whole-of-fund* (or *European*) waterfalls.

- Deal-by-deal waterfalls are more advantageous to the GP because performance fees are collected on a per-deal basis, allowing the GP to get paid before LPs receive both their initial investment *and* their preferred rate of return (i.e., the hurdle rate) on the entire fund.
- In whole-of-fund waterfalls, all distributions go to the LPs as deals are exited and the GP does not participate in any profits until the LPs receive their initial investment and the hurdle rate has been met. In contrast to deal-by-deal waterfalls, whole-of-fund waterfalls occur at the aggregate fund level and are more advantageous to the LPs.

Exhibit 10 and Exhibit 11 illustrate how the cash flow to the GP differs in a deal-by-deal waterfall with a clawback provision versus a whole-of-fund waterfall, respectively. In the first instance, the fund initially grants the GP payouts of $2 million, $3 million, and $8 million because Investments 1, 2, and 3 generate a profit when sold. However, all subsequent investments either break even or return a loss, meaning that over the course of the fund's life, it breaks even at an aggregate level. Thus, the GP must return all early payouts, to compensate for subsequent losses.

Exhibit 10: Deal-by-Deal (American) Waterfall Example—with Clawback Provision

	Year		Amount ($mm)		Profit		
Investment no.	**Invested**	**Sold**	**Invested**	**Sold**	**$mm**	**%**	**GP at 20%**
1	1	4	$10	$20	$10	26.0%	$2
2	2	5	$20	$35	$15	20.5%	$3
3	2	7	$40	$80	$40	14.9%	$8
4	3	7	$20	$20	—	—	—
5	3	8	$35	$25	($10)	neg	($2)
6	4	9	$25	$20	($5)	neg	($1)
7	5	9	$30	$—	($30)	neg	($6)
8	5	10	$20	$—	($20)	neg	($4)
Total	1	10	$200	$200	—	—	—

In the second instance, the GP would receive no payouts until the LPs have received their initial investment and the hurdle rate has been met at the aggregate level. Since the fund only breaks even at the aggregate level, the GP would receive no performance payouts.

Exhibit 11: Whole-of-Fund (European) Waterfall Example

	Year		Amount ($mm)		Profit		
Investment no.	**Invested**	**Sold**	**Invested**	**Sold**	**$mm**	**%**	**GP at 20%**
1	1	4	$10	$20	$10	26.0%	—
2	2	5	$20	$35	$15	20.5%	—
3	2	7	$40	$80	$40	14.9%	—
4	3	7	$20	$20	—	—	—

	Year		Amount ($mm)		Profit		
Investment no.	Invested	Sold	Invested	Sold	$mm	%	GP at 20%
5	3	8	$35	$25	($10)	neg	—
6	4	9	$25	$20	($5)	neg	—
7	5	9	$30	$—	($30)	neg	—
8	5	10	$20	$—	($20)	neg	—
Total	1	10	$200	$200	—	—	—

QUESTION SET

1. Compensation structures for alternative investments *most likely* are:

   A. less complex than those of traditional investments.

   B. equally complex as those of traditional investments.

   C. more complex than those of traditional investments.

   Solution:

   C is correct. The illiquidity, complexity, and long-term nature of alternative investments require more complex structures to bridge potential gaps between manager and investor interests. Alternative investment structures may explicitly address both the roles and responsibilities of investors and managers to address these gaps. In addition, alternative investment structures tailor the distribution of returns between these two parties to minimize the divergence of incentives between manager and investor. A is incorrect because the compensation structures for alternative investments are more complex, not less complex, than those for traditional investments. B is incorrect because the compensation structures for alternative investments are more complex than, not equally complex as, those for traditional investments.

2. Identify the following statement as true or false: Limited partners (LPs) are involved in the management of the alternative investment fund in which they invest; they assist the general partner (GP) in the operations and decisions of the fund.

   A. True

   B. False

   Solution:

   False. LPs play passive roles and are not involved in the management of the fund (although co-investment rights allow LPs to make additional direct investments in the portfolio companies); the operations and decisions of the fund are controlled solely by the GP.

3. Calculate the general partner's performance fee earned based on the following terms:

Single-period fund rate of return	20%
Hard hurdle rate	10%

GP performance fee	18%
Catch-up clause	none

A. 1.6%

B. 1.8%

C. 2.0%

Solution:

The correct answer is B, 1.8%, determined as follows:

A GP's rate of return when there is no catch-up clause is calculated as

r_{GP}=max[0, $p(r - r_h)$],

where

Symbol	Stands for
r_{GP}	GP's rate of return
p	GP's performance fee
r	Single-period fund rate of return
r_h	Hard hurdle rate

Using the terms noted results in a rate of return for the GP of 1.8%:

r_{GP} = max[0, 18%(20% – 10%)].

r_{GP} = 1.8%.

A is incorrect because it is calculated using a single-period fund rate of return of 18%, a hard hurdle rate of 10%, and a GP performance fee of 20%.

C is incorrect because it is calculated using a single-period fund rate of return of 18%, a hard hurdle rate of 8%, and a GP performance fee of 20%.

4. Determine the correct answers to fill in the blanks: A ____________agrees to manage a fund's operations under an agreed standard of care and to perform such activities as buying or selling assets, borrowing funds, establishing reserves, or entering into contracts on behalf of the fund. A ____________________ establishes the terms of a limited partnership and governs the actions and decisions of the limited partnership.

Solution:

A *general partner* agrees to manage a fund's operations under an agreed standard of care and to perform such activities as buying or selling assets, borrowing funds, establishing reserves, or entering into contracts on behalf of the fund. A *limited partnership agreement (LPA)* establishes the terms of a limited partnership and governs the actions and decisions of the limited partnership.

5. Identify the investment type in which each of the following investments *best* fits.

Investment	Traditional Investment	Alternative Investment
A. Alibaba shares traded on the Frankfurt Stock Exchange		
B. Real estate holdings		
C. Hedge fund shares invested in common stock		
D. An investment in an infrastructure project via a public–private partnership		
E. The most junior tranche in an asset-backed security		

Solution:

Investment	Traditional Investment	Alternative Investment
A.	Publicly traded equity shares are a traditional, not an alternative, investment.	
B.		Real estate is a real, tangible physical asset that will generate current and/or future cash flows.
C.		Hedge funds are private investment vehicles, not traditional ones, even though they may invest in public equities or fixed income, private capital, and/or real assets. They are distinguished by their investment approach rather than the types of investments they make via the fund.
D.		Infrastructure is a special type of real asset typically involving land, buildings, and other long-lived fixed assets that are intended for public use and provide essential services. When private investors get involved in such projects, they participate through a public–private partnership.
E.	The most junior tranche in an asset-backed security is still a fixed-income instrument. Fixed-income instruments are traditional investments.	

PRACTICE PROBLEMS

1. Which of the following documents provides tailored terms for a specific investor?

   A. A side letter

   B. An excusal right

   C. A limited partnership agreement

2. Identify the fee approach that *most directly* encourages private equity fund managers to invest selectively, not just quickly. Management fees:

   A. based on committed capital

   B. combined with an incentive fee

   C. based on a fixed percentage of assets under management

3. Which performance fee modification grants limited partners the right to reclaim a portion of the general partner's performance fee?

   A. Catch-up clause

   B. High-water mark

   C. Clawback provision

4. Which of the following features is *most likely* associated with an alternative investment rather than a traditional one?

   A. Illiquidity

   B. Smaller capital outlays

   C. Shorter investment time horizons

5. Assets developed through a public–private partnership typically involve:

   A. long-lived fixed assets intended for public use.

   B. ownership capital used in the early life cycle of a venture.

   C. commercial real estate where private business activity is the primary cash flow source.

6.

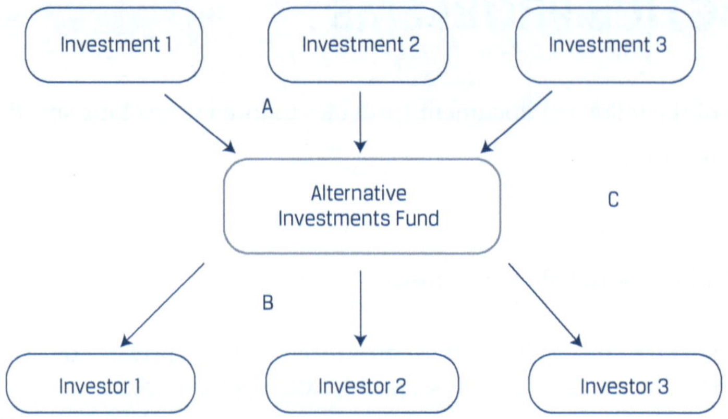

Referring to the diagram above, identify the label (A, B, or C) that *best* corresponds to each of the following financial measures

A.	1. Management fee
B.	2. Net return
C.	3. Gross return

7. Which of the following options is the *most likely* ranking of the alternative investment methods—from most desirable to least—for the following pension fund?A well-endowed university pension fund with significant in-house knowledge, skills, and oversight capabilities is seeking alternative investments to diversify its existing asset portfolio and produce higher returns than more traditional investments while retaining as much control as possible.

   A. fund investment, co-investment, direct investment

   B. direct investment, co-investment, fund investment

   C. co-investment, direct investment, fund investment

8. From the following options, identify the *most important* reason that investors in alternative funds compensate managers using a performance-based fee structure. To:

   A. penalize managers for poor or declining performance over time

   B. better align manager and investor incentives over longer periods

   C. protect themselves from paying managers twice for the same returns

SOLUTIONS

1. The correct answer is A. In addition to limited partnership agreements (LPAs), a supplemental document known as a side letter also may be negotiated. Side letters are agreements between the general partner and one or more limited partners that exist outside the LPA and whose terms override or modify the original limited partnership agreement terms. A side letter is negotiated to address the unique legal, regulatory, or reporting requirements of a specific investor. B is incorrect because an excusal right gives an investor the right to forgo a capital contribution or to not participate in a particular type of investment. An excusal right is granted when it has been stipulated in a side letter, not independently. C is incorrect because the limited partnership agreement establishes and governs the terms of a limited partnership; its terms apply to all limited partners, not just to a specific investor who requires tailored terms.

2. The correct answer is A. Private equity funds typically calculate their management fee based on committed capital, which is the total amount that the limited partners have promised to fund future investments, rather than based on assets under management. The committed-capital basis for management fees is an important distinction from hedge funds, whose management fees are typically based on assets under management. Having committed capital as the basis for management fee calculations reduces the incentive for GPs to deploy the committed capital as quickly as possible to grow their fee base and thus allows the GPs to be selective about deploying capital into investment opportunities. B is incorrect because alternative investment funds usually combine a management fee with a performance fee paid when fund returns exceed a specified hurdle rate. Although this combined fee approach is typical for alternative investment funds, it is not what encourages managers to invest selectively, rather than quickly. C is incorrect because typically hedge funds and REITs charge a management fee on assets under management, while private equity funds instead levy management fees on committed capital.

3. C is correct. A clawback provision grants limited partners the right to reclaim a portion of the general partner's performance fee. Clawback provisions are usually activated when a GP exits successful deals early on but incurs losses on deals later in the fund's life. A is incorrect because a catch-up clause allows a general partner to accelerate performance fees once a fund exceeds a specified soft hurdle rate. B is incorrect because the high-water mark identifies the fund's peak value as of a performance calculation date net of fees; it is not a performance fee modification.

4. A is correct. Investors are often attracted to alternative investments if they are seeking greater diversification and higher expected returns than traditional investments can deliver; alternative investments are often longer-term, illiquid investments in less efficient markets. B is incorrect because alternative investments often require larger capital outlays, not smaller ones than traditional investments. C is incorrect because alternative investments typically require long investment time horizons compared to those of traditional investments.

5. A is correct. In a public–private partnership (PPP), both governments and private investors are involved in funding and completing long-lived fixed assets intended for public use and/or to provide essential services. B is incorrect because ownership capital used for non-public companies in the early life cycle of a venture pertains to venture capital, not to public–private partnerships. C is incorrect because typically a public–private partnership is used to fund and develop infrastructure (i.e., long-lived fixed assets intended for public use and to provide

essential services), not commercial real estate for private business activity.

6. A. 3 is correct. The returns generated by fund investments are gross returns. From these, management deducts its fees, paying the remainder (net fees) to fund investors.

   B. 2 is correct. In alternative fund investing, the fund manager pays the net return (gross return less management fees) to investors.

   C. 1 is correct. Management fees and performance fees are how alternative fund managers are compensated for managing the fund and its investments.

7. B is correct. It shows the three alternative investment methods from most control to least. Direct investing offers investors maximum flexibility and control when it comes to investment choice, methods of financing, and timing. Co-investors gain more control than fund-only investors but not as much as direct investors. Fund investors have the least control; their decisions are limited to either investing in the fund or not. A is incorrect because it ranks the three investment methods from least control to most. C is incorrect because it puts co-investment, the alternative investment method with some control but not the most, in front of direct investment, which offers maximum control and flexibility.

8. B is correct. Investors in alternative funds usually compensate managers using a performance-based, versus flat, fee structure to better align manager and investor incentives over longer periods. A is incorrect because while performance fees/fee structures can penalize managers for declining performance, that is not the most important reason for a performance-based fee structure. C is incorrect because although calculation of a manager's performance may include reference to a fund's peak value (high-water mark) in order to avoid paying twice for the same returns, this is not the most important reason that investors in alternative funds compensate using a performance-based fee structure.

LEARNING MODULE

2

Alternative Investment Performance and Returns

LEARNING OUTCOMES

Mastery	*The candidate should be able to:*
☐	describe the performance appraisal of alternative investments
☐	calculate and interpret alternative investment returns both before and after fees

INTRODUCTION

1

Investment performance measurement on common asset classes, such as public equity and debt, is relatively straightforward. In alternative investments, there are unique features that make this asset class somewhat complicated when it comes to measurement of investment risk and return. In this learning module, we first discuss these unique characteristics and the challenges they pose to performance appraisal. Then we explain the various features in the complex fee arrangement in alternative investments and the nuances when it comes to calculating investor returns.

LEARNING MODULE OVERVIEW

- Alternative investments differ from traditional asset classes in that they involve longer time horizons, unique patterns of cash flows, the use of leverage, illiquid positions, more complex fee structures, different tax and accounting treatment, and so on. In addition, returns are usually less normally distributed for alternative investments than for traditional investments.
- The investment life cycle is usually longer and involves three phases: capital commitment, capital deployment, and capital distribution.
- Internal rate of return (IRR) is often the preferred measure for alternative investment returns. The multiple of invested capital (MOIC) is often used as a shortcut measure, but it ignores the timing of cash flows.

- Customized and complex compensation arrangements seek to align manager and investor incentives. Special provisions also exist for the lockup and redemption of capital from investors.
- In addition to a base management fee, alternative investments often charge additional performance fees based on a percentage of periodic fund returns. When calculating fees and investors' net returns, different features have to be considered, such as founder share class, either/or fee structure, hurdle rate, and high-water mark and clawback clauses.
- It is difficult to generalize performance appraisal for these investments because returns may vary depending on how and when a particular investor invested in a particular vehicle.

LEARNING MODULE SELF-ASSESSMENT

1. In which part of the investment life cycle of a private equity investment should investors generally expect a positive cash flow?

   A. Capital commitment

   B. Capital deployment

   C. Capital distribution

   Solution:

   C is correct. In the initial capital commitment phase, fees and expenses are immediately incurred prior to capital deployment, and assets may generate little or no income during this first phase. In the capital deployment phase, cash outflows typically exceed inflows as funds are deployed. Only in the capital distribution phase can excess income be generated from the invested properties and substantial capital gains be realized upon the sale of assets.

2. Why is IRR preferred for performance measurement for alternative investments?

   A. IRR is commonly used for other asset classes.

   B. IRR is easy and intuitive to calculate.

   C. IRR takes into account the timing of cash flows in long-lived alternative investments.

   Solution:

   C is correct. IRR is seldom used to measure investment performance of other asset classes with publicly quoted market prices. Although IRR is complicated to calculate and involves assumptions on opportunity costs and reinvestment rates, it is the best metric to evaluate long-lived alternative investments because it takes into account the unique timing of cash flows in the investment life cycle of alternative investments.

3. Which of the following statements regarding hedge fund fee structure is correct?

   A. The periodic returns of all investors in the same fund must be identical.

   B. Hedge funds usually charge a performance fee based on a percentage of periodic return above a certain threshold.

C. The management and performance fee rates are always the same for all investors in the same fund.

Solution:

B is correct. A hedge fund usually charges both a flat management fee and an additional performance fee based on a percentage of periodic fund returns. Periodic performance results may vary based on which investor has invested and when the investor invested into the fund. Besides, a particular investor may face significantly lower incentive fees if she invests more capital in a fund at an earlier phase or is willing to accept greater restrictions on redemptions.

4. A $100 million hedge fund charges all its investors a 2% management fee and a 20% performance fee if the periodic return, net of management fee, exceeds a 5% hard hurdle rate. All fees are deducted based on the end-of-year value. If the fund makes a gross return (before fees) of 8% for the year, what is the investor's return, net of fees, *closest* to (ignoring any high-water mark provisions)?

A. 4.67%

B. 5.67%

C. 5.84%

Solution:

B is correct. If the hedge fund makes 8% gross return for the year, its net asset value has grown to $108 million before any fees are deducted.

Management fee = $108 × 2% = $2.16 million.

Performance fee = [($108 – $2.16) – ($100 × $1.05%)] × 20% = $0.168 million.

Net asset value after fee deduction = $108 – $2.16 – $0.168 = $105.672 million.

Net investor return = ($105.672 – $100)/$100 ≈ 5.67%.

5. A €100 million private equity fund has a preferred return of 5% per annum, 20% carried interest with full catch-up, and standard clawback clauses. The fund realizes a gross gain of 50% in two years before it distributes all its capital back to its LPs. Ignoring management fees, the total carried interest to the GP for the two years is *closest* to:

A. €8 million.

B. €10 million.

C. €16 million.

Solution:

B is correct. After two years, the net asset value of the fund has grown to €100 million × 150% = €150 million shortly before distribution. The preferred return to the LPs for the two years totaled €100 million × 5% × 2 = €10 million. (Note that annual preferred return is typically not compounded.) Next, the GP is allowed full catch-up until the GP's carried interest has caught up to the 20% of the total profit accounted for so far, or €2.5 million (€10 million/0.8 × 0.2). The remaining profit of 50 – 10 – 2.5 = €37.5 million is then split 80/20 between the LPs and GP; that is, the GP will get another €7.5 million (€37.5 million × 20%). Therefore, the total carried interest to the GP is 2.5 + 7.5 = €10 million, which is exactly 20% of the €50 million gain.

2 ALTERNATIVE INVESTMENT PERFORMANCE

- [ ] describe the performance appraisal of alternative investments

The unique features, form, and structure of alternative investments must be considered when evaluating the relative performance *between* alternative investments and when comparing their performance to that of more common asset classes over time. In particular, such features as staggered capital commitments over time, longer required investment horizons, reduced liquidity, and less efficient markets highlighted in prior lessons must be factored into the performance appraisal for alternative investments. Alternative investment returns are usually less normally distributed and therefore require different measures of risk and return than those used for more traditional asset classes.

Alternative Investment Performance Appraisal

Appraising the performance of alternative investments requires more scrutiny in certain areas than traditional asset classes do.

Comparability with Traditional Asset Classes

Public equity and debt securities share several characteristics that facilitate the comparison of their performance over a particular period. These standardized claims involve no further required capital commitments and provide identical claims to periodic cash flows, such as dividends in the case of shareholders or contractual bond coupons and principal for debtholders. Prices of publicly traded securities are often continuously quoted, with large peer groups of similar investments available and common indexes used to benchmark returns. Performance appraisal of publicly traded securities is thus straightforward to implement and evaluate.

In contrast, alternative investments are customized investments whose distinctive features complicate performance appraisal between investments and across asset classes. These features include

- the *timing* of cash inflows and outflows for specific investments,
- the use of borrowed funds,
- the *valuation* of individual portfolio positions over specific phases of the investment life cycle, and
- more complex fee structures and tax and accounting treatment.

Performance Appraisal and Alternative Investment Features

When appraising alternative investments, four areas to focus on include the life cycle phase of the investment, the amount of borrowed funds used to maintain the market position, the valuation of the assets, and the fee structure of the fund.

Investment Life Cycle

Unlike public debt or equity securities purchased in the primary or secondary market, alternative investments usually involve a longer investment life cycle with distinct phases characterized by net cash outflows and inflows that complicate periodic return comparisons. Life cycle phases and timing vary across alternative investment types but generally fall into three distinct periods, as shown in Exhibit 1.

Exhibit 1: Investment Life Cycle

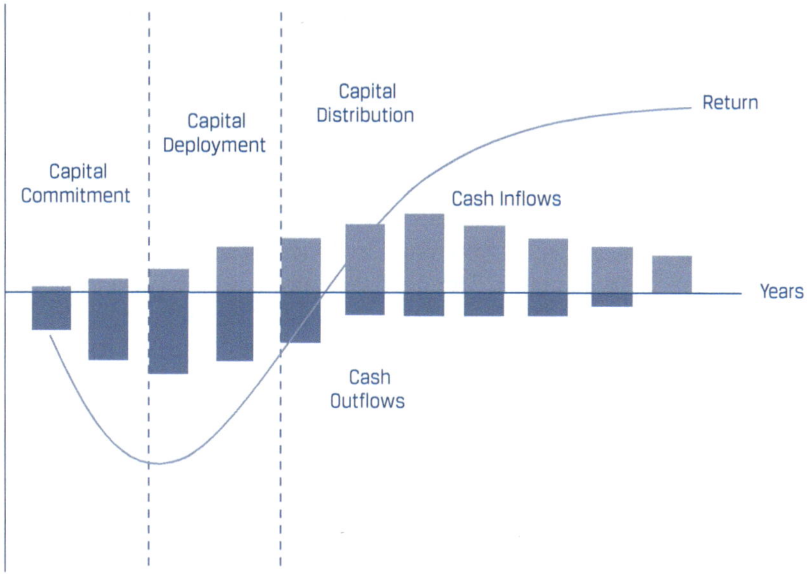

- **Capital commitment:** Alternative managers identify and select appropriate investments with either an immediate or a delayed commitment of capital (known as a capital call) that may be in an early-stage company in the case of venture capital, a more mature firm for private equity, or one or more properties in the case of real estate. Returns are usually negative over this phase because fees and expenses are immediately incurred prior to capital deployment and assets may generate little or no income during this first phase.
- **Capital deployment:** Over this second phase, alternative managers deploy funds to engage in construction or make property improvements in the case of real estate or infrastructure, incur expenses in the turnaround phase of a mature company in the case of private equity, or initiate operations for a startup using venture capital. Cash outflows typically exceed inflows, with management fees further reducing returns.
- **Capital distribution:** When the turnaround strategy, startup phase, or property improvements are completed and if the investment is successful, the underlying assets appreciate in price and/or generate income in excess of costs, causing fund returns to accelerate. The fund may realize substantial capital gains from liquidating or exiting its investments, which may involve an initial public offering (IPO) for venture capital or the sale of properties in the case of real estate.

The so-called **J-curve effect** (because it resembles the letter J) shown in Exhibit 1 represents the initial negative return in the capital commitment phase followed by an acceleration of returns through the capital deployment phase. Returns often level off as capital is distributed to investors, investments are sold, and the fund is closed.

As a result of the cash inflows and outflows that occur over the investment life cycle, an internal rate of return is often used as an initial approach to calculate investment returns for these investments, which include private equity and real estate investments.

The performance assessment in both private equity and real estate investments depends far more on the timing and magnitude of cash flows in and out of the investments, and these are often hard to standardize and anticipate. Given the long time horizon, the application of different tax treatments can have a non-trivial impact on after-tax investment returns.

As a general rule, the best way to start evaluating such investments is with the IRR, taking into account the respective cash flows into an investment and the timing thereof, versus the magnitude and the timing of the cash flows returned by the investment (inclusive of tax benefits).

In an independent, fixed-life private equity fund, the decisions to raise money, take money in the form of capital calls, and distribute proceeds are all at the discretion of the private equity manager. Timing of cash flows is an important part of the investment decision process. The private equity manager should thus be rewarded or penalized for the results of those timing decisions, and the calculation of an IRR is key for doing so.

Although the determination of an IRR involves certain assumptions about a financing rate to use for outgoing cash flows (typically a weighted average cost of capital) and a reinvestment rate to use for incoming cash flows (which must be assumed and may or may not actually be earned), the IRR is the key metric used to assess longer-term alternative investments in the private equity and real estate worlds. IRR calculations will be covered in more depth in the Corporate Issuers topic area.

EXAMPLE 1

Peterburgh Capital, LLC

Peterburgh Capital, LLC, a private equity vehicle, is considering investment in various companies and is expecting the following cash flow pattern from these investments:

Year	Cash Inflow (USD)	Cash Outflow (USD)
0	—	2,500,000
1	—	4,000,000
2	—	1,700,000
3	500,000	1,000,000
4	1,000,000	—
5	3,000,000	—
6	12,500,000	—

IRR can be calculated by the standard formula $\sum_{t=0}^{n} \frac{CF_i}{(1+r)^i} = 0$, or using a financial calculator, r ≈ 14.596%.

As is true for any IRR calculation, assumptions regarding the opportunity cost of outgoing cash flows and the reinvestment rate for incoming cash flows will affect the results.

Because of this complexity, a shortcut methodology often used by both private equity and real estate managers involves simply citing a **multiple of invested capital (MOIC)**, or money multiple, on total invested capital (which is paid-in capital less management fees and fund expenses). Here, one simply measures the total value of all realized investments and residual asset values (assets that may still be awaiting their ultimate sale) relative to an initial total investment. MOIC is calculated as follows:

MOIC = (Realized value of investment + Unrealized value of investment)/Total amount of invested capital. (1)

Although the MOIC ignores the timing of cash flows, it is easier to calculate, and it is intuitively easier to understand when someone says he received two or three times his initial investment. But how long it takes to realize this value does matter. A 2× return on one's initial investment would be great if the return were collected over two years but far less compelling if it took 15 years to realize.

In general, because private equity and real estate investments involve longer holding periods, there is less emphasis on evaluating them in terms of shorter-term portfolio correlation benefits. After a private equity fund has fully drawn in its monetary commitments, interim accounting values for a private equity partnership become less critical for a period of time because no incoming or outgoing cash flows may immediately hinge on such valuations. During this "middle period" in the life of a private equity fund, accounting values may not always be particularly reflective of the future potential realizations (and hence the expected returns) of the fund. It is not that the value of the investments is not actually rising and falling in the face of economic influences; rather, accounting conventions simply leave longer-lived investments marked at their initial cost for some time or make only modest adjustments to carrying value until clearer impairments or realization events take place.

KNOWLEDGE CHECK: MOIC CALCULATION

Himitsu, a private equity firm, makes an initial investment of JPY3.8 billion into ZZZ company in Year 0. Eight years later, it sells its stake in ZZZ for JPY8.5 billion. Additional capital investments were made in Year 2 and in Year 3 for JPY1.2 billion and JPY200 million, respectively.

1. Calculate the MOIC.

Solution:

MOIC = 8.5/(3.8 + 1.2 + 0.2) = 1.63×.

	Amount	Year
Invested Capital	(3,800,000)	0
	—	1
Additional Capital	(1,200,000)	2
Additional Capital	(200,000)	3
Liquidity Event	8,500,000	8
MOIC	**1.63×**	
IRR	**20%**	

Use of Borrowed Funds

Alternative investments may use borrowed funds to increase investment returns. This form of financial leverage has the effect of magnifying both gains and losses by allowing investors to take a market position that is larger than the capital committed. Consider a cash investment V_c with a periodic rate of return r. If we assume an investor is able to borrow at a periodic rate of r_b to increase the size of its investment by borrowed funds of V_b, we can calculate a simple *leveraged* rate of return r_L for the period as follows:

$$r_L = \text{Leveraged portfolio return/Cash position} = [r \times (V_c + V_b) - (V_b \times r_b)]/V_c. \quad (2)$$

We can rearrange Equation 2 to show the relationship between the cash portfolio return, r, and the leveraged rate of return, r_L, as follows:

$$r_L = r + V_b/V_c(r - r_b). \quad (3)$$

Hedge funds leverage their portfolios by using derivatives or borrowing capital from **prime brokers**, negotiating with them to establish margin requirements, interest, and fees in advance of trading. In a typical **margin financing** arrangement, the prime broker essentially lends the hedge fund the shares, bonds, or derivatives, and the hedge fund deposits cash or other collateral into a margin account with the prime broker based on certain fractions of the investment positions. The margin account represents the hedge fund's net equity in its positions. The minimum margin required depends on the riskiness of the investment portfolio and the creditworthiness of the hedge fund.

Leverage is a large part of the reason that some hedge funds either earn larger-than-normal returns or suffer significant losses. If the margin account or the hedge fund's equity in a position declines below a certain level, the lender initiates a margin call and requests that the hedge fund put up more collateral. An inability to meet margin calls can have the effect of magnifying or locking in losses because the hedge fund may have to liquidate (close out) the losing position. This liquidation can lead to further losses if the order size is sufficiently large to move the security's market price before the fund can sufficiently eliminate the position. Under normal conditions, the application of leverage may be necessary for yielding meaningful returns from given quantitative, arbitrage, or relative value strategies. But with added leverage comes increased risk.

EXAMPLE 2

Leverage by Lupulus Opportunity Fund LLC

Lupulus Opportunity Fund LLC, a hedge fund that has USD100 million of capital, ordinarily uses leverage to invest in a variety of equity-linked notes.

Scenario 1: Suppose Lupulus's underlying positions return 8%. If it could add leverage of USD50 million to the portfolio at a funding cost of 4%, what would have been the leveraged return?

Using Equation 3, the leveraged return can be calculated as follows:

$V_c = 100$; $V_b = 50$.

$r_L = 0.08 + (50/100)(0.08 - 0.04) = 10\%$.

Scenario 2: Suppose Lupulus's underlying positions incur a loss of 2% instead of earning a gain. What would have been the leveraged return if Lupulus had borrowed USD50 million at 4%?

Again, using Equation 3, $V_c = 100$ and $V_b = 50$

$r_L = -0.02 + (50/100)(-0.02 - 0.04) = -5\%$.

In other words, Lupulus would have magnified its portfolio loss from –2% to –5% by adding leverage of USD50 million.

Scenario 3: If Lupulus's underlying positions make a gain of 6%, what is the breakeven borrowing rate at which Lupulus is indifferent to adding leverage to the portfolio?

From Equation 3, Lupulus would be indifferent about adding leverage when the magnification effect of leverage equals 0; that is,

when $r_L = r$, or $(V_b/V_c)(r - r_b) = 0$,

$r_b = r = 6\%$.

As the previous example shows, the leveraged rate of return will exceed that of an equivalent cash portfolio if the market return on assets exceeds the borrowing rate. This example assumes the investor has unlimited access to borrow freely on an unsecured basis. The access to borrowed funds or lack thereof is an important factor in evaluating the risk of leveraged investments.

Valuation

Alternative assets are often characterized by illiquidity, which makes performance appraisal over time challenging and periodic comparison with common asset classes difficult. Accounting rules dictate that investments must be recorded at their **fair value** for financial reporting purposes. The fair value of an investment is a market-based measure based on observable or derived assumptions to determine a price that market participants would use to exchange an asset or liability (often referred to as the *exit price* for a seller) in an orderly transaction at a specific time. Assumptions used to measure fair value follow a three-level hierarchy, as shown in Exhibit 2:

Exhibit 2: Fair Value Hierarchy

Level	Description	Sample Application and Method
Level 1	Quoted prices in active markets for identical asset/liability that may be accessed as of measurement date	Exchange-traded public equity securities (observed closing market price)
Level 2	Inputs other than quoted market prices in Level 1 that are directly or indirectly observable for an asset/liability	Over-the-counter interest rate derivatives (pricing model using quoted market prices)
Level 3	Unobservable inputs are used to measure fair value for asset/liability in which there is little, if any, market activity as of the measurement date	Private equity or real estate investments (cash flow projection models with reasonably available market participant assumptions)

While common asset classes often rely on Level 1 inputs, the interim valuation of private equity, real estate, and other less frequently traded assets based on Level 3 inputs is more challenging. Interim accounting values may be less critical for the partnership itself over a period where no incoming or outgoing cash flows are expected. The lack of new market information over time may thus anchor the value of these long-lived investments at or near initial cost, with adjustments to carrying value when impairments or realization events occur. The relatively stable accounting valuations of these strategies may give investors a false sense that they are less correlated with and less volatile than other investments, although a more realistic picture may emerge if managers are forced to liquidate a portfolio prematurely.

For Level 3 asset pricing, regardless of the model used by a manager in such circumstances, that model should be independently tested, benchmarked, and calibrated to industry-accepted standards to ensure a consistency of approach. Because of the potential for conflicts of interest when applying estimates of value, hedge funds must develop procedures for in-house valuation, communicate these procedures to clients, and adhere to them consistently.

Notwithstanding best practice, the very nature of assets that can be valued only on a "mark-to-model" basis can and should be a focus for the alternative asset investor. A model may reflect an imperfect theoretical valuation and not a true liquidation value. The illiquid nature of these assets means that estimates, rather than observable transaction prices, may well have factored into any valuation. As a result, returns may be smoothed or overstated and the volatility of returns, understated. As a generalized statement, any investment vehicle that is heavily involved with Level 3 priced assets deserves increased scrutiny and due diligence.

Fees

Alternative investment fees also vary from those for common asset classes, which typically involve a flat management fee. Alternative investments often levy additional performance fees based on a percentage of periodic fund returns. Performance appraisal for these investments can be difficult to generalize, because results may vary significantly based on *which* investor has invested *when* in a particular vehicle.

For example, an investor may face significantly lower incentive fees if she invests *more* capital in a fund at an *earlier* phase or is willing to accept *greater* restrictions on redemptions. Also, an investor entering an alternative fund following a sharp drop in value may incur performance fees if the fund rises, while an earlier investor who experienced the sharp decline in value from its peak may be exempt from such fees for the same period. These and other details of these complex alternative investment fee arrangements and their effect on investment return are the subject of the following lesson.

QUESTION SET

1. Which of the following is *not* a factor that makes comparison of performance between alternative investments and public securities difficult?

   A. Alternative investments charge higher fees.

   B. The use of leverage in alternative investments magnifies their risk and return measures.

   C. The fair value of portfolio positions in alternative investments may not be readily available.

   Solution:

   A is correct. Although an alternative investment may charge a higher fee, it is not the absolute fee level but the complexity of the fee arrangement that makes alternative investment appraisal unique compared to other common asset classes.

   Alternative investments often involve the use the of explicit leverage, which has the effect of magnified gains and losses. Alternative assets are often characterized by illiquidity with unobservable market prices, making performance appraisal over time and periodic comparison with common asset classes challenging.

2. Describe the J-curve effect in alternative investments.

Solution:

The J-curve effect in alternative investments describes the initial negative return in the capital commitment phase followed by an acceleration of returns through the capital deployment phase. Returns often level off as capital is distributed to investors, investments are sold, and the fund is closed.

3. A private equity closes a fund with a capital commitment of €750 million. It has a capital call of €500 million initially and another €250 million at the end of Year 1. The management fee is 2% per annum. At the end of Year 5, a total of €1.0 billion is distributed to its investors, and the fund is left with €500 million in asset value. The multiple of invested capital (MOIC) after five years is *closest* to:

A. 1.3×.

B. 2.0×.

C. 2.2×.

Solution:

C is correct. Using Equation 1, MOIC = (Realized value of investment + Unrealized value of investment)/Total amount of invested capital, where invested capital equals total paid-in capital less management fees and fund expenses. MOIC is different from the IRR measure because it ignores the timing of cash flows.

Total paid-in capital = 500 + 250 = 750.

Total management fee for 5 years = 750 × 0.02 × 5 = 75.

Total invested capital = 750 – 75 = 675.

MOIC = (1,000 + 500)/675 ≈ 2.2×.

4. If the market return of underlying portfolio positions is expected to be 10% and the fund manager adds 100% explicit leverage to its capital at a borrowing rate of 3%, what is the expected leveraged return?

Solution:

Using Equation 3,

$$r_L = r + (V_b/V_c)(r - r_b) = 0.10 + (100/100)(0.10 - 0.03) = 17\%.$$

5. Match the fair value classification of assets to their description for financial reporting purpose:

Fair Value Classification	Description
1. Level 1 assets	(a) Inputs other than quoted market prices are directly or indirectly observable for valuation on measurement date
2. Level 2 assets	(b) Unobservable inputs are used to evaluate fair value for the assets
3. Level 3 assets	(c) Quoted prices in active markets for identical asset available on measurement date

Solution:

1. Level 1 assets: (c) Quoted prices in active markets for identical asset available on measurement date

2. Level 2 assets: (a) Inputs other than quoted market prices are directly or indirectly observable for valuation on measurement date

3. Level 3 assets: (b) Unobservable inputs are used to evaluate fair value for the assets

3 ALTERNATIVE INVESTMENT RETURNS

☐ calculate and interpret alternative investment returns both before and after fees

Hedge funds often use complex strategies to achieve outsized returns with low correlation with the broader market. These more complex strategies require more sophisticated portfolio management tools and a larger range of skills, making them more expensive to run. Rather than paying a very high flat management fee, investors demand that some of the compensation is aligned to the performance delivered by the strategy in the form of a performance fee.

Apart from the performance fee, there are also other customized, complex compensation arrangements that seek to align manager and investor incentives. These structures are designed to reward investors for early involvement, larger investments, and/or longer lockup periods. Managers benefit from applying specialized knowledge and skills to achieve steadily rising returns in excess of a designated hurdle rate. These complex fee structures impact returns for different investors in the same fund, as well as returns before and after fees across various alternative investments.

Another factor that can lock in or magnify losses for hedge funds is investor redemptions. Redemptions frequently occur when a hedge fund is performing poorly. Redemptions may require the hedge fund manager to liquidate some positions and potentially receive particularly disadvantageous prices when forced to do so by redemption pressures, while also incurring transaction costs.

Funds sometimes charge a **redemption fee** to discourage redemption and to offset the transaction costs for remaining investors in the fund. A **notice period** is a period (typically 30–90 days) in advance that investors may be required to notify a fund of their intent to redeem some or all their investment. This notice period allows the fund manager an opportunity to liquidate a position in an orderly fashion without magnifying the losses. A **lockup period** is the minimum holding period before investors are allowed to make withdrawals or redeem shares from a fund. This provision is intended to allow the hedge fund manager the required time to implement and potentially realize a strategy's expected results. If the fund receives a drawdown request shortly after a new investment, the lockup period forces the investors who made the request to stay in the fund for a period of time rather than be allowed to immediately withdraw. In addition, funds sometimes impose a **gate**, a provision that when implemented limits or restricts redemptions for a period of time, usually at the discretion of the fund manager. Investors should be aware of their liquidity needs before investing in a fund with restrictive provisions.

A hedge fund's ability to demand a long lockup period while raising a significant amount of investment capital depends a great deal on the reputation of either the firm or the hedge fund manager. Funds of hedge funds may offer more redemption flexibility than is afforded to direct investors in hedge funds because of special redemption arrangements with the underlying hedge fund managers, the maintenance of added cash reserves, access to temporary bridge-loan financing, or the simple avoidance of less liquid hedge fund strategies.

Ideally, redemption terms should be designed to match the expected liquidity of the assets being invested in, but even with careful planning, an initial drawdown can turn into something far more serious when it involves illiquid and obscure assets. These left-tailed loss events are not easily modeled for hedge funds.

Alternative Investment Returns

Custom Fee Arrangements

Alternative investments often involve customized fee arrangements combining management and performance-based fees that vary based on the size, timing, and/or terms of investor participation in the investment over time. Examples include the following:

- **Fees based on liquidity terms and asset size:** Limited partnerships may charge different rates depending on the liquidity terms that an investor is willing to accept (longer lockups resulting in lower fees), and managers may discount their fees for larger investors or for placement agents who introduced these investors. Different investors in the same fund may face different fee structures. For example, management fees for large LPs might range from 0.5% to 1.5%, with incentive fees reduced to 10%–15%, depending on the mandate. Such reductions can be meaningful in terms of net realized returns. However, smaller funds with strong performance (and capacity constraints) are able to maintain higher fees and may even decline business from larger investors rather than agree to a lower fee.
- **Founders shares:** As a way to entice early participation in startup funds, managers sometimes offer incentives known as **founders class shares**. Founders shares entitle investors to a lower fee structure, such as a 1.5% management fee and a 10% performance fee rather than a more standard 2% management fee and a 20% performance fee, and may apply only to the first $100 million in assets invested, although cutoff thresholds vary. Another alternative is to reduce the fees for early founders share investors once the fund achieves a critical mass or performance targets.
- **"Either/or" fees:** Major institutional investors, such as the Teacher Retirement System of Texas, have demanded that alternative investment funds accept an **either/or fee** agreement by choosing *between* fixed management and variable performance fees. Managers agree *either* to charge a lower, 1% management fee (to cover expenses during down years) *or* to accept a higher, 30% incentive fee above a mutually agreed-upon annual hurdle (to incentivize and reward managers during up years), whichever is greater. Major investors offering larger commitments may negotiate such novel fee structures designed to reward returns in excess of a benchmark, while smaller investors, such as high-net-worth individuals with smaller commitments, usually face more traditional fees.

Alternative Investment Return Calculations

Return calculations vary among alternative investments based on the form of the investments, as described in an earlier lesson. While more liquid alternative investments, such as REITs, commodity index exchange-traded funds, or other frequently traded investments, have a simple management fee structure similar to common assets, those with longer life cycles, illiquidity, and less transparency, such as private equity, hedge funds, and real estate, often use performance fees with modifications to create incentives for managers to act in the best interest of investors.

The impact of different fee arrangements and their effect on the resulting returns to investors is best illustrated using a series of examples. If we assume fixed GP management fees as a percentage of assets under management (AUM) of r_m, beginning-of-period assets of P_0, end-of-period assets of P_1, and a GP performance fee (p) that is a percentage of total return, the GP's return in currency terms (R_{GP}) is as follows:

$$R_{GP} = (P_1 \times r_m) + \max[0, (P_1 - P_0) \times p]. \quad (4)$$

And we may solve for an investor's periodic rate of return, r_i, as follows:

$$r_i = (P_1 - P_0 - R_{GP})/P_0. \quad (5)$$

EXAMPLE 3

Kettleside Timberland LP

Kettleside is a timberland investment management organization with $100 million of initial investment capital. It charges a 1% management fee based on year-end AUM (r_m) and a 20% performance fee (p). In its first year, Kettleside generates a 30% return. Assume management fees are calculated using an end-of-period valuation.

1. What are Kettleside's fees if the performance and management fees are calculated independently? What is an investor's effective return given this fee structure?

   Solution:

   Using Equation 4 with P_0 equal to \$100 million, P_1 of \$130 million, r_m = 1%, and p = 20%,

   $$R_{GP} = \$130\text{ million} \times 1\% + \max[0, (\$130\text{ million} - \$100\text{ million}) \times 20\%]$$

   $$= \$7.3\text{ million.}$$

   $$r_i = (\$130\text{ million} - \$100\text{ million} - \$7.3\text{ million})/\$100\text{ million}$$

   $$= 22.7\%.$$

2. What are Kettleside's fees if the performance fee is calculated from the return *net* of the management fee? What is an investor's net return given this fee structure?

   Solution:

   In order to solve for GP return where performance fee is calculated *net* of management fees, we must modify Equation 4 as follows:

$$R_{GP(Net)} = (P_1 \times r_m) + \max\{0, [P_1(1 - r_m) - P_0] \times p\}. \quad (6)$$

Using Equation 6 with P_0 of \$100 million, P_1 of \$130 million, r_m = 1%, and p = 20%,

$R_{GP(Net)}$ = \$130 million × 1% + max{0, [\$130 million(0.99) – \$100 million] × 20%}

= \$7.04 million.

r_i = (\$130 million – \$100 million – \$7.04 million)/\$100 million

= 22.96%.

The previous example demonstrates how fee calculations affect investor returns, with a higher return when fees are calculated on a net basis. Alternative investment databases and indexes usually report fund performance net of aggregated fees. If fee structures vary, the actual net-of-fee returns earned by various investors may vary from the quoted return.

One fee structure variation involves the modification of performance fees using hurdle rates and high-water marks. In the next example, we consider the effect of both on investor returns using the same details from the prior example.

EXAMPLE 4

Kettleside Timberland LP Performance Fee Modifications

As in the prior case, Kettleside Timberland LP has initial capital of \$100 million, charging a 1% management fee based on year-end AUM (r_m) and a 20% performance fee (p).

1. If Kettleside's fee agreement specifies a 6% hurdle rate with performance fees based on returns *in excess of* the hurdle rate, what are Kettleside's fees assuming the performance fee is calculated *net* of the management fee? What is an investor's net return given this fee structure?

Solution:

To solve for Kettleside's fees with a hard hurdle rate calculated net of management fees, we make a further adjustment to Equation 4 by incorporating the hurdle rate, r_h, as follows:

$$R_{GP(Net\ with\ Hurdle)} = (P_1 \times r_m) + \max\{0, [P_1(1 - r_m) - P_0 \times (1 + r_h)] \times p\} \quad (7)$$

$R_{GP(Net\ with\ Hurdle)}$
= \$130 million × 1% + max{0, [\$130 million(0.99) – \$100 million(1.06)] × 20%}

= \$5.84 million.

r_i = (\$130 million – \$100 million – \$5.84 million)/\$100 million

= 24.16%.

2. In the second year, Kettleside fund value declines to \$110 million. The fee structure is as specified in Question 1 of Example 3 but also includes the use of a high-water mark (P_{HWM}) computed net of fees. What are Kettleside's

fees in the second year? What is an investor's net return for the second year given this fee structure?

Solution:

We must again alter Equation 4 to include the high-water mark (P_{HWM}) provision, as follows:

$$R_{GP(High\text{-}Water\ Mark)} = (P_2 \times r_m) + \max[0, P_2((1-r_m) - P_{HWM}) \times p] \quad (8)$$

where P_{HWM} is defined as the maximum fund value at the end of any *previous* period net of fees. We may solve for investor return r_i in Period 2 as follows:

$$r_i = (P_2 - P_1 - R_{GP})/P_1. \quad (9)$$

$R_{GP(High\text{-}Water\ Mark)}$

$= \$110 \text{ million} \times 1\% + \max[0, (\$110 \times 0.99 - \$124.16) \times 20\%]$

$= \$1.1 \text{ million}.$

$r_i = (\$110 \text{ million} - \$124.16 \text{ million} - \$1.1 \text{ million})/\$124.16 \text{ million}$

$= -12.291\%.$

The beginning capital position in the second year for the investors is \$130 million – \$5.84 million = \$124.16 million. The ending capital position at the end of the second year is \$110 million – \$1.1 million = \$108.9 million.

3. In the third year, Kettleside's fund value increases to \$128 million. The fee structure is as specified in Questions 1 and 2 of Example 4. What are Kettleside's fees in the third year? What is an investor's net return for the third year given this fee structure?

Solution:

We amend Equation 8 and Equation 9 to reflect returns for the third period and calculate as follows:

$$R_{GP(High\text{-}Water\ Mark)} = (P_2 \times r_m) + \max[0, P_2((1-r_m) - P_{HWM}) \times p]$$

$$r_i = (P_3 - P_2 - R_{GP})/P_2.$$

Note that the high-water mark, P_{HWM}, is the highest value of the fund after fees in all previous years. In Kettleside's case, it was \$122.7 million, the ending value in the first year, P_1.

Kettleside Timberland LP Performance Fee Modifications

Year	Fund Value ($m), after Fees	
0	100.00	
1	122.70	← High-Water Mark
2	108.90	

$R_{GP(High\text{-}Water\ Mark)}$

$= \$128 \text{ million} \times 1\% + \max[0, (\$128 \times 0.99 - \$124.16) \times 20\%]$

$= \$1.792 \text{ million}.$

$r_i = (\$128 \text{ million} - \$108.9 \text{ million} - \$1.792 \text{ million})/\$108.9 \text{ million}$

= 15.89%.

The beginning capital position in the third year for the investors is \$110 million − \$1.1 million = \$108.9 million. The ending capital position for the third year is \$128 million − \$1.792 million = \$126.208 million, which represents a new high-water mark to be applied the following year for this investor.

Performance fee modifications may have similar or different effects on the periodic investor returns depending on the timing of an investment. For example, if two Kettleside investors were to purchase the fund at different times and had otherwise similar fee structures, they would both realize a fee reduction in the case of a hard hurdle equal to $P_t \times r_h \times p$, or the product of the end-of-period fund value for year *t*, the hurdle rate, and the performance fee. However, in the case of a high-water mark, the time-dependent nature of this fee modification gives different results for an investor who enters the fund at a later date, as in the following example.

EXAMPLE 5

Kettleside Timberland LP High-Water Mark for New Investor

At the end of Year 2, Kettleside Timberland LP has capital of \$108.9 million. Consider the Year 3 returns of a *new* investor assuming the same fund performance and fee structure—namely, a 1% management fee based on year-end AUM (r_m), a 20% performance fee (p), and a high-water mark provision.

$$R_{GP(High\text{-}Water\ Mark)} = (P_3 \times r_m) + \max[0, (P_3 - P_{HWM}) \times p].$$

$$r_i = (P_3 - P_2 - R_{GP})/P_2.$$

$$R_{GP(High\text{-}Water\ Mark)}$$

$$= \$128 \text{ million} \times 1\% + \max[0, (\$128 \text{ million} - \$108.9 \text{ million}) \times 20\%]$$

$$= \$5.1 \text{ million}.$$

$$r_i = (\$128 \text{ million} - \$108.9 \text{ million} - \$5.1 \text{ million})/\$108.9 \text{ million}$$

$$= 12.856\%.$$

Note that the new investor in Example 5 realizes *no* high-water mark reduction in fees as in the prior case and therefore faces a *lower* periodic return than the investor participating since the fund's inception.

In other instances, the timing of returns can have a meaningful impact on manager fees and investor returns, as shown in the following example of a clawback provision.

EXAMPLE 6

Tenderledge Opportunity Fund LP—Clawback Provision

Tenderledge Opportunity Fund makes \$20 million in new investments, evenly divided with \$10 million into Arguston Inc. (a leveraged buyout) and \$10 million to Heartfield Digital (an early-stage venture) One year later, Arguston is sold to a strategic buyer for \$22 million after costs. Two years later, Heartfield Digital fails and Tenderledge is unable to recoup any of its original investment.

1. If Tenderledge's fee agreement as general partner (GP) specifies a 20% performance fee of aggregate profits (p) with a clawback provision, which performance fees will Tenderledge accrue and what will it ultimately receive?

   Solution:

   Gain in the Arguston investment: \$22 million – \$10 million = \$12 million.

   Loss in the Heartfield Digital investment: \$0 – \$10 million = –\$10 million.

   Aggregate gain of Tenderledge after two years = \$12 million – \$10 million = \$2 million.

   Tenderledge would initially accrue 20% of the \$12 million aggregate profit from the sale of Arguston at the end of the first year, or \$12 million × 20% = \$2.4 million. This amount is typically held in escrow for the benefit of the GP but not paid.

   The failure of Heartfield Digital in Year 2 reduces the original \$12 million gain by \$10 million, so the aggregate fund gain at the end of Year 2 is only \$2 million. This net profit results in a performance fee of \$400,000 (= \$2 million × 20%). Tenderledge would then have to return \$2 million of the previously accrued performance fees to LP investor capital accounts due to the clawback provision.

KNOWLEDGE CHECK FEE AND RETURN CALCULATIONS

AWJ Capital is a hedge fund with \$100 million of initial investment capital. It charges a 2% management fee based on year-end AUM and a 20% incentive fee. In its first year, AWJ Capital has a 30% return. Assume management fees are calculated using end-of-period valuation.

1. What are the fees earned by AWJ if the incentive and management fees are calculated independently? What is an investor's effective return given this fee structure?

   Solution:

   AWJ fees:

   \$130 million × 2% = \$2.6 million management fee.

   (\$130 million − \$100 million) × 20% = \$6 million incentive fee.

   Total fees to AWJ Capital = \$8.6 million.

2. What are the fees earned by AWJ assuming that the incentive fee is calculated from the return net of the management fee? What is an investor's net return given this fee structure?

   Solution:

   \$130 million × 2% = \$2.6 million management fee.

   (\$130 million − \$100 million − \$2.6 million) × 20%
   = \$5.48 million incentive fee.

   Total fees to AWJ Capital = \$8.08 million.

   Investor return = (\$130 million − \$100 million − \$8.08 million)/\$100 million

= 21.92%.

3. If the fee structure specifies a hurdle rate of 5% and the incentive fee is based on returns in excess of the hurdle rate, what are the fees earned by AWJ assuming the performance fee is calculated net of the management fee? What is an investor's net return given this fee structure?

Solution:

$130 million × 2% = $2.6 million management fee.

($130 million − $100 million − $5 million − $2.6 million) × 20%
= $4.48 million incentive fee.

Total fees to AWJ Capital = $7.08 million.

Investor return = ($130 million − $100 million − $7.08 million)/$100 million
= 22.92%.

4. In the second year, the fund value declines to $110 million. The fee structure is as specified for Question 1 but also includes the use of a high-water mark (computed net of fees). What are the fees earned by AWJ in the second year? What is an investor's net return for the second year given this fee structure?

Solution:

$110 million × 2% = $2.2 million management fee.

No incentive fee because the fund has declined in value.

Total fees to AWJ Capital = $2.2 million.

Investor return = ($110 million − $2.2 million − $121.4 million)/$121.4 million
= −11.20%.

The beginning capital position in the second year for the investors is $130 million − $8.6 million = $121.4 million. The ending capital position at the end of the second year is $110 million − $2.2 million = $107.8 million.

5. In the third year, the fund value increases to $128 million. The fee structure is as specified in Questions 1 and 4. What are the fees earned by AWJ in the third year? What is an investor's net return for the third year given this fee structure?

Solution:

$128 million × 2% = $2.56 million management fee.

($128 million − $121.4 million) × 20% = $1.32 million incentive fee.

The $121.4 million represents the high-water mark established at the end of Year 1.

Total fees to AWJ Capital = $3.88 million.

Investor return = ($128 million − $3.88 million − $107.8 million)/$107.8 million = 15.14%. The ending capital position at the end of Year 3 is $124.12 million. This amount is the new high-water mark.

Relative Alternative Investment Returns and Survivorship Bias

Investors seeking higher risk-adjusted returns with low correlation with common asset classes in alternative investments often track their performance based on *relative* returns. As is the case for more common asset classes, returns on individual alternative investments are usually compared to a benchmark of investments with similar features. These benchmarks may be interpreted differently or take on different characteristics in the case of alternative investments. For example, the use of a composite benchmark for private equity or real estate investments may be misleading if a specific investment is in a different life cycle phase than most of its peers. However, return comparisons between such investments of the same vintage year on an annual or "since inception" basis lead to more accurate results. That said, lockups and illiquidity may prevent an investor from reacting to underperformance by selling an investment.

Hedge fund indexes deserve greater scrutiny given changes to the universe of funds included in a benchmark over time. For example, studies suggest that over a quarter of all hedge funds fail within the first three years due to performance problems that lead to investor defections and fund closure. The exclusion of failed funds from a given benchmark is a form of selection bias that can lead investors to overly optimistic return expectations known as **survivorship bias**. Survivorship bias is a major problem among hedge fund indexes that include only current investment funds and exclude those funds that are no longer available. A second form of bias relates to how and when hedge fund returns are initially included in a benchmark index. For example, a fund manager may launch several hedge fund investments at once and include only the most successful funds in an index a couple of years after inception. The subsequent inclusion or "backfilling" of prior performance data on a selective basis serves to increase average reported returns in what is known as **backfill bias**. Because of survivorship and backfill biases, hedge fund indexes may not reflect actual average hedge fund performance but, rather, only the returns of those hedge funds that initially performed best and/or have not failed.

EXAMPLE 7

Comparison of Returns: Investment Directly into a Hedge Fund or through a Fund of Hedge Funds

An investor is contemplating investing €100 million in either the ABC Hedge Fund (ABC HF) or the XYZ Fund of Funds (XYZ FOF). XYZ FOF has a "1 and 10" fee structure and invests 10% of its AUM in ABC HF. ABC HF has a standard "2 and 20" fee structure with no hurdle rate. Management fees are calculated on an annual basis on AUM at the beginning of the year. For simplicity, assume that management fees and incentive fees are calculated independently. ABC HF has a 20% return for the year before management and incentive fees.

1. Calculate the return to the investor from investing directly in ABC HF.

   Solution:

   ABC HF has a profit before fees on a €100 million investment of €20 million (= €100 million × 20%). The management fee is €2 million (= €100 million × 2%), and the incentive fee is €4 million (= €20 million × 20%). The return to the investor is 14% [= (20 − 2 − 4)/100].

2. Calculate the return to the investor from investing in XYZ FOF. Assume that the other investments in the XYZ FOF portfolio generate the same

return before management fees as those of ABC HF and that XYZ FOF has the same fee structure as ABC HF.

Solution:

XYZ FOF earns a 14% return, or €14 million profit after fees on €100 million invested with hedge funds. XYZ FOF charges the investor a management fee of €1 million (= €100 million × 1%) and an incentive fee of €1.4 million (= €14 million × 10%). The return to the investor is 11.6% [= (14 – 1 – 1.4)/100].

3. Why would the investor choose to invest in a fund of funds instead of a hedge fund given the effect of the "double fee" demonstrated in the answers to Questions 1 and 2?

Solution:

This scenario assumes that returns are the same for all underlying hedge funds. In practice, this result will not likely be the case, and XYZ FOF may provide due diligence expertise and potentially valuable diversification. In addition, the underlying hedge fund might be closed to new investors and investing in the FOF may be the only way to access the hedge fund.

QUESTION SET

1. Soft Hurdle

A real estate investment fund has deployed $100 million initial capital to purchase a property. The fund has a soft hurdle preferred return to investors of 8% per annum and an 80%/20% carried interest incentive split thereafter (with a standard catch-up clause). At the end of Year 2, the property is sold for a total of $160 million.

Ignoring management fees, what are the correct distributions to the LPs and the GP?

Solution:

With a soft hurdle arrangement, the carried interest is calculated on the entire annual gross return as long as the set hurdle is exceeded. To calculate the distributions of gain, one needs to construct a waterfall of cash flows.

First, the LPs would be due their $100 million initial investment.

Then, they would be due $16 million (8% preferred return on initial capital for two years).

The soft hurdle has been met, and the GP is due the carried interest until 20% of the profits generated is received, or $4 million (2% for two years), which would be paid to the GP next as a catch-up to the achieved hurdle return.

The residual amount would be $160 million – $100 million – $16 million – $4 million = $40 million. This amount would then be split 80% to the LPs and 20% to the GP, or $32 million and $8 million, respectively.

So, the total payout with a soft annual hurdle of 8% of the $160 million would end up with the following waterfall:

	LP	GP
Return of Capital	$100 m	
8% Preferred per Annum	$16 m	
GP Catch-Up 20%		$4 m
80%/20% Split	$32 m	$8 m
Total Payout	$148 m	$12 m

2. Hard Hurdle

Following Question 1, how would the distributions to the LPs and GP have been different if the real estate investment fund had a hard hurdle of 8% per annum and no catch-up clause?

Solution:

If the fund had a hard hurdle rate instead (i.e., no catch-up clause), only the amount above the $100 return of capital and $16 million preferred return would be subject to the 20% carried interest incentive to the GP: 20% × $44 million = $8.8 million—quite a bit less than the carried interest payment with the soft hurdle. The LPs would be due the balance of $35.2 million (= $44 million – $8.8 million incentive). This would result in the following total payout:

	LP	GP
Return of Capital	$100 m	
8% Preferred per Annum	$16 m	
80%/20% Split above Hurdle	$35.2 m	$8.8 m
Total Payout	$151.2 m	8.8 m

3. Calculating Net Return

Capricorn Fund of Funds invests GBP100 million in each of Alpha Hedge Fund and ABC Hedge Fund. Capricorn Fund of Funds has a "1 and 10" fee structure. Management fees and incentive fees are calculated independently at the end of each year. After one year, net of their respective management and incentive fees, Capricorn's investment in Alpha is valued at GBP80 million and Capricorn's investment in ABC is valued at GBP140 million. The annual return to an investor in Capricorn Fund of Funds, net of fees assessed at the fund-of-funds level, is closest to:

A. 7.9%.

B. 8.0%.

C. 8.1%.

Solution:

A is correct, because the net investor return is 7.9%, calculated as follows:

First, note that "1 and 10" refers to a 1% management fee and a 10% incentive fee.

End-of-year capital = GBP140 million + GBP80 million = GBP220 million.

Management fee = GBP220 million × 1% = GBP2.2 million.

Incentive fee = (GBP220 million − GBP200 million) × 10% = GBP2 million.

Total fees to Capricorn = GBP2.2 million + GBP2 million = GBP4.2 million.

Investor net return = (GBP220 − GBP200 − GBP4.2)/GBP200 = 7.9%.

If, however, the incentive fee is calculated after deduction of management fees (instead of being calculated independently), then the incentive fee would become (GBP220 million – GBP200 million – GBP2.2 million) × 10% = GBP1.78 million

Investor net return would have become (GBP220 – GBP200 – GBP2.2 – GBP1.78)/GBP200 ≈ 8.0%.

4. IRR vs. MOIC

Match the advantages and disadvantages of IRR and MOIC as performance measures for long-lived alternative investments:

Return Metrics	Advantages/Disadvantages
1. IRR	A. ignores timing of cash flows.
	B. considers timing of cash flows.
	C. is more complicated to calculate.
2. MOIC	D. is easy to calculate and understand.
	E. requires assumptions on opportunity costs and reinvestment rates.
	F. is the preferred measure for long-lived alternative investments.
	G. is commonly used by private equity and real estate investors as a shortcut.

Solution:

1. IRR (F) is the preferred measure for long-lived alternative investments, because it (B) considers timing of cash flows, but it (C) is more complicated to calculate and (E) requires assumptions on opportunity costs and reinvestment rates.
2. MOIC (G) is commonly used by private equity and real estate investors as a shortcut, because it (D) is easy to calculate and understand, but it (A) ignores timing of cash flows.

5. Either/or Fee Structure

A closed-end infrastructure fund with initial capital of €100 million has an either/or fee structure under which the GP can either charge a 1% management fee or accept a higher 25% incentive fee, whichever is higher. All fees are calculated based on end-of-period net asset value. Standard high-water mark provisions apply.

The fund returns for the first five years are as follows:

Year	NAV (€ millions)	Gross Return
1	98.00	-2%
2	93.10	-5%
3	108.00	16%
4	129.60	20%
5	176.26	36%

Please calculate the fees received by the GP for each of the five years.

Solution:

The management and incentive fees that can be received by the GP in each year are tabulated as follows:

Year	NAV (€ millions)	Gross Return	Management Fee (%)	Incentive Fee (%)	Total Fee (€ millions)
1	98.00	–2%	1%	—	0.98
2	93.10	–5%	1%	—	0.93
3	108.00	16%	—	25% (108 – 100) × 25%	2.00
4	129.60	20%	—	25% (129.6 – 108.0) × 25%	5.40
5	176.26	36%	—	25% (176.26 – 129.60) × 25%	11.67
				Cumulative fees	**20.98**

Note that because the fund made a loss in Year 1 and in Year 2, there is no incentive fee and the GP can receive only the 1% management fee. In Year 3, when the fund made a profit, the incentive fee can be charged on the gain above the last high-water mark, which was the initial €100 million in Year 0. Since the management fee for Year 3 would have been just €1.08 million (= €108 million × 1%), the GP will be better off receiving the incentive fee of €2 million. Likewise, for Years 4 and 5, the GP can choose to receive the incentive fee at 25% of the profits in those two years without earning any management fee.

6. Hedge Fund Indexes

A common problem with hedge fund indexes is the upward bias due to:

A. backfill bias only.

B. survivorship bias only.

C. both backfill and survivorship bias.

Solution:

C is correct. Both backfill bias and survivorship bias are common in hedge fund indexes.

Survivorship bias refers to the selection bias in the index due to the exclusion of failed funds from a given benchmark. It leads to overly optimistic return expectations. Backfill bias refers to hedge funds including only the most successful funds in an index a few years after inception. The subsequent inclusion or "backfilling" of prior performance data on a selective basis serves to increase average reported returns. Both of these biases result in an upward bias in hedge fund indexes because they may reflect not actual average hedge fund performance but, rather, only the returns of those funds that initially performed best and/or have not failed.

PRACTICE PROBLEMS

1. The following information applies to Rotunda Advisers, a hedge fund:

   - $288 million in AUM as of prior year end
   - 2% management fee (based on year-end AUM)
   - 20% incentive fee calculated:
     - Net of management fee
     - Using a 5% soft hurdle rate
     - Using a high-water mark (high-water mark is $357 million)
   - Current-year fund gross return is 25%.

   The total fee earned by Rotunda in the current year is closest to:

   A. $7.20 million.

   B. $20.16 million.

   C. $21.60 million.

2. A hedge fund with net capital of GBP500 million has borrowed an additional GBP200 million at 4.5% per annum. The current-year return of the fund is 15%. What would have been the return if the fund had not added any leverage?

   A. 10.7%

   B. 12.0%

   C. 19.2%

3. A common problem for the "mark-to-model" valuation of private equity funds is *most likely*:

   A. a violation of accounting rules.

   B. an understatement of portfolio risk.

   C. an understatement of interim portfolio return.

4. A commodity hedge fund has three investors:

   - €100 million from Investor A invested at Year 0,
   - €100 million from Investor B invested at the beginning of Year 2, and
   - €100 million from Investor C invested at the beginning of Year 3.

   The gross returns before fees of the fund are as follows:

Year	Annual Gross Return	Investor A's Investment (€ millions)	Investor B's Investment (€ millions)	Investor C's Investment (€ millions)
0	—	100		—
1	20%	—		—
2	–15%	—	100	—

Year	Annual Gross Return	Investor A's Investment (€ millions)	Investor B's Investment (€ millions)	Investor C's Investment (€ millions)
3	15%	—		100
4	10%	—		—

The management fee is 2% based on end-of-year value. The incentive fee is 20% above the high-water mark and is calculated based on end-of-year value net of management fee.

Which investor has earned the highest net return after the end of Year 4?

A. Investor A

B. Investor B

C. Investor C

The following information relates to questions 5-6

Buyout Capital, LLC, is a private equity fund that has the following characteristics:

- Capital committed: $200 million
- Preferred return: 8% soft hurdle, with full catch-up
- Fund distribution: after five years
- Management fee: none
- Carried interest: 20% above preferred return
- Waterfall structure: American (deal by deal) with clawback

The fund made five investments, tabulated as follows:

Investment No.	Year		Amount ($ m)		Profit	
	Invested	Sold	Invested	Sold	$ m	%
1	0	4	40	60	20	10.67%
2	0	4	40	100	60	25.74%
3	1	5	40	50	10	5.74%
4	1	5	40	120	80	31.61%
5	2	5	40	30	(10)	neg.
Total			**200**	**360**	**160**	**12.47%**

5. What is the total carried interest to the GP?

   A. $30 million

   B. $32 million

   C. $34 million

6. Buyout Capital, LLC, is a private equity fund that has the following

characteristics:

- Capital committed: $200 million
- Preferred return: 8% soft hurdle, with full catch-up
- Fund distribution: after five years
- Management fee: none
- Carried interest: 20% above preferred return
- Waterfall structure: European (whole of fund)

The fund made five investments that are tabulated as follows:

Investment No.	Year		Amount ($ m)		Profit	
	Invested	Sold	Invested	Sold	$ m	%
1	0	4	40	60	20	10.67%
2	0	4	40	100	60	25.74%
3	1	5	40	50	10	5.74%
4	1	5	40	120	80	31.61%
5	2	5	40	30	(10)	neg.
Total			**200**	**360**	**160**	**12.47%**

What is the total carried interest to the GP?

A. $30 million

B. $32 million

C. $34 million

7. A hedge fund has the following fee structure:

- Annual management fee based on year-end AUM: 2%
- Incentive fee: 20%
- Hurdle rate before incentive fee collection starts: 4%
- Current high-water mark: $610 million

The fund has a value of $583.1 million at the beginning of the year. After one year, it has a value of $642 million before fees. The net percentage return to an investor for this year is closest to:

A. 6.72%.

B. 6.80%.

C. 7.64%.

SOLUTIONS

1. A is correct. Although the gross return of Rotunda results in a \$360 million gross NAV, the deduction of the \$7.2 million management fee brings NAV to \$352.8 million, which is below the prior high-water mark. Rotunda earns a management fee of \$7.20 million but does not earn an incentive fee because the year-end fund value net of management fee does not exceed the prior high-water mark of \$357 million. Since Rotunda is still also below the prior-year high-water mark, the hurdle rate of return is also basically irrelevant in this fee calculation.

   The specifics of this calculation are as follows:

   End-of-year AUM = Prior year-end AUM × (1 + Fund return) = \$288 million × 1.25 = \$360 million.

   \$360 million × 2% = \$7.20 million management fee.

   \$360 million − \$7.2 million = \$352.8 million AUM net of management fee.

   The year-end AUM net of fees do not exceed the \$357 million high-water mark. Therefore, no incentive fee is earned.

2. B is correct.

   Using Equation 2,

   r_L = Leveraged portfolio return/Cash position = $[r \times (V_b + V_c) - (V_b \times r_b)]/V_c$.

   Or, after re-arranging the formula,

   $$r = \frac{(V_c \times r_L) + (V_b \times r_b)}{(V_c + V_b)}.$$

   Substituting $r_L = 0.15$, $V_b = 200$, $V_c = 500$, $r_b = 0.045$,

   $r = (500 \times 0.15) + (200 \times 0.045)/(200 + 500) = 12\%$.

   Since leverage magnifies return when the borrowing cost is lower than asset returns, the unleveraged asset return must be lower than 15%.

3. B is correct. Accounting rules require that investments be recorded at their fair value for financial reporting purposes. The fair value of private equity that owns illiquid assets requires certain estimates, rather than observable transaction prices, to be factored into valuation. A model that relies on Level 3 inputs may reflect an imperfect theoretical valuation and not a true liquidation value. The lack of new market information over time may anchor the interim valuation at or near initial cost. The relatively stable accounting valuations may give investors a false sense that they are less volatile. At the same time, there is a potential conflict of interest for the GP to overstate interim return because of the implication for carried interest. As a result, returns may be smoothed or overstated and the volatility of returns understated.

4. C is correct. Despite investing for the shortest period of time in the fund (i.e., two years), Investor C has earned the highest net return compared to the other two investors. The following table illustrates the calculations based on the "2 and 20" fee structure and the high-water marks facing each investor in any particular year; in each case, the incentive fee is calculated using Equation 8:

   $R_{GP(High\text{-}Water\ Mark)} = (P_2 \times r_m) + \max[0, (P_2 - P_{HWM}) \times p]$.

The net return is calculated using Equation 9:

$r_i = (P_2 - P_1 - R_{GP})/P_1$.

Year	Annual Gross Return	Investor A's Investment	Year-End AUM (Before Fee)	High-Water Mark	Management Fee (2%)	Incentive Fee (20%)	Year-End AUM (After Fee)
							(Before Fee)
0	—	100.00	100.00	—	—	—	100.00
1	20%	—	120.00	100.00	2.40	3.52	114.08
2	-15%	—	96.97	114.08	1.94	—	95.03
3	15%	—	109.28	114.08	2.19	—	107.10
4	10%	—	117.81	114.08	2.36	0.27	115.18
Investor A's net return							**15.18%**

Year	Annual Gross Return	Investor B's Investment	Year-End AUM (Before Fee)	High-Water Mark	Management Fee (2%)	Incentive Fee (20%)	Year-End AUM (Before Fee)
0	—	—	—	—	—	—	—
1	20%	—	—	—	—	—	—
2	-15%	100.00	85.00	100.00	1.70	—	83.30
3	15%		95.80	100.00	1.92	—	93.88
4	10%	—	103.27	100.00	2.07	0.24	100.96
Investor B's net return							**0.96%**

Year	Annual Gross Return	Investor C's Investment	Year-End AUM (Before Fee)	High-Water Mark	Management Fee (2%)	Incentive Fee (20%)	Year-End AUM (Before Fee)
0	—	—	—	—	—	—	—
1	20%	—	—	—	—	—	—
2	-15%	—	—	—	—	—	—
3	15%	100.00	115.00	100.00	2.30	2.54	110.16
4	10%	—	121.18	110.16	2.42	1.72	117.03
Investor C's Net Return							**17.03%**

5. A is correct. The distribution of profit of each investment is as follows:

	Year		Amount ($ m)		Profit			
Investment No.	**Invested**	**Sold**	**Invested**	**Sold**	**$ m**	**%**	**LPs at 80%**	**GP at 20%**
1	0	4	40	60	20	10.67%	16	4
2	0	4	40	100	60	25.74%	48	12
3	1	5	40	50	10	5.74%	10	0
4	1	5	40	120	80	31.61%	64	16

	Year		Amount ($ m)		Profit			
Investment No.	**Invested**	**Sold**	**Invested**	**Sold**	**$ m**	**%**	**LPs at 80%**	**GP at 20%**
5	2	5	40	30	(10)	neg.	(8)	(2)
Total			**200**	**360**	**160**	**12.47%**	**130**	**30**

Since the preferred return of the LP is 8%, Investments 1, 2, and 4 all meet the criterion and the profit is split 80/20 between the LPs and GP. Investment 3 does not earn the GP any carry because it fails to meet the preferred return; neither does Investment 5, whose profit is negative. Because of the clawback clause, the GP's carry is reduced by $2 million (or 20% of the loss on Investment 5). Therefore, the total carried interest adds up to $30 million, or 30/160 = 18.75% of the total profit made by the fund.

6. B is correct. A European waterfall occurs at the aggregate fund level. As long as the fund exit IRR exceeds 8% after five years, the GP will be eligible for the full 20% carried interest on the profit made from all investments—that is, $160 million × 20% = $32 million.

	Year		Amount ($ m)		Profit			
Investment No.	**Invested**	**Sold**	**Invested**	**Sold**	**$ m**	**%**	**LPs at 80%**	**GP at 20%**
1	0	4	40	60	20	10.67%		
2	0	4	40	100	60	25.74%		
3	1	5	40	50	10	5.74%		
4	1	5	40	120	80	31.61%		
5	2	5	40	30	(10)	neg.		
Total			**200**	**360**	**160**	**12.47%**	**128**	**32**

7. C is correct. The management fee for the year is $642 million × 0.02 = $12.84 million.

   Because the ending gross value of the fund of $642 million exceeds the high-water mark of $610 million, the hedge fund can collect an incentive fee on gains above this high-water mark but net of the hurdle rate of return. The incentive fee calculation becomes

   {$642 – [$610 × (1 + 0.04)]} × 0.20 = $1.52 million.

   The net return to the investor for the year is

   [($642 – $12.84 – $1.52)/$583.1] – 1 = 0.07638 ≈ 7.64%.

LEARNING MODULE

3

Investments in Private Capital: Equity and Debt

LEARNING OUTCOMES

Mastery	The candidate should be able to:
☐	explain features of private equity and its investment characteristics
☐	explain features of private debt and its investment characteristics
☐	describe the diversification benefits that private capital can provide

INTRODUCTION

1

This Learning Module and the subsequent four Learning Modules explain the investment characteristics of specific alternative asset types, starting with private equity and private debt. The subsequent Learning Modules focus on real assets, natural resources, hedge funds, and digital assets. Each Learning Module introduces core characteristics, distinguishing features, and risk–return characteristics for the specific asset class. Alternative assets differ from the traditional asset classes—debt and equity—due to their unique return, risk, and information profiles and historically show low levels of correlation with debt and equity. Moreover, alternative assets often require highly specialized knowledge to select, manage, and divest these assets. Since these alternative assets are generally considered to be less liquid than traditional asset classes, understanding the valuation and return characteristics is a specialized skill.

LEARNING MODULE OVERVIEW

- Private equity is a form of private capital funding sourced from outside public markets through non-traditional sources, such as venture capital and leveraged buyout firms. It can be injected at various stages of business development, from initial idea to final transition to public company status.
- The duration of a private equity investment also varies, with funds conducting their exits typically by the strategies of trade sales to strategic buyers or public listings through IPOs or special acquisition

companies (SPACs). Other strategies include recapitalizations, secondary sales, and liquidations, with all the strategies having their unique advantages and drawbacks.

- Compared to traditional investments, private equity can offer better returns combined with higher risks. This contrast is a function of private equity's distinct choice set, greater management control, and greater leverage. Data ambiguities make it challenging to reliably measure the benefits of private equity investing.
- Private debt primarily refers to the various forms of debt provided by investors directly to private entities. Its four major categories are direct lending, mezzanine loans, venture debt, and distressed debt, and it also includes unitranche debt of blended loans and other specialty loans.
- As in private equity investment, private debt can be arranged on a direct or indirect basis, with funds deployed over the corporate life cycle straight from an investor or intermediated through a fund. Investors receive interest payments and the return of principal after a designated term, with debt typically secured and having protections/covenants.
- Private debt has potentially higher returns and risks than traditional fixed income, with its investors needing specialized knowledge to adjust exposures for differences across company funding stages, debt structures, and underlying assets.
- Private debt and equity are distinct in terms of risks and performance from their public counterparts due to illiquidity and concentration risk and to the often-greater uncertainties of both their underlying businesses and the means to hedge away their risks. And a fundamental timing characteristic for private capital is its vintage year, with the valuation and economic environment at the origin of a private equity fund having a potentially substantial effect on realized results over the fund's set lifespan.
- To offset the potentially adverse performance effects of an ill-timed fund launch at an unfavorable stage of the business cycle, investors can diversify exposure across fund vintage years.
- Investments in private capital vary in terms of risk and return across the corporate capital structure hierarchy, with a diversified mix of private equity and debt investments potentially balancing private capital risks and returns. And when combined with public stocks and bonds, investments in private capital funds can add a moderate diversification benefit with opportunities for excess returns due to private capital's additional leverage, market, and liquidity risks.

SELF-ASSESSMENT

These initial questions are intended to help you gauge your current level of understanding of this learning module.

1. At the conclusion of a public company's leveraged buyout, the amount of its market-traded stock is substantially:

   A. reduced.

B. increased.

C. unaffected.

Solution:

A is correct. After the transaction, the target company becomes or remains a privately owned company. Leveraged buyouts are sometimes called "going-private" transactions because after the acquisition of a publicly traded company, the target company's equity is substantially no longer publicly traded.

2. Which of the following financing tools would *most likely* be used at the later stage of venture capital investment?

   A. Common stock

   B. Preferred stock

   C. Convertible debt

Solution:

B is correct. Preferred stock can be deployed as late into a company's maturity as later-stage venture capital, when preferred stock can offer more protection to venture investors as a company transitions toward an IPO. A and C are incorrect because these instruments are more typically used in the earlier pre-seed and seed stages.

3. Which of the following transaction features is associated with mezzanine debt?

   A. Warrants

   B. Lines of credit

   C. Fixed payment schedules

Solution:

A is correct. Mezzanine debt often comes with additional features, such as warrants or conversion rights. These provide equity participation to lenders/investors. B is incorrect because lines of credit are associated with venture debt, which entrepreneurs may seek to obtain additional financing without further diluting shareholder ownership. C is incorrect because fixed payment schedules are associated with direct lending, in which, as with typical bank loans, payments are usually received on a fixed schedule.

4. In using private debt for a syndicated leveraged mortgage portfolio, the financial ratio of loan to value (LTV) is important at:

   A. origination and to the real estate fund sponsor.

   B. syndication and to the private debt fund lender.

   C. both transaction phases and to each of the parties.

Solution:

C is correct. LTV plays a significant role in both legs of this transaction. For a sponsor to be able to borrow and for a lender to be able syndicate the loans, the aggregate LTV ratio cannot be breached, and any deviation from LTV on an individual property level needs to be cured. As the loan amortizes, its outstanding principal declines, decreasing LTV. However, if the value of the real estate were to drop, then the sponsor will be required to raise additional collateral to maintain the LTV level.

5. Vintage diversification is an advisable policy for implementation by private capital:

   A. funds.

   B. investors.

   C. users, such as company managers.

   Solution:

   B is correct. The vintage year, the time when fund deployment begins, is important for comparing PE and VC investments with other funds in the same year. Because of changing business and valuation environments, funds of a certain vintage have a relative advantage based on their start-up timing. That is why investors are encouraged to pursue vintage diversification by investing in multiple vintage years. A is incorrect because once capital commitments from a fund begin, all subsequent transactions are classified as part of the same vintage year. C is incorrect because the terms and conditions of capital use are more a function of the circumstances of their company than of the origin point of their fund source.

6. The potential diversification benefits from private capital investment are *most likely* related to its:

   A. wide range of exit strategies.

   B. various types of fee structures.

   C. lower correlation with public asset returns.

   Solution:

   C is correct. Investments in private capital funds can add a moderate diversification benefit to a portfolio of publicly traded stocks and bonds. Correlations with public market indexes vary from 0.63 to 0.83. A is incorrect because different exit strategies can offer funds the opportunity to maximize returns but do not necessarily reduce the volatility of returns over time. B is incorrect because while different fee structures may more effectively align the interests of funds and their investors, they do not necessarily change the risks of the underlying investments.

2 PRIVATE EQUITY INVESTMENT CHARACTERISTICS

☐ explain features of private equity and its investment characteristics

Private capital is the broad term for funding provided to companies that is not sourced from the public markets, such as from the sale of equities, bonds, and other securities on exchanges, or from traditional institutional providers, such as a government or bank. Capital raised from sources other than public markets and traditional institutions and in the form of an equity investment is called **private equity**. Comparably sourced capital extended to companies through a loan or other form of debt is referred to as **private debt**. Private capital relates to the entire capital structure, comprising private equity and private debt.

Private equity strategies include **leveraged buyout (LBO)**, venture capital (VC), and growth capital. Leveraged buyouts, or highly leveraged transactions, arise when private equity firms establish buyout funds (or LBO funds) to acquire public companies or established private companies, with a significant percentage of the purchase price financed through debt. The target company's assets typically serve as collateral for the debt, and the target company's cash flows are expected to be sufficient to service the debt. The debt becomes part of the target company's capital structure after the buyout occurs. After the transaction, the target company becomes or remains a privately owned company. LBOs are sometimes called "going private" transactions because after the acquisition of a publicly traded company, the target company's equity is substantially no longer publicly traded.

The LBO may also be of a specific type. In a **management buyout** (MBO), the current management team participates in the acquisition, and in a **management buy-in** (MBI), the current management team is replaced with the acquiring team involved in managing the company. LBO managers seek to add value by improving company operations, boosting revenue, and ultimately increasing profits and cash flows. Cash flow growth, in order of contribution, comes from organic revenue growth, cost reductions and restructuring, acquisitions, and then all other sources. The financial returns in this category, however, depend greatly on the use of leverage. If debt financing is unavailable or costly, LBOs become less attractive and are less likely to take place. As business conditions and the availability of financing change, private equity managers may change focus.

A manager may manage many private equity funds, each composed of several investments, and the companies owned are called **portfolio companies** because they will be part of a private equity fund portfolio.

There are certain similarities and differences between private equity and public equity. Both types of equity represent direct ownership and control of the corporation. Owners are shareholders and as such have voting rights at the annual general meeting of shareholders electing the board, setting strategy, and making impactful decisions for the future of the company. Additionally, all owners have a direct and proportional claim to residual cash flow rights in the form of dividends. Ultimately, because of significant shareholdings, private equity ownership allows more direct control over decisions than public equity. Because of this, managing a direct private investment exposure requires specialized knowledge specific to the industry and sector the firm is in. Capital gains are typically the largest driver of returns, either through price appreciation or from free cash flow generated by the holdings.

Equity investment, whether in public or private companies, has historically exhibited higher returns at the expense of greater risk compared with debt. The potential pay off for equity investors is unlimited upside with the downside limited to the amount invested. However, there are some differences as well.

Private Equity Investment Categories

Private equity investments can be direct, through a single private equity fund, or indirect, through a fund-of-funds vehicle with stakes in various other private funds. With a direct private equity investment, the investment is made in a single, specific asset, but there may also be co-investments where the investor will participate alongside a lead sponsor who sources, structures, and executes the transaction.

Non-public equity is often categorized by the investor's *entry* point in a company's life cycle (venture capital versus private equity), as Exhibit 1 shows.

Exhibit 1: Private and Venture Capital across the Corporate Life Cycle Stages

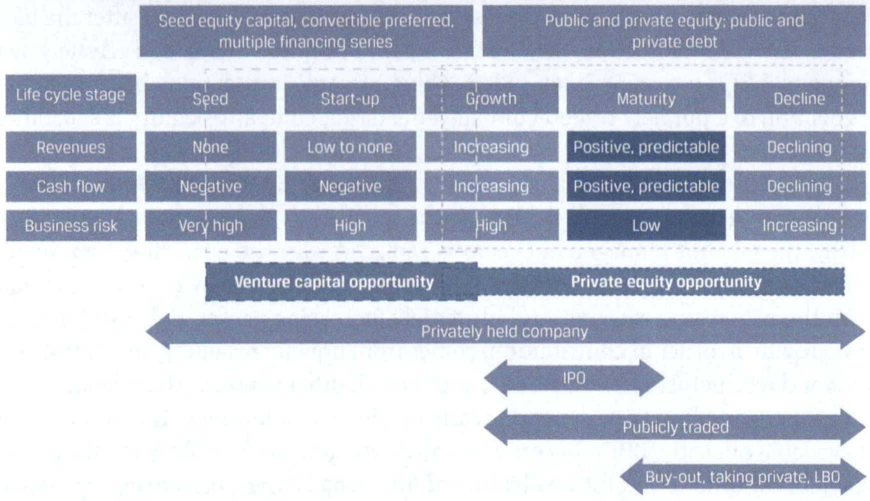

Venture capital entails investing in or providing financing to private companies with high growth potential. Typically, these are start-ups or young companies, but venture capital can be injected at various stages, ranging from concept creation for a company or near the point of a company's IPO (initial public offering) launch or its acquisition. The investment return required varies with the company's stage of development. Investors in early-stage companies will demand higher expected returns relative to later-stage investors because the earlier the stage of development, the higher the risk.

Venture capitalists, like all private equity managers, are active investors directly involved with their portfolio companies.

VC funds typically invest in companies and receive an equity interest but may also provide financing in the form of debt (commonly, convertible debt). Exhibit 2 summarizes the financing stages at different phases of the venture.

Exhibit 2: Stages of Venture Capital

Stage	Pre-seed	Seed	Early stage | Later stage
Investors	• Founders • Friends and family • Angel investors	• Seed funds • Angel investors	• Venture capital funds • Corporate venture funds • Private equity investors • Strategic investors
Typical investment amount	USD5k–USD500k	USD25k–USD5mil	USD5mil+
Source of capital	Mainly individuals	Funds	• Institutional investors • Family offices • Strategic investors

- *Pre-seed capital*, or *angel investing*, is capital provided at the idea stage. Funds may be used to develop a business plan and to assess market potential. The amount of financing here is typically small and sourced from individuals, often friends and family, rather than by VC funds.

- *Seed-stage financing*, or *seed capital*, generally supports product development and marketing efforts, including market research. This is the first stage at which VC funds usually invest.
- *Early-stage financing* (early-stage VC), or *start-up stage financing*, goes to companies moving toward operation but prior to commercial production or sales, in both of which early-stage financing may be injected to initiate.
- *Later-stage financing* (expansion VC) comes after commercial production and sales have begun but before an IPO. Funds may be used to support initial growth, a major expansion (such as a physical plant upgrade), product improvements, or a major marketing campaign.

Later-stage financing generally involves management selling control of the company to the VC investor; financing is provided through equity and debt, although the fund may also use convertible bonds or convertible preferred shares. The VC fund offers debt financing for reasons of recovery and the control of assets in a bankruptcy situation, not to generate income. Simply put, debt financing affords the VC fund more protection than equity does.

Mezzanine-stage financing (mezzanine venture capital) prepares a company to go public as it continues to expand capacity and enhance its growth trajectory. It represents the bridge financing needed to fund a private firm until it can execute an IPO or be sold. The term *mezzanine-stage financing* is used because it is infused between private and public company status, principally distinguished by the timing of the financing rather than its method. While the terms sound quite similar, mezzanine financing is different from mezzanine-stage financing. Mezzanine financing relates to the use of equity–debt hybrid instruments, such as convertible debt or convertible preferred. Mezzanine-stage financing can use mezzanine financing, but typically at this stage the main financing is either equity-like (to capture potential gains from the planned IPO) or short-term debt.

Convertible preferred shares are often used in start-ups to raise private capital from venture capital funds. Since convertible preferred shares include an option for the holder to convert the preferred shares into a fixed number of common shares after a predetermined date and in some cases at a predetermined price, they provide incentive alignment between the entrepreneurs in the start-up and the investor. The conversion value is ultimately based on the valuation of the start-up. Investing in a start-up is risky because the investor is financing a new and unproven business. Preferred convertible equity provides investors with additional protections that are not available to common shareholders. Most importantly, in the event of a liquidation, preferred convertible shareholders have seniority over common shareholders and are entitled to recover the entire value of their investment before common shareholders receive any of the proceeds.

When investing, the manager of the venture capital fund is largely confident that the portfolio company's management team is competent and armed with a solid business plan showing strong prospects for growth. Because these companies are immature businesses without years of operational and financial performance history, estimating company valuations and their future prospects is highly subjective.

Once venture capital sees an exit opportunity, private equity can take over. Private equity firms specialized in the later-stage life cycle phase seek to generate returns by directly influencing management and implementing strategy changes, particularly for both publicly traded and privately held companies that are underperforming their peers. Here, private equity focuses on increasing the value of the core business by adaptively changing the overall business strategy by eliminating poor-performing business lines or businesses that do not generate sufficiently high returns. These strategic changes can generate value that can be extracted either from the assets in place (selling underperforming assets) or by creating a more sustainable strategy and selling the company at a higher valuation.

Established companies in a transition phase may seek minority equity interest to expand, restructure, or acquire other companies. A private equity firm that engages in minority equity investing, also known as growth equity or growth capital, takes a less-than-controlling interest in more mature companies looking for capital to expand or restructure operations, enter new markets, or finance major acquisitions. Many times, minority equity investing is initiated and sought by the management of the investee company. The management's motive is to realize earnings from selling a portion of its shares before the company can go public but still retain control and participation in the success of the company. Although this scenario occurs most commonly with private companies, publicly quoted companies can seek private equity capital through PIPEs (private investments in public equities).

EXAMPLE 1

Tenderledge and Arguston—Buyout

A private equity firm, Tenderledge Opportunity Fund LLC, is evaluating Arguston Inc. Arguston is a mid-sized manufacturing firm operating in a mature industry and has seen both its revenues and earnings drop. Arguston does not have the needed capital to make the necessary long-term investments in technological upgrades to maintain its competitiveness or to recapture and extend its dwindling market share. The company is closely held, but the current owners and its management do not have the financial capacity to make the necessary investments and are willing to be bought out by Tenderledge.

To make the investment in Arguston, Tenderledge would not only provide needed capital but also restructure Arguston's operations to create efficiencies by reducing unnecessary redundancies and streamlining production, operations, and administration. It would likely replace management and install its own board members.

Tenderledge is likely to reduce overhead costs and cut employment levels. Once the restructuring and technological investments bear fruit, Tenderledge may also opt to consider acquiring some of Arguston's competitors to create additional growth through economies of scale and scope. Ultimately, the objective is to increase the value of Arguston and exit from the investment at a much higher price.

A **PIPE (private investment in public equity)** transaction is a private offering to select investors with fewer disclosures and lower transaction costs that allows the issuer to raise capital more quickly and cost effectively than with other means that may be more regulated, expensive, and lengthy. In a traditional PIPE transaction, either newly issued common stock or shares sold by existing stockholders—or a combination of both—in an already-publicly traded company are made available to certain investors. These investors, typically investment firms, mutual funds, or other institutional investors, enter into a definitive purchase agreement with the issuer and commit to purchase securities at a fixed price. These transactions are common in work-out or rescue situations where there is a material difference in the market price and valuations. A special case of PIPE is capital raised through convertible debt or convertible preferred stock. PIPE transactions are also dilutive to existing shareholders, and the new investors require a discount to market on the purchase price, which can introduce incentive conflicts between existing shareholders and new shareholders.

EXPEDIA AND PIPE DURING COVID-19

Private investment in public equity often signals confidence in a company's prospects and offers companies an accelerated approach to raise capital by selling large chunks of its equity to investors who often take board seats to directly get involved in setting business strategy. But these transactions can be costly.

In March 2020, the early stages of the COVID-19 pandemic led to a severe decline in travel, creating crisis conditions for the industry. Expedia, an online business and retail travel platform operating several brands, sold USD1.2 billion of preferred shares to two private equity managers, gave each firm a seat on its board, and issued USD2 billion of additional debt.

The preferred shares pay a fixed rate of 9.5% and warrants to purchase common stock. All in all, Expedia accumulated over USD4 billion in liquidity to weather the business disruption caused by the pandemic.

Expedia may redeem these preferred shares at preset prices during certain time periods and at preset periods.

Time period	Redemption price
Up to the first year of issuance	105.0%
Between first and second year of issuance	103.0%
Between second and third year of issuance	102.0%
Between third and fourth year of issuance	101.0%
After the fourth year of issuance	100.0%

When redeeming these shares, Expedia also has to pay any unpaid and accrued dividends. Additionally, Expedia also issued warrants to purchase 8.4 million shares of common equity at an exercise price of USD72.00 per share; these warrants have an expiration of 10 years.

Finally, Expedia also issued debt with an aggregate principal amount up to USD855 million. Its euro-denominated debt paid up to a 2.35% annual interest rate until 31 December 2021 and after that date paid up to 1.75%.

Assuming the adverse business conditions recovered fairly quickly to enable Expedia redemption of the financing at the midpoint (2 years) of the term sheet and it had not paid any preferred dividends beforehand, Expedia's cost would be $[(1.02) + (0.095 \times 2)]$(USD1.2 billion) = USD1.45 billion, or USD250 million in excess of the preferred fund raise, plus the potential dilutive effects on earnings of 8.4 million extra common shares if their market price exceeded the USD72 warrant exercise price. As a benchmark comparison, the dividend yield of the largest US market preferred ETF, iShares Preferred and Income Securities, was approximately 5.6% in the summer of 2020, a substantially lower yield.

Private Equity Exit Strategies

Private equity firms seek to improve new or underperforming businesses and then exit them at higher valuations, buying and holding companies for an average of five years. Holding time, however, can range from less than six months to more than 10 years. Before deciding on an exit strategy, private equity managers assess the dynamics of the industry in which the portfolio company competes, the overall economic cycle, interest rates, and company performance.

Instead of a long-term buy-and-hold strategy that managers and owners of publicly held equity funds espouse, private equity seeks to aggressively maximize investment return by selling or even auctioning holdings in private assets to the highest bidder. The added value that private equity investors can realize by strategically connecting firms and entities can further increase the value of the transaction and the returns to the private equity investors.

Typically, a private equity fund has an investment period of approximately five years and a subsequent harvesting period when exit occurs and the valuation environment becomes more relevant. Moreover, private equity fund investments are not made in one single payment but are spread over time using committed capital over several years, which provides managers a great deal of flexibility to optimize when their entry and exit points occur.

There are two main exit strategies: trade sale and public listing, which can take the form of IPOs, direct listings, or SPACs

Trade Sale

There are two main exit strategies: trade sale and public listing. In a **trade sale**, a portion or a division of the private company is sold either via direct sale or auction to a strategic buyer interested in increasing the scale and scope of the existing business. Because the transaction may have an impact on the competitive environment, it may face regulatory scrutiny and approval or management or employee resistance.

A key advantage of a trade sale is that a strategic investor will be willing to pay a premium as they price in potential synergies with their existing business. Other advantages of a trade sale include the relatively fast and simple execution of the transaction, which compared with an IPO may be shorter and incur lower transaction costs. Since these are privately negotiated transactions, there is a higher confidentiality because there are just a few parties involved in the transaction or the auction. Additionally, the strategic buyers can better evaluate the fit with their existing business without external scrutiny, which potentially makes strategic buyers willing to pay more from anticipating synergies with their own business.

The disadvantages of trade sales include potential resistance from existing members of management, who may fear their job security and may wish to avoid ownership by a competitor. Similarly, management and employees may resist a private transaction because a public listing would monetize the shares and potentially attain a higher sale price. Finally, the universe of trade buyers may be limited, which can potentially raise regulatory scrutiny and reduce prices.

EXAMPLE 2

Tenderledge and Arguston—Exit

After Tenderledge Opportunity Fund LLC, bought out Arguston Inc., the mid-sized manufacturing firm operating in a mature industry, Tenderledge restructured Arguston's operations and acquired some of Arguston's direct competitors to increase its economies of scale. Additionally, it acquired one of Arguston's smaller, strategic suppliers to create a strategically resilient and efficient entity. To realize the efficiencies from streamlining production, operations, distributions, and administration, Tenderledge is now considering exiting from this investment.

Trade sale may be an alternative Tenderledge considers, particularly because there still are some competitors that may benefit from a strategic alliance with a more cost-efficient peer. Tenderledge has turned to BridgeRock LLC, another private equity firm, which owns one of Arguston's main competitors, Tetrawolf Inc., about merging the two companies before exiting from the investment by listing the companies on the market.

Public Listing

Public listing on an exchange can take place either as an initial public offering (IPO), a direct listing, or a special acquisition company (SPAC). IPOs are the most common means of raising capital in public equity markets using financial intermediaries to underwrite the offering. When a private equity firm or company founder takes a company public, the portfolio company sells its shares, including some or all of those held by the private equity firm, to public investors.

There are several benefits of an IPO as an exit strategy. An IPO may potentially realize the highest price for the company, may increase the visibility of the company, and would continue to provide an upside for the private equity company because it retains a share in the new public entity. Moreover, the success of an IPO builds on management support and approval, and it is likely that management will be retained, which provides job security.

There are several disadvantages with an IPO and public listing. Apart from the high transaction fees to investment banks and lawyers, the time to complete the transaction may be long, and it requires onerous disclosure. The public equity market introduces stock market volatility, and the potential lockup period (mandating the private equity firm to retain an equity position for a specified period post-IPO) may limit a quick realization of value. Moreover, not all companies are suitable for an IPO; smaller companies and those operating in out-of-favor industries, ones with unclear strategic priorities and unstable financial position, or those that have limited operating histories may not be ideal candidates for an IPO. A less commonly used approach to exit from a private equity position is **direct listing**, where the equity of the entity is floated on the public markets directly, without underwriters, reducing the complexity and cost of the transaction.

A **special purpose acquisition company** (SPAC) is a technique also used for a public exit. Such a "blank check" company exists solely for the purpose of acquiring an unspecified private company within a predetermined period; otherwise, it must return capital to investors. Companies suitable for an IPO would be appropriate SPAC candidates, but the two strategies have different valuation methods: here a single counterparty sets SPAC terms, which reduces the uncertainty around the valuation.

There are several advantages of an SPAC exit; these transactions provide an extended time for public disclosure on company prospects to build investor interest, flexibility of transaction structure to best suit the company's context, and association with potentially high-profile and seasoned sponsors and their extensive investor network. Moreover, the valuation of the entity is fixed in advance and does not change, which reduces both the volatility and the uncertainty of share pricing. Finally, SPACs are allowed to provide more forward formal guidance on a company's prospects than is allowed under an IPO.

There are some noteworthy shortcomings of using SPACs for market access and exit. First, SPAC transactions increase the cost of capital because the various capital instruments, such as warrants, have dilutive effects. Second, there is a valuation spread between the value of the SPAC equity and the equity purchased by the SPAC. This can be further complicated by possible dilution effects: The shares and warrants of a SPAC can be issued and then traded separately. Third, there may also be specific deal risk associated with the successful execution of the definite purchase and merger agreement. Fourth, regulatory authorities, such as the US SEC, are reconsidering the classification of SPACs under long established rules that could impose more stringent standards on their operations. Finally, there may be significant trading in the SPAC equity in the months after the purchase transaction is announced that can lead to **stockholder overhang**, the downward pressure on the share price as large blocks of shares are being sold on the open market.

EXAMPLE 3

Tenderledge and BridgeRock—SPAC Transaction

After Tenderledge Opportunity Fund LLC and BridgeRock merged their two companies Arguston Inc. and Tetrawolf Inc., they continued to operate the merged company, Aurora Inc., each holding a 50% share in the merged entity. As both private equity firms are considering exiting from the investment at the same time, they were evaluating various exit alternatives.

For private equity, having an exit strategy is critical. Tenderledge and BridgeRock are evaluating various alternatives. Although IPOs and direct listings are popular exit strategies, SPACs have the ability to raise capital as companies such as Aurora enter the public market. Given the future uncertainty about valuations, the private equity firms chose to go the SPAC route and enter into a merger with a SPAC to bring Aurora to market a few months faster and at a higher price than the companies would have realized had they chosen an IPO or a direct listing.

Exhibit 3: Pros and Cons of Common Private Equity Exit Strategies

Strategy	Advantage	Disadvantage
Trade Sale	1. Immediate cash exit 2. Higher price from synergy-seeking strategic buyers 3. Fast and simple execution 4. Streamlined process on transaction cost, disclosure, and confidentiality from dealing with only one party	1. Potential management opposition 2. Limited set of buyers 3. Reduced financial appeal to employees due to forgone monetization of ownership stakes/options
IPO	1. Highest potential share price 2. Likeliest management approval 3. Notoriety to private equity sponsor' 4. Sharing in potential share price appreciation from ongoing ownership stake	1. High transaction costs 2. Long lead time 3. Stock market volatility creating value uncertainty 4. Onerous disclosure 5. Potential lockup period freezing capital committed to deal 6. Suitable mainly for large and fast-growing companies
SPAC	1. Extended disclosure time and ability to provide forward guidance to develop investor interest 2. Fixed valuation with lower share price volatility 3. Transaction structure flexibility 4. Involvement of high-profile, seasoned sponsors and their investor networks	1. Potential higher capital costs of dilution, warrants, and fees 2. Divergence between announced and true equity value due to dilution 3. Deal and capital risk of potential redemptions 4. Prolonged post-merger stockholder overhang and churn

Other Exit Strategies

In addition to the previously discussed exit strategies, other exit strategies include **recapitalization**, **secondary sale**, and **write-off/liquidation**.

- *Recapitalization.* Recapitalization via private equity describes the steps a firm takes to increase or introduce leverage to its portfolio company and pay itself a dividend out of the new capital structure. A recapitalization is not a true exit strategy, because the private equity firm typically maintains control; however, it does allow the private equity investor to extract money from the company to pay its investors and improve its internal rate of return (IRR).
- *Secondary sale.* This approach represents a sale of the company to another private equity firm or group of financial buyers. With the considerable amount of funds raised by global PE, there has been an increase in the proportion of secondary sale exits.
- *Write-off/liquidation.* A write-off occurs when a transaction has not gone well, and the investment is likely to lose value. The private equity firm then revises the value of its investment downward or liquidates the portfolio company before moving on to other projects.

The exit strategies we have discussed may be pursued individually or in combination with others or may be used for a partial exit strategy, such as divesting a self-contained product or business line. For example, private equity funds may sell a portion of a portfolio company to a competitor via a trade sale and then complete a secondary sale to another private equity firm for the remaining portion. Company shares may also be distributed directly to the investors (LPs) of the private equity fund, although such a move is unusual.

Risk–Return from Private Equity Investments

Private equity investors expect ownership capital returns—cash flows from dividends and proceeds from exit—subject to underlying market conditions of the industry. However, private equity investments have distinct entry and exit points between which managers exercise greater direct control and apply specialized knowledge to add value over a specific life cycle phase. While both involve investment selection (stock selection using filings and financial statement analysis for public companies, target selection for private equity), vintage year is important for private equity for comparative purposes.

The higher-return opportunities that private equity funds may provide relative to traditional investments are due to their ability to invest in private companies, their influence on portfolio companies' management and operations, and their use of leverage. Investing in private equity, including venture capital, is riskier than investing in common stocks and requires a higher return for accepting its higher risk, including illiquidity and leverage risks.

Published private equity indexes may be an unreliable measure of performance. Measuring historical private equity performance is challenging; as with hedge funds, which will be discussed later, private equity return indexes typically rely on self-reporting and are subject to survivorship, backfill, and other biases. This typically leads to an overstatement of returns. Moreover, prior to the global financial crisis of 2008–2009, in the absence of a liquidity event, private equity firms did not necessarily mark their investments to market. Failure to mark to market combined with the lag to mark investments due to inherent illiquidity will understate measures of volatility and correlations with other investments. Thus, data adjustments are required to more reliably measure the benefits of private equity investing. As a result, many investors expect companies to be marked on a quarterly or annual basis, preferably by an independent party. Investors should require a higher return for accepting a higher risk, including illiquidity and leverage risks.

QUESTION SET

1. Determine the correct answers to fill in the blanks:
   ______________ is the broad term for funding provided to companies that is not sourced from the public markets, with its two primary sub-categories being ______________ and ______________.

   Solution:

   Private capital is the broad term for funding provided to companies that is not sourced from the public markets, with its two primary sub-categories being *private equity* and *private debt*.

2. Identify the following statement as true or false: Both public and private equity represent direct ownership and control of the corporation. Additionally, all owners have a direct and proportional claim to residual cash flow rights in the form of dividends.

   Solution:

   True. These are two of the similarities shared by public and private equity.

3. Describe a funding situation to which a PIPE transaction is well suited.

   Solution:

   A PIPE (private investment in public equity) transaction is a private offering to select investors with fewer disclosures and lower transaction costs that allows the issuer to raise capital more quickly and cost effectively than other means that may be more regulated, expensive, and lengthy. These transactions are common in work-out or rescue situations where there is a material difference in the market price and valuations.

4. Match each form of private capital investment with the combination of corporate life cycle characteristics *most appropriate* for it.

Investment Form	Corporate Life Cycle Characteristics
1. Private Equity	i. Negative cash flow, high business risk
2. Venture Capital	ii. Increasing cash flow, high business risk
3. Both Private Equity and Venture Capital	iii. Declining cash flow, increasing business risk

   Solution:

Investment Form	Corporate Life Cycle Characteristics
1. Private Equity	iii. Declining cash flow, increasing business risk
2. Venture Capital	i. Negative cash flow, high business risk
3. Both Private Equity and Venture Capital	ii. Increasing cash flow, high business risk

   As shown in Exhibit 1, the "iii" combination of characteristics is typical of the decline stage, when private equity would have the best fit. The "i" combination of characteristics is typical of the start-up stage of the corporate life

> cycle, when venture capital is most appropriate. Finally, the "ii" combination is typical of the growth stage, when the opportunities for the forms of investment overlap and either type would be suitable.

PRIVATE DEBT INVESTMENT CHARACTERISTICS 3

- [ ] explain features of private debt and its investment characteristics

Private debt primarily refers to the various forms of debt provided by investors directly to private entities. In the past decade, the expansion of the private debt market has been largely driven by private lending funds filling the gap between borrowing demand and reduced lending supply from traditional lenders in the face of tightened regulations following the 2008 financial crisis.

We can organize the primary methods of private debt investing into four categories: direct lending, mezzanine loans, venture debt, and distressed debt. The broad array of debt strategies offers not only diversification benefits but also exposure to other investment spheres, such as real estate and infrastructure.

Private Debt Categories

Analogous to private equity investment, an investor wanting to include private debt in a portfolio has various alternatives along a comparable direct versus indirect distinction. In direct private debt investment, the investor makes a loan directly to a specific operating company. In the indirect approach, the investor takes an intermediated path, purchasing an interest in a fund that pools contributions typically on behalf of multiple participants to buy into the debt from a set of operating companies. For both approaches, in exchange for the debt, the investors receive interest payments and the return of principal after a designated term. The debt is typically secured and has various protections/covenants in place. Exhibit 4 depicts the role of private debt in the corporate life cycle.

Exhibit 4: Private Debt and Corporate Life Cycle

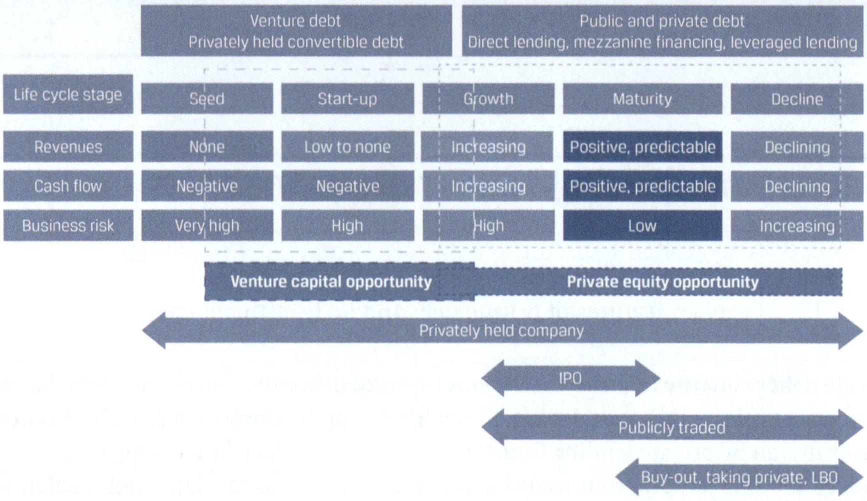

Venture debt is private debt funding that provides venture capital backing to start-up or early-stage companies that may be generating little or negative cash flow. Entrepreneurs may seek venture debt, often in the form of a line of credit or term loan, to obtain additional financing without further diluting shareholder ownership. Venture debt can complement existing equity financing, allowing current shareholders to maintain ownership and control for a longer period. Similar to mezzanine debt, venture debt may carry additional features that compensate the investor/lender for the increased risk of default or for the start-up and early-stage companies that lack substantial assets for debt collateral. One such feature could grant the lender rights to purchase equity in the borrowing company under certain circumstances.

Private debt investors get involved in **direct lending** by providing capital directly to borrowers and subsequently receiving interest, the original principal, and possibly other payments in exchange for their investment. As with typical bank loans, payments are usually received on a fixed schedule. The debt itself typically is senior and secured and has covenants in place to protect the lender/investor. It is provided by a small number of investors to private and sometimes public entities and differs from traditional debt instruments, such as bonds, which can be issued to many participants and be publicly traded.

Direct lending primarily involves private debt firms (or private equity firms with private debt arms) establishing funds with money raised from investors desiring higher-yielding debt. Fund managers will then seek financing opportunities, such as providing a loan to a mid-market corporation or extending debt to another private equity fund that is seeking funds for acquisitions. In general, private debt funds provide debt, at higher interest rates, to entities needing capital but lacking good alternatives to traditional bank lenders, which themselves may be uninterested or unable to transact with these borrowers. As in private equity, private debt fund managers conduct thorough due diligence before investing.

In direct lending, many firms may also provide debt in the form of a **leveraged loan**, a loan that is itself levered. Private debt firms that invest in leveraged loans first borrow money to finance the debt and then extend it to another borrower. By using leverage, a private debt firm can enhance the return on its loan portfolio.

EXAMPLE 4

Peterburgh Real Estate Fund, LLC—Syndicated Leveraged Mortgages

The Peterburgh Real Estate Fund, LLC, has acquired a portfolio consisting of six commercial properties for a total of GBP100 million. From its investors, the fund secured GBP30 million in equity financing, and it turned to BridgeRock Credit Opportunities LLP, a private debt fund that underwrites commercial mortgages before syndicating them.

In this specific transaction, properties valued at GBP100 million serve as collateral for a total of GBP75 million mortgages, giving an aggregate loan to value (LTV) of 0.75, which provides GBP25 million excess collateral to BridgeRock. The terms of the mortgage are MRR + 150 bps, with a maturity of 15 years, GBP5 million in annual amortization, and all mortgages being secured by the first lien on the property. The lender, BridgeRock, then sells or syndicates the mortgages to other banks or institutional investors. The LTV plays a significant role in both legs of this transaction. For Peterburgh to be able to borrow and for BridgeRock to be able syndicate the loans, the aggregate LTV ratio cannot be breached, and any deviation from the LTV on an individual property level needs to be cured. As Peterburgh amortizes the loan, the outstanding principal of the mortgages decline, which decreases the LTV value. However, if the value of the real estate were to drop, then Peterburgh will be required to raise additional collateral to maintain the LTV.

In private debt, **mezzanine debt** refers to private credit subordinated to senior secured debt but senior to equity in the borrower's capital structure. Mezzanine debt is a pool of additional capital available to borrowers beyond senior secured debt, often used to finance LBOs, recapitalizations, corporate acquisitions, and similar transactions. Because of its typically junior ranking and its usually unsecured status, mezzanine debt is riskier than senior secured debt. To compensate investors for this heightened risk, investors commonly demand higher interest rates and may require options for equity participation. Mezzanine debt often comes with additional features, such as warrants or conversion rights. These provide equity participation to lenders/investors, conveying the option to convert their debt into equity or purchasing the equity of the underlying borrower under certain circumstances.

Involvement in **distressed debt** typically entails buying the debt of mature companies in financial difficulty. These companies may be in bankruptcy, have defaulted on debt, or seem likely to default on debt. Some investors identify companies with a temporary cash flow problem but a good business plan to help the company survive and ultimately flourish. These investors buy the company's debt expecting both the company and its debt to increase in value. Turnaround investors buy debt with an aim to be more active in distressed company management and direction, seeking to restructure and revive the company. Overall, investors concentrating on distressed debt need to develop specialized knowledge related to assessing the likelihood of default and the possible recovery rates because distressed debt is priced to the expected recovery rate, but occasionally recovery rates mistake the underlying risk of the exposures and have long time horizons. Bankruptcy procedures can be lengthy, complex, and capital intensive. Similarly, distressed debt investors need to understand how to restructure companies and restructure debt. Several distressed debt funds focus on debtor-in-possession (DIP) financing, which provides operating funds for firms already in bankruptcy.

HERTZ AND DIP FINANCING

Hertz entered Chapter 11 reorganization in May 2020 after filing for bankruptcy due to COVID-19's near total shutdown of the global travel industry. In October 2020, it negotiated USD1.65 billion in operating funds secured through debtor-in-possession financing. That committed Hertz to pay creditors up to a market reference rate of (MRR) + 725 bps, permitting drawdowns from the facility in individual tranches of at least USD250 million. Up to USD1 billion was allowed for vehicle acquisition, and as much as USD800 million was allowed to fund working capital and general corporate needs.

The DIP financing was projected to provide Hertz with liquidity to support its continued operations throughout 2021, when the loan matured. Private capital firms Apollo Global Management, Diameter Capital Partners, and Silver Point Capital provided this funding. DIP financing is often a signal that lenders are confident in the company's ability to reorganize and pay the debt back in time.

Another type of debt that could be directly extended to borrowers is **unitranche debt**. Unitranche debt consists of a hybrid or blended loan structure combining different tranches of secured and unsecured debt into a single loan with a single, blended interest rate. Since unitranche debt is a blend of secured and unsecured debt, its interest rate will generally fall in between the interest rates often demanded on secured and unsecured debt. The unitranche loan will usually be structured between senior and subordinated debt in priority ranking.

Private debt firms may also provide *specialty loans*, extended to niche borrowers in specific situations. For example, in litigation finance, a specialist funding company provides debt to clients, usually plaintiffs in litigation, for their legal fees and expenses in exchange for a share of judgements.

Risk–Return of Private Debt

Private debt investments may provide higher-yielding opportunities to fixed-income investors seeking increased returns relative to traditional bonds. Private debt funds may generate higher returns by taking opportunistic positions based on market inefficiencies. Private lending funds filled the financing gap left by traditional lenders following the 2008 financial crisis. Investors in private debt could realize higher returns from the illiquidity premium, which is the excess return investors require to compensate for lack of liquidity. Investors also benefited from increased portfolio diversification by owning these securities.

The interest rate of private debt is often expressed relative to a reference rate—for example, the Secured Overnight Financing Rate (SOFR) + 375 bps. As a result, the coupon varies in line with changes to the reference rate brought about by changes to the interest rate environment.

Differences between public and private debt include the distinct entry and exit points with lenders, which offer borrowers greater flexibility in arranging financing. Specialized knowledge for private debt financing is needed in order to add value for the investor. First, the financing and return on debt depends on the specific period of a company's phase of life cycle. Earlier debt financing typically carries higher risks and provides higher returns. Second, the structure of the debt is also of importance; for instance, CLOs (collateralized loan obligations) with the market reference rate, or MRR, as the base rate require specialized knowledge. Finally, the investor needs to have special knowledge about underlying assets, particularly for secured lending, such as real estate.

The potential for higher returns is connected to higher levels of risk. Private debt investments vary in risk and return, with senior private debt providing a steadier yield and moderate risk and mezzanine private debt carrying higher growth potential, equity upside, and higher risk than senior private debt. Overall, investing in private debt is riskier than investing in traditional bonds. Investors should be aware of these risks, including illiquidity and heightened default risk when loans are extended to riskier entities or borrowers in riskier situations. Modeling private equity or debt returns is not straightforward, due to a lack of good-quality data and artificially smooth returns.

QUESTION SET

1. Identify two categories of private debt that would typically be relied on in the growth stage or a later stage of the corporate life cycle.

   Solution:

   As shown in Exhibit 4, three private debt categories are featured in the later stages of the corporate life cycle:

   1. Direct lending
   2. Mezzanine financing
   3. Leveraged lending

2. **Determine the correct answers to fill in the blanks:** Similar to mezzanine debt, ______________ may carry additional features that compensate the investor/lender for ________________________ or for the start-up and early-stage companies that ______________________.

   Solution:

   Similar to mezzanine debt, *venture debt* may carry additional features that compensate the investor/lender for *the increased risk of default* or for the start-up and early-stage companies that *lack substantial assets for debt collateral.*

3. Describe the borrowing cost of unitranche debt.

   Solution:

   Unitranche debt consists of a hybrid or blended loan structure combining different tranches of secured and unsecured debt into a single loan with a single, blended interest rate. Since unitranche debt is a blend of secured and unsecured debt, its interest rate will generally fall in between the interest rates often demanded on secured and unsecured debt.

4. Identify the following statement as true or false: Modeling private debt returns is fairly straightforward because they are a function of a benchmark public debt return.

   Solution:

   False. While private debt and public debt share a reference point in being marked up from a benchmark return, modeling private equity or debt returns is not straightforward, due to a lack of good-quality data, more security-specific risk between assets, and artificially smooth returns.

4 DIVERSIFICATION BENEFITS OF PRIVATE CAPITAL

☐ describe the diversification benefits that private capital can provide

Since the performance of private debt and private equity greatly depend on the specific phase of a company's life cycle, performance, and risk, comparison of public debt and equity may not be appropriate. First, investing in a start-up carries greater risk than investing in a well-established firm. Second, investing in a company in a declining or disintermediated industry is unlikely to offer positive return over longer time horizons. Moreover, performance risk of a continuous investment in public equity and debt can easily be hedged away.

The vintage year is important for comparing private equity and VC investments with other funds in the same year. Each private equity fund carries a **vintage year**, typically defined as the year in which the fund makes its first investment. Typically, a private equity fund operates over a 10- to 12-year period, which is often segmented into an initial investment period and a subsequent harvesting period. The investment period usually is the first five years during which the capital is sourced from the limited partners and invested in various companies. The harvesting period is the remaining years of the fund, when the fund looks to exit its existing investments and to return capital to limited partners.

Because of changing business and valuation environments, funds of a certain vintage have the advantage of starting in a low-valuation, low-risk appetite, economic recovery phase and benefit from riding the wave of an economic recovery. Other vintages may be less fortunate and invest the bulk of their capital in a high-valuation environment preceding a market crash or a period of prolonged economic contraction. That is why investors are encouraged to pursue vintage diversification by investing in multiple vintage years.

The performance realized by the fund is greatly determined by the vintage year and the phase of the business cycle in which the vintage year occurred, as Exhibit 5 shows. Funds seeded during the expanding phase of the business cycle tend to earn excess returns if they fund early-stage companies. Funds seeded during the contracting phase of the business cycle tend to earn excess returns if they fund distressed companies.

Exhibit 5: US Private Equity Index Vintage Year Returns, Net Fund-Level Performance

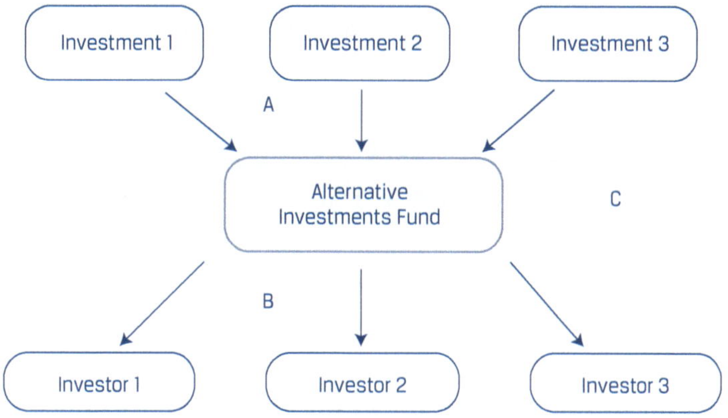

Vintage Year	2007	2011	2012	2013	2014	2015	2016	2017	2018
2020 Return	10.3%	14.7%	24.8%	29.6%	29.0%	33.9%	40.4%	29.7%	43.5%

Source: Cambridge Associates, data as of December 31, 2020. https://www.cambridgeassociates.com/benchmarks/us-pe-vc-benchmark-commentary-calendar-year-2020/

Investments in private capital vary in terms of risk and return across the corporate capital structure hierarchy. Typically, private equity, as the riskiest alternative, offers the highest returns, with private debt returns declining on a continuum down to the safest, most secured form of debt—infrastructure debt. Exhibit 6 outlines various private equity and private debt categories by their risk and return levels (mirroring the risk–return pathway for traditional equity and debt investing, note the trade-off as investors select between junior and senior debt and between equity and debt).

Exhibit 6: Private Capital Risk and Return Levels by Category

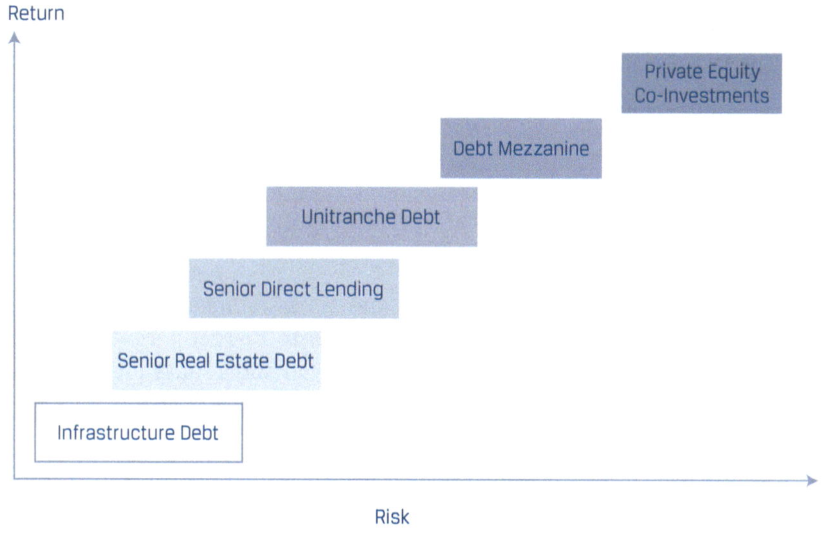

Source: Based on a graph from Leon Sinclair, "The Rise of Private Debt," IHS Markit (7 August 2017).

Investments in private capital funds can add a moderate diversification benefit to a portfolio of publicly traded stocks and bonds. Correlations with public market indexes vary from 0.63 to 0.83, as shown in Exhibit 7. And if investors identify skillful fund managers, benefits from excess returns given the additional leverage, market, and liquidity risks are possible.

Exhibit 7: Private Capital's Average Correlations with Public Market Indexes, March 2008–June 2021

	S&P 500 Total Return	Russell 2000 Total Return	MSCI World Total Return
Preqin, Private Equity	0.80	0.76	0.81
Preqin, Venture All Stage	0.65	0.67	0.63
Preqin, Buyout	0.82	0.76	0.83
Preqin, Private Debt	0.82	0.77	0.86

Source: Annualized quarterly returns of Private Capital Quarterly Index rebased to 31 December 2007, provided by Preqin.

QUESTION SET

1. State a private debt and equity investment factor that can make performance/risk comparisons with public debt and equity inappropriate.

   Solution:

   There are several private debt and equity investment factors that can invalidate such comparisons:

   - Start-up investments carry greater risks than those of established firms.
   - Investments in declining industries are unlikely to sustain gains over the long term.
   - Ongoing performance risk in private investments can't be easily hedged.

2. Describe the life cycle segments of a private equity fund.

   Solution:

   The year in which a private equity fund makes its first investments is called its vintage year. Typically, operations span a 10- to 12-year period, which is often segmented into an initial investment period and a subsequent harvesting period. The investment period usually is the first five years during which the capital is sourced from the limited partners and invested in various companies. The harvesting period is the remaining years of the fund, when the fund looks to exit its existing investments and to return capital to limited partners.

3. Identify the following statement as true or false:

   A private equity fund whose vintage dates to a high-valuation environment *most likely* starts with an advantage in having rich prices for its assets.

   Solution:

   False. Funds starting in a low-valuation, low-risk appetite, economic recovery phase benefit from riding the wave of an economic recovery and have an advantage over other vintages investing the bulk of their capital in a high-valuation environment preceding a market crash or a period of prolonged economic contraction.

4. Match the form of private capital investment with its *most likely* position on the risk/return continuum.

Investment Form	Risk/return combination
1. Mezzanine Financing	i. Lowest risk and return
2. Private Equity	ii. Intermediate risk and return
3. Senior Direct Lending	iii. Highest risk and return

   Solution:

   Investing in private debt and equity mirrors the risk–return pathway for traditional equity and debt investing. As investors select between senior and junior debt and between equity and debt, the potential risks and returns increase. Therefore, the lowest risk and return come from senior direct lending, and the highest risk and return are from private equity, while mezzanine financing falls in between the two.

Investment Form	Risk/return combination
1. Mezzanine Financing	ii. Intermediate risk and return
2. Private Equity	iii. Highest risk and return
3. Senior Direct Lending	i. Lowest risk and return

PRACTICE PROBLEMS

1. Which of the following is *most likely* to participate in early-stage financing?

   A. Founders

   B. Angel investors

   C. Strategic investors

2. Private equity funds are *most likely* to use:

   A. leveraged buyouts.

   B. option-based strategies.

   C. merger arbitrage strategies.

3. A shared advantage of IPO and SPAC exit strategies for a private equity fund is their:

   A. fast and simple execution.

   B. ability to win market attention.

   C. transaction structure flexibility.

4. Which of the following combinations of financial characteristics *most likely* would be associated with a venture debt transaction?

   A. Positive revenues and cash flow

   B. Declining revenues and cash flow

   C. Low revenues and negative cash flow

5. In contrast to direct lending and distressed debt, mezzanine debt *most likely* requires higher interest rates for its investors due to its:

   A. reliance on leverage.

   B. overall ranking and status in company debt structure.

   C. need for management involvement over an extended time.

6. A feature that private debt and public debt share in the setting of their investment returns is their:

   A. relationship to benchmark interest rates.

   B. need for specialized investment knowledge.

   C. opportunity for illiquidity premiums in market crises.

7. The *most likely* effect on a portfolio's diversification when exposure to direct lending commences is that it:

   A. decreases.

B. remains the same.

C. increases.

8. Private equity funds whose vintage year occurs in the expanding phase of the business cycle tend to earn excess returns by investing in companies that are:

   A. mature.

   B. distressed.

   C. early stage.

9. The private capital category *most likely* to offer the highest diversification benefit for portfolios holding public stock and bonds is:

   A. private debt.

   B. private equity.

   C. venture capital.

SOLUTIONS

1. C is correct. Strategic investors typically join in at early-stage to later-stage financing. A is incorrect because founders are typically part of the investor group at the earliest, pre-seed stage. B is incorrect because angel investors are typically involved in the beginning stages, either pre-seed or seed.

2. A is correct. Many private equity transactions involve leveraged buyouts to acquire public companies or established private companies. B and C are incorrect because these are strategies implemented by other types of alternative investors, such as hedge funds.

3. B is correct. IPOs can gain public attention for sponsors by high-profile business launches, and SPACs often have high-profile, seasoned sponsors and their investor networks as participants. A is incorrect because this is an advantage of a trade sale exit strategy. C is incorrect because it is a benefit specific to SPACs, with IPOs having fairly rigid and defined features, such as onerous disclosure requirements and lock-up periods.

4. C is correct. These financial characteristics are typical of the start-up stage in the corporate life cycle, when it is suitable to rely on venture debt. A is incorrect because these are features of the maturity stage, when direct lending, mezzanine financing, and leveraged lending are customary. B is incorrect because these are features of the maturity stage, when direct lending, mezzanine financing, and leveraged lending are customary.

5. B is correct. Because of its typically junior ranking and its usually unsecured status, mezzanine debt is riskier than senior secured debt. To compensate investors for this heightened risk, investors commonly demand higher interest rates. A is incorrect because leverage is typically a feature of a form of direct lending in which firms may also provide debt in the form of a leveraged loan, a loan that is itself levered with borrowing costs figuring into returns. C is incorrect because operational involvement over a possibly lengthy time with unpredictable risks describes the role of turnaround investors involved with distressed debt.

6. A is correct. For both public debt and private debt, return on debt capital tends to follow and change with the benchmark interest rate environment. B is incorrect because there is a need for specialized knowledge for private debt financing to add value to the investor through consideration of such factors as the debt's life cycle timing, its place in the financial structure, and the quality of underlying assets. C is incorrect because in market disruptions, such as the 2008 financial crisis, private debt exclusively benefited from an illiquidity premium when private lending funds filled the financing gap left by traditional lenders because traditional lenders were reluctant to underwrite public debt.

7. C is correct. Private capital can have overall positive contributions to diversification. Note, however, that direct lending can involve a large capital commitment to a single borrower, with increased concentration risk and reduced diversification

8. C is correct. Fund performance is greatly determined by the vintage year and the coinciding phase of the business cycle. Funds seeded during the expanding phase tend to earn excess returns investing in early-stage companies. Funds seeded during the contracting phase tend to do best with distressed companies. Results may be intermediate with mature, stable companies.

9. C is correct. Research on the correlations between portfolios holding these public assets shows that venture capital has the lowest correlations across all major market indexes. This relationship implies a higher diversification benefit for venture capital.

LEARNING MODULE

4

Real Estate and Infrastructure

LEARNING OUTCOMES

Mastery	The candidate should be able to:
☐	explain features and characteristics of real estate
☐	explain the investment characteristics of real estate investments
☐	explain features and characteristics of infrastructure
☐	explain the investment characteristics of infrastructure investments

INTRODUCTION

1

Broadly defined, real estate comprises land and buildings. Real estate investments involve developed land, including commercial and industrial real estate and residential real estate. Real estate has some unique features, including heterogeneity (no two properties are identical), long lives, and fixed geographical or physical location.

Raw land and less developed land used in agriculture and forestry are categorized as *natural resource* investments, while *infrastructure* involves land, buildings, and other fixed assets developed by public entities or public–private partnerships for economic use. Investments in real estate and infrastructure are included in many portfolios because they tend to exhibit low correlations with traditional asset classes and provide risk and return combinations across a broad spectrum. Here, as in other alternative assets, investors need specialized knowledge in selecting, acquiring, managing, and divesting these assets.

LEARNING MODULE OVERVIEW

- Real estate includes two major sectors: residential and commercial. Residential real estate is the largest sector, totaling 75% of the global market. Commercial real estate includes office buildings, shopping centers, and warehouses.
- Real estate investing has some unique features, including heterogeneity (no two properties are identical), fragmentation, price discovery challenges, and costly and time-consuming transactions.

- Real estate investments can be direct or indirect, in the public market (e.g., REITs) or private transactions, and in equity.
- The return on real estate investments comes from income or asset appreciation or a combination of both. More than half of the returns commercial real estate investors earn are derived from income, and throughout an economic market cycle, real estate income is a more consistent source of return than capital appreciation.
- Investing in real estate can generate either lower-risk, bond-like cash flows from leases or higher-risk, equity-like speculative returns from realizing value from development projects or price appreciation.
- Real estate offers diversification benefits to portfolios. However, during certain market conditions, equity REIT correlations with market benchmarks increase, particularly during steep market downturns.
- Infrastructure consists of assets that are capital intensive and long lived and that are intended to provide essential services for public use.
- Infrastructure investments can take many forms, both direct and indirect. They can be broadly categorized as either economic (e.g., transportation, utility, and energy assets) or social (e.g., educational assets). They can also be categorized based on the underlying asset's stage of development as greenfield, secondary stage, or brownfield. The greenfield investment life cycle common among public–private partnerships is called the build-operate-transfer (BOT) life cycle.
- Most infrastructure assets are financed, owned, and operated by governments, and infrastructure is increasingly being financed privately through public–private partnerships by local, regional, and national governments. Investments in construction and development of new infrastructure are made with expectations to generate cash from either income or capital appreciation.
- Of the three stages of infrastructure investments, greenfield investments offer the highest expected return and have the highest expected risk, and secondary stage investments offer the lowest expected return and have the lowest expected risk.
- Infrastructure investors primarily expect the assets to generate stable long-term cash flows that also adjust for economic growth and inflation and secondarily expect capital appreciation, depending on the type and timing of their investment.
- Infrastructure investments provide an income stream, increase portfolio diversification by adding an asset class with typically low correlation with other public investments, provide some protection for changes in GDP growth, and offer some protection against inflation.

LEARNING MODULE SELF-ASSESSMENT

These initial questions are intended to help you gauge your current level of understanding of this learning module.

1. The two categories of real property are:

   A. residential and commercial.

   B. privately held and publicly traded.

C. individual market and institutional market.

Solution:

The correct answer is A. The two categories of real property are residential and commercial.

2. The preferred investment vehicles for public investors to own income-producing real estate are:

   A. real estate funds.

   B. mortgage-backed securities.

   C. real estate investment trusts.

Solution:

The correct answer is C. Real estate investment trusts (REITs) are the preferred investment vehicles for owning income-producing real estate for both private and public investors.

3. Which of the following entails the least risk?

   A. Value-add real estate

   B. Investment-grade commercial mortgage-backed securities

   C. Residential real estate with long-term leases and many lessors

Solution:

The correct answer is B. Of these three, investment-grade commercial mortgage-backed securities (CMBS) entail the least risk, and value-add real estate investments entail the most.

4. Which of the following entails the most risk?

   A. Mezzanine debt

   B. Core-plus real estate strategies

   C. Redevelopment of an existing property

Solution:

The correct answer is A. Of these three, mezzanine debt entails the most risk, and core-plus strategies entail the least.

5. The first stage of development of an infrastructure asset is typically called:

   A. bluesky.

   B. greenfield.

   C. early stage.

Solution:

The correct answer is B. The first stage of development of an infrastructure asset is typically called greenfield. Greenfield investing involves developing new assets and new infrastructure with the intention either to lease or sell the assets to the government after construction or to hold and operate the assets. Greenfield investors typically invest alongside strategic investors or developers that specialize in developing the underlying assets. The subsequent stages of development of infrastructure assets are typically called secondary stage and brownfield.

6. Direct infrastructure investment involves assets that are:

   A. illiquid.

B. securitized.

C. exchange traded.

Solution:

The correct answer is A. Like real estate, direct investment in existing infrastructure involves acquiring unique, illiquid assets with distinct location, features, and uses. Investors concerned about liquidity and diversification may invest indirectly using publicly traded infrastructure securities.

7. Which of the following types of infrastructure investments has the highest expected return?

   A. Greenfield

   B. Brownfield

   C. Secondary stage

Solution:

The correct answer is A. Greenfield investments offer the highest expected return of the three. They also entail the highest expected risk. Secondary stage offers the lowest expected return and the lowest expected risk.

8. Which of the following tends to make the largest allocations to the infrastructure asset class?

   A. Pension funds

   B. Sovereign wealth funds

   C. Life insurance companies

Solution:

The correct answer is B. Sovereign wealth funds tend to make the largest allocations to the infrastructure asset class—around 5%–6% of total AUM, according to Preqin.

2 REAL ESTATE FEATURES

☐ explain features and characteristics of real estate

Both individuals and institutions invest in real property: either in residential or commercial real estate. Residential real estate, or the housing market, consists of individual single-family detached homes and multi-family attached units, which share at least one wall with another unit, such as condominiums, cooperatives, townhouses, or terraced housing. Commercial real estate includes primarily office buildings, retail shopping centers, commercial and residential rental properties, and warehouses. In contrast to the owner-occupied market, rental properties are leased to tenants.

Residential real estate is by far the largest market sector by value and size. Savills World Research estimated in July 2018 that residential real estate accounted for more than 75% of global real estate values. Although the average value of a home is less than the average value of an office building, the aggregate space required to house people is much larger than that needed to accommodate office use and retail shopping.

Real Estate Investments

Real estate investments exhibit general similarities to and differences from traditional equity and debt classes. Real estate can be held privately or traded publicly through real estate investment trusts (REITs). Equity investment involves direct or indirect ownership with claims to residual cash flows from the property. Depending on the property investment, these cash flows can be variable or fixed. Debt investment typically involves direct mortgage lending from financial intermediaries, part of which then can be securitized and then traded through various types of mortgage-backed securities (MBS). The main features of residential and commercial real estate are shown in Exhibit 1.

Exhibit 1: Main Features of Residential and Commercial Real Estate

	Residential real estate	Commercial real estate
Typical property	Owner-occupied, single residences; single-family residential property	Residential properties owned for lease or rental Office, retail, industrial, warehouse, hospitality, and mixed-use properties
Source of equity	Owners	Privately held by owners Publicly held through investors
Source of debt	Directly: Lenders (banks) through residential mortgages Indirectly: Investors in MBS that package residential mortgages	Directly: Lenders (banks) through commercial mortgages Indirectly: Investors in MBS that package commercial mortgages
Source of return to investors	Enjoyment of the property Price, or capital, appreciation	Income, or cash flow, generated by the property Price, or capital, appreciation

Real estate is uniquely different from other asset classes in several ways:

- The initial investment is typically large.
- Real estate is unique and distinct because there aren't two identical properties; each piece of real estate is heterogeneous and is uniquely characterized in terms of location, age, tenant credit mix, lease term, and market demographics.
- There are multiple types of real estate investment alternatives available: direct and indirect investment options spanning the spectrum from relatively liquid investments in stable, income-producing properties to illiquid investments over a long development life cycle across the purchase, construction/upgrade, occupancy, and sales phases.
- Diversification across all different types of real estate investment alternatives may be difficult to attain.
- Private market indexes replicating the performance of real estate are not directly investable.

Additionally, the price discovery process in the private real estate markets is opaque, for multiple reasons:

- Historical prices may not reflect prevailing market conditions.

- Transaction costs are typically high. Buying and selling real estate can be a time-consuming process, involving real estate professionals, banks, lawyers, and others needed to facilitate these transactions.
- Transaction activity may be limited in certain markets due to either supply or demand conditions.

Because of distinct and unique features—geographic location and potential uses—real estate markets are typically fragmented, with the local demand and supply conditions determining the value of the property. Consequently, the heterogeneity unique to real estate demands specialized skills. Selecting, valuing, acquiring, managing, and divesting a real estate portfolio is often more complicated than managing a portfolio made up of listed corporate debt and equity.

Real Estate Investment Structures

Real estate investments take on a variety of public and private forms across equity and debt capital alternatives, as summarized in Exhibit 2.

Exhibit 2: Selected Forms of Real Estate Investment

	Debt	Equity
Private	Mortgage debt Construction loans Mezzanine debt	**Direct ownership** Sole ownership Joint ventures Limited partnerships **Indirect ownership** Real estate funds Private REITs
Public	MBS/CMBS/CMOs Covered bonds Mortgage REITs Mortgage ETFs	**Publicly traded shares** Construction Operating Development Public REITs UCITS/Mutual funds/ETFs

Direct Real Estate Investment

Direct private investing involves purchasing a property and originating debt for one's own account. Ownership can be free and clear, whereby the property title is transferred to the owner(s) unencumbered by any financing liens, such as from outstanding mortgages. Initial purchase expenses associated with direct ownership may include legal expenses, survey costs, engineering/environmental studies, and valuation (appraisal) fees. There are distinct advantages to owning real estate directly for property investors:

- *Control.* Only the owner can decide when to buy or sell, when and how much to spend on capital projects, whom to select as tenants based on credit quality preference and tenant mix, and what types of lease terms to offer. Owners generate cash flow returns from the use and enjoyment of the property, the receipt of lease payments, and the potential for capital appreciation.

- *Tax benefits.* The owners can reduce their taxable income using non-cash property depreciation expenses and tax-deductible interest expenses.
- *Diversification.* Historically, real estate has exhibited low correlation with other asset classes, and adding real estate to a portfolio has been demonstrated to increase portfolio diversification and reduce portfolio risk.

There are also disadvantages to investing directly in property:

- *Complexity.* The owners need to dedicate time to manage the property. Making the purchase itself is more complicated as well, with requirements including property selection, negotiating terms, performing due diligence, title search, contract review, and property inspection.
- *Need for specialized knowledge.* The owners need to understand both general and local market characteristics, which requires local market knowledge.
- *Significant capital needs.* The owners need to have access to a potentially significant amount of debt and equity capital because of the large initial capital outlay needed for real estate investments.
- *Concentration risk.* Owners, particularly smaller investors, cannot create a well-diversified real estate portfolio through direct investment.
- *Lack of liquidity.* It is typically difficult to quickly buy or sell direct investments in real estate, and transaction costs are typically high.

Real estate investors may choose to handle all aspects of investing in and operating the property internally. However, commercial real estate investors often hire advisers to identify investments, negotiate acquisition and lease terms, perform due diligence, conduct real estate operations, and assist with the eventual disposal. Institutional investors that hire advisers or managers to manage their direct real estate investment can also use a separate account structure that allows the investor to control the timing and value of acquisitions and dispositions.

Owners can also borrow from mortgage lenders to fund the acquisition. Additional debt closing costs are incurred when owners take out loans to fund their investments.

Indirect Real Estate Investment

Indirect investment in real estate pools assets from different investors to acquire one or several properties; here the exposure is indirect through a variety of investment vehicles. These can be public or private, such as limited partnerships, mutual funds, equities, REITs, and exchange-traded funds (ETFs). Sometimes investors form joint ventures with other investors to invest in real estate. Joint ventures are especially common when one party can uniquely contribute something of value, such as land, capital, development expertise, debt due diligence, or entrepreneurial talent.

Tax-advantaged trusts that own, operate, and sometimes develop income-producing real estate property are known as real estate investment trusts. Their structure is shown in Exhibit 3. There are three main forms of REIT: equity REITs, which invest in properties outright or through partnerships and joint ventures; mortgage REITs, which underwrite loans to real estate (mortgages) or invest in MBS; and hybrid REITs, which invest in both these types.

Exhibit 3: Real Estate Investment Trust Structure

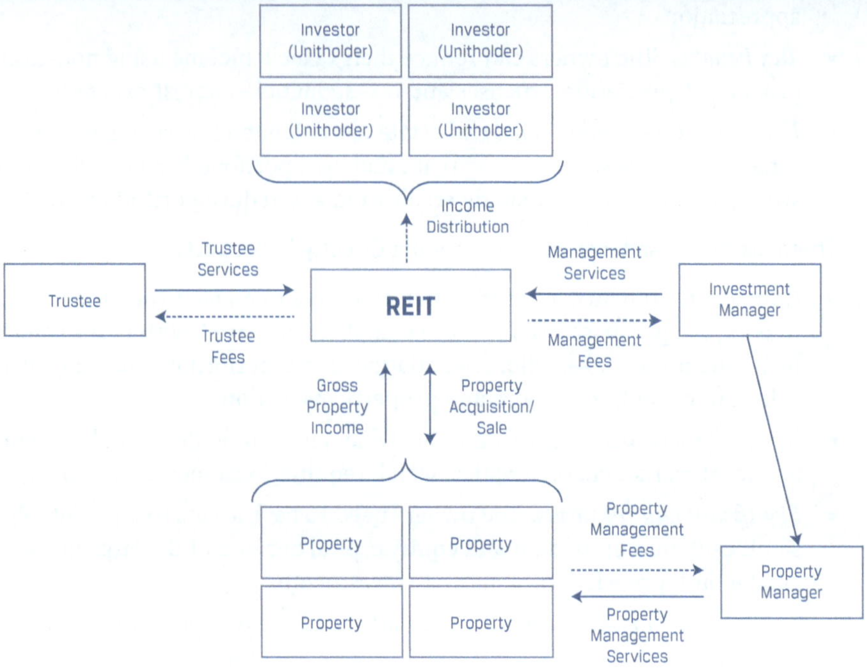

REITs are the preferred investment vehicles for owning income-producing real estate for both private and public investors. The main appeal of the REIT structure is the elimination of double corporate taxation. Corporations pay taxes on their income, from which they make dividend distribution to their owners from after-tax earnings. The shareholders, in turn, are taxed at their personal tax rate. REITs can avoid corporate income taxation by distributing dividends equal to 90%–100% of taxable net rental income.

The business strategy for equity REITs is simple: Maximize property occupancy rates and rents while minimizing ongoing operating and maintenance expenses to maximize cash income and dividends. REITs are a popular investment vehicle both in the United States, where they originated, and in other countries. REITs and REIT-like structures have similar legal and taxation structures and provide unique tax advantages to investors and the corporate entity.

Equity REITs, like other public companies, must report earnings per share based on net income as defined by generally accepted accounting principles (GAAP) or International Financial Reporting Standards (IFRS). Many report non-traditional measures, such as net asset value or variations of gross cash flow, such as funds from operations (FFO), which makes adjustments for depreciation, distributions, and preferred dividends, to better estimate future dividends, because non-cash depreciation expenses can be high for asset-intensive businesses.

These publicly traded REITs address many of the disadvantages related to private real estate investing. These REITs provide investors with greater transparency. Additionally, a REIT investor only needs to buy or sell REIT shares instead of buying or selling real estate directly. The REIT is not forced to sell the company's underlying real estate like open-end funds experiencing mass redemptions. Finally, REITs have the know-how to manage the properties in order to align the interests of the REIT with those of its investors. However, a disadvantage of REITs is their higher correlation with the public equity markets when compared to private real estate.

EXAMPLE 1

Luxury Dreams REIT

Luxury Dreams Real Estate Investment Trust acquires high-quality, income-oriented, high-end real estate around the world and offers investment alternatives for investors looking for long-term, stable, predictable cash flows, price appreciation in the underlying properties from the inclusion of properties, and active management of the properties, at generally lower volatility because of its focus on high-end real estate.

The REIT invests at least 75% of assets in high-end residential properties and up to 25% of assets in privately held, real estate-related securities, mortgage debt, and cash. The REIT is capped at USD5 billion. Because this REIT is not traded publicly, shares in the trust can be redeemed at the end of each month at a price equal to the prior month's net asset value (NAV) per share in increments of USD10,000. NAV per share is determined at the end of each month and is released to holders within 15 business days after the end of the month. Each shareholder is limited to transact 2% of the total NAV per month and 5% of NAV per quarter.

REITs and other private real estate funds are structured as infinite-life, open-end funds and allow investors to contribute or redeem capital throughout the life of the fund in a fashion parallel to mutual fund structures. Open-end funds generally offer exposure to well-leased, high-quality commercial and residential real estate in the best markets, also called **core real estate strategies**. Investors expect core real estate to deliver stable returns, primarily from income from the property.

Investors seeking higher returns may also accept additional risks from development, redevelopment, repositioning, and leasing. For such opportunistic investment preferences, finite-life, closed-end funds are more commonly used. Investors may focus on **core-plus real estate strategies**, value-add investments that require modest redevelopment or upgrades to lease any vacant space together with possible alternative use of the underlying properties. To earn higher returns, investors may engage in **value-add real estate strategies**, such as larger-scale redevelopment and repositioning of existing assets. The most **opportunistic real estate strategies** include major redevelopment, repurposing of assets, taking on large vacancies, or speculating on significant improvement in market conditions.

Mortgage REITs and hybrid REITs invest in real estate debt, typically MBS (covered elsewhere in the curriculum. These debt REITs can be both private and publicly traded funds.

QUESTION SET

1. True or false: The distinct and unique features of real estate make managing a real estate portfolio less complex than managing a portfolio of listed corporate bonds.

   Solution:

   False. Selecting, valuing, acquiring, managing, and divesting a real estate portfolio is often more complicated than managing a portfolio made up of listed corporate debt. The heterogeneity unique to real estate demands specialized skills, and real estate markets are typically fragmented, with the local demand and supply conditions determining the value of the property.

2. The largest sector of the real estate market is:

   A. residential real estate.

   B. real estate investment trusts.

   C. publicly traded mortgage-backed securities.

   Solution:

   The correct answer is A. Residential real estate is by far the largest market sector by value and size. Savills World Research estimated in July 2018 that residential real estate accounted for more than 75% of global real estate values.

3. Describe the business strategy for equity REITs.

   Solution:

   The business strategy for equity REITs is to maximize property occupancy rates and rents while minimizing ongoing operating and maintenance expenses to maximize cash income and dividends.

4. When a property title that is transferred to a new owner is unencumbered by any financing liens, such as from outstanding mortgages, the new ownership is considered:

   A. privately held.

   B. free and clear.

   C. direct equity ownership.

   Solution:

   The correct answer is B. "Free and clear" refers to the lack of any financing liens on a purchased property. If a direct private investor purchases a property and receives a title that is unencumbered by any financing liens, that ownership is considered free and clear.

3 REAL ESTATE INVESTMENT CHARACTERISTICS

☐ explain the investment characteristics of real estate investments

Investments in real estate provide competitive long-term total returns from income generation combined with potential price appreciation. Many commercial real estate companies offer multiple-year leases with fixed rents; hence, the income earned from these leases is typically both predictable and stable. Moreover, real estate tends to provide inflation protection because the lease payments are regularly adjusted, which allows for a clear valuation and pricing of the property. Finally, real estate historically has low correlations with other asset classes, and adding real estate to an investment portfolio provides diversification benefits at relatively lower levels of risk. There are a variety of indexes globally designed to measure total and component real estate returns for listed securities and non-listed investment vehicles.

Source of Returns

The return on real estate investments comes from income or asset appreciation or a combination of both. Income-producing real estate generates income primarily from the collection of rental or lease payments, including lease renewals. Expenses include direct and indirect management expenses, such as maintenance and improvement costs. Income-producing real estate investment is mostly low-risk direct investment that depends on the timely receipt of lease payments. Investors relying on capital appreciation typically expect that their longer-term property development projects are successful and the exit price will exceed the aggregate investments and any cash flow that they can generate in the meantime.

The risk and return spectrum for real estate investments, depicted in Exhibit 4, includes strategies across both debt and equity investment. Investing in real estate can generate either lower-risk, bond-like cash flows from leases or higher-risk, equity-like speculative returns from realizing value from development projects or price appreciation. Moreover, most real estate strategies are financed by a combination of debt and equity, with the proportion depending on the type of real estate.

Exhibit 4: Real Estate Risk–Return Spectrum

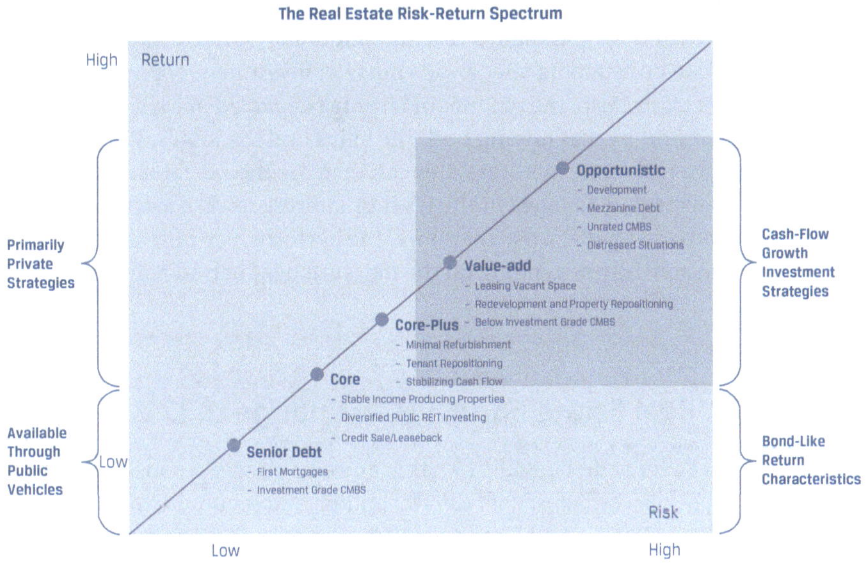

The low-risk/low-return part of the spectrum, starting in the lower left section of the exhibit, is made up by relatively low-risk, senior debt, such as first mortgages and investment-grade commercial mortgage-backed securities (CMBS). Since the underlying assets are bonds, both the risks and returns are bond-like.

The second part of the of spectrum is made up of the core, stable income-producing REITs, investing in properties that generate stable cash flows either from properties with long-term leases and with many lessors (typically residential real estate) or from sale-leaseback transactions. Because in a sale-leaseback transaction the owner of the property sells the property to an investor and leases the property for continued use, the risk of default is low, providing investors a stable and relatively safe return. Additionally, real estate investors often use sale leaseback structures to secure financing in a cost-efficient way or to reduce their leverage. Overall, the returns are relatively higher compared to low-risk senior debt and are generally bond-like because the main source of return comes from long-term lease payments.

The third and fourth parts of the spectrum offer higher, riskier, and less predictable potential returns; the main source of return moves away from the predictable, bond-like, contractual cash flows and is replaced by more speculative sources from potential price appreciation. The main source of return for core-plus holdings comes from leases, but the cost of acquiring these leases and maintaining and updating the underlying properties may become significant, particularly when the property needs refurbishment, renovation, and redevelopment. For value-add real estate, the returns are increasingly equity-like, with the price appreciation component becoming progressively meaningful.

The final, fifth phase of the spectrum provides the greatest return potential at the expense of the highest levels of risk from opportunistic real estate. For instance, investments in distressed properties and in property development are subject to greater risks than investments in properties in sound financial condition or with stable operations, such as core real estate. The increasing equity-like return reflects that property development is subject to special risks, including regulatory issues, construction delays, and cost overruns. Environmental regulation is one regulatory hurdle, as is the failure to receive zoning, occupancy, and other approvals and permits. Because the lifecycle of such projects can be very lengthy, economic conditions may change. All these issues may increase construction time or delay successful leases, which increases construction costs and reduces the level of rents relative to initial expectations. This could result in a reduction of IRR versus expectation—leaving the investor uncompensated for the higher risk and illiquidity of real estate investment.

In sum, real estate investments offer a wide range of investment opportunities along the risk/return spectrum. Also, the amount of leverage deployed in each strategy shifts the risk/return trade-off by magnifying both the gains and the losses. Particularly for the more speculative real estate investors, this can increase their default risk, especially when there are unexpected changes in the level of interest rates, access to financing, or government land-use regulations. Therefore, the performance of real estate investments can vary substantially depending on the measurement period being considered.

EXAMPLE 2

Peterburgh Real Estate Fund, LLC—Change to LTV

The Peterburgh Real Estate Fund, LLC, has acquired a portfolio consisting of six commercial properties for a total of GBP100 million and secured GBP75 million in mortgages from BridgeRock Credit Opportunities LLP, a private debt fund that syndicated them. The terms of the mortgage are MRR + 150 bps, with a maturity of 15 years, GBP5 million in annual amortization, and all mortgages being secured by the first lien on the property. The loan agreements stipulated that the loan to value (LTV) should remain at 0.75. But after one year, the economic environment worsened substantively and the assessed value of some of the commercial properties owned by Peterburgh declined by GBP8 million to GBP92 million, breaching the LTV of 0.75. More specifically, the outstanding mortgage balance was reduced through amortization by GBP5 million to GBP70 million and the value of the property is GBP92 million, which gives an LTV of 0.76. BridgeRock and the other members of the syndicate would now require that Peterburgh fix the breach by adding GBP1.3 million in collateral to bring the LTV down to 0.75.

Returns to both debt and equity investors in real estate depend to a large extent on the ability of the owners or their agents to successfully operate the underlying properties. Property values vary with global, national, and local conditions. Real estate tends to provide inflation protection if leases provide regular contractual rent step-ups or can be frequently marked to market. Research suggests that inflation-hedging ability varies significantly by geographic location, market segment, and time period. In particular, the inflation-hedging potential of real estate may be more difficult to detect if the high-inflation period of the late 1970s and early 1980s is excluded from the period of study. In addition to these macro and micro conditions, the prevailing level of interest rates influence valuation, returns, and risk.

Real Estate Investment Diversification Benefits

Investors in real estate—whether direct or indirect, public or private, debt or equity—seek high, stable, and steady returns. Real estate investments generate bond-like cash flows from their medium- to long-term property leases and offer bond-like returns. The variability of these returns can be reduced by longer-term leases, better credit quality of tenants, and the possibility of rent increases.

Real estate investments offer the opportunity for capital appreciation from the underlying assets that can bolster returns. In fact, more than half of the returns commercial real estate investors earn are derived from income, with the rest coming from long-term price appreciation. Additionally, throughout an economic market cycle, the real estate income is a more consistent source of return than capital appreciation. This reduces the risk from investing for real estate investors and provides a source of diversification: stock market returns mostly derive from long-term capital appreciation. Effectively, investment in real estate is somewhat like a convertible bond but with several advantages: steady cash flows, the possibility of capital appreciation, and low correlation between real estate price appreciation and equity market price appreciation.

Different investors have differing views on how to approach investments in REITs. Some institutional investors consider it a separate alternative asset class, some consider it a sub-sector of the broader real estate market, some consider it a fixed-income/equity hybrid, and others consider it a fixed-income asset with an incremental yield advantage over investment-grade corporate bonds.

Whether listed real estate behaves like stocks or private real estate is a matter of ongoing debate. The market prices listed REITs continuously, whereas private real estate is appraised perhaps once a year. This mismatch in appraisal timing leads to correlation numbers that are artificially low. Additionally, equity investors in public real estate discount future cash flows, while appraisers of private real estate place heavy emphasis on current market conditions and recent trends. The various real estate strategies provide different diversification benefits, as Exhibit 5 shows.

Exhibit 5: Historical Correlation between Real Estate Investment Strategies and Market Returns, March 2008–June 2021

Correlation	S&P 500 Total Return	MSCI US REIT Total Return	MSCI World Total Return
Preqin, real estate	0.51	0.49	0.46
Preqin, real estate debt	0.40	0.48	0.38

Source: Annualized quarterly returns of Private Capital Quarterly Index rebased to 31 December 2007, provided by Preqin.

Moreover, during certain market conditions, equity REIT correlations with market benchmarks increase, particularly during steep market downturns, such as the 2007–08 financial crisis. As these high correlations remained high during the post-crisis recovery, they lifted the value of most asset classes. Similar patterns in financial asset prices and real estate prices appear to have been observed during the COVID-19 recovery.

All in all, there appears to be a consensus that real estate offers diversification benefits to portfolios. Real estate markets around the world can be highly idiosyncratic and often have low correlations with traditional asset classes. For example, Oxford Economics studied the expected performance of listed European real estate as an asset class, comparing it with equities, fixed income, and commodities.[1] "A substantial allocation to listed real estate," the authors concluded, "does enhance the risk–return characteristics of a multi-asset portfolio." They went on to recommend larger allocations to real estate for European investors.

QUESTION SET

1. True or false: Real estate historically has high correlations with other asset classes.

   Solution:

   False. Real estate historically has low correlations with other asset classes, and adding real estate to an investment portfolio provides diversification benefits at relatively lower levels of risk.

2. The sources of long-term return for real estate investments are _______ and _______.

   Solution:

   income generation, potential price appreciation

3. In what ways are real estate investments similar to bond investments?

   Solution:

   Real estate investments can be similar to bond investments in that they are stable, predictable, lower-risk cash flows from leases that are similar to bond coupon payments

4. In what ways are real estate investments similar to equity investments?

   Solution:

   Real estate investments can be similar to equity investments in that they are speculative returns that can be realized from price appreciation of the real estate asset

1 Listed Real Estate in A Multi-Asset Portfolio: A European Perspective, pg. 2, Oxford Economics , EPRA September 2019.

INFRASTRUCTURE INVESTMENT FEATURES

4

☐ explain features and characteristics of infrastructure

Infrastructure investments have a societal purpose; facilitate broad economic, technological, and social development purposes; and usually combine land, buildings, and other long-lived fixed assets. Infrastructure supports public transportation, airports, utilities (water, gas, and electricity), and more recently, information (telecommunication, cable, and wireless networks). Early infrastructure investments were typically financed by private corporations to realize profits. Subsequently, many governments took on a larger proportion of infrastructure investment and by the second half of the 20th century became the main source of investments. The late 20th century saw waves of privatizations of public transportation, and the scope of private infrastructure investment expanded to assets that governments had historically financed, owned, and operated themselves. The market for privately funded infrastructure is sizeable.

Infrastructure Investments

Infrastructure investments are real, capital-intensive, and long-lived assets intended for public use and provide essential services, such as airports, health care facilities, and sewage treatment plants. These investments have similarities to and differences from common equity and debt. Investments include equity, with its usual claims to residual cash flows, and debt, to finance and maintain such investments. Like real estate, investment in existing infrastructure involves acquiring unique, illiquid assets with distinct locations, features, and uses. Investments in construction and development of new infrastructure are made with expectations to generate cash either from income or from capital appreciation.

Infrastructure investments often involve a consortium that combines one or several strategic partners that have specialized operational or technical skills with the financial investors. Rather than leases or rentals from commercial or residential tenants, infrastructure cash flows in most cases arise from contractual payments, such as the following:

- *Availability payments*, which are payments that are received to make the facility available
- *Usage-based payments*, such as tolls and fees for using the facilities
- *"Take-or-pay" arrangements*, which obligate buyers to pay a minimum purchase price to sellers for a pre-agreed volume.

Allocations to infrastructure investments are driven both by the increased demand for infrastructure and by many governments' search for alternative funding sources for infrastructure investments, such as investors interested and experienced in building, managing, and running infrastructure. Investors have an interest in financing infrastructure investments, demand-side growth. As governments provide more opportunities by expanding infrastructure assets, they also continue to privatize government services.

Most infrastructure assets are financed, owned, and operated by governments, and a substantive proportion of these investments comes from public sources in the developing world. However, increasingly infrastructure is being financed privately through public–private partnerships (PPPs) by local, regional, and national governments. A **public–private partnership** is typically defined as a long-term contractual relationship between the public and private sectors for the purpose of having the private sector deliver a project or service traditionally provided by the public sector.

Infrastructure investors may intend to lease the assets back to the government, to sell newly constructed assets to the government, or to hold and operate the assets until they reach operational maturity or perhaps for even longer.

Infrastructure investments are also made in partnership with development finance institutions, which are specialized financial intermediaries that provide risk capital for economic development projects on a non-commercial basis. There are global, international, national, and local development finance institutions. For instance, the European Bank for Reconstruction and Development (EBRD) invests to improve municipal services, including infrastructure, and regularly taps global financial markets to finance infrastructure and other types of investments.

Categories of Infrastructure Investments

To categorize infrastructure investments, investors frequently rely on the underlying assets, with the broadest categorization distinguishing between economic and social infrastructure assets, as shown in Exhibit 6.

Exhibit 6: Categorizing Infrastructure Investments

Economic Infrastructure Investments			
Transportation Assets	**Information and Communication Technology Assets**	**Utility and Energy Assets**	**Social Infrastructure Investments**
▫ roads ▫ bridges ▫ tunnels ▫ airports ▫ seaports ▫ railway systems	▫ telecommunication towers ▫ data centers	▫ electrical grid ▫ power generation, transmission, distribution ▫ potable water production ▫ gas storage and distribution ▫ liquefied natural gas terminals ▫ oil and gas infrastructure ▫ solid waste treatment	▫ educational assets ▫ health care assets ▫ social housing ▫ correctional facilities ▫ government/municipal buildings

Economic infrastructure investments support economic activity through transportation assets, information and communication technology (ICT) assets, and utility and energy assets:

- *Transportation assets* include roads, bridges, tunnels, airports, seaports, and heavy and light/urban railway systems. Income will usually be linked to demand based on traffic, airport and seaport charges, tolls, and rail fares and hence is deemed to carry market risk.
- *ICT assets* include infrastructure that stores, broadcasts, and transmits information or data, such as telecommunication towers and data centers.
- *Utility and energy assets* generate power and produce potable water; transmit, store, and distribute gas, water, and electricity; and treat solid waste.

Utility investments encompass environmentally sustainable development, with an increasing focus on renewable technologies, including solar, wind, and waste-to-energy power generation. Other energy assets may encompass downstream oil and gas infrastructure, the electrical grid, and liquefied natural gas terminals. The income earned from utility assets may also carry demand risk because buyers' energy and natural resources needs fluctuate. Alternatively, utilities can institute "take-or-pay" arrangements, locking buyers into minimum purchases whether supply is needed or not. Buyers usually have recourse if the utility falls short on performance or delivers supplies that are late or of inferior quality.

Social infrastructure investments are directed toward human activities and include such assets as educational, health care, social housing, and correctional facilities, with the focus on providing, operating, and maintaining the asset infrastructure. The relevant services administered through those facilities are usually provided separately by the public authority or by a private service provider contracted by the public authority. In some countries, this model has been extended to other public infrastructure, including government and municipal buildings. Income from social infrastructure is typically derived from a type of lease payment that depends on availability payments and on managing and maintaining the asset according to predefined standards.

EXAMPLE 3

Clarkswood Infrastructure Fund LP

Clarkswood Infrastructure Fund LP invests its assets in equity and equity-like securities and debt issued by issuers that own or operate infrastructure assets in developed and developing countries. Infrastructure lays the foundation of basic services, facilities, and institutions on which the growth and development of a nation and country directly depend. More specifically, in several developed countries, such as the United States, the United Kingdom, and Australia, many infrastructure assets have been privatized as national, state, and local governments spend less on building, investing, maintaining, and operating infrastructure. The private sector has stepped in to provide equity financing to fund infrastructure.

For instance, the fund invests in an operator of Australian toll roads listed on the Australian Stock Exchange, as well as the operator of the Auckland Airport (New Zealand's largest airport), also listed on a stock exchange. It also invests in several corporations that provide infrastructure services in both the developing world and the developed world, including China and India, that see significant demand for infrastructure products and services and seek private sector investments. The fund invests up to 50% of its assets in US assets, up to 30% in infrastructure assets located in OECD (Organisation for Economic Co-operation and Development) countries, up to 30% in assets in non-OECD countries, and no more than 10% in any country with no more than 5% in any infrastructure provider.

Stages of Infrastructure Development

Infrastructure investments can also be categorized by the underlying assets' stage of development. Typically, we distinguish among greenfield investments, secondary-stage investments, and brownfield investments.

Greenfield investments, developing new assets and new infrastructure, are opportunistic investments. The intent may be to lease or sell the assets to the government after construction or to hold and operate the assets. If they are held, it can be over the long term or for a shorter period until operational maturity, with subsequent sale to new investors, thus ensuring capital appreciation to reflect the construction and commissioning risk. Greenfield investors typically invest alongside strategic investors or developers that specialize in developing the underlying assets.

The greenfield investment life cycle common among public–private partnerships is called the build-operate-transfer (BOT) life cycle and is shown in Exhibit 7. The build phase is often characterized by an initial longer approval and construction phase with negative cash flows. The subsequent operate phase is governed by a concession agreement in which the private investor generates income based on pre-agreed parameters. In the final transfer phase, the investment is transferred to a government entity based on pre-determined parameters, sold to a third party, or decommissioned.

Exhibit 7: Illustrative Build-Operate-Transfer Model for Greenfield Infrastructure

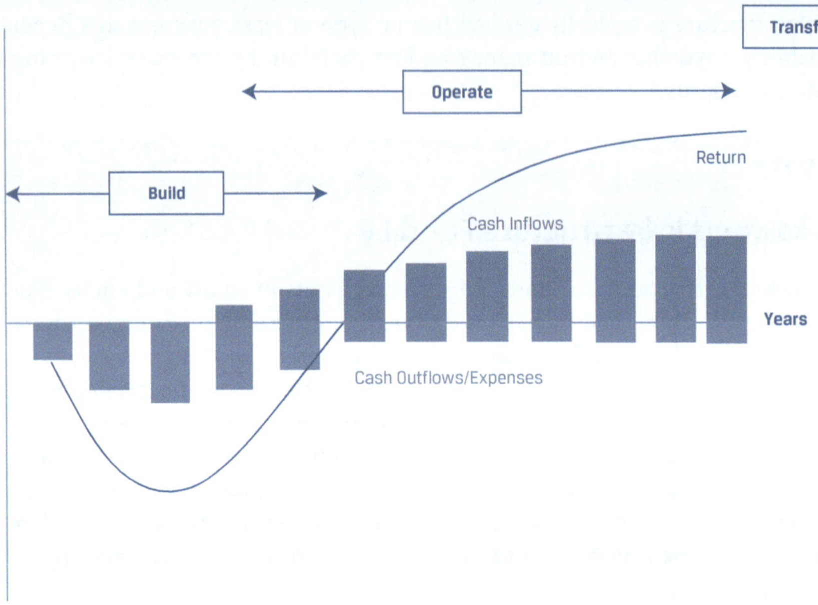

Brownfield investments expand existing facilities and may involve privatization of public assets or a sale leaseback of completed greenfield projects. They are characterized by a shorter investment period with immediate cash flows and an operating history. Typically, some of the assets' financial and operating history is available, and so brownfield investments may be sought after by both strategic investors specializing in operating the assets and—particularly with privatizations—financial investors focused on long-term, stable returns.

Secondary-stage investments invest in existing infrastructure facilities or fully operational assets that do not require further investment or development over the investment horizon. These assets generate immediate cash flow and returns expected over the investment period. Some assets never reach this stage because they continuously require additional capital and development.

Forms of Infrastructure Investment

As with real estate investments, infrastructure investments come in a variety of forms. The choice affects liquidity, cash flow, and income streams. Infrastructure investments can be direct or indirect. The vast majority of investors focus on equity investments, with some interest in pure debt (infrastructure bonds) and convertible debt.

- *Direct investment in the underlying infrastructure* provides control and the opportunity to capture full value. It requires a large investment and results in both concentration and liquidity risks while the assets are managed and operated. Because of this risk and the typical long-term horizon, direct infrastructure investment usually takes place with a group or consortium of strategic investors that share the financial risk and/or assume a specific role in building, operating, or managing the assets. Such strategic partners, such as large pension funds or sovereign wealth funds, are frequent direct investors because they are better placed to manage certain risks to limit individual concentration risk. Frequently these funds invest under specific mandates in infrastructure projects and specifically prioritize domestic infrastructure needs.

EXAMPLE 4

Public–Private Partnership, Iguá Saneamento S.A.

In March 2021, the Canada Pension Plan Investment Board paid CAD270 million (BRL1,178 million) for a 45% stake in Iguá Saneamento S.A. (Iguá), a water and sewage service company operating 18 concessions and contracts across five Brazilian states. The company serves more than 6 million people, provides sanitation services, and is the third-largest Brazilian private water and sewage treatment service provider.

The objective of the transaction is to support Iguá's growth objectives and to maintain operating funds to support its operations. Iguá is considering acquiring additional water and sanitation concessions in Brazil, including the formation of public–private partnerships there. Other institutional investors include Alberta Investment Management Corporation (39%), BNDES Participações S.A. (11%), and IG4 Capital Group (11%).

- *Indirect investments* include infrastructure funds (similar in structure to private equity funds and either closed end or open end), infrastructure ETFs, and holding equity in publicly traded infrastructure providers, or master limited partnerships (MLPs). Investors concerned about liquidity and diversification may choose publicly traded infrastructure securities. Publicly traded infrastructure securities benefit from liquidity, reasonable fees, transparent governance, observable market prices, and transparent pricing, in addition to diversification among underlying assets. An investor should be aware, however, that publicly traded infrastructure securities represent a small segment of infrastructure investment: S&P Dow Jones Indices reported a total global market cap of USD2.23 trillion as of 31 December 2021.[2] Publicly traded infrastructure investments also tend to be clustered in certain asset categories.

Master limited partnerships (MLPs) trade on exchanges, are pass-through entities like REITs, and share the income pass-through structure taxation rules that minimize double taxation for investors. MLPs are most commonly used in energy transportation, processing, or storage; generate relatively stable cash flows from fee-based income; and distribute larger parts of their free cash flow to their investors.

Debt financing for infrastructure projects can be both private debt and publicly traded debt. Normally, the terms are flexible to accommodate periods of zero cash flow and long development or investment horizons. Publicly issued debt, such as the Airport Authority of Hong Kong perpetual bonds and Indonesian Infrastructure Fund US dollar bonds highlighted in earlier fixed-income modules are other approaches to financing infrastructure projects.

2 S&P Dow Jones Indices, "Approaches to Benchmarking Listed Infrastructure" (June 2022, p. 3). www.spglobal.com/spdji/en/documents/research/research-approaches-to-benchmarking-listed-infrastructure.pdf.

QUESTION SET

1. Infrastructure cash flows primarily arise from:

   A. dividends.

   B. commercial tenants.

   C. contractual payments.

   Solution:

   The correct answer is C. Rather than leases or rentals from commercial or residential tenants, infrastructure cash flows arise from contractual payments, such as: availability payments (payments are received to make the facility available), usage-based payments (e.g., tolls and fees for using the facilities), and "take-or-pay" arrangements (which obligate buyers to pay a minimum purchase price to sellers for a pre-agreed volume).

2. Most infrastructure assets are financed, owned, and operated by:

   A. governments.

   B. public–private partnerships.

   C. development finance institutions.

   Solution:

   The correct answer is A. Most infrastructure assets are financed, owned, and operated by governments, and a substantive proportion of these investments comes from public sources in the developing world. However, increasingly infrastructure is being financed privately through public–private partnerships by local, regional, and national governments. Infrastructure investments are also made in partnership with development finance institutions, which are specialized financial intermediaries that provide risk capital for economic development projects on a non-commercial basis.

3. Which of these statements about infrastructure investing is true? Infrastructure investments:

   A. can generate cash income.

   B. are intended to be non-profit.

   C. do not have capital appreciation.

   Solution:

   The correct answer is A. Investments in construction and development of new infrastructure are made with expectations to generate cash either from income or from capital appreciation.

4. Which of the following is a characteristic of direct investment in infrastructure?

   A. High liquidity

   B. Concentration risk

   C. Short-term horizon

   Solution:

   The correct answer is B. Direct investment in infrastructure requires a large investment and results in both concentration and liquidity risks while the assets are managed and operated. Because of these risks and the typical long-term horizon, direct infrastructure investment usually takes place with a group or consortium of strategic investors that share the financial risk and/or assume a specific role in building, operating, or managing the assets.

INFRASTRUCTURE INVESTMENT CHARACTERISTICS 5

☐ explain the investment characteristics of infrastructure investments

The type of the underlying infrastructure investment, its stage of development, its geographic location, and the way the investment is structured define the expected risk and returns, as Exhibit 8 depicts.

Exhibit 8: Infrastructure Investment Characteristics

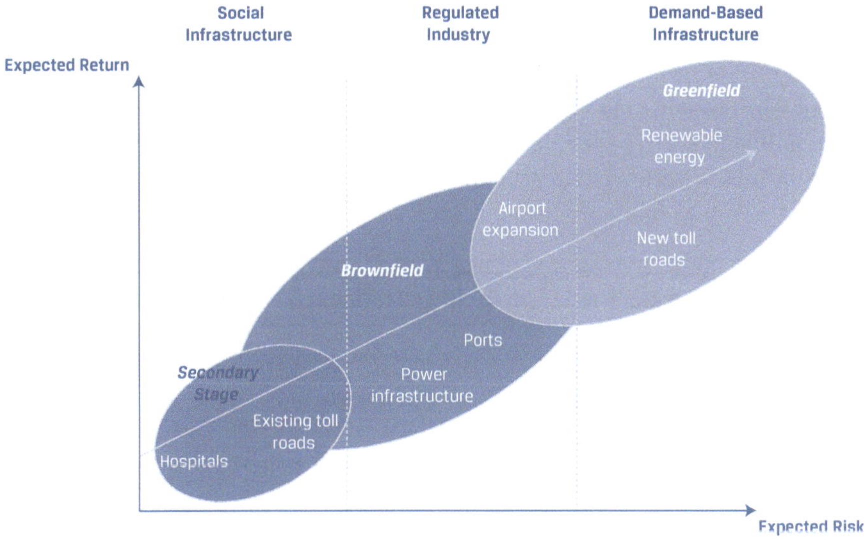

In the three groupings of the infrastructure development cycle—greenfield, operational secondary-stage, and brownfield—the operational secondary-stage assets with an existing track record of generating steady, bond-like cash flows possess the lowest risk and offer the lowest return to the investors. Brownfield investments, redevelopment of existing infrastructure, are incrementally riskier, and greenfield projects are the riskiest. Exhibit 9 shows the historical risk and return statistics for infrastructure assets compared to other real asset categories.

Exhibit 9: Historical Annualized Return and Standard Deviation of Return for Infrastructure and Real Assets, March 2008–June 2021

Annualized	Average return	Standard deviation	Coefficient of variation
Preqin, infrastructure	8.57%	0.07	0.82
Preqin, natural resources	3.29%	0.09	2.66
Preqin, real estate	3.43%	0.10	2.86
S&P Infrastructure Total Return	3.52%	0.19	5.52
MSCI US REIT Total Return	7.77%	0.26	3.38

Source: Annualized quarterly returns of Private Capital Quarterly Index rebased to 31 December 2007, provided by Preqin.

Additionally, the type of infrastructure investment is material in determining the risk and return. While investments in basic social services infrastructure or existing regulated industries typically involve less risk and lower expected return, demand-based infrastructure projects often build on projections of future economic growth and increased usage demands and are riskier.

In developing market economies, where infrastructure investments are needed to underpin economic, social, and societal growth and benefit from increased wealth created by the economy, risks are considerable, but the returns—over long time horizons—are considerable. Greenfield infrastructure projects in developing countries offer exceptional return opportunities over very long time horizons. Exhibit 10 shows the risk profiles of various infrastructure projects.

Exhibit 10: Private Infrastructure Fund Illustrative Target Returns

High-Risk Profile	Medium-Risk Profile	Low-Risk Profile
Greenfield projects without guarantees of demand upon completion—e.g., variable electricity prices, uncertain traffic on roads and through ports	Mostly brownfield assets (with some capital expenditure requirements) and some greenfield assets (with limited construction and demand risk)	Brownfield assets with mitigated risks—e.g., fully constructed with contracted/regulated revenues
Located in OECD countries and emerging markets	Located primarily in OECD countries	Located in the most stable OECD countries
High weighting to capital appreciation	Mix of yield and capital appreciation	High weighting to current yield
Target equity returns of 14%+	**Target equity returns of 10%–12%**	**Target equity returns of 6%–8%**

Note: Target equity returns are net of fees.
Source: Cambridge Associates, "Digging In: Assessing the Private Infrastructure Opportunity Today," Research Note (April 2017).

Most infrastructure funds gravitate toward the medium- and low-risk profiles, generating an average long-term annual return around 10%. As for other alternative investments, less liquid forms of direct equity ownership investments tend to offer the highest expected return with the greatest risk, while publicly traded forms of debt offer the lowest potential returns. Assets backed by stable long-term concession arrangements provide the most stable returns.

Infrastructure Diversification Benefits

Infrastructure investors expect the assets to primarily generate stable long-term cash flows that also adjust for economic growth and inflation and secondarily expect capital appreciation, depending on the type and timing of their investment. Because infrastructure investments typically support services that face inelastic demand and/or benefit from high barriers to entry, generate steady cash returns, and have a longer life cycle, equity investments in infrastructure offer lower correlation with public market equities and the broader economy. Effectively, infrastructure investments provide an income stream, increase portfolio diversification by adding an asset class with typically low correlation with other public investments, provide some protection for changes in GDP growth, and offer some protection against inflation. Exhibit 11 summarizes the diversification benefits of infrastructure investments and shows the low correlation between infrastructure and other market returns. It is notable that public and private infrastructure returns exhibit low correlations.

Exhibit 11: Historical Annualized Correlations for Infrastructure Assets, March 2008–June 2021

Correlation	S&P 500 Total Return	S&P Infrastructure Total Return	MSCI US REIT Total Return	MSCI World Total Return
Preqin, infrastructure	0.12	0.14	0.33	0.08
Preqin, natural resources	0.68	0.67	0.61	0.68
Preqin, real estate	0.51	0.39	0.49	0.46

Source: Annualized quarterly returns of Private Capital Quarterly Index rebased to 31 December 2007, provided by Preqin.

Most institutional investors consider infrastructure investments to balance public equity holdings because infrastructure has proven to be relatively resilient to swings in the equity markets. Given the stable underlying nature of cash flows, infrastructure debt tends to experience lower default rates and higher recovery than similar fixed-income instruments, and it is less subject to fluctuation over the economic cycle.

Additionally, infrastructure may better match the longer-term liability structure of certain investors, such as pension funds, superannuation schemes, and life insurance companies. It also suits the longer-term horizon of sovereign wealth funds, which tend to make the largest allocations to this asset class—around 5%–6% of total assets under management, according to Preqin. Long-term correlation benefits also result from the fact that most infrastructure assets have a link to inflation through regulation, concession agreements, or other fee contracts whose rates rise to or above the rate of inflation.

QUESTION SET

1. True or false: Greenfield infrastructure projects in developing countries offer exceptional return opportunities over very long time horizons.

   Solution:

   True. In developing market economies, where infrastructure investments are needed to underpin economic, social, and societal growth and benefit from increased wealth created by the economy, risks are considerable but the returns—over long time horizons—are also considerable.

2. Which of these types of infrastructure investment has the highest expected risk?

   A. Regulated industry

   B. Social infrastructure

   C. Demand-based infrastructure

Solution:

The correct answer is C. Demand-based infrastructure investments have the highest expected risk of the three. Social infrastructure has the lowest.

3. Which of the following has the highest weighting to capital appreciation?

   A. Greenfield assets with limited construction and demand risk

   B. Fully constructed brownfield assets with contracted revenues

   C. Greenfield assets without guarantees of demand upon completion

Solution:

The correct answer is C. Greenfield projects without guarantees of demand upon completion—for example, variable electricity prices, uncertain traffic on roads and through ports—have a high weighting to capital appreciation. Greenfield assets with limited construction and demand risk have a mix of yield and capital appreciation. Brownfield assets with mitigated risks (e.g., fully constructed with contracted/regulated revenues) that are located in the most stable OECD countries have a high weighting to current yield.

4. Which of the following is true regarding infrastructure investments?

   A. Infrastructure investments typically generate volatile cash returns.

   B. Infrastructure investments typically support services that face inelastic demand and/or benefit from high barriers to entry.

   C. While public infrastructure returns have low correlation with market returns, private infrastructure returns have high correlation with market returns.

Solution:

The correct answer is B. Because infrastructure investments typically support services that face inelastic demand and/or benefit from high barriers to entry, generate steady cash returns, and have a longer life cycle, equity investments in infrastructure offer lower correlation to public market equities and the broader economy. It is notable that public and private infrastructure returns exhibit low correlations.

PRACTICE PROBLEMS

1. A REIT is considered to be "hybrid" if it invests in both:
   A. equity REITs and mortgage REITs.
   B. sole ownership and joint ventures.
   C. direct and indirect property ownership.

2. A direct private real estate investor can reduce taxable income using:
   A. double taxation.
   B. cash depreciation expenses.
   C. tax-deductible interest expenses.

3. The main appeal of the REIT structure is the elimination of:
   A. dividend distributions.
   B. double corporate taxation.
   C. the requirement to report earnings per share.

4. An advantage of REITs is:
   A. low non-cash depreciation expenses.
   B. more transparency than private real estate markets.
   C. lower correlation with the public equity markets compared to private real estate.

5. Which of the following tends *not* to characterize real estate investments?
   A. Predictability
   B. Protection from inflation
   C. High correlations with other asset classes

6. Akasaka Investment Company established a portfolio of warehouse properties with a total market value of THB3.60 billion. It secured mortgage financing of THB2.61 billion. The terms of the mortgage required Akasaka to maintain a loan-to-value ratio of 0.725.
   After 18 months, the portfolio value had dropped to THB3.23 billion and the mortgage liability was THB2.35 billion.
   By how much must Akasaka reduce its mortgage liability to return its LTV back to the required level?
   A. THB6.00 million
   B. THB8.25 million
   C. THB9.19 million

7. Unlike appraisers, equity investors tend to place heavy emphasis on:
   A. recent trends.
   B. discounted cash flows.
   C. current market conditions.

8. Infrastructure investments can be categorized based on the nature of their underlying assets as:
   A. economic or social.
   B. local, regional, or national.
   C. usage-based or take-or-pay.

9. Which of these would most likely appeal to an investor who wants long-term, stable returns?
   A. Greenfield investments
   B. Brownfield investments
   C. Secondary-stage investments

10. Which of the following is true regarding infrastructure investments?
    A. They cannot be made using publicly traded securities.
    B. Master limited partnerships minimize double taxation for investors.
    C. Large pension funds are frequent members of direct investment consortiums because of their preference for a short-term horizon.

11. Which of the following types of infrastructure investments entails the lowest expected risk?
    A. Greenfield
    B. Brownfield
    C. Secondary stage

12. Which of the following has the highest weighting to current yield?
    A. Greenfield assets with limited construction and demand risk
    B. Fully constructed brownfield assets with contracted revenues
    C. Greenfield assets without guarantees of demand upon completion

13. Compared with similar fixed-income instruments, infrastructure debt:
    A. has higher recovery rates.
    B. experiences higher default rates.
    C. has more fluctuation over the economic cycle.

SOLUTIONS

1. The correct answer is A. There are three main forms of REIT: (1) equity REITs that invest in properties outright or through partnerships and joint ventures, (2) mortgage REITs that underwrite loans to real estate (mortgages) or invest in MBS, and (3) hybrid REITs that invest in both of these types.

2. The correct answer is C. Direct private real estate owners can reduce their taxable income using *non*-cash property depreciation expenses and tax-deducible interest expenses.

3. The correct answer is B. The main appeal of the REIT structure is the elimination of double corporate taxation. Corporations pay taxes on their income, from which they make dividend distributions to their owners from after-tax earnings. The shareholders, in turn, are taxed at their personal tax rate. Equity REITs, like other public companies, must report earnings per share based on net income as defined by generally accepted accounting principles or International Financial Reporting Standards.

4. The correct answer is B. An advantage of REITs is more transparency than private real estate markets. As an asset-intensive business, REITs can have high non-cash depreciation expenses. REITs have higher correlation with the public equity markets compared to private real estate, and this is a disadvantage of REITs.

5. The correct answer is C. Real estate has historically low correlations with other asset classes, and adding real estate to an investment portfolio provides diversification benefits at relatively lower levels of risk. Many commercial real estate companies offer multiple-year leases with fixed rents; hence, the income earned from these leases is typically both predictable and stable. Moreover, real estate tends to provide inflation protection because the lease payments are regularly adjusted.

6. The correct answer is B.

   LTV = Mortgage liability/Portfolio value.

   Mortgage liability = LTV × Portfolio value.

   Required mortgage liability = Required LTV × Portfolio value.

   Required reduction in mortgage liability = Mortgage liability – Required mortgage liability.

   Required reduction in mortgage liability = Mortgage liability – (Required LTV × Portfolio value).

   $8.25 = 235 - (0.725 \times 323)$.

7. The correct answer is B. Equity investors in public real estate discount future cash flows, while appraisers of private real estate place heavy emphasis on current market conditions and recent trends.

8. The correct answer is A. To categorize infrastructure investments, investors frequently rely on the underlying assets, with the broadest categorization distinguishing between economic and social infrastructure assets.

9. The correct answer is B. With brownfield investments, typically some of the financial and operating history is available. Therefore, brownfield investments may be sought after by both strategic investors specializing in operating the assets

and—particularly with privatizations—financial investors focused on long-term, stable returns.

10. The correct answer is B. Master limited partnerships trade on exchanges, are pass-through entities like REITs, and may also share with REITs taxation rules that minimize double taxation for investors.

    Investors concerned about liquidity and diversification may choose publicly traded infrastructure securities.

    Because of the concentration and liquidity risks and the typical long-term horizon, direct infrastructure investment usually takes place with a group or consortium of strategic investors that share the financial risk and/or assume a specific role in building, operating, or managing the assets. Such strategic partners, such as large pension funds or sovereign wealth funds, are frequent direct investors because they are better placed to manage certain risks to limit individual concentration risk.

11. The correct answer is C. In the three groupings of the infrastructure development cycle—greenfield, operational secondary stage, and brownfield—the operational secondary-stage assets with an existing track record of generating steady, bond-like cash flows possess the lowest risk and offer the lowest return to the investors. Brownfield investments, redevelopment of existing infrastructure, are incrementally riskier, and greenfield projects are the riskiest.

12. The correct answer is B. Brownfield assets with mitigated risks (e.g., fully constructed with contracted/regulated revenues) that are located in the most stable OECD countries have a high weighting to current yield. Greenfield assets with limited construction and demand risk have a mix of yield and capital appreciation. Greenfield projects without guarantees of demand upon completion—e.g., variable electricity prices, uncertain traffic on roads and through ports—have a high weighting to capital appreciation.

13. The correct answer is A. Given the stable underlying nature of cash flows, infrastructure debt tends to experience lower default rates and higher recovery than similar fixed-income instruments, and it is less subject to fluctuation over the economic cycle.

LEARNING MODULE

5

Natural Resources

LEARNING OUTCOMES	
Mastery	*The candidate should be able to:*
☐	explain features of raw land, timberland, and farmland and their investment characteristics
☐	describe features of commodities and their investment characteristics
☐	analyze sources of risk, return, and diversification among natural resource investments

INTRODUCTION

1

Natural resources comprise commodities and raw land used for agricultural purposes, specifically farming and timber. Managing this asset class requires specialized knowledge of the features of natural resources. An increasing number of portfolios include natural resources, which justifies a separate examination of the sector. There has been rapid development in offering indirect investment in natural resources through exchange-traded funds (ETFs), limited partnerships, REITs, swaps, and futures.

Commodities, such as crude oil, soybeans, copper, and gold, are seen as investments. Investments in commodities can be either "hard" (those mined, such as copper, or extracted, such as oil) or "soft" (those grown over a period of time, such as livestock, grains, and cash crops, such as coffee).

Timberland investment involves ownership of raw land and the harvesting of its trees for lumber, thus generating an income stream and the potential for capital gain, and timberland has been included in large institutional portfolios for decades. Farmland as an investment is a more recent phenomenon, with only a few dedicated funds involved. With population growth, weather, and water management becoming more topical, however, investors may turn to these assets to actively address sustainability.

LEARNING MODULE OVERVIEW

- Investments in farmland and timberland are similar in certain respects to real estate investments but also exhibit several important differences.

- While raw land's investment returns occur strictly from price changes of the asset, both farmland and timberland generate returns from the assets' income stream in addition to price changes of the assets.
- Timberland's income stream differs from that of farmland in that the harvest time of timber can be chosen while crops from farmland are harvested on a regular cycle.
- Commodity investments are typically entered into via derivative markets, although some investors may find value in investment in physical commodities directly or through specialized funds.
- The prices available on commodities through derivative markets must be related to the prices on the same commodities in physical markets to prevent arbitrage opportunities.
- The forward price of a commodity will be greater than the spot price on the same commodity only if the carrying costs of owning the physical commodity are greater than the non-cash benefits of owning the physical commodity.
- Investing in commodities is motivated by its potential for high expected return, its potential for diversifying a portfolio of traditional assets, and inflation protection. Commodities exhibit high correlation with inflation over the last 30 years, suggesting that commodities are an effective inflation hedge.
- Farmland and timberland investments trade infrequently and in non-public markets. As a result, they are likely to appear as less volatile than commodities and other publicly traded risky assets (such as stocks), despite the fact that both asset classes face significant risks, such as weather-related threats.
- Farmland and timberland provide diversification potential to portfolios consisting primarily of traditional assets (i.e., stocks and bonds). Historical correlations between these asset classes and traditional assets have been close to zero.

LEARNING MODULE SELF-ASSESSMENT

These initial questions are intended to help you gauge your current level of understanding of this learning module.

1. Which of the following asset characteristics is shared by both farmland and real estate investments?

   A. Both are liquid investments.

   B. Both are illiquid investments.

   C. Physical improvements are a primary focus of the investment value for both.

   Solution:

   B is correct. Farmland and real estate share a feature of illiquidity: It is costly to find a buyer when sale of the investment is desired. A is incorrect given that both are illiquid investments. C is incorrect because physical improvements are a focus of value only for real estate investments, not for farmland investments.

2. Which of the following natural resource investments is least likely to use the real estate investment trust (REIT) ownership structure?

   A. Farmland

   B. Raw land

   C. Timberland

   Solution:

   B is correct. Raw land is typically acquired through direct ownership or a partnership structure. Also, raw land has no inherent income stream and returns accrue purely from price appreciation, making the income pass-through REIT structure less relevant. Both A and C are incorrect because both farmland and timberland investments are included in REIT structures, as well as other ownership forms.

3. Which type of investor is likely to prefer investing in commodities using exchange-traded products?

   A. Those seeking simplified trading through a brokerage account

   B. Those seeking to gain access to dynamic commodity trading strategies

   C. Those seeking expertise in a specific commodity sector

   Solution:

   A is correct. Exchange-traded products allow investors to gain commodity exposure through a simple exchange-traded instrument that can be accessed via a brokerage account. B is incorrect because it describes investors who choose to use commodity trading advisors. C is incorrect because this type of investor will choose a specialized commodity fund for its expertise.

4. Which of the following describes a non-cash benefit of holding a physical commodity rather than a derivative contract on the same commodity?

   A. Interest

   B. Convenience yield

   C. Storage

   Solution:

   B is correct. In market environments in which physical inventories of a commodity become low, investors in that commodity will prefer to hold the physical asset rather than a derivative contract with the asset as an underlying. The premium on the spot price resulting from this preference is called the convenience yield. A and C are both incorrect because interest and storage reflect costs associated with owning the physical commodity.

5. Which of the following statements most correctly reflects commodity supply and demand fundamentals?

   A. Supply of commodities adjusts equally to demand for commodities.

   B. Supply of commodities adjusts more rapidly than does demand for commodities.

   C. Supply of commodities adjusts more slowly than does demand for commodities.

   Solution:

   C is correct. Commodity supply adjusts slowly to demand because of long production times; for example, agricultural crops require a growing cycle.

6. Which of the following measures is best used to assess the potential for portfolio diversification when adding farmland or timberland to a portfolio of traditional assets?

   A. Returns of other asset classes

   B. Volatility of other asset classes

   C. Correlation between other asset classes

   Solution:

   C is correct. Correlation between asset classes best reflects the potential for portfolio diversification. An asset class that exhibits lower (i.e., closer to zero) correlation with traditional asset classes (such as stocks and bonds) has better diversification potential compared to an asset class exhibiting higher (i.e., closer to one) correlation. A and B are incorrect because returns and volatility strictly reflect reward and risk for the asset class without consideration as to how the asset class performs compared to other asset classes.

2 NATURAL RESOURCES INVESTMENT FEATURES

☐ explain features of raw land, timberland, and farmland and their investment characteristics

Natural resources comprise different production inputs that are basic to the economy and everyday life: plants and animals (i.e., soft commodities); energy and minerals (hard commodities); and metals and industrial goods used to manufacture goods and produce services. A notable proportion of natural resource investments are directly through farmland, raw land with exploration and mining rights, and timberland. Direct ownership spans a broad spectrum: from farmers producing grain to institutional investors building solar farms.

Many large institutional investors create exposure to natural resources outright by purchasing land with rights to farm agricultural commodities; to extract oil and gas; to build facilities for alternative energy generation, such as solar and wind farms; or to mine commodities, such as iron, coal, and other industrial metals. By investing in these assets, institutional investors often seek to fulfil their environmental, social, and governance (ESG) objectives, such as sustainability, water conservation, and other environmental goals.

Land Investments vs. Real Estate

Farmland, timberland, and raw land are similar to real estate investments in that they are unique, illiquid assets with distinct geographic location and features, where the latter two characteristics have an influence on the value of the resource itself. They involve forms of ownership capital (claims to residual cash flows). In the case of developed real estate and farmland, there may also be steady cash flow streams (leases).

Less developed land includes farmland, timberland, and raw land, as well as associated mineral or drilling rights. Sources of return include expected price appreciation over time and cash flows, such as farm lease payments (for an owner), farm operating income (owner-operator), farm timberland income, and mineral and drilling royalties.

Estimates suggest nearly half of private investable timberland globally is in the United States. The next biggest timberland regions are Central and Eastern Europe, Latin America, Australia, and New Zealand.

There are several differences between real estate investments and raw land, farmland, and timberland investments. The first difference is that unlike real estate, there is limited or no focus on the physical improvements to the land. It is not the value of buildings, construction, and development that matters but, rather, the quality of the soil, climate features (farmland, timberland), or geology (mineral rights). In contrast, it is the actual, potential, and planned improvements that determine the value of the property in real estate investments. The location of land is also important; the closer it is to transportation and markets, the higher the price. While the proximity to transportation is also a factor for real estate, transportation expenses can be a significant component of the price of the products paid by the end-user of timberland and farmland.

To make investments in raw land, timberland, or farmland, investors need specialized knowledge and understanding of the specifics of the natural resource. Investors investing directly in timberland need forest investment expertise to manage a forest over its life cycle. Many large institutional investors that do not have this expertise rely on **timberland investment management organizations** (TIMOs), entities that support institutional investors by managing their investments in timberland by analyzing and acquiring suitable timberland holdings.

Both commercial and residential real estate offer a wide variety of financing alternatives; however, there are fewer alternatives for farmland, timberland, and raw land. Often these investments are financed through bank loans or direct, private debt investment. Finally, these are illiquid assets that have a limited number of potential buyers and sellers due to the specialized knowledge and capital needed for these transactions. These features are outlined in Exhibit 1.

Exhibit 1: Raw Land, Farmland and Timberland

	Raw land	Farmland	Timberland
Return drivers	Price of land	Harvest quantities Commodity prices Price of land	Biological growth Harvest quantities Lumber prices Price of land
Source of direct revenue	Price appreciation Lease revenue	Sale of crops and other agricultural products Price appreciation Lease revenue	Sale of trees, wood, and other timber products Price appreciation Lease revenue
Value	Physical location	Physical location Growth cycle Soil quality	Physical location Quality of timber Phase in timber production
Main risks	Best alternative use	Weather factors and climate change Biological factors, diseases	
Owners	Mostly institutional, some individual	Mostly individuals, some institutional	Mostly institutional, some individual
Ownership structure	Direct ownership, partnership	Direct ownership, partnership, REIT	Direct ownership, partnership, REIT, TIMO

Features and Forms of Farmland and Timberland Investment

Sustained interest in farmland and timberland investments stems from their common nature (everyone eats and requires shelter), the recurring income from crops, inflation protection from holding land, and their degree of insulation from financial market volatility. US farmland, for example, enjoyed positive returns both during periods when US GDP declined significantly (1973–1975 and 2007–2009) and when the United States experienced higher-than-normal inflation (1915–1920, 1940–1951, and 1967–1981).

Timberland has been part of institutional and ultra-high-net-worth portfolios for decades, typically trading in large units of land (several thousands of acres or hectares). One of the main challenges of these investments is their long market cycle, particularly in new-growth forest and crops that are picked, such as fruit. In contrast, farmland can be found in much smaller sizes—perhaps tens of or a few hundred acres or hectares. Many farms are still family owned, as is 98% of US farmland. Globally, farmland remains a main source of family wealth.

Investments in farmland and timberland—owned directly, owned indirectly, or leased—generate returns from selling crops and timber. Farmland consists mainly of row crops that are planted and harvested (more than one round of planting and harvesting can occur in a year depending on the crop and the climate) and permanent crops that grow on trees or vines. Farmland may also be used as pastureland for livestock. Farm products must be harvested when ripe, with little flexibility in production. By contrast, timberland serves as both a factory and a warehouse. Timber (trees) can be grown (i.e., timberland's factory characteristic) and easily stored by simply not harvesting the trees (i.e., timberland's warehouse characteristic). This characteristic offers the flexibility of harvesting when timber prices are up and delaying harvests when prices are down.

As part of the returns generated by selling the output from the land, both farmland and timberland generate returns from price changes in their output. The market prices for agricultural products and timber may fluctuate considerably over time, and these prices combined with harvest quantities dictate the revenue generated by the sale of the land's output. Finally, the value of the land may change over time for both farmland and timberland, and these land price changes also contribute to the return on farmland and timberland investments. The return drivers are summarized in the first row of Exhibit 1.

For centuries, direct farmland and timberland ownership has been the initial dominant form, with a focus on long-term tax-exempt investors, such as pension funds, foundations, and endowments. That is why the primary investment vehicles of smaller investors for timber and farmland are investment funds, whether offered on the public markets, such as real estate investment trusts in the United States, or administered privately through limited partnerships. Direct timberland investors use TIMOs to select, manage, and sell assets in accordance with investor objectives. TIMOs are often used in conjunction with indirect investment alternatives, such as limited partnerships, limited liability corporations (LLC), and private REITs.

Larger investors can consider direct investments for assets with appeal. For example, Middle Eastern sovereign wealth funds have made investments in farmland in Africa and Southeast Asia. Increasingly, farmland funds and limited partnerships and publicly traded farmland REITs have been launched.

These indirect investment vehicles usually involve separately managed accounts that distinguish between owner and owner-operator models; in the former case, owners rent land used for row crops (i.e., grains, etc.), while in the latter, they retain some operating control in the case of permanent crop properties (orchards, vineyards, etc.). Cash flows are typically fixed in the former case and variable in the latter, with investors taking on some operating risk.

Owning physical farmland opens the door to a wider variety of foodstuffs: spices, nuts, fruits, and vegetables—a much broader array than the corn, soy, and wheat offered by futures investment. However, there is limited price transparency or information to guide investment decisions without the assistance of sector specialists. The illiquidity of direct farmland and timberland investments is also limiting.

In terms of risk, farmland is highly sensitive to unexpected weather changes and climate developments that can easily destroy crops and eradicate revenue. The impact of weather spans the entire growing season, making agricultural volumes and prices difficult to predict. That is why agricultural commodity futures contracts can be combined with farmland holdings to generate an overall hedged return. A farm has an inherent long position in its crop and, therefore, will sell futures for delivery at the time of the harvest. The following discussion provides a more detailed case study of climate risks associated with timberland investing.

There is an indirect benefit from farmland and timberland investments: These natural resources consume carbon as part of the plant life cycle and their value comes not just from the harvest but also from the carbon offset to human activity. Water rights are also part of the direct and implied value of these properties; conservation easements may create value by supporting traditions and nature conservation. Demand for arable land may rise as interest in investments that adhere to ESG considerations grows.

CASE STUDY

Investing Responsibly in Timberland Assets: A Climate-Conscious Case Study

Campbell Global (CG) is a global investment manager focused on forest and natural resources investments. Based in Portland, Oregon, with offices in 14 US states and New Zealand, the firm has nearly four decades of experience in sustainable value creation. CG is committed to managing its forests in a manner that promotes the best long-term interests of its clients, while also striving to address economic and ESG considerations. In addition to their economic value, forests serve as vast carbon sinks, with trees removing atmospheric CO_2 and providing carbon storage. In one year, a single Douglas fir tree, a common commercial timber species in the US Pacific Northwest, stores the CO_2 equivalent of driving 400 miles in a standard automobile. Globally, the Earth's forests are estimated to absorb as much as 30% of human-induced CO_2 emissions.

Sustainably harvested wood products and materials also store atmospheric CO_2 long after removal from a forest, with one cubic meter of wood capturing nearly a metric ton of CO_2. In addition to carbon sequestration, forests provide benefits of clean water and wildlife habitat, recreational opportunities, and a source of living-wage jobs in rural communities. These attributes agree with the UN's Sustainable Development Goals and contribute to advancing the UN's mission for a sustainable future globally. With these effects, there is increasing awareness that well-managed forests are a critical component of any global climate change strategy.

CG uses scenario analyses to identify climate-related risks beginning at a broad country-level scale, narrowing down to a specific property, and then testing the impact of various risks to a site's present and future suitability. Factors analyzed to gauge climate risks include precipitation patterns, temperature fluctuations, severity of weather events, presence of pests or disease, and annual average growth rates for commercial tree species. While many climate-related risks in forestry are mitigated through active management, during this iterative process, CG analyzes the potential positive and negative impacts associated with these risks to assess potential changes in net asset value. The following table illustrates climate risks evaluated, their impact on the forest, and the ability to mitigate the risks.

Climate Risk	Implication	CG Mitigants
Change in temperature	Increased fire danger	Property-specific fire plans; re-evaluate target regions/countries for investment
Change in precipitation patterns	Changes in tree species range; increased drought and related fire risk	Vegetation suitability modeling and genetic tree improvement; re-evaluate target regions/countries for investment
Frequency of extreme weather events	Loss of standing timber from wind events	Re-evaluate target regions; property-specific response plans; geographically diverse portfolio construction
Presence of pests or disease	Early onset and increased frequency of individual tree mortality	Immediate treatment, which may include removal of affected trees to prevent further spread of pests or disease in the forest
Change in growth	Increased or decreased growth rates	Effects will vary by region, may influence planting stock decisions; re-evaluate forest growth model assumptions

Climate change opportunities and challenges highlighted in the CG investment process include the following:

- Identifying afforestation (establishment of new forest) opportunities that mitigate climate change by sequestering CO_2 emissions from the atmosphere in trees and soil, while offering many important co-benefits for communities, biodiversity, and soil and water quality.
- Protecting existing carbon stocks by minimizing impacts to carbon stored on the forest floor through tailored forest management practices.
- Enhancing forest carbon sequestration by replanting areas as soon as possible so the new forest will quickly begin removing CO_2 from the atmosphere.

The ability to quantify, evaluate, and report the year-over-year changes in the carbon footprint of a forest can influence the impacts an organization has on the environment, leading to increased transparency and more-informed business decisions. Incorporating climate change factors in its investment process not only mitigates climate-related risks; it also promotes and enhances the natural solutions forests provide. Understanding and measuring the comprehensive carbon stores of forests may lead to business decisions improving carbon sequestration, critical for addressing climate change.

QUESTION SET

1. Identify the three primary return drivers of investing in timberland.

   Solution:

   The three primary return drivers of investing in timberland are (1) the biological growth of the timber to be harvested in the future, (2) the price of lumber, and (3) changes in the price of the land.

2. Which of the following statements provides the most accurate description of timberland investment management organizations?

   A. TIMOs are entities that use their forest investment expertise to analyze and acquire suitable timberland holdings on behalf of institutional investors.

   B. TIMOs are investment funds that raise money from individual investors to buy timberland.

   C. TIMOs are entities that only facilitate direct ownership of timberland by institutional investors.

   Solution:

   A is the correct response. Timberland requires asset-specific expertise, and TIMOs use their expertise to analyze and acquire timberland holdings either directly or indirectly for institutional investors. B is incorrect because TIMOs are not investment funds. C is incorrect because TIMOs can be used by institutional investors in conjunction with indirect investing in timberland.

3. Describe one important similarity and one important difference between investing in timberland versus investing in real estate.

   Solution:

   Similarities between timberland and real estate include the fact that both asset classes involve investing in unique assets with distinct geography and the fact that both asset classes have a high degree of illiquidity.

   An important difference between the two asset classes is the degree to which value reflects physical improvements to the land. Specifically, real estate investing values actual and potential improvements while timberland investing does not.

4. Describe a significant difference in the income component of farmland investing versus timberland investing.

   Solution:

   Timberland provides flexibility in the timing of harvesting trees. Unlike timberland, farm products must be harvested when ripe, with little flexibility in production.

COMMODITY INVESTMENT FORMS 3

☐ describe features of commodities and their investment characteristics

Commodity Investment Features

Commodities themselves do not generate cash flows but usually incur costs (*cost of carry* introduced in derivatives learning modules), such as those for transportation, storage, and insurance for physical commodities. Investors seek to benefit from commodity price appreciation (in excess of carry cost) based on their future economic value rather than actual use of the underlying asset.

Moreover, governments have realized the importance of controlling natural resources and taken an increasingly important role in natural resource markets. For instance, many governments provide food price subsidies to customers and price support to farmers.

Governments often control extractable natural rights, such as energy resources and mining. In many emerging markets, governments or government-owned enterprises control strategic energy production or mining resources. For instance, SOCAR, the State Oil Company of Azerbaijan Republic, is the fully state-owned national oil and gas company of the country and extracts oil and natural gas from onshore and offshore fields of the Caspian Sea. Moreover, it operates Azerbaijan's only oil refinery and operates several oil and gas export pipelines. It is a major source of income for the country. In other countries, owners of land may only be able to cultivate the soil and may extract only certain minerals. Often the government owns and manages subsurface rights and has the right to extract certain resources, such as oil, gas, coal, gold, and silver.

Environmental factors play a direct role in natural resource investments, because governments are increasingly implementing environmental safeguards to meet climate objectives and control activities with climate impact, such as mining, agriculture, and energy extraction and production. More specifically, global climate change policies seek to reduce reliance on fossil fuels (coal, oil) and increase renewable energy use. To do so, countries are in the process of adopting national programs that intend to increase renewable energy (wind, solar, biomass) and reduce the reliance on fossil fuels.

The policy objective of reducing the reliance on fossil fuels has shifted focus to electric vehicles and advances in battery technology. A potential impact of the reliance on low-carbon energy technologies is the higher demand for many minerals and metals, such as lithium, cobalt, and nickel. As mining activities for these critical metals will increase, there will be significant impacts on local water systems, ecosystems, and communities.

Finally, there is growing interest from ESG investors seeking to promote sustainable farming practices or use timberland investments for carbon offsets.

Distinguishing Characteristics of Commodity Investments

Commodity sectors include precious and base (i.e., industrial) metals, energy products, and agricultural products. Exhibit 2 offers examples of each type. The relative importance, amount, and price of individual commodities evolve with society's preferences and needs. Increasing industrialization of emerging markets has driven strong global demand for commodities. These markets need increasing amounts of oil, steel, and other materials to support manufacturing, infrastructure development, and the consumption demands of their populations. Emerging technologies, such as advanced cell phones and electric vehicles, create demand for new materials and destroy demand for old resources as markets for specific commodities evolve over time.

Exhibit 2: Examples of Commodities

Sector	Sample Commodities
Energy	Oil, natural gas, electricity, coal
Base metals	Copper, aluminum, zinc, lead, tin, nickel
Precious metals	Gold, silver, platinum
Agriculture	Grains, livestock, coffee
Other	Carbon credits, freight, forest products

Commodities may be further classified by physical location and grade or quality. For example, there are many grades and delivery locations for crude oil and wheat. Commodity derivative contracts thus specify quantity, quality, maturity date, and delivery location.

The majority of commodity investing is implemented through derivatives. Physical commodities often generate unwelcome tax obligations and costs arising from storage, insurance, brokerage, and transportation. Additionally, physical commodity markets lack price transparency. As such, commodity investments are usually made through financial derivative instruments, most frequently commodity futures and forwards and occasionally options on futures. Using derivatives to establish exposures to natural resources has several benefits: Because these instruments are traded on organized exchanges, they are very liquid and provide opportunities for price discovery.

Futures contracts are obligations to buy or sell a specific amount of a given commodity at a fixed price, location, and date in the future. Futures contracts are exchange traded, are marked to market daily, and may or may not be settled on delivery or receipt of the physical commodity at the end of the contract. This delivery obligation becomes dramatically important during stressful periods. For example, with oil during the global financial crisis in 2008 and during the COVID-19 pandemic in 2020, as demand collapsed, oil producers could not find buyers and global storage filled suddenly. Even commodity-related ETFs were affected, forcing some to close and impose large losses on investors.

For futures contracts, counterparty risk is managed through the settlement process between the clearinghouse/exchange and clearing brokers. Commodity exposure can be achieved through means other than direct investment in commodities or commodity derivatives, including the following:

- *Exchange-traded products.* ETPs, either funds (ETFs) or notes (ETNs), may be suitable for investors restricted to equity shares or seeking simplified trading through a standard brokerage account. ETPs may invest in commodities or commodity futures. For example, the SPDR Gold Shares ETF seeks to track the price of physical gold by holding bullion in vaults. It owned just under USD53 billion in gold bullion as of December 2022. ETPs may use leverage and may replicate the pay-offs from a long or short position, with the latter form considered inverse or "bearish." Similar to mutual funds or unit trusts, ETPs charge fees included in their expense ratios.
- *Investing with commodity trading advisers.* CTAs are another way to gain commodity exposure. CTAs are managed futures funds that make directional investments primarily in futures markets based on technical and fundamental strategies. A commodity-focused CTA might concentrate on a specific commodity (such as grains) or be broadly diversified across commodities. However, one would need to find a fund focused solely on the desired commodity, because modern CTAs often invest in a variety of futures, including commodities, equities, fixed income, and foreign exchange. Individual investors may establish accounts that are managed in

accordance with their specific investment preferences and risk tolerance called **separately managed accounts** (SMAs). These types of individual accounts are common for commodity investments. More details on CTAs and managed futures are covered in the learning module on hedge funds.

- *Specialized funds investing in specific commodity sectors.* An example of specialized funds is private energy partnerships, which are similar in structure to private equity funds and enable institutional exposure to the energy sector. Management fees can range from 1% to 3% of committed capital, with a typical life span of 10 years and extensions of 1- and 2-year periods. Publicly available energy mutual funds and unit trusts typically focus on the oil and gas sector, often acting as fixed-income investments to pay dividends from rents or capital gains. They may focus on upstream (drilling), midstream (refineries), or downstream (chemicals). Their management fees are comparable with those of other public equity managers and range from 0.4% to 1%.

Commodity investments are typically direct underwriting of the acquisition, management, and extraction of the natural resource itself. These investments usually involve direct or indirect claims to *physical* assets themselves and not claims on residual (equity) or fixed (debt) cash flows.

This indirect approach, however, comes with the added risks from financing and operations and, when privately held, the impact of additional illiquidity.

Basics of Commodity Pricing

Investors seeking to benefit from direct commodity price exposure typically use derivative instruments, such as exchange-traded futures and options and forwards, with individual commodities or an index as the underlying asset. Different commodity indexes are composed of different commodities and have materially different index weights, which determines varying exposures to not only specific commodities but also commodity sectors. However, as we will see later in this module, the correlation between commodities and traditional asset classes is typically low, which means improved portfolio diversification is possible regardless of the index chosen.

Since commodities trade in both physical and financial markets, there is a direct relationship between their prices in both the physical cash markets and the financial derivative markets. Such no-arbitrage conditions, which we have encountered earlier in the derivatives readings, dictate that the difference in prices between the cash or spot markets and derivative markets is equal to the *cost of carry*, which is the opportunity cost of holding these assets, and mirrors the risk-free rate and the cost of storing, transporting, and insuring the commodity. The holder of the physical commodity should expect to be compensated via a higher forward price, $F_0{}^{+}(T)$, than the prevailing cash price.

However, there may be non-cash benefits from holding the physical commodity instead of gaining exposure using a derivative. Such *convenience yield* may arise under conditions when the market participants prefer to hold the physical commodity; for instance, the owners want to ensure that they have continuous access to this commodity. Usually, the convenience yield is related inversely to inventory levels of the underlying commodity. Because convenience yield is a benefit and *accrues* to the owner, it *reduces* the forward price.

The pricing relationship between cash, S_0, and derivative markets can be expressed under continuous compounding as

$$F_0(T) = S_0 e^{(r+c-i)T}, \qquad (1)$$

where c is the cost of carry, i is the convenience yield, r is the risk-free rate, and T is the time to the expiration of the forward contract. Effectively, the relationship between commodity forward and spot prices over time depends on the relative relationship between the cost of carry and the convenience yield.

Looking at the relationship between the convenience yield and the cost of carry, there are two relationships. When the spot price is above the forward prices, there is **backwardation**, a downward-sloping, or inverted, forward curve. This can occur for physically settled contracts when the convenience yield is positive and the benefit of holding the commodity outright exceeds the cost of carry. When the spot price is below the forward prices, there is **contango** because the cost of ownership exceeds the benefit of a convenience yield and the forward price will be above the underlying spot asset price. As a rule of thumb, a contango scenario generally lowers the return of the long-only investor, and a backwardation scenario enhances it. The following example shows how market changes can lead to significant shifts in the shape of the commodity forward curve:

EXAMPLE 1

Crude Oil Going from Backwardation to Contango

In April 2020, the price of crude oil futures on the New York Mercantile Exchange (NYMEX) fell below zero for the first time ever; sellers paid buyers to take on an exposure to oil. This situation is highly unusual and was caused by the lockdowns in the wake of the COVID-19 pandemic that eroded the demand for oil. Producers could not cut crude oil production quickly enough, and storage facilities were overflowing with oil. This caused oil inventories to skyrocket. Exhibit 3 shows the NYMEX oil futures price from January to June 2020.

Exhibit 3: NYMEX Oil Futures Price (US dollars per contract), January–June 2020

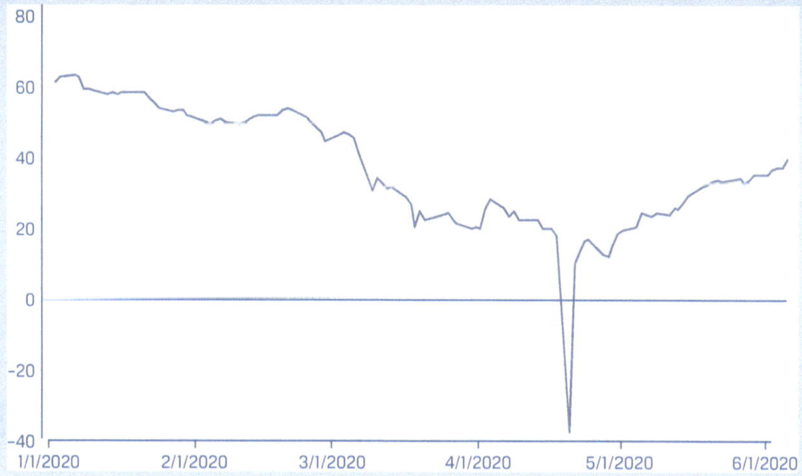

Source: Bloomberg.

The sudden disappearance of the demand for oil impacted the shape of the oil futures curve, the series of oil futures contract prices with different forward settlement dates. Prior to the outbreak of the COVID-19 pandemic in January 2020, the US oil markets had the lowest inventory levels in over a year and expected a continued healthy demand from a vibrant economy. Because of low inventory levels, the oil futures curve was in backwardation at the beginning of January 2020 because the benefit of holding oil outright exceeded the cost of carry of having oil in inventory (see Exhibit 4).

Exhibit 4: NYMEX Oil Futures Curve, January 2020

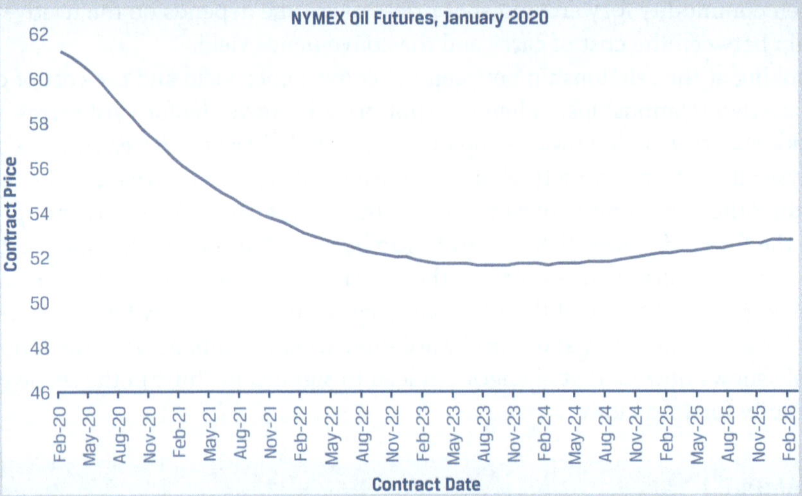

As lockdowns continued into mid-2020, US oil market inventory approached near all-time high levels but demand remained muted. Carry costs then outweighed any benefit of storing oil for production purposes (and there was hardly any open storage capacity available), and the oil futures curve was in *contango* at the beginning of May 2020 (see Exhibit 5).

Exhibit 5: NYMEX Oil Futures Curve, May 2020

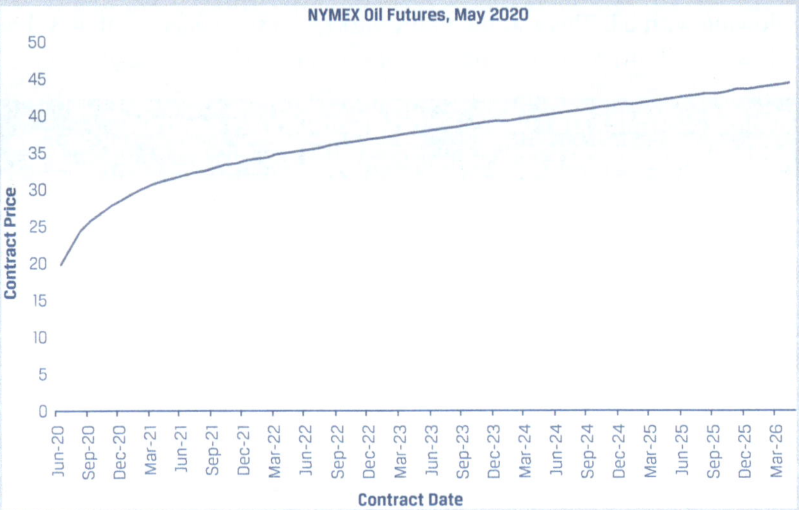

QUESTION SET

1. Compare farmland investment to commodity investment with respect to sources of value.

   Solution:

   A similarity between the two is that both forms of investment rely on changes in the price of underlying. A difference between the two is that commodity investments, which typically rely on derivative contracts, do not generate cash flows while farmland investment generates cash flows through the income generated from harvesting the agricultural crops.

2. Which of the following statements is most correct about investors seeking commodity exposure through a commodity trading adviser (CTA)?

   A. The investor is seeking to make direct investment in commodities.

   B. The investor is seeking to benefit from an income stream from commodities.

   C. The investor is seeking to profit from specific directional trends in commodity futures contracts.

   Solution:

   C is correct. Commodity trading advisers devise trading strategies using derivative contracts on commodities that are focused on predicting upcoming bull or bear trends. A is incorrect because CTAs do not advise on physical commodity transactions. B is incorrect for a similar reason, because the income stream from most commodities would require direct or indirect land ownership, which produces commodities.

3. Discuss how the relationship between costs of carry and benefits of owning a commodity outright affect the relationship between the forward price and spot price of the commodity.

   Solution:

   A simple framework for expressing the relationship between forward price and spot price in terms of costs and benefits of owning the underlying commodity is as follows:

   Forward price = Spot price + Costs of carry – Benefits of ownership.

   Thus, if costs of carry exceed benefits of ownership, then forward price is greater than spot price for the commodity. In contrast, forward price is less than spot price if benefits exceed costs.

4. Explain why low inventories of a commodity may result in backwardation for the commodity.

   Solution:

   Backwardation reflects a downward-sloping term structure of prices for a commodity. In the near term, backwardation implies forward price below spot price. Low inventories of a commodity cause investors to prefer to hold the physical commodity over derivative contracts (i.e., forwards). This preference will cause price for the physical asset to be bid higher, and if this noncash benefit of owning the physical commodity (also known as convenience yield) exceeds costs of ownership of the commodity (such as interest and storage), then the spot price of the commodity exceeds its forward price.

NATURAL RESOURCE INVESTMENT RISK, RETURN, AND DIVERSIFICATION 4

☐ analyze sources of risk, return, and diversification among natural resource investments

Commodity prices have risk and return drivers that are often related to but do not always directly coincide with the timing of the economic cycle affecting the prices of common equity and debt securities. Commodities, farmland, and timberland have different return drivers and cycles. Commodities are priced on a second-by-second basis on public exchanges, whereas land generally has an infrequent pricing mechanism and may include imprecise estimates, as opposed to actual transactions. Keeping these market structure differences in mind helps investors consider their relative benefits and challenges.

Commodities

Physical commodity supply dynamics are determined by production (in the case of hard commodities), seasonal crop yields (for soft commodities), and inventory levels in the short term, while commodity end user/consumer use of these basic inputs drives ultimate demand. Supplies of physical commodities are determined by production and inventory levels and secondarily by the actions of non-hedging investors. Demand for commodities is determined by the needs of end users and secondarily by the actions of non-hedging investors. Investor actions can both dampen and stimulate commodity price movements, at least in the short term. Gold, a physical commodity and a precious metal, is often a preferred safe haven given its historical use as a store of value among investors and as a non-currency based reserve among central banks.

Producers cannot alter commodity supply levels quickly because extended lead times are often needed to affect production levels. For example, agricultural output may be altered by planting more crops and changing farming techniques, but at least one growing cycle must pass before there are results. And at least one factor beyond the producer's control—the weather—will significantly affect output. Building the necessary infrastructure for increased oil and mining production may take many years, involving both developing the mine itself and the necessary transportation and smelting components. For commodities, suppliers' inability to quickly respond to changes in demand may result in supply too low in times of economic growth and too high when the economy slows. And despite advancing technology, the cost of new supply may grow over time.

Investing in commodities is motivated by its potential for returns, portfolio diversification, and inflation protection. Investors may choose commodities if they believe prices will increase in the short or intermediate term. Commodity futures contracts may offer investors a liquidity premium or other trading opportunities, creating the prospect for a positive real return. In the 30-year period referenced in Exhibit 6, commodity investments outperformed global stocks and global bonds but with much higher volatility.

Exhibit 6: Historical Returns of Commodities, Q3 1992–Q2 2022 (quarterly data)

	Global Stocks	Global Bonds	Commodities
Annualized return			
1992:Q3–2022:Q2	6.89%	4.39%	7.81%
Annualized standard deviation			
1992:Q3-2022:Q2	16.76%	6.14%	24.39%
Worst calendar year	−43.54%	−5.17%	−42.80%
	(2008)	(1999)	(2008)

	Global Stocks	Global Bonds	Commodities
Best calendar year	31.62%	19.66%	50.30%
	(2003)	(1995)	(2009)

Sources: Global stocks, MSCI ACWI; global bonds, Bloomberg Barclays Global Aggregate Index; commodities, S&P GSCI Total Return.

Exhibit 6 shows a summary of investment performance and volatility of global stocks, global bonds, and commodities over a 30-year time horizon from Q3 1992 through Q2 2022. Commodities exhibit the highest average return and the highest volatility among the three asset classes. The worst performance for both global stocks and commodities occurred during 2008, coinciding with the middle of the global financial crisis of 2007–2009. As global economies began recovering in 2009, commodities exhibited their best calendar-year performance. While the data may imply that commodities behave similarly to global stocks, we directly address the correlation between these two asset classes later in this lesson. Overall demand levels are influenced by global manufacturing dynamics and economic growth. When demand levels and investors' orders to buy and sell during a given period change quickly, the resulting mismatch of supply and demand may lead to price volatility.

Farmland and Timberland

Farmland and timberland, in contrast, are far less frequently traded and derive their value from different sources. In the case of farmland, it is multiple growing seasons over time that generate the return. In the case of timberland, it is the longer forest/tree growth cycle and the demand for lumber that determine returns once the lumber has been cut down. The size of the global investable farmland market is estimated at approximately USD1 trillion, with a relatively small proportion, less than 5%, held by institutional investors. Institutional investors hold about one-quarter of the global investable timberland base, valued at roughly USD285 billion. A large majority of timberland held by these investors is located in the United States, Australia, and New Zealand.

Turning to land, Exhibit 7 provides a comparison of returns on US timber and farmland. The National Council of Real Estate Investment Fiduciaries (NCREIF) constructs a variety of appraisal-based indexes for property, timberland, and farmland. Over the 30-year time period from Q3 1992 to Q2 2022, farmland had the higher annualized return and timber had the higher standard deviation.

Exhibit 7: Historical Returns of US Real Estate Indexes, Q3 1992–Q2 2022 (quarterly data)

	NCREIF Data	
	Timberland	Farmland
Annualized return	8.69%	10.95%
Annualized standard deviation	6.76%	5.88%
Worst calendar year	–5.30%	2.02%
	(2001)	(2001)
Best calendar year	22.36%	33.90%
	(1993)	(2005)

Although the data in Exhibit 7 make farmland appear to be a very attractive investment, it has definite risks. Liquidity is very low, the risk of negative cash flow is high because fixed costs are relatively high (land requires care and crops need fertilizer, seed, and so on), and revenue is highly variable based on weather. The risks of timberland and farmland are similar to those of real estate investments in raw land, but weather is a unique and more exogenous risk for these assets and does not have the same impact on traditional commercial and residential real estate properties. Drought and flooding can dramatically decrease the harvest yields for crops and thus the expected income stream.

In contrast to the local nature of real estate, farmland and timberland are exposed to more global risks given that these investments generate commodities that are globally traded and consumed. For example, there have been interruptions in world trade, and growing agricultural competition has resulted in declining grain prices. Therefore, it seems difficult to repeat these returns over the next 30 years. Timberland and farmland investments should consider the international context as a major risk factor.

Finally, investment in vacant or raw land that has not been developed or prepared for construction generally involves greater risk than farmland or timberland.

Inflation Hedging and Diversification Benefits of Natural Resource Investments

Investors often consider commodity investments as a hedge against inflation and as a source of portfolio diversification relative to a portfolio of traditional assets (i.e., stocks and bonds).

Hedge against Inflation

The argument for commodities as a hedge against inflation derives from some commodity prices being components of inflation calculations. Commodities, especially energy and food, affect consumers' cost of living. The volatility of commodity prices, especially energy and food, is much higher than that of reported consumer inflation. Consumer inflation is computed from many products, including housing, whose prices change more slowly than commodity prices, and inflation calculations use statistical smoothing techniques and behavioral assumptions. Exhibit 8 shows a summary of calendar year returns on global stocks, global bonds, commodities, farmland, and timberland segmented by whether the US CPI (i.e., inflation) is above or below its median of 2.26%.

Exhibit 8: Historical Asset Class Returns Divided by Median US CPI, 1993–2021 (annual returns)

	Global Stocks	Global Bonds	Commodities	Farmland	Timberland
Higher inflation	+9.40%	+5.66%	+22.87%	12.78%	10.44%
Lower inflation	+5.43%	+4.18%	−9.26%	9.85%	5.70%

Sources: Global stocks, MSCI ACWI; global bonds, Bloomberg Barclays Global Aggregate Index; commodities, S&P GSCI Total Return; Farmland and Timberland, NCREIF

The data from Exhibit 8 covering 29 full calendar years are consistent with the idea that investments in commodities perform well when inflation is higher and perform poorly when inflation is lower. This difference also holds if the 29 calendar years are split into low, middle, and high inflation rates. In fact, the performance distinctions on commodities are even larger using the three inflation categories instead of only two. However, there is less evidence that investment performance of farmland or timberland differs significantly in differing inflation environments.

As an alternative to presenting asset class returns during higher or lower inflation, Exhibit 9 shows average return data for commodities, global bonds, and global stocks when inflation has moved lower, higher, or very little. Here, stable inflation is defined as a less than a 10 bp move from year to year, so falling and rising inflation regimes are those years with larger year-to-year changes in inflation.

Exhibit 9: Annual Asset Class Returns in Falling, Rising, and Stable Inflation Environments, 1993–2021

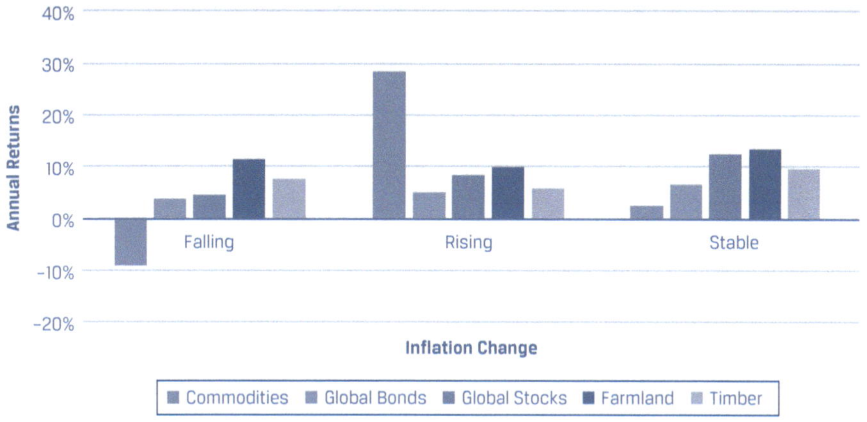

Sources: Global stocks, MSCI ACWI; global bonds, Bloomberg Barclays Global Aggregate Index; commodities, S&P GSCI Total Return Farmland and Timber, NCREIF

Consistent with the data shown in Exhibit 8, the returns presented in Exhibit 9 highlight that commodities provide greater returns in rising inflation environments at a cost of negative returns as inflation rates decline. In stable inflation environments, commodity returns have tended to be low but positive. None of the other asset classes, including farmland and timberland, demonstrate such large contrasts in performance based on changing inflation.

Portfolio Diversification

Farmland, timberland, and commodities exhibit potential for portfolio diversification. Historically, all three of these asset classes have low correlations with investment returns from traditional assets (i.e., stocks and bonds) during the business cycle. Exhibit 10 shows the quarterly correlation between farmland, timberland, selected commodities, global equity, and global bond indexes from Q3 1992 through Q2 2022. All three of the alternative asset classes show correlations of approximately zero with global bonds. Timberland shows the lowest correlation of the alternative asset classes with global stocks, at approximately 0.02. Farmland's correlation with global stocks is still low, at approximately 0.12, while commodities demonstrate the least diversification potential with global stocks, given the correlation of 0.41. The correlations of stocks, bonds, and commodities are expected to be positive because all the assets have some exposure to the global business cycle. The commodity index, the S&P GSCI (Goldman Sachs Commodity Index), is heavily weighted toward the energy sector, with each underlying commodity possibly exhibiting unique behavior.

The data in Exhibit 10 also complement the earlier discussion of the potential for asset classes to serve as inflation hedges. The correlation between commodities and inflation of 0.54 is much higher than that of other asset classes with inflation and is consistent with the idea of commodities as an inflation hedge. Neither farmland (–0.17) nor timberland (0.02) shows a high degree of correlation with inflation, implying that these asset classes are less effective as inflation hedges. However, the prior section suggests that the lack of correlation has more to do with their investment performance not suffering during periods of low or declining inflation. Commodity returns, in contrast, are negative during low or declining inflation, as shown earlier.

Exhibit 10: Historical Commodity Return Correlations, 1990–Q1 2020 (quarterly data)

	Farmland	Timberland	Commodities	Global Bonds	Global Stocks	Inflation
Farmland	1					
Timberland	0.4352	1				
Commodities	−0.1276	−0.1180	1			
Global Bonds	−0.0209	−0.0047	0.0006	1		
Global Stocks	0.1221	0.0215	0.4106	0.1465	1	
Inflation	−0.1724	0.0166	0.5404	−0.2180	0.0954	1

Sources: Global stocks, MSCI ACWI; global bonds, Bloomberg Barclays Global Aggregate Index; commodities, S&P GSCI Total Return; Farmland and Timberland, NCREIF

Overall, investments in natural resource assets exhibit significant portfolio diversification potential because of low correlations with traditional asset classes. Farmland and timberland display somewhat high correlation with each other (approximately 0.44), but each of these asset classes has slightly negative correlations with commodities.

Finally, commodity prices are often more sensitive to geopolitical factors and natural phenomena, such as weather conditions. Also, commodity investments frequently employ leverage and seek to capitalize on expected price changes based on more complex strategies, such as futures contract delivery timing and location, which will be addressed in later lessons.

QUESTION SET

1. Contrast the pricing of commodities with the pricing of farmland/timberland investments.

   Solution:

   Commodities are priced on public exchanges, and their pricing reflects the latest information. Land investments, such as farmland and timberland, are traded only when actual transactions occur; thus pricing is infrequent and relies on imprecise estimates.

2. Explain why commodity supply is usually slow to adjust to changes in demand for the commodity.

   Solution:

   Commodity supply adjusts slowly to changes in commodity demand because producers are unable to alter supply quickly due to the need for extended lead times to affect production levels. For example, increased demand for a specific agricultural crop requires at least one growing cycle to produce more supply.

3. Explain one rationale as to why consumer price inflation is likely to be less volatile than commodity prices.

   Solution:

   - One possible rationale is that consumer price inflation reflects many additional products beyond commodities (such as housing), which dampens the effect of commodity prices on inflation.
   - Another possible rationale is that statistical techniques used to compute consumer price inflation cause smoothing in the data while commodity prices reflect real-time changes on public exchanges.

4. Analyze the results in Exhibit 9 as to how different asset classes perform as inflation changes.

   Solution:

   Commodities clearly perform well in periods of rising inflation and clearly exhibit negative performance as inflation declines. Global stocks and bonds do not exhibit such clear differences in performance related to inflation. Both global stocks and bonds perform best during periods of stable inflation.

PRACTICE PROBLEMS

1. Which of the following possible value drivers does *not* apply to both raw land and farmland investments?

   A. Lease revenue

   B. Sale of agricultural products

   C. Price appreciation of property

2. Which of the following most correctly describes a significant difference between farmland and timberland investment?

   A. Timberland provides environmental benefits because of the ability of trees to absorb carbon, while farmland does not.

   B. Farmland provides a resource necessary for human existence, while timberland does not.

   C. Farmland is commonly family owned, while timberland is commonly owned by institutional investors.

3. Which of the following best reflects an advantage of institutional ownership of physical farmland as opposed to buying exposure to crops through futures contracts?

   A. Liquidity of physical farmland

   B. Price transparency of farmland

   C. Flexibility to gain price exposure to a wider variety of agricultural products

4. Which of the following is most consistent with backwardation in a commodity market?

   A. The convenience yield is negative.

   B. The benefit of holding the physical commodity exceeds the cost of carry.

   C. The forward price is above the spot price.

5. Which of the following futures market price conditions would be most expected in a period of low commodity inventories?

   A. Backwardation

   B. Falling prices

   C. Contango

6. Which of the following characteristics is *not* a benefit of derivative instruments (compared to ownership of the physical commodity) as a means of gaining commodity exposure?

   A. Price transparency

   B. Non-cash benefits

C. Liquidity

7. Which of the following statements most correctly describes why commodity investments are thought to provide a hedge against inflation?

   A. The returns on commodity investing are driven by commodity price changes, and inflation partially reflects these changes.

   B. Commodity prices increase after inflation rates increase.

   C. Expectations of higher inflation cause commodity prices to increase.

8. Which of the following statements is most correct about commodity investments?

   A. Commodity investments are expected to perform worse in inflationary environments.

   B. Commodity investments exhibit high risk because of high leverage.

   C. Commodity investments provide weak portfolio diversification because of their high risk.

9. Which of the following statements is most correct if you observe that the correlation between farmland and inflation is significantly lower than the correlation between commodities and inflation (and that both correlations are positive)?

   A. Commodities are expected to provide a better inflation hedge than farmland.

   B. Farmland is expected to provide a better inflation hedge than commodities.

   C. Differences in correlation do not provide any information that is useful in assessing whether an asset class is an inflation hedge.

SOLUTIONS

1. B is correct. Raw land's value is derived solely from lease revenue and price appreciation. Farmland, in contrast, also generates value from the production and sale of agricultural products.

2. C is correct. Timberland tracts typically consist of thousands (or more) of acres of land, while farmland is quite frequently owned in smaller tracts of tens or hundreds of acres. As such, farmland is much more suited to family ownership, while timberland is more commonly owned by institutions. A is incorrect because carbon offset is capable in both trees (i.e., timberland) and crops (i.e., farmland). B is incorrect because the lumber from timberland provides the raw material for housing, which is a basic human need.

3. C is correct. Futures contracts are available on a very limited number of common crops (i.e., wheat, corn, etc.). Ownership of physical farmland opens up the possibilities of growing crops not traded on futures exchanges, thus providing a larger universe of agricultural product price exposures. A and B are incorrect because futures contracts provide greater liquidity and price transparency than available in physical farmland, which is not traded on public exchanges.

4. B is correct. Backwardation in a commodity market implies that forward prices are lower than spot prices. This can occur only if the total benefits of physical ownership of the commodity exceed the total costs. A is incorrect because convenience yield cannot be negative. C is incorrect because this statement implies a contango market.

5. A is correct. Low inventories of a specific commodity create incentives for market participants to own the physical commodity rather than a derivative contract. This incentive drives up spot prices relative to forward prices and can lead to spot prices being greater than forward prices (i.e., backwardation). B is incorrect because low inventories of a commodity indicate scarcity and would be more likely to contribute to a rising price for the commodity. C is incorrect because a contango market is the opposite of a market in backwardation.

6. B is correct. Non-cash benefits refer to the convenience yield, which causes a preference for owning the physical commodity rather than a derivative contract. A is incorrect in that derivatives provide price transparency while the market for physical commodities is much less transparent. C is incorrect in that the more frequent trading of derivatives on organized exchanges enhances liquidity while physical commodity markets are characterized by infrequent trading and thus poor liquidity.

7. A is correct. Commodity prices are a significant portion of consumer prices because commodities include aspects of everyday life, such as food and energy, and thus consumer price inflation will incorporate the effects of commodity price changes. By investing in commodities, an investor is, at least partially, hedged against the inflation that occurs with rising commodity prices. B is incorrect because inflation and commodity prices do not move together, but instead, changes in the inflation rate lag behind changes in commodity prices. C is incorrect because in this case, commodity price increases occur before inflation changes.

8. B is correct. Commodity investments are typically entered into through derivative contracts, which are highly leveraged financial instruments. As a result, observed returns are highly volatile. A is incorrect because commodity investments

are expected to perform better during inflationary environments. C is incorrect because commodity investments tend to exhibit low correlations with traditional assets and thus are typically used as portfolio diversifiers.

9. A is correct. An effective hedge exhibits relatively high correlation relative to the risk exposure being hedged. Thus, the higher correlation between commodities and inflation implies that commodities provide a better hedge against inflation compared to farmland.

LEARNING MODULE

6

Hedge Funds

LEARNING OUTCOMES

Mastery	The candidate should be able to:
☐	explain investment features of hedge funds and contrast them with other asset classes
☐	describe investment forms and vehicles used in hedge fund investments
☐	analyze sources of risk, return, and diversification among hedge fund investments

INTRODUCTION

1

Hedge funds originally started as an equity investment vehicle in which offsetting short and long positions protected the overall portfolio against major stock market moves. Today, the name *hedge funds* is a misnomer. They are not restricted to equities or just hedging strategies. Hedge funds are private pooled investment vehicles that can invest in a wide variety of products, including equities, fixed income, derivatives, foreign exchange, private capital, and real assets. It is the investment *approach* rather than the underlying investments that distinguish hedge funds. Many hedge funds operate in all kinds of financial markets by using leverage, short selling, or using financial instruments that are not often used by other similar commingled funds, such as mutual funds. This may result in a very different risk and return profile than owning underlying assets themselves.

The hedge fund industry is in a state of constant change as several hundred new funds are launched each year, with a similar number of funds exiting or being liquidated. While several jurisdictions around the world regulate hedge funds, often they are lightly regulated compared with other investment vehicles.

LEARNING MODULE OVERVIEW

- Hedge funds are private investment vehicles with pooled funds from institutions and high-net-worth (HNW) investors. Hedge funds typically have more flexible investment strategies than other options, such as mutual funds and ETFs.

- Hedge funds are not an asset class but are a variety of investment vehicles driven by a set of disparate investment strategies. Most hedge funds utilize some form of leverage to enhance potential returns.
- Hedge funds are typically classified by strategy. A variety of classifications are possible, which helps in the selection of appropriate investment strategies and appropriate performance benchmarks and in reviewing aggregate performance.
- Most hedge funds are set up as limited partnerships, with the portfolio manager acting as a general partner (GP) and the institutional investors acting as limited partners (LPs). This is the direct form of hedge fund setup. For smaller and retail investors, indirect forms, such as funds of funds, help obtain a hedge fund exposure.
- The legal and contractual relationship between the GPs and LPs is governed by the fund offering documents. In addition, a manager could draft a "side letter" applicable to some investors only, with different legal, regulatory, tax, operational, or reporting requirements.
- Hedge funds use several strategies, such as market-neutral, relative value, and event-driven strategies, to obtain diversification benefits and to attempt to outperform equity markets on a risk-adjusted basis.
- Hedge fund strategies are classified by a combination of the instruments in which they are invested, the trading philosophy followed, and the types of risks assumed.

LEARNING MODULE SELF-ASSESSMENT

These initial questions are intended to help you gauge your current level of understanding of this learning module.

1. Which statement about hedge funds is most accurate?

   A. Hedge funds are investment products offered to the public and are traded daily on the OTC market.

   B. Hedge funds are benchmarked to an index or industry/sector, and managers use complex strategies to mimic the index or industry/sector.

   C. Hedge funds are private pooled funds, applying strategies with a goal of maximizing returns while reducing risk.

   Solution:

   C is correct. A hedge fund is a pooled investment vehicle that uses complex trading (using leverage, short selling, using derivatives, etc.) and risk management techniques to enhance performance for a private group of accredited investors.

   A is incorrect. Mutual funds, not hedge funds, are regulated investment products offered to the public and available for daily trading.

   B is incorrect. Exchange-traded funds (ETFs) are normally benchmarked to an index or industry/sector and typically track a specific industry or index. Hedge funds are benchmarked to either a hedge fund index or performance measured in absolute returns.

2. Which of the following statements about relative value strategies is *least accurate*?

   A. Relative value strategies seek to profit from a price or return discrepancy between securities based on a short-term relationship.

   B. Relative value funds are inherently structured to minimize net market risk and credit risks.

   C. The investments made under a relative value strategy are all within a single asset class or sector, using assets with a sufficient price differential to arbitrage their movements to equilibrium prices.

   Solution:

   C is correct because it is the least accurate statement. Relative value strategies often involve investments in different asset classes. A and B are true.

3. Which of the following statements is *least accurate* about hedge funds?

   A. Merger arbitrage strategies generally assume that an acquirer will be overpaying for the target.

   B. Event-driven hedge funds flourish in a stable market environment, where minor deviations in asset prices quickly converge to equilibrium.

   C. An activist strategy expects to realize higher returns due to the manager being more effective in driving the corporate policies or strategic direction of the investment.

   Solution:

   B is correct because it is the least accurate statement. Event-driven hedge funds thrive in a rising market environment with a high level of corporate activity in a strong economy. These are the times that accelerate merger and acquisition activity. A and C are accurate statements.

4. Which of the following is *not* a characteristic of hedge funds?

   A. Hedge funds are mostly illiquid, with little trading possibilities.

   B. Hedge fund managers use leverage; however, the overall risk is lower.

   C. Hedge funds are a different asset class, with a distinct risk/reward profile.

   D. Managers demand higher remuneration and have more discretionary freedom in the choice of investments.

   Solution:

   C is correct. Hedge funds invest in traditional asset classes but use a specific investment strategy. They are not a distinct asset class.

5. In January, HedgeAway, a new hedge fund, started operations with an initial amount of USD100 million. The fund charges a management fee of 1.6% based on end-of-year value and a performance fee of 18% on gross returns payable on the excess over a hurdle rate of 8% after fees. The fund ended the year with assets under management (AUM) of USD120 million. What was the investors' return during the year?

   A. 16.38%

   B. 18.08%

C. 18.19%

Solution:

A is correct.

Management fee = 1.6% of 120 million = 1.92 million.

Growth during the year = 20 million, excess over the hurdle

= 20 million – (100 million × 0.08) – 1.92 million = 10.08 million.

Performance fee = 10.08 million × 0.18 = 1.81 million.

Total fees = 1.92 million + 1.81 million = 3.72 million.

Return to the investors = 20 million – 3.72 million = 16.38 million.

Investors' return = 16.38%.

2 HEDGE FUND INVESTMENT FEATURES

☐ explain investment features of hedge funds and contrast them with other asset classes

As private investment vehicles, hedge funds are distinguished by their investment approach rather than the underlying investments. Hedge funds combine traditional debt and equity instruments with leverage, derivatives, short selling, and other strategies to generate and enhance their returns. The objective of a hedge fund is to generate high returns, either in an absolute sense or on a risk-adjusted basis relative to its portfolio-level volatility. The strategies hedge funds use can make benchmarking their performance relative to traditional index performance benchmarks difficult. Thus, many hedge funds evaluate their performance using an absolute return standard instead of tracking a benchmark. Hedge funds are attractive for their diversification effects because their returns typically demonstrate low correlation with traditional asset investing.

Hedge funds normally apply common principles that seemingly increase portfolio risk, such as borrowing money to invest, using leverage (derivatives), and short selling. On their own, they do not hedge risky positions against a market move; on the contrary, they seem to amplify the risks. It may seem like the name *hedge funds* is a misnomer. However, the investment strategy splits a portfolio such that each component helps hedge the risks from the other. Thus, by internally neutralizing market risk and by managing the portfolio components, the hedge fund manager can obtain enhanced risk-adjusted returns.

While mutual funds and hedge funds seem similar, in that they both invest clients' money to achieve a better risk/reward profile, there are some major differences. Mutual funds managers are paid a fixed compensation and may not necessarily invest in the funds they manage. Hedge fund managers are paid a performance-based fee, and many require the managers to invest in the hedge fund. Some hedge funds incorporate a high-water mark, in which the manager will get a performance fee only when the returns exceed the previous highest value of the fund.

Normally, hedge fund managers have a great deal of freedom to make trading decisions and to decide how to allocate client funds. Mutual funds are highly regulated since they are available to public investors. Hedge funds are available only to institutional and accredited investors.

Hedge funds are different from other fund types, such as mutual funds, ETFs, bond funds, and REITs, in that a hedge fund is privately owned. And unlike many of these funds, hedge funds are lightly regulated. They are different from private equity funds, in that hedge funds typically have a shorter time horizon and invest in more liquid asset classes.

Hedge funds select investments from one or more asset classes (equities, credit, fixed income, commodities, futures, foreign exchange, loans, and sometimes even hard assets, such as real estate). Some hedge funds implement strategies focused on one specific asset class, while others combine multiple asset classes. Hedge funds can also be geographically focused or agnostic and implement their strategies across different geographic regions.

Leverage—through short selling, borrowing, or derivatives and occasionally combining all three—is often used by hedge funds to enhance returns. Since leverage is often a core component of the strategy, hedge funds continuously need to monitor the value of their exposures. This is particularly important when a hedge fund takes both long and short positions (when possible) solely using derivatives.

Hedge funds are typically classified by strategy. One such classification includes five broad categories of strategies:

- equity hedge funds,
- event-driven hedge funds,
- relative value hedge funds,
- opportunistic hedge funds, and
- multi-manager hedge funds.

Many hedge funds trade sovereign and corporate debt, commodities, futures contracts, options, derivatives, and even real estate investments. However, not all hedge funds maintain short positions or use leverage. Instead, many simply exploit niche areas of expertise in a sophisticated manner; hedging and leverage may or may not be involved. Finally, there are funds of hedge funds that create a diversified portfolio of hedge funds. These vehicles are attractive to smaller investors without the resources to select individual hedge funds and build a portfolio of them.

Hedge fund categorization allows investors to review aggregate performance data, select strategies with which to build a portfolio of funds, and select or construct appropriate performance benchmarks. Exhibit 1 shows examples of the five broad strategy hedge fund categories mentioned above.

Exhibit 1: Hedge Fund Strategies

Equity	Event Driven	Relative Value	Opportunistic	Multi-Manager
Long/Short Equity	Merger Arbitrage	Convertible Bond Arbitrage	Global Macro	Fund of Funds
Short Biased	Distressed	Fixed-Income Arbitrage	Managed Futures	
Market Neutral	Special Situations	Multi-Strategy		
	Activist			

Equity Hedge Fund Strategies

Hedging long positions through short selling can be considered the original hedge fund category. Long/short equity funds focus on public equity markets and take long and short positions in equity and equity derivative securities. Most equity hedge strategies use a "bottom-up" security-specific approach—company-level analysis, followed by overall industry analysis, followed by overall market analysis—with relatively balanced long and short exposures. A contrasting "top-down" approach entails global macro analysis, followed by sector/regional analysis, followed by individual company analysis or any market-timing approach. Some equity long/short strategies may use index-based short hedges to reduce market risk or single-name shorts for portfolio alpha and added absolute return. The following are examples of equity hedge strategies.

- **Fundamental long/short**: In this strategy, the hedge fund takes long positions in companies that are trading at inexpensive levels compared to their potential intrinsic value and shorts those that trade in the other direction, with the intention of reversing this trade to obtain alpha.

  In all cases, the strategy takes a long position in those securities (buys stocks or call options) whose valuations are underestimated/undervalued by the market or have a potential for growth that the market has not yet identified. The strategy also concurrently shorts stocks or an index to reduce the risk. The manager typically maintains a net long exposure but may adjust the amount of net market risk depending on his or her market forecast.

  Most hedge funds that use a long/short strategy have a long bias, which differentiates this strategy from the short bias strategy.
- **Fundamental growth**: These strategies use fundamental analysis to identify companies expected to exhibit high growth and capital appreciation. The hedge fund will take a long position in these stocks. The fund will short companies with business models that are under downward pressure and expected to exhibit low or negative growth and suffer capital depreciation. Effectively, the spread between growth and value expectations drives the investment strategy and portfolio performance. Most of these portfolios tend to end up long biased; hence, they may not be market neutral and their returns may exhibit a non-zero beta.
- **Fundamental value**: These strategies use fundamental analysis to identify undervalued and unloved companies for which there is the possibility that a corporate turnaround, with future revenue and cash flow growth, will result in higher valuations. The hedge fund takes long positions in these companies to capture expected future stock price rises. Effectively, it is the spread between value and growth expectations that drives portfolio performance.
- **Short biased**: These strategies use quantitative, technical, and fundamental analysis to short the overvalued equity securities with limited or no long-side exposures. Managers are often forensic in their fundamental analysis and sometimes try to expose previously unrecognized accounting or business flaws. The expectation is that company share price will fall and thus improve the profitability of the fund's portfolio. These funds vary their short exposure over time. Short-biased managers tend to be contrarian; they are shorting shares in otherwise successful companies. These funds can be useful additions to larger portfolios during periods of market stress. Short-biased managers, however, have had a difficult time overall posting meaningful long-term returns during the past 30 years of generally positive market conditions.

- **Market neutral**: These strategies use quantitative, fundamental, and technical analysis to identify under- and overvalued equity securities. The hedge fund takes long positions in undervalued securities and short positions in overvalued securities, while seeking to maintain a market-neutral net position. Ideally, the manager achieves an overall beta relative to the market close to zero.

  The intent is to profit from the movements of individual securities, undervalued ones rising and overvalued ones falling, while avoiding movements in the overall market. To achieve a meaningful return, market-neutral portfolios may require the application of leverage. These portfolios generally seek stable, single-digit returns that are independent of the market (market neutral), but because leverage is used to amplify the returns, these funds may experience higher risk during periods of unexpected volatility unless they reduce their leverage.

EXAMPLE 1

Tenderledge Investments LLC—Equity Strategies

Tenderledge Investments, a fund-of-funds hedge fund, is benchmarking the performance of various equity strategies as measured by monthly hedge fund returns over a 10-year period, shown in the following tables.

Equity Strategies: Monthly Returns	Market Index	Fundamental Value	Market Neutral	Fundamental Growth	Short Bias
Average	0.30%	0.03%	−0.04%	0.03%	−0.5%
Standard deviation	2.0%	1.0%	0.5%	1.5%	2.3%
Coefficient of variation	14.8%	2.6%	−7.4%	1.9%	−20.1%
Max.	5.2%	2.2%	1.0%	3.5%	7.2%
Min.	−8.1%	−4.0%	−2.7%	−10.4%	−11.3%

Equity Strategies: Correlation of Monthly Returns	Market Index	Fundamental Value	Market Neutral	Fundamental Growth	Short Bias
Market Index	1.00				
Fundamental Value	0.80	1.00			
Market Neutral	0.22	0.24	1.00		
Fundamental Growth	0.67	0.64	0.38	1.00	
Short Bias	−0.72	−0.53	−0.23	−0.60	1.00

The market index, measured by the S&P 500 Index, outperformed each strategy both in absolute terms as measured by the average monthly returns and in relative terms as measured by the coefficient of variation of returns. Moreover, analyzing the correlations between these strategies shows that fundamental value and growth have exhibited high correlation with the market index.

Market-neutral funds have the lowest positive correlation with the market index, reflecting the fact that these strategies intend to generate returns without taking on market-level exposure. As expected, the short-bias funds have a negative correlation with the other strategies. Note that over short time frames, short-bias strategies are negatively correlated with the market index–based strategies. However, in the long term, similar correlations may not hold.

Event-Driven Strategies

These bottom-up strategies seek to profit from defined events that are expected to change valuations, typically involving changes in corporate structure, such as an acquisition or restructuring. Event-driven strategies may include long and short positions in common and preferred stocks, debt securities, and options. Further subdivisions of this category by Hedge Fund Research (HFR) include the following:

- **Merger arbitrage**: Generally, these strategies involve going long (buying) the stock of the company being acquired at a discount to its announced takeover price and going short (selling) the stock of the acquiring company when the merger or acquisition is announced. The manager may expect to profit once this initial deal spread (the price between the buyer and the object of the acquisition) narrows to the closing value of the transaction after it is fully consummated. This spread exists because of timing and uncertainty over the closure of the deal due to legal and regulatory hurdles, or the acquirer may decide to step away. Shorting the acquirer is also a way to express the risk of merger overpayment. The primary risk in merger arbitrage is that the announced combination fails to occur and the value of the fund holdings are negatively impacted before it can unwind its position. Since the expected risk and return on a merger arbitrage strategy stems from the modest spread in prices, leverage is regularly used to amplify returns but also increases losses when the strategy fails.
- **Distressed/restructuring**: These strategies focus on securities of companies either in or perceived to be near bankruptcy. In one approach, hedge funds simply purchase fixed-income securities trading at a significant discount to par but that are still senior enough to be backed by sufficient corporate assets. The expectation is that these securities should be valued at par or at least at a significant premium to the current bond purchase price in a bankruptcy reorganization or liquidation. Alternatively, a fund may purchase a debt instrument that is expected to be converted into new equity upon restructuring or bankruptcy, typically called a *fulcrum* security, and then either hold onto the equity or exit.
- **Special situations**: These strategies focus on opportunities to buy equity of companies engaged in security issuance or repurchase, special capital distributions, rescue finance, asset sales/spin-offs, or other catalyst-oriented situations.
- **Activist**: The term "activist" is short for "activist shareholder." Here, managers secure sufficient equity holdings to allow them to seek a position on the company board and influence corporate policies or direction. They seek to create business changes that move the investment towards a desired outcome. For example, an activist hedge fund may advocate for divestitures, restructuring, capital distributions to shareholders, or changes in management and company strategy affecting their equity holdings. Such hedge funds are distinct from private equity because they operate primarily in the public equity market.

Event-driven strategies tend to be long biased, with merger arbitrage having the least bias; the time to complete a merger transaction typically takes somewhere between 6 and 24 months, while a bankruptcy or a reorganization can take years to complete.

EXAMPLE 2

Activism of Carl Icahn and Hertz

Carl Icahn, an activist hedge fund manager, has been financially successful in several cases where he took a controlling interest in companies to direct their operations for an increase in enterprise value. Hertz, a car rental company, is an interesting example. In 2014, Icahn started investing in Hertz and in 2020 held more than 55 million, or 39%, of its common shares. During May 2020, Hertz sought bankruptcy protection because of the impact of COVID-19 and the collapse of the global travel industry. Before Hertz filed for bankruptcy protection, Icahn's holdings were worth around USD2.3 billion. After Hertz filed, he sold his shares at a loss of USD2 billion, even though he acquired 11 million shares only a few weeks earlier.

Originally, Icahn acquired his stake in Hertz starting in 2014 based on his notion that Hertz had a strong brand and operational foundation but was lacking discipline and management. And Icahn accumulated a more than USD1.1 billion position in the company by the end of that year. When Icahn entered Hertz, the company was emerging from years of operational, strategic, and financial problems that eroded its financial strength. Icahn put new board members and a new management in place, which in the ensuing years instilled fiscal and operational discipline. The company restated previous years' earnings, finished the integration of various enterprise-wide systems, and secured a qualified management team. At the same time, the car rental industry was impacted by two strategic shifts: One was the increased preference for SUVs, and the other was the emergence of ride-hailing apps. While the company showed higher revenue and increasingly consistent profits, the cost of restoring the company eroded its financial and liquidity position. After Hertz came out of bankruptcy proceedings in July 2021, Icahn has been closely following the company.

Relative Value Strategies

Relative value strategies seek to profit from a pricing discrepancy between related securities based on an unusual short-term relationship. The expectation is the short-term discrepancy will be resolved over time. Examples of relative value strategies include the following:

- *Convertible bond arbitrage.* This conceptually market-neutral investment strategy seeks to exploit a perceived mispricing between a convertible bond and its component parts: the underlying bond and the embedded call option. There may be relative mispricing between equity and the convertible bond. The strategy typically involves buying convertible debt securities and simultaneously selling a certain amount of the same issuer's common stock based on the delta of the embedded call option. This strategy can be sensitive to bankruptcy risks; however, they may be hedged away using either equity put options or credit default swap derivatives on the issuer.
- *Fixed income (general).* These strategies focus on the relative value within the fixed-income markets, with an emphasis on sovereign debt (relative value rates) and sometimes the relative pricing of investment-grade corporate debt (relative value credit). Strategies may incorporate long–short trades between two different issuers, between corporate and government issuers, between different parts of the same issuer's capital structure, or

between different parts of an issuer's yield curve. Here, spread and currency dynamics together with considerations around the shape of government yield-curve considerations drive investment choices and returns.

- *Fixed income (asset backed, mortgage backed, and high yield).* These strategies focus on the relative value of various higher-yielding securities, such as asset-backed securities, mortgage-backed securities, high-yield loans and bonds, and their derivatives. Hedge funds seek to generate an attractive and highly secured coupon return and to exploit relative security and quality mispricings.
- *Multi-strategy.* These strategies trade relative value within and across asset classes or instruments. Rather than focusing on one type of trade (e.g., convertible arbitrage), a single basis for a trade (e.g., merger arbitrage), or a particular asset class (e.g., fixed income), this strategy instead looks for any available investment opportunities, often with different pods of managers executing unique market approaches. The goal of a multi-strategy manager is to initially deploy (and later redeploy) capital efficiently and quickly across various strategy areas as conditions change.

Opportunistic Strategies

There are also funds that focus on macro events and commodity trading. These strategies may often use index ETF securities or derivatives in addition to individual securities.

- *Macro strategies* emphasize a top-down approach to identify economic trends. Trades are made on the basis of expected movements in economic variables. Generally, these funds trade opportunistically in fixed-income, equity, currency, and commodity markets. Macro hedge funds use long and short positions to profit from a view on overall market direction as it is influenced by major economic trends and events. Because these funds generally benefit most from periods of higher volatility, the active moves by national authorities, such as central banks, to smooth out economic shocks likely shrink their investment sphere.
- *Managed futures* funds are actively managed funds making diversified directional investments primarily in the futures markets on the basis of technical and fundamental strategies. Managed futures funds are also known as commodity trading advisers (CTAs) because they historically focused on commodity futures. However, CTAs may include investments in a variety of futures, including commodities, equities, fixed income, and foreign exchange. CTAs generally use models that measure trends and momentum over different time horizons. CTA investments can be useful for portfolio diversification, particularly in times of strong trending market conditions and especially during periods of extended market stress when other fundamental strategies may be expected to perform poorly. CTAs can be relied on to profit from having purchased short positions in falling markets. However, mean-reverting markets, which may cause false momentum breakout signals, can lead to extended drawdown periods before strong trends emerge for the CTA. To the extent that many CTAs have migrated to trade more and more financial products (such as stock index futures and bond futures), the reliability of CTA diversification benefits has diminished.

Commodity-focused managed futures funds are unique (versus global macro) because there is a constant price tension between suppliers and consumers: High prices cripple demand (tending to lower prices), and low prices shut in supply (and thus raise prices). This situation creates a unique balance absent in traditional stocks and bonds.

Distinguishing Characteristics of Hedge Fund Investments

The key characteristics distinguishing hedge funds and their strategies from traditional investments include the following:

1. Less legal and regulatory constraints
2. Flexible mandates permitting the use of shorting and derivatives
3. A larger investment universe on which to focus
4. Aggressive investment styles that allow concentrated positions in securities offering exposure to credit, volatility, and liquidity risk premiums
5. Relatively liberal use of leverage
6. Liquidity constraints that include lockups and liquidity gates
7. Relatively high fee structures involving management and incentive fees

While hedge funds frequently invest in publicly traded equity or debt instruments and often use financial statement analysis techniques to value securities, their return and risk characteristics generally differ from those of exchange-traded funds and mutual funds. The typical relative value hedge fund generates returns using a combination of long and short positions in equities, increases its asset base using borrowed funds, and implements opportunistic positions in special situations, seeking to earn very different risk–return profiles than those of common long-only funds.

Hedge funds are also subject to much lighter regulatory, compliance, and transparency requirements. With more flexibility in portfolio construction, hedge funds enjoy leeway to invest in situations in which time may be needed to generate an expected return and thus are unsuitable for a mutual fund offering daily liquidity. Investors in modern hedge funds are subject to extended holding periods (known as *lockup periods*) and subsequent *notice periods* before an investment redemption is possible. Some hedge funds partially limit fund redemptions through a liquidity gate provision so that assets can be liquidated over a longer time period. Compared to, for example, many mutual funds allowing easier redemption and guaranteed liquidity on one day's notice, such lengthy mandatory lockup and notice periods allow hedge funds more flexibility than mutual funds or other types of investments.

A redemption fee may be charged, typically payable to the fund itself (rather than the manager) to protect remaining investors in the fund, particularly in circumstances where the redemption takes place during the lockup period. This characteristic is called a *soft lockup*, and it offers a path (albeit an expensive one) to redeem early.

With reduced operating constraints, hedge funds may avail themselves of less liquid and unnoticed opportunities, the true valuation of which may at times be opaque. For instance, several hedge fund strategies—long/short, activist, distressed, and arbitrage—build on highly concentrated, long-term, leveraged holdings in equities, debt, and derivatives. Building up such an exposure may take a longer time to execute and unwinding such a position can be complex and quite time consuming, particularly when financial markets are under transitory stress. That is why restrictions on *redemptions* are typically imposed.

There is also reduced transparency for more complex hedge fund investments and asymmetric information between managers and investors. This leads to incentive-based performance fees to bridge the gap between the manager's and the investor's interests. Investors look to earn high returns, and sharing some proportion of these high returns with the managers incentivizes managers to perform in the interest of the shareholders. Hedge funds are generally deemed riskier from an oversight (fraud risk) point of view, but some hedge funds take less absolute market risk in their portfolio construction than is taken by registered products available to retail investors. A hedge fund's true market risk and its distinction between regulatory risk and illiquidity risk can thus often be confused.

Hedge funds generally utilize active management by experienced managers and an integrated risk management approach. A variety of strategies are possible, which makes each hedge fund uniquely different from others. They can be customized for a specific investor preference. They provide an ability to generate alpha and uncorrelated risk-adjusted returns. Some of the strategies also implement guardrails to insure against significant losses. Such attributes help an investor build a diversified portfolio that stabilizes market volatility within a multi-asset class portfolio.

Investors should consider several issues when choosing a hedge fund. Broadly, they should review the limited partner capabilities, including their operational framework, risk management practices, and hands-on monitoring of portfolio performance. As for the GP performance, the investor should consider their fiduciary management guidelines, manager experience, and alignment of interests towards the fund's strategies.

There have been quite a few reported incidents of fraud in the hedge fund space, including setting up a fund as a Ponzi scheme and reporting false performance data. Some hedge funds had complex strategies that failed during market turmoil. The reduced regulatory oversight, along with the large investments that are typically required to participate in a hedge fund, opens the door for some unscrupulous fund managers to take advantage of investors' trust in them.

While evaluating the investment, the investor should take into account its strategy, transparency, liquidity, and reporting practices. In addition, the investor should thoroughly evaluate the fund manager's past performance and be aware of how the fund compensates the fund managers and calculates the fees charged to investors.

QUESTION SET

1. Both hedge funds and private equity invest in equity stock of public or private enterprises, and there are many commonalities between them. The following statements are some of the commonalities, and one of these statements is false. Choose the *false* statement.

   A. Both are structured as partnerships of investors with private pooling of funds and are primarily intended for high-net-worth individuals.

   B. Both utilize leverage to invest in a variety of marketable securities.

   C. Both are less liquid than mutual funds or ETFs.

   D. Both are less regulated, and the transparency/reporting requirements are not strict.

   Solution:

   B is false. Hedge funds normally invest in public securities (including debt, equity, and derivatives), while private equity funds invest directly in private operating companies, which are not marketable securities, nor do private equity firms apply leverage to their fund.

2. Both hedge funds and private equity invest in equity shares of public or private enterprises. However, there are many differences between them. The

following statements lists some of their differences. Choose the statement that is *false*.

A. Private equity funds invest for the long term, while hedge funds invest in equities for the shorter term.

B. Typical hedge funds are transaction oriented; they make several offsetting trades. Private equity funds make stable, long-term investments in few companies.

C. An investor normally funds the hedge fund at the start of the investment, while private equity funds are committed at the start and funded over time, upon demand.

D. Private equity is redeemable on a periodic basis, while hedge funds require a longer-term commitment.

Solution:

D is the correct answer choice because the statement is false. Hedge funds are redeemable on a periodic basis, and private equity funds require a longer-term commitment. The other statements are correct.

3. Hedge funds versus mutual funds: Choose the *false* statement.

A. Mutual funds are open to any investor and are generally more liquid instruments with minimal constraints on redemptions.

B. Hedge fund fees are typically negotiable by an investor, while mutual funds operate with the same fees for all investors.

C. Hedge funds are more restricted in what they can trade compared to mutual funds.

Solution:

C is the false statement. Hedge funds are less restricted than mutual funds as to the securities they can trade. They are also subject to less disclosure and transparency requirements. A and B are true statements.

4. How many of the following statements comparing hedge funds and ETFs are true?

1. ETFs are exchange-traded public securities, while hedge funds are private partnership funds.

2. Any investor can invest in an ETF, while specific restrictions apply to who can invest in a hedge fund.

3. ETFs have very low fees and expense ratios compared to hedge funds.

4. ETFs are highly regulated, with specific reporting requirements, while hedge funds are lightly regulated.

A. One of the statements is true.

B. Two of the statements are true.

C. Three of the statements are true.

D. Four of the statements are true.

Solution:

D is correct. All the statements are true.

5. Select the statements that are true:

   A. The primary drivers of returns from stocks are growth projections, dividends, and retained earnings.

   B. The primary drivers of returns from a bond are interest rates, credit risk, and coupon payments.

   C. The primary drivers of return from hedge funds are market volatility and market inefficiency.

   Solution:

   A, B, and C are all true.

3 HEDGE FUND INVESTMENT FORMS

☐ describe investment forms and vehicles used in hedge fund investments

A common structural characteristic of a hedge fund is that it is set up as a private investment partnership either onshore or in a tax-advantaged offshore location. Under certain legal restrictions (which vary by jurisdiction), the offering can be open only to a limited number of investors meeting certain income and net worth guidelines.

Hedge funds, like private equity funds, are legally typically incorporated and organized as private limited partnerships or limited liability companies with a general partner or managing member who is the hedge fund manager. The partnership or the managing member receives a management fee, and the general partner receives compensation based on fund performance. Hedge fund investors purchase a share of the fund or partnership and receive in return a fixed percentage of the fund returns, minus applicable fees.

The fund documents—private placement memorandum, the partnership agreement, or the articles of incorporation—lay out the legal and contractual relationship between the fund manager and the fund investor and create the operational framework for the fund. Normally, the fund structures are incorporated as perpetual legal entities, but in reality, as the hedge funds close, they are liquidated on a regular basis.

Direct Hedge Fund Investment Forms

A common hedge fund form is a master feeder structure. The master feeder structure is set up for optimum tax efficiency and consists of an offshore feeder fund and an onshore feeder fund—both feeding into a master fund that invests the capital based on its contractual partnership agreements. This structure is depicted in Exhibit 2.

Exhibit 2: Sample Master-feeder Structure

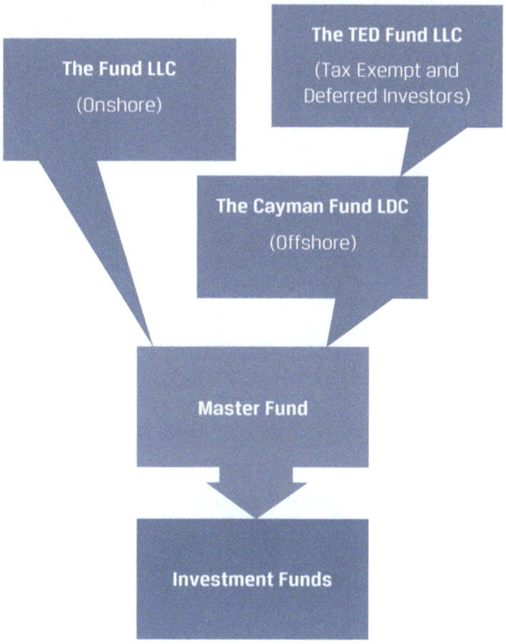

A common hedge fund fee structure is known as "two and twenty." In this setup, the hedge fund partnership entity that operates and administers the fund receives a 2% management fee. The general partner, who manages the fund investments, receives 20% of the fund's net profits. The investment returns, after management and performance fees, flow back to the feeder funds to the investors. Recently, the fee structure has been changing due to pressure from investors. Some of the newer funds are offered with a fee of 1 or 30, where the manager receives the greater of a 1% management fee or an incentive fee of 30% of the fund's alpha or outperformance against a benchmark, instead of a performance fee based simply on total profits.

In addition to the partnership agreement that delineates responsibilities, hedge funds often use side letters to address the specific legal, regulatory, tax, operational, and reporting requirements of an investor. Such side letters complement and can occasionally supersede the terms of the fund's documents and are typically used when a hedge fund investor requires concessions without changing the private placement memorandum, the partnership agreement, or the articles. Occasionally, specific rights are conferred to a particular investor, such as enhanced information rights.

For larger investors, the hedge fund structure could be a fund of one or a separately managed account (SMA). These are separate investment accounts over which the investor retains more influence. In the case of a fund of one structure, the hedge fund is created for one investor, and in the case of an SMA, the investor creates his or her own investment vehicle and the underlying assets are held and registered in the name of the investor. However, the day-to-day management of the account is delegated to the hedge fund manager. These structures may require additional agreements and service providers to operate efficiently and seamlessly. Exhibit 3 shows a typical structure.

Exhibit 3: Separately Managed Hedge Fund Investment Account

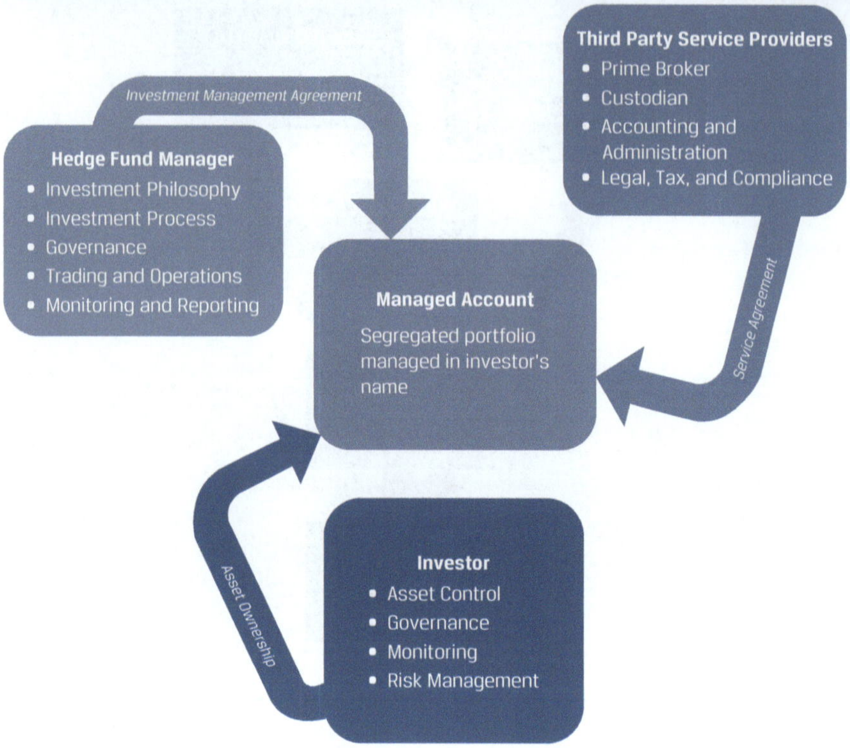

Source: KPMG. https://assets.kpmg/content/dam/kpmg/pdf/2015/09/hedge-fund-managed-accounts.pdf.

An SMA structure allows for a customizable portfolio, with investor-specific investment mandates, better transparency, efficient capital allocation, and higher liquidity, over which the investor can exercise enhanced control while keeping the fees lower. However, SMAs are operationally more complex and also demand greater governance oversight. That is why these accounts are more appropriate for larger, institutional investors.

An SMA structure has some downsides as well. Unlike a commingled fund, the managers do not have a stake in the fund investments. The investors negotiate lower fees and fund expenses but in return, may receive allocations only to the fund manager's most liquid investment trades. Hence, the overall motivation of the managers for investment performance could be reduced. Structuring in favor of incentive fees can mitigate this problem.

Indirect Hedge Fund Investment Forms

Indirect investment in hedge funds aims to make hedge fund exposures more accessible to smaller institutional and larger retail investors or to those who may lack specialized skills in managing certain asset types or want to create multiple and concurrent exposures to different strategies. The choice of indirect exposure is often motivated by reducing management costs, increasing performance transparency, and improving liquidity. Often the choice is the fund-of-hedge-funds approach, which is a managed portfolio of hedge funds.

Funds of hedge funds pool funds from investors and invest the proceeds in a diversified portfolio of hedge fund investments across a variety of hedge funds. This approach provides direct diversification benefits across fund strategies, investment regions, and management styles. These funds offer generally lower investment minimums, reduced lockup periods, and typically better exit liquidity.

For the investor, all this comes with a higher fee structure—often an additional 1%—because the manager of the fund of funds adds its own fees on top of the hedge fund management fees. Fund-of-funds investors often face a 10% incentive fee in addition to those fees charged by underlying hedge funds. The incentive fee is typically calculated on profits net of management fees at both the hedge fund level and the fund-of-funds level. This raises the cost for the investors, but at the same time, they gain access to hedge funds in which they otherwise would not have been able to invest in a diversified pool of funds. Fee layering reduces the end investor's initial gross investment returns and may result in an investor paying fees more than once for management of the same assets. Despite the additional fees, investors choose funds of funds since they provide an opportunity to invest in an underlying hedge fund that might be closed to new investors otherwise. Greater liquidity in funds of funds may result in weaker performance due to fund redemptions in times of market turmoil.

The fund-of-hedge-fund managers must have expertise in conducting hedge fund due diligence, must monitor both absolute and relative performance, and are often able to negotiate better redemption or fee terms than individual investors can.

EXAMPLE 3

Tenderledge Investments LLC—Comparing strategies

Tenderledge Investments, a fund-of-funds hedge fund, is benchmarking the performance of various hedge fund strategies as measured by the annual strategy returns over a 10-year period. Focusing on the correlation between various hedge fund strategies, the highest correlation between fund-of-funds returns is with fundamental growth, and the lowest is with short-bias funds.

Correlation between Annual Returns	Fund of Funds
Fundamental Growth	0.91
Convertible Arbitrage	0.89
Distressed/Restructuring	0.84
Multi-Strategy	0.83
Credit	0.74
Equity Market Neutral	–0.02
Macro/CTA	–0.16
Short Bias	–0.84

An increasing number of exchange-traded products, such as ETFs, seek to replicate hedge fund investment *styles* without directly investing in hedge funds themselves. Exhibit 4 shows where these investments are on the liquidity spectrum.

Exhibit 4: Liquidity Spectrum of Various Investment Alternatives

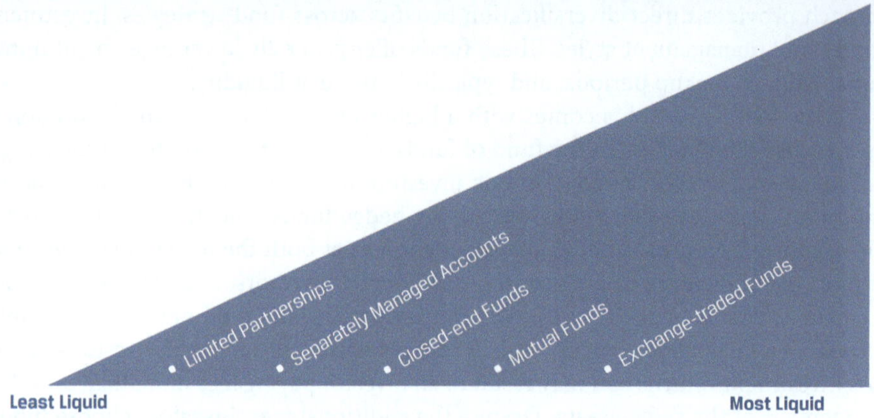

These funds can deliver returns similar to many popular hedge fund strategies, such as long/short equity, market neutral, and event driven, through indexing or active management using liquid assets. Effectively, hedge fund replication ETFs seek to generate returns with high correlations with actual hedge fund returns. By relying on quantitative tools, they imitate a broad spectrum of hedge fund returns or a specific style return. However, the returns from these strategies often fall short compared to pure hedge fund strategies because these instruments are publicly traded, are subject to a much heavier regulatory burden, do not impose restrictions on redemptions, and cannot use leverage to the same level. Yet, these investments benefit from greater liquidity, lower fees, and increased transparency than comparable hedge fund or fund-of-funds strategies and seek to match the monthly returns of hedge fund indexes, as in the following example.

EXAMPLE 4

Tenderledge Investments LLC—Creating a Hedge Fund ETF

Tenderledge is in the process of developing a hedge fund ETF that would track, before fees and expenses, the performance of a fund-of-hedge-funds strategy index. The strategy index seeks to replicate the risk-adjusted return characteristics of fund of hedge funds and underlying multiple hedge fund investment styles—more specifically, long/short equity, market neutral, event driven, fixed-income arbitrage, and distressed situations.

Although Tenderledge is a fund of hedge funds, the ETF will not invest in any hedge funds but, rather, incorporates Tenderledge's experience and knowledge in selecting hedge fund investments for the incorporation of its flagship fund of funds. Tenderledge will use quantitative tools to select traded debt and equity instruments, as well as certain derivatives, to replicate the performance of these five hedge fund strategies.

This ETF intends to achieve portfolio diversification by tracking the performance of the hedge fund universe and the five styles it seeks to replicate, generating returns with high correlation with these strategies over the long-term. Moreover, by combining these distinct strategies, the ETF will reduce its exposures to traditional sources of risk, such as interest rate volatility and equity market risk factors, such as beta.

QUESTION SET

1. Choose the correct statements regarding benefits of a master feeder structure.

   A. It allows investors in taxable jurisdictions to invest in an offshore hedge fund without any tax liability.

   B. Pooling funds from offshore and onshore funds creates economies of scale.

   C. This structure allows hedge funds to accept funding from global investors with relative ease.

   D. Many regional regulatory requirements can be avoided by such a structure.

   Solution:

   B, C, and D are correct. A is incorrect because investors in taxable jurisdictions do not avoid taxes by investing in offshore funds.

2. Which of the following statements about SMAs is *least* accurate?

   A. SMAs are a preferred choice of high-net-worth investors with specific investment mandates because they are highly customizable.

   B. SMAs provide better transparency for the investor than other fund structures.

   C. SMAs are characterized by simpler fee structures compared to mutual funds.

   D. The potential for conflicts of interest exists for SMAs since managers are not personally invested in the funds and the regulation requirements are light.

   Solution:

   C is correct because it is the least accurate statement. Mutual fund fees are clearly disclosed in the fund prospectus. The SMA fees are negotiated with the manager for each account and require sufficient care to structure in a way to incentivize the manager. A, B, and D are accurate statements.

3. Which of the following is *least* likely an investor objective that would help inform the choice of a specific fund structure?

   A. Reduce tax leakage and enhance returns by efficient tax planning

   B. Ensure an appropriate amount of investor control on companies and strategies

   C. Maximize the net returns on the investments

   D. Reduce the regulatory and compliance requirements

   Solution:

   C is correct because it is the least likely investor objective. The objective of the investment manager is to maximize the returns, while the objective of the structure is to ensure that the other options (Choices A, B, and D) are taken care of.

4. Identify the investment structure most appropriate for the investor.

A. Managed futures

B. SMA

C. Fund of funds

1. A high-net-worth investor who requires tax-efficient investment channels with a high degree of control over allocation decisions	
2. An institutional investor intending to invest in commodity markets	
3. A small investor who would like hedge fund exposure at a lower risk	

Solution:

1. A high-net-worth investor who requires tax-efficient investment channels with a high degree of control over allocation decisions	B. SMA
2. An institutional investor intending to invest in commodity markets	A. Managed futures
3. A small investor who would like hedge fund exposure at a lower risk	C. Fund of funds

Choice A: Managed futures funds are also known as commodity trading advisers because they historically focused on commodity futures. However, CTAs may include investments in a variety of futures, including commodities, equities, fixed income, and foreign exchange.

Choice B: An SMA structure allows a customizable portfolio, with investor-specific investment mandates, better transparency, efficient capital allocation, and higher liquidity, over which the investor can exercise enhanced control while keeping fees lower. However, SMAs are operationally more complex and also demand greater governance oversight. That is why these accounts are more appropriate for larger investors.

Choice C: Funds of funds allow smaller investors to make investments in hedge funds for which the minimum investment and research requirements would otherwise be overly burdensome. Volatility is generally low in these offerings because the fund-of-funds manager invests in many different hedge funds.

HEDGE FUND INVESTMENT RISK, RETURN, AND DIVERSIFICATION

4

☐ analyze sources of risk, return, and diversification among hedge fund investments

Hedge fund portfolios approach return generation differently from traditional portfolios, as Exhibit 5 shows. The most significant difference is that hedge funds seek to limit market exposure and returns from beta and primarily focus on generating idiosyncratic returns by identifying sources of unique return, or alpha. The primary source of hedge fund excess return is market inefficiencies (which may be short lived) and the skills of the manager in leveraging them.

Exhibit 5: Comparing Traditional and Hedge Fund Portfolio Sources of Return

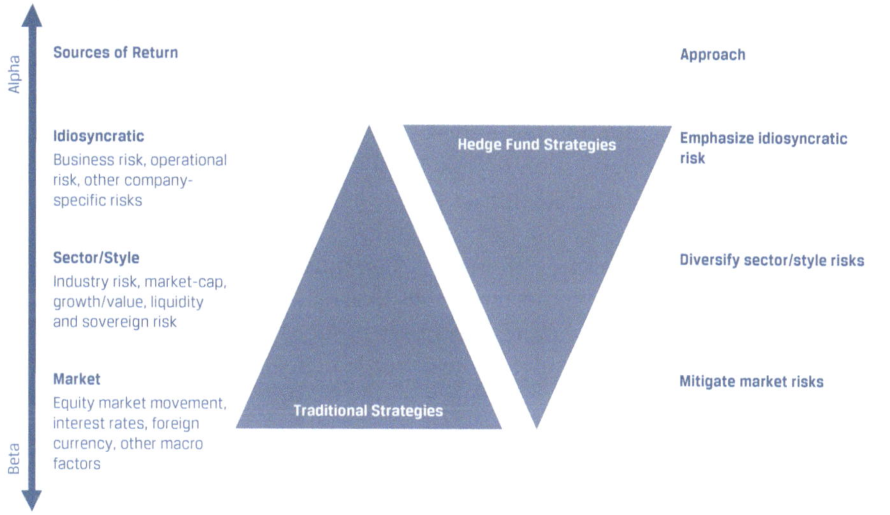

Some specific sources of alpha are the manager skills in specific stock selection and utilizing higher-return strategies that minimize risks. The performance of hedge funds can be attributed to three distinct sources:

- Market beta—the broad market beta that can be realized using market index–based funds/ETFs
- Strategy beta—the beta attributed to the investment strategy of the hedge fund applied across the broad market
- Alpha—the manager-specific returns, due to the selection of specific positions

The managers can realize the strategy beta and alpha returns due to their skills in identifying mis-priced securities and sectors, correctly timing the market, and utilizing operational control on the company business model, as well as using leverage to amplify the results.

This does not suggest that the traditional asset pricing models are incorrect. They operate within a set of assumptions—not the least of which is that the markets are efficient. The returns from hedge funds are due to systematic and idiosyncratic alternative risk factors not considered by the model.

Typically, investors do not realize the full returns from the hedge fund. Hedge funds are characterized by higher fees, which reduce the alpha generated by them. Some underperforming hedge funds that close out for performance issues face another problem. The capital redeemed from liquidated positions may result in a lower payout, effectively diminishing the total return from the fund.

To compare the risk-adjusted return characteristics of individual hedge funds and aggregate hedge fund strategies, we use hedge fund indexes that are created using publicly available hedge fund performance data. There are several vendors that create such indexes, and each index has its own features, but there are some general considerations around these indexes that distinguish them from other indexes used for performance comparison. Most hedge fund indexes are based on information reported by the hedge fund managers and others who receive performance information with the right to share that information. It should also be noted that the reporting by any hedge fund is voluntary. This situation introduces several sources of bias and suggests that hedge fund performance is likely overestimated.

Selection bias can be an issue. Individual funds are allocated to strategy peer groups in an inconsistent manner: sometimes based on the prospectus, sometimes based on historical style analysis, sometimes using a combination of approaches, each of which adds and compounds bias. Indexes may also have inconsistent sources of the underlying data. A handful of these indexes operate with transparent and constant inclusion, selection, and exclusion of individual managers and/or their funds. Some index providers impose requirements on AUM, vintage, and whether the hedge fund is open to new investors.

Survivorship bias can also be an issue. When funds that have stopped reporting are removed from the index, the index will likely show better performance. This effect can be mitigated by including the returns of funds of funds that are active and those that have stopped reporting. For instance, a hedge fund manager consistently underperforming a peer group may have limited incentives to continue to highlight underperformance, particularly if the manager is actively sourcing new investors or launching new funds. Hence, the manager may discontinue reporting poor performance, which overestimates reported performance.

Additionally, hedge funds that are closed to new investors or closed because of underperformance are treated equally. Their performance is excluded from the index value. Additionally, the hedge fund performance data are published with a delay, normally a time lag of four weeks or one month. Since these indexes are non-investable and illiquid, replicating their performance may be difficult.

In addition, backfill bias can be an issue. When a successful fund starts reporting performance for the first time, it is very likely that its past performance was stellar, since typically only hedge funds with favorable returns are reported. When such funds are added to an index, the benchmarks will overstate the actual performance. This is a variation of the survivorship bias that results when a new hedge fund is included in a given index and its past performance is "backfilled" into the index's database. Typically, larger indexes have less backfill bias.

A large majority of hedge fund indexes are not weighted by assets under management. In these hedge fund indexes, each hedge fund receives an equal index weighting in the performance peer group. As a result, comparison of large and small funds can be skewed compared to the performance of a size-weighted index.

Hedge Fund Investment Risks and Returns

Many traditional investment funds, such as long-only mutual funds and index ETFs, diversify away much of the idiosyncratic risks in their holdings by investing in a large number of stocks and achieve most of their returns primarily by bearing the systematic market risk (beta). Unlike in traditional funds, hedge funds use a variety of instruments across asset classes and techniques in seeking to generate absolute returns in all market environments.

The structure of a hedge fund complicates the benchmarking of the returns on a frequent basis. Due to the high degree of flexibility the managers have over the investments and the minimal level of disclosure (as well as the frequency of disclosure) they offer, it is hard to conduct any performance attribution analysis. Additionally, the relative illiquidity of investments held by the funds makes marking to market a problematic and potentially futile process.

Hence, attributing the sources of returns and risks is a composite process that is further complicated by the complexity of the strategies and compounded using various sources of leverage. That is why risk and return comparisons are typically made to fund-of-funds composite indexes to minimize return distortions. That approach controls for the effects of self-reporting and selection biases. Furthermore, it ensures that the fund-of-funds benchmark index is investable.

Nonetheless, over the long term (since 1990), hedge funds have enjoyed higher returns (at least prior to fees and expenses) than either stocks or bonds and a standard deviation nearly identical to that of bonds. Specifically, Exhibit 6 compares the returns, risk, and performance measures for the HFRI Fund of Funds Composite Index, the MSCI ACWI Index, and the Bloomberg Barclays Global Aggregate Index. The HFRI Fund of Funds Composite Index is an equally weighted performance index of funds of hedge funds included in the HFR Database.

As mentioned earlier, hedge fund indexes typically build on data that each hedge fund reports. Because these data are self-reported, there is a degree of survivorship bias that the HFRI Fund of Funds Composite Index mitigates by reflecting the actual performance of portfolios of hedge funds. The measures shown here may reflect a lower reported return because of the added layer of fees, but they likely represent a fairer, more conservative, and more accurate estimate of average hedge fund performance than HFR's composite index of individual funds. The returns are likely biased toward equity long/short funds since these are frequently a substantial portion of funds of funds' allocation mix. There are also other hedge fund indexes, allowing a more thorough analysis of the source of returns.

As shown in Exhibit 6, over the 25-year period between 1990 and 2014, hedge funds had higher returns than either stocks or bonds and a standard deviation almost identical to that of bonds. This, however, depends on the benchmarks used, which typically are broad market benchmarks. In the 1990- 2014 period, hedge funds had modest overall correlation with global stock returns (0.56) and negligible correlation with global bond returns (0.07) over this 25-year period. Hedge funds certainly offered added value to institutional investors as a portfolio diversification agent in this time period.

Exhibit 6: Historical Risk–Return Characteristics of Hedge Funds and Other Investments, 1990–2019

	FoF	Global Stocks	Global Bonds
Annualized return			
1990–2014	7.2%	6.9%	6.3%

	FoF	Global Stocks	Global Bonds
2015–2019	*2.48%*	*10.41%*	*2.42%*
Annualized volatility			
1990-2014	6.0%	16.5%	5.8%
2015–2019	*1.08%*	*11.42%*	*1.33%*
FoF correlation (avg. monthly)			
1990–2014		0.56	0.07
2015–2019		*0.86*	*0.03*
Percentage of positive months	69.3%	61.3%	62.7%
Best month	6.8%	11.9%	6.2%
Worst month	–7.5%	–19.8%	–3.8%
Worst drawdown	–22.2%	–54.6%	–10.1%

Sources: Fund-of-funds (FoF) data are from the HFRI Fund of Funds Composite Index; global stock data are from the MSCI ACWI Index; global bond data are from the Bloomberg Barclays Global Aggregate Index.

Notably, Exhibit 6 shows that for the subsequent five-year period between 2015 and 2019, the absolute return of funds of funds relative, in particular, to global equities has declined, while their performance correlation with equity markets actually increased. This trend has made hedge fund allocations arguably less useful and also somewhat less popular. But some allocators have continued to find value to maintain or actually increase their allocation to a mix of hedge funds as a bond market substitute in their overall portfolio building.

Looking at the performance of various hedge fund strategies over time, an approach is to examine the relationship between hedge fund returns and the risk measured by the standard deviation of returns. Exhibit 7 shows the log returns and standard deviation of returns for selected hedge fund strategies on an annualized monthly basis as reported by Hedge Fund Research. The data cover the period from January 2008 to November 2021, a period of almost 14 years.

Exhibit 7: Return and Risk of Selected Hedge Fund Strategies, 2008–2021

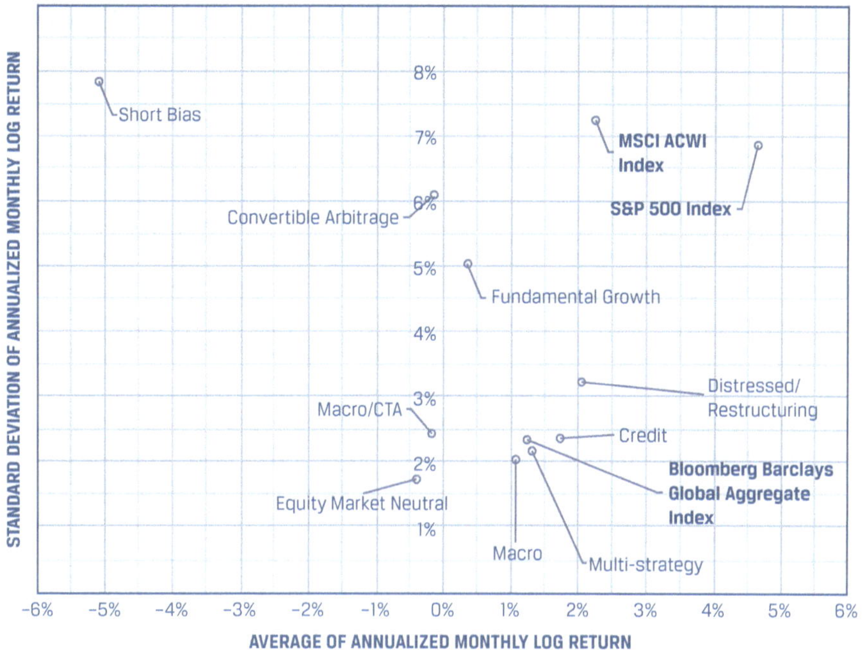

Source: Hedge Fund Research (HFR), annualized monthly log returns.

Some of the hedge fund strategies generated negative returns on average. Short-bias strategies underperformed all the other strategies in terms of both return and risk measured by standard deviation. For comparison, the S&P 500, MSCI ACWI, and Bloomberg Barclays Global Aggregate Index returns are also plotted to show that many strategies have widely varying risk/return characteristics compared to common equity and fixed income benchmarks.

Another approach to analyze the benefits from investing in hedge funds looks at the risk/return trade-off measured by the coefficient of variation of annual hedge fund returns. The coefficient of variation can be thought as the price of return in terms of risk or the relative return adjusted for risk: A higher coefficient of variation provides greater return for the same amount of risk.

Diversification Benefits of Hedge Fund Investments

The original hedge fund strategy was a market-neutral strategy in which the long and short positions made the portfolio beta neutral and generated a positive alpha. Stated differently, hedge funds initially kept their portfolios' net market sensitivity exposure to the market benchmark index at zero. By holding long and short positions, they sought to create value for their investors with minimal exposure to the market.

Over time, hedge fund investments have evolved from these equity hedge strategies with little or no equity market correlation to complex strategies across various asset classes. While hedge fund strategies vary widely, market-neutral, relative value, and event-driven strategies tend to outperform equity markets during market downturns and when individual stock correlations fall and tend to have weaker performance when correlations are high (reducing relative value opportunities) and equities move uniformly higher.

The diversification benefits of hedge funds first came to prominence with the dot-com bubble unwinding in 2000–2002, when they generally performed well compared with traditional long-only investment products. Starting with funds of funds, institutional investors increased their hedge fund exposure and then expanded it through direct allocations following the 2008 financial crash. Seeking better diversification and risk mitigation, despite high hedge fund fees, the investors sought absolute and uncorrelated risk-adjusted returns rather than outsized upside performance. In the early 2000s, when hedge funds came to prominence, the primary drivers were the absolute excess returns, regardless of market direction. The verification efforts from investors on hedge fund operations were minimal. The 2008 crisis (including Lehman Brothers' bankruptcy and the Bernie Madoff fraud) brought to light the need for additional due diligence. The correction after the 2008 crisis brought several changes. The inflow from high-quality institutional investors and pension funds increased. Such investors demanded additional transparency and control over the fund's investment process, fund operations, leverage applied, and managers' performance. This change has benefited only the highest-quality funds, and most other hedge funds failed to keep pace with the positive equity and bond market advances of 2009–2019. They continue to have a place in institutional asset allocations because of their risk-diversification properties.

Exhibit 8 shows return relationships between hedge funds and US stock and bond indexes from 2001 to 2021. Although diversification is typically used to reduce idiosyncratic risk, diversification using hedge fund investments seeks to add idiosyncratic outperformance.

While hedge fund risk diversification benefits can merit investigation, experience also reflects that their prospective advantage can vary over time. Investors need to be thorough in conducting due diligence when selecting a hedge fund manager. Hedge fund performance has a very low correlation with that of traditional asset classes, such as investment bonds and currencies/cash. For traditional investors in these asset classes, hedge funds provide an enhanced opportunity for portfolio diversification and for generating consistent returns over time. Adding hedge funds to a traditional 60/40 portfolio typically decreases the total portfolio standard deviation and increases the Sharpe ratio, thus enhancing portfolio diversification and risk-adjusted return.

Exhibit 8: Historical Hedge Fund Monthly Return Correlations, 2001–2021

	Hedge Funds	S&P 500	Investment-Grade Bonds
Hedge Funds	1	0.82	0.10
S&P 500		1	−0.06
Investment-Grade Bonds			1

Notes: Hedge funds = Dow Jones Credit Suisse Hedge Fund Index. Investment-grade bonds = Bloomberg Barclays US Aggregate Bond Index.

As Exhibit 8 shows, hedge funds have a fairly high correlation with equities and a low correlation with investment-grade bonds.

QUESTION SET

1. Selecting investment trades with high idiosyncratic risk is *most likely* associated with the management of which type of fund?

   A. Equity index ETF

   B. Long-only equity mutual fund

   C. Long/short equity hedge fund

   Solution:

   C is correct. Long/short equity hedge funds are the most likely type of funds to seek out trades with high idiosyncratic risk, so their performance is driven primarily by stock selection and less by other factors, such as sector and market exposures. B is incorrect because long-only mutual funds are more likely to seek returns from market risk and sector risks with less emphasis on undiversifiable, security-specific risks. A is incorrect because equity index funds do not seek out idiosyncratic risk and simply try to mimic the performance of an index.

2. Hedge funds are not obligated to report their performance to the public. Many do, however, to attract additional investors. Hedge fund benchmarks and indexes are created using the reported data. Which of the following is *least likely* a bias that hedge fund investors should be aware of when evaluating the performance of hedge fund benchmarks and indexes?

   A. Survivorship bias: Unsuccessful and liquidated hedge funds are removed from an index, resulting in their underperformance not being accounted for in the index.

   B. Self-reporting bias: Hedge funds have the freedom to not report their performance, and only the ones that report are included in an index.

   C. Societal bias: This relates to the perception of hedge funds at a societal level, where hedge funds that are perceived to be high performing are included in the index.

   Solution:

   C is correct. Societal bias is not one of the biases that hedge fund investors need to be aware of when evaluating hedge fund performance. A and B are biases that distort the performance of hedge fund benchmarks and indexes.

3. An investor wants to invest in a diversified hedge fund that minimizes the return correlation with the traditional asset classes but would prefer the fund to be more liquid and transparent while minimizing the leverage obtained by borrowing or shorting. What would be the *most* appropriate hedge fund the investor can choose?

   A. Fundamental value

   B. Managed futures

   C. Multi-strategy

   D. Fund of funds

   Solution:

   B is correct. Managed futures have, historically, exhibited low correlation with traditional assets and invest in active futures in liquid commodities and foreign exchange markets. They are also able to increase exposure without resorting to borrowing or shorting.

PRACTICE PROBLEMS

1. Choose the *false* statement about hedge funds:

   A. While traditional fund managers charge mainly a management fee, hedge fund managers charge both a management fee and a performance-based incentive fee.

   B. Redemption of funds from a hedge fund prior to its liquidation is very hard, due to the initial lockup period and specific terms of redemption.

   C. Individual retail investors cannot invest in hedge funds, and only institutional investors can.

2. A fundamental long/short hedge fund manager is evaluating specific securities to build a portfolio's positions. Which of the following is the strategy the manager would *least likely* adopt?

   A. Long securities that have an upside potential relative to current price

   B. Short sectors with macro trends negatively impacting the company

   C. Long securities that trade at a significant discount, expecting an increased valuation in case of a bankruptcy

3. Which of the following fund structures is most likely to be suitable for an institutional hedge fund investor that seeks a highly customizable offering with negotiable fees?

   A. Separately managed hedge funds

   B. Commingled hedge funds (master feeder funds)

   C. Mutual funds

   D. Funds of funds

4. Which of the following parties is responsible for the portfolio management of a fund of hedge funds?

   A. Accredited investor

   B. General partner

   C. Limited partner

5. Which of the following best explains why it is unlikely a poor-performing hedge fund would be added to an index?

   A. Survivorship bias

   B. Backfill bias

   C. Selection bias

6. The strategy that identifies opportunities for future merger, bankruptcy, or

spin-offs and seeks profit from pricing inefficiencies is known as:

A. event driven.

B. relative value.

C. opportunistic.

7. A money manager was reviewing the automobile sector and identified that the stock of General Motors (GM) is relatively overvalued compared to Ford. A money manager purchases 100 shares of Ford and shorts 150 shares of GM. It turned out that the manager's perception was right. At the end of the quarter, she unwinds both positions, making a profit on both positions. What is this strategy called?

A. Equity long/short

B. Event driven

C. Relative value

SOLUTIONS

1. C is correct because it is a false statement. Accredited retail investors can invest in various types of hedge funds. A and B are true.

2. C is correct. Participating in a potential bankruptcy situation would be characteristic of an event-driven hedge fund manager and not a fundamental long/short manager. B is incorrect because a fundamental long/short manager would invest in securities expected to exhibit high growth and capital appreciation. C is incorrect because a fundamental long/short manager would short securities in sectors that project negative growth.

3. A is correct. A hedge fund SMA can be tailored to a single investor seeking a tailored portfolio with negotiated fees. The other fund structures do not generally offer customization or negotiable fees.

4. B is correct. The general partner is responsible for choosing the hedge funds in a fund of hedge funds. A and C are incorrect because they refer to customers or investors in the fund.

5. C is correct. Selection bias refers to when the benchmark inclusion criteria cover only those funds that have good performance and hence report their performance to attract new investors. A is incorrect; survivorship bias is when the benchmark stops including funds that have ceased operations, most likely due to poor performance, and hence does not fully represent the hedge fund universe. B is incorrect; backfill bias occurs when an index retroactively includes the performance of a fund before it is added to the index.

6. A is correct. Event-driven strategies include mergers, bankruptcies, and spin-offs. Relative value strategies (Choice B) seek to profit from a price or return discrepancy between securities based on a short-term relationship. Opportunistic strategies (Choice C) use managed futures and macro strategies.

7. A is correct. Equity long/short strategies purchase undervalued stocks and sell short overvalued stocks. Event-driven managers (Choice B) participate in such events as mergers and spin-offs. Relative value managers (Choice C) seek to arbitrage values between related securities.

LEARNING MODULE

7

Introduction to Digital Assets

LEARNING OUTCOMES	
Mastery	*The candidate should be able to:*
☐	describe financial applications of distributed ledger technology
☐	explain investment features of digital assets and contrast them with other asset classes
☐	describe investment forms and vehicles used in digital asset investments
☐	analyze sources of risk, return, and diversification among digital asset investments

INTRODUCTION

1

As introduced in Alternatives Learning Module 1, digital assets are a relatively new investment class that covers assets that can be created, stored, and transmitted electronically and have associated ownership or use rights. This class includes a wide variety of digital assets, including cryptocurrencies, tokens, and digital collectables. Based on the innovative distributed ledger technology (DLT), or blockchain technology, digital assets utilize advanced encryption techniques that assure the authenticity of digital assets. While cryptocurrencies have their own blockchains, crypto-tokens are built on an existing blockchain.

As with other types of alternative investments, digital assets have characteristics distinct from traditional investments. Since the advent of Bitcoin in 2009, when it was a niche concept in the technology world, digital assets have gradually become more mainstream alternative investments for investors worldwide. We will give an overview of the common forms of digital asset investments and discuss the key concepts and pitfalls in this space.

Despite their special features and technological characteristics, digital assets offer investors diversification while providing higher expected returns than traditional investments provide. However, their risks are also higher. We will discuss the sources of risks in digital assets to provide a better understanding of this evolving asset class.

LEARNING MODULE OVERVIEW

- Blockchain and distributed ledger technology might offer a new way to store, record, and track digital assets on a secure, distributed basis. Additionally, DLT could bring efficiencies to post-trade and compliance processes through automation, smart contracts, and identity verification.
- DLT can take the form of either permissionless or permissioned networks.
- A consensus protocol is a set of rules that govern how blocks are cryptographically chained together in a blockchain network for the verification of the complete and immutable history of transaction records. Two broad types of consensus protocols are "proof of work" (PoW) and "proof of stake" (PoS).
- Digital assets are frequently seen as an alternative asset class. As digital assets become more developed, institutional investors may continue to seek some exposure to these assets for their higher returns and possible diversification benefits.
- Digital assets differ from traditional financial assets in terms of their inherent value, transaction validation approach, uses as a legal medium of exchange, and legal and regulatory protection.
- The most common digital assets are cryptocurrencies, including Bitcoin and altcoins (including stablecoins and meme coins). There are also digitalized tokens that include non-fungible tokens, security tokens, utility tokens, and governance tokens.
- Many cryptocurrencies are designed with self-imposed limits on the total supply through complex computer algorithms. Such limits could help maintain a value from a technical perspective, yet there is no economic consensus on how they should be valued. Cryptocurrency exchanges are classified into centralized exchanges and decentralized exchanges. Both centralized and decentralized exchanges face problems with fraud and manipulation because they are not subject to rigorous oversight and are generally not regulated as financial exchanges.
- Investment in digital assets can take the form of direct ownership of cryptocurrencies and other digital assets on the blockchains or indirect investment in exchange-traded products, hedge funds, trusts, futures, and thematic stocks.
- Asset-backed tokens are digital claims on physical assets, financial assets, or financial instruments and are collateralized by these underlying assets.
- The push for financial decentralized applications based on open-source codes and smart contracts has grown into a movement known as decentralized finance, or DeFi. DeFi seeks to design, combine, and develop decentralized financial applications as building blocks for sophisticated financial products and services.
- The price of Bitcoin and other digital assets are driven by expectations on future asset appreciation rather than any underlying cash flow. The market demand for the limited supply of cryptocurrencies is a significant driver of prices.

- The performance of the first widely traded digital asset, Bitcoin, has been characterized by high return, high volatility, and low correlations with traditional asset classes.
- Due to the historically low correlations with other asset classes, digital assets offer potential diversification benefits to a well-diversified portfolio. But the correlations are observed to have risen, especially during periods of high market uncertainty.

LEARNING MODULE SELF-ASSESSMENT

These initial questions are intended to help you gauge your current level of understanding of this learning module.

1. The consensus protocol on a distributed ledger technology network refers to:

   A. the standardized approach that governs how digital assets generated from a blockchain network should be valued.

   B. programs embedded in electronic transaction records that are coded to self-execute according to predetermined conditions.

   C. the set of rules governing how blocks are cryptographically linked to the chain to become immutable on the distributed ledger network.

   Solution:

   The correct answer is C. When transactions enter a node of the distributed ledger, they are bundled into "blocks" and cryptographically "chained" together to facilitate verification of the prior history. How blocks are chained together is determined by the consensus protocol, a set of rules governing how blocks can join the chain and become the immutable "truth." The consensus protocols are designed to resist attempts at malicious manipulation up to a certain level of security.

2. Cryptocurrencies are a common form of digital asset that:

   A. can be mined only through "proof of work" on blockchain networks.

   B. exist both in physical forms and electronic records with rights to use, buy, or sell by owners.

   C. can be used to transfer or store value, which allows time-efficient transactions between parties without the need for an intermediary.

   Solution:

   The correct answer is C. Cryptocurrencies are used to transfer or store value, which allows near-real-time transactions between parties without the need for an intermediary. As electronic mediums of exchange, cryptocurrencies lack physical form and exist only as electronic records on distributed ledgers. Depending on the particular consensus protocols used, cryptocurrencies can be generated either by "proof of work" or "proof of stake" by miners or validators on networks.

3. Digital assets differ from traditional financial securities in that:

   A. digital assets are subject to a broader legal protection framework.

   B. digital assets are not valued based on their expected future cash flow.

C. transaction records of digital assets require a centralized intermediary.

Solution:

The correct answer is B. Most digital assets do not have a fundamental value based on underlying assets or on the potential cash flow or earnings they are expected to generate. To date, the legal and regulatory frameworks for digital assets are still evolving, and there is generally less legal protection compared to traditional financial securities. Digital asset transactions are recorded on a distributed ledger, and no centralized intermediary is required in the process.

4. A special type of cryptocurrency that is backed by and pegged to a fiat currency is called:

   A. altcoin.

   B. stablecoin.

   C. meme coin.

   Solution:

   The correct answer is B. A stablecoin is designed to maintain a stable value by pegging its value to another asset and is collateralized by a basket of assets, typically a fiat currency, precious metals, or other cryptocurrencies.

5. An indirect investment in digital assets can be made through:

   A. entering into cryptocurrency futures.

   B. purchasing Bitcoins on cryptocurrency wallets.

   C. participating in the initial coin offering of a new digital token.

   Solution:

   The correct answer is A. Investors interested in an indirect investment in digital assets can trade cryptocurrency futures on established exchanges, such as the Chicago Mercantile Exchange. However, the purchase of Bitcoins and buying new tokens through an initial coin offering are direct forms of investment.

6. A cryptocurrency ETF seeks to:

   A. gain exposure to cryptocurrencies through cash and cryptocurrency derivatives.

   B. replicate digital asset investment returns by investing directly in cryptocurrencies.

   C. gain exposure to the cryptocurrency theme by investing in public equities related to the digital asset sector.

   Solution:

   The correct answer is A. A cryptocurrency ETF seeks to replicate digital asset investment returns by cash and cryptocurrency derivatives.

7. Bitcoin as an alternative investment has historically exhibited:

   A. low return, low risk, and high correlations with traditional assets.

   B. high return, high risk, and low correlations with traditional assets.

C. high return, high risk, and high correlations with traditional assets.

Solution:

The correct answer is B. Despite no future cash flow generation, Bitcoin as an alternative investment has been characterized by high return, high volatility, and low correlations with traditional asset classes.

8. Early investors in cryptocurrencies have enjoyed significant price appreciation but many later-stage investors suffered huge losses most likely because:

   A. blockchain technology favors early-stage investors.

   B. there are substantial price fluctuations in cryptocurrencies.

   C. cryptocurrencies have increased their appeal to institutional investors.

   Solution:

   The correct answer is B. Because cryptocurrencies are a relatively new innovation, their market is subject to rapid price swings, changes, and uncertainty. Their prices have been extremely volatile over the years, and price drawdowns were often much more substantial than for traditional asset classes. As a result, later-stage investors may suffer huge losses depending on their points of entry and exit.

DISTRIBUTED LEDGER TECHNOLOGY 2

☐ describe financial applications of distributed ledger technology

Distributed ledger technology (DLT) based on a distributed ledger (defined later) represents a technological development and offers potential improvements to delivering financing services and financial record keeping. DLT networks are being considered as a means to create, exchange, and track ownership of financial assets on a peer-to-peer (P2P) basis. Potential benefits of using this technology include greater accuracy, transparency, and security in record keeping; faster transfer of ownership; and P2P interactions. However, the technology is not fully secure, and breaches in privacy and data protection are possible. Additionally, the computational processes underlying DLT generally require massive amounts of energy to verify transaction activity.

A **distributed ledger** is a type of database that can be shared among potentially infinite numbers of entities in a network. In a distributed ledger, entries are recorded, stored, and distributed across a network of participants so that each participating entity has a matching copy of the digital database, making each copy of the database a verified record of all current and previous transactions. Basic elements of a DLT network include a digital ledger, a consensus mechanism used to confirm new entries, and a participant network.

The consensus mechanism is the process by which the computer entities (or nodes) in a network agree on a common state of the ledger. Consensus generally involves two steps: transaction validation and agreement on ledger update by network parties. These features enable the creation of records that are, for the most part, considered immutable, or unchangeable, yet they are transparent and accessible to network participants on a near-real-time basis. There are various approaches to establishing consensus.

Features of DLT include the use of **cryptography**—an algorithmic process to encrypt data, making the data unusable if received by unauthorized parties—which enables a high level of network security and database integrity. For example, DLT uses cryptographic methods of proof to verify network participant identity and for data encryption.

DLT has the potential to accommodate "**smart contracts**," which are computer programs that self-execute on the basis of pre-specified terms and conditions agreed to by the parties to a contract. Examples of smart contract use are the automatic execution of contingent claims for derivatives and the instantaneous transfer of collateral in the event of default.

Exhibit 1 illustrates a distributed ledger network in which all participants (nodes) are connected to one another, each having a copy of the distributed ledger. The term "consensus" is shown in the center of the network and represents the consensus mechanism in which the nodes agree on new transactions and ledger updates.

Exhibit 1: Distributed Ledger Network Setup

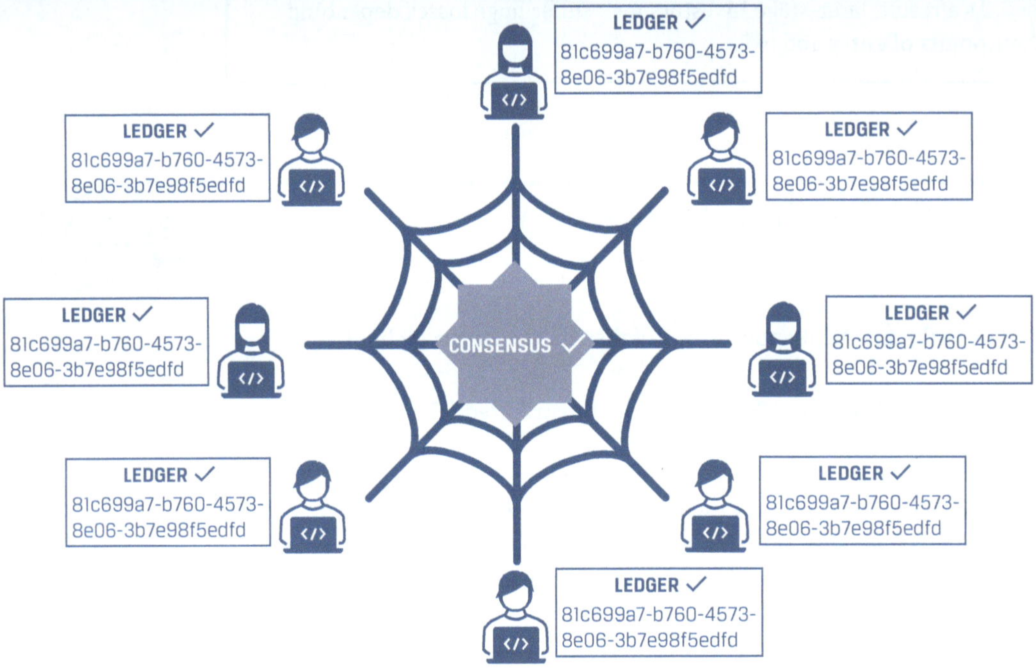

Blockchain is a type of digital ledger in which information, such as changes in ownership, is recorded sequentially within blocks that are then linked or "chained" together and secured using cryptographic methods. The steps outlining adding a new transaction to the network are outlined in Exhibit 2. There are several key steps a transaction must go through before it is added to the blockchain.

Exhibit 2: Adding a Transaction to the Blockchain

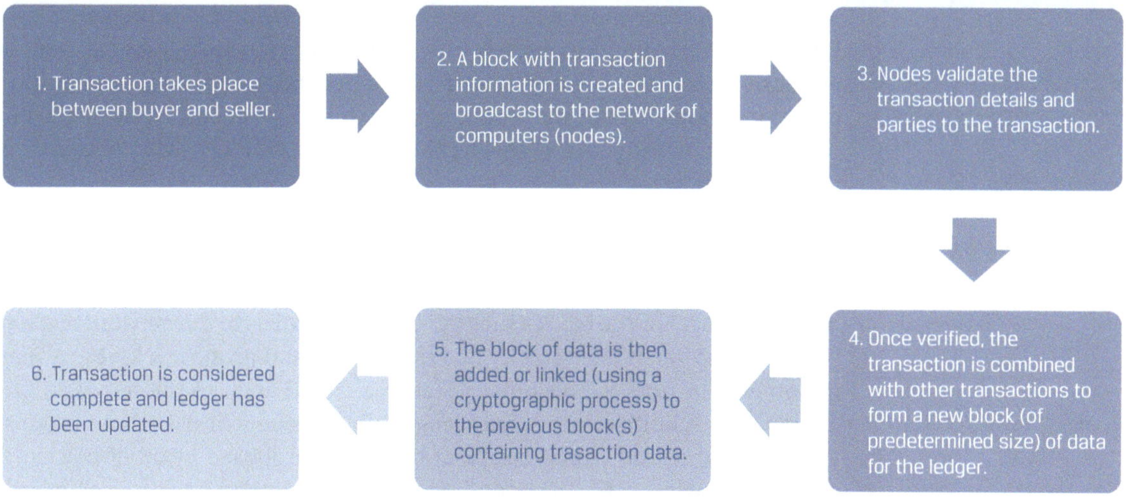

Each block contains a grouping of transactions (or entries) and a secure link (known as a hash) to the previous block. New transactions are inserted into the chain only after validation via a consensus mechanism in which authorized members agree on the transaction and the preceding order, or history, in which previous transactions have occurred.

Proof of Work vs. Proof of Stake

Fundamentally, blockchains are software protocols that enable many parties to interact under common assumptions and knowledge without having to trust each other. When transactions enter into a node of the blockchain, they are bundled into "blocks" and cryptographically "chained" together to facilitate verification of the prior history. How blocks are chained together is determined by the **consensus protocol**, a set of rules governing how blocks can join the chain and become the immutable "truth." The consensus protocols are designed to resist attempts at malicious manipulation up to a certain level of security. We distinguish between two main types of protocols.

The Proof of Work (PoW) Protocol

The proof of work protocol determines which specific block to add through a computationally costly lottery. The PoW consensus mechanism used to verify a transaction involves a cryptographic problem that must be solved by some computers on the network (known as miners) each time a transaction takes place. **Miners** use powerful computers and significant amounts of energy to solve complex algorithm puzzles to validate and lock blocks of transactions into the blockchain, earning cryptocurrency for themselves in the process. The "proof of work" consensus process to update the blockchain can require substantial amounts of computing power, making it very difficult and extremely expensive for an individual third party to manipulate historical data. To manipulate historical data, an individual or entity would have to control most nodes in the network. The success of the network, therefore, relies on broad network participation.

Participants on the network agree that the *longest chain* of blocks is the only truthful representation of all previous transactions. If a malicious attacker wanted to make a longer chain including fraudulent transactions, it must outperform the entire network's computational power, which theoretically requires most of the network's available computational power. This is the famous 51% attack threshold and serves as the boundary of the PoW protocol's security standards. Amassing this much network power on the most widely used blockchains behind cryptocurrencies, such as Bitcoin or Ethereum, is extremely difficult for any individual, organization, or group of coordinated actors. Even if most of the network's computational power can be controlled momentarily, the length of block history that can be altered is limited by the duration of this control. This has been the most widely used consensus protocol for digital assets.

The Proof of Stake (PoS) Protocol

This protocol requires selected participants on the networks, the validators, to pledge capital to vouch for the block's validity. This stake signals to the network that a validator is available to verify the veracity of a transaction and propose a block. A majority of the other validators, who similarly staked a digital asset to the network, must then attest to the validity of proposed block. Validators benefit from both proposing and attesting to the validity of blocks that have been proposed by other participants in a similar staking process. The boundary of the PoS protocol's security standards builds on a group of stakers (and their pledged stake) controlling the network's computational power and protecting access from malicious parties gaining a majority.

Under both consensus protocols, the validation of the transactions comes with rewards: mining. Successful miners that validate the transaction obtain a new digital asset, whether it is a cryptocurrency or a token. The rate of mining and the speed at which new transactions on the network are validated generally control the amount of a new digital asset that can be created on a specific digital ledger network.

Permissioned and Permissionless Networks

DLT can take the form of either permissionless or permissioned networks. **Permissionless networks** are open to any user who wishes to make a transaction, and all users within the network can see all transactions that exist on the blockchain. In a permissionless, or open, DLT system, any network participant can perform all network functions.

The main benefit of a permissionless network is that it does not depend on a centralized authority to confirm or deny the validity of transactions, because this takes place through the chosen consensus mechanism. This means no single point of failure exists because all transactions are recorded on a single distributed database and every node stores a copy of the database. Once a transaction has been added to the blockchain, it cannot be changed, barring manipulation; the distributed ledger becomes a permanent and immutable record of all previous transactions. In a permissionless network, trust between transacting parties is not a requirement.

Bitcoin is a well-known use of an open permissionless network. Bitcoin was created in 2009 to serve as the public ledger for all transactions occurring on its virtual currency. Since the introduction of Bitcoin, many more cryptocurrencies, or digital currencies, which use permissionless DLT networks, have been created.

In **permissioned networks**, network members might be restricted from participating in certain network activities. Controls, or permissions, can be used to allow varying levels of access to the ledger, from adding transactions (e.g., a participant) to viewing transactions only (e.g., a regulator) to viewing selective details of the transactions but not the full record. Exhibit 3 compares the salient features of permissioned and permissionless blockchains.

Exhibit 3: Features of Permissioned and Permissionless Blockchains

	Permissioned blockchain	Permissionless blockchain
Speed	Faster as only a limited number of members participate or are authorized to validate transactions	Slower as a large number of members have to reach consensus, which decreases network speed and scalability
Cost	Cost-effective as few members are required to validate each transaction	Not cost-effective as many members are required to validate each transaction
Decentralization	Partially decentralized as there are a limited number of members in the chain	Decentralized as all members can access the network
Access	Membership is limited.	Membership is unlimited.
Governance	The governance is determined by a centralized organization.	The governance is decentralized and is maintained by the members.

Based on their decentralized nature, permissionless distributed ledgers are fully open to all, but that high level of decentralization usually requires more processing power and bandwidth, making them less cost-effective. The opposite holds true for permissioned blockchains. Governance and transaction verification are two other aspects that are specific to the type of blockchain.

Types of Digital Assets

Potential applications of DLT to financial services and investment management include the creation of digital assets, such as cryptocurrencies, and the process to deliver financial services more efficiently, such as processes tokenization, post-trade clearing and settlement, and compliance. Exhibit 4 summarizes different digital assets.

Exhibit 4: Different Digital Assets

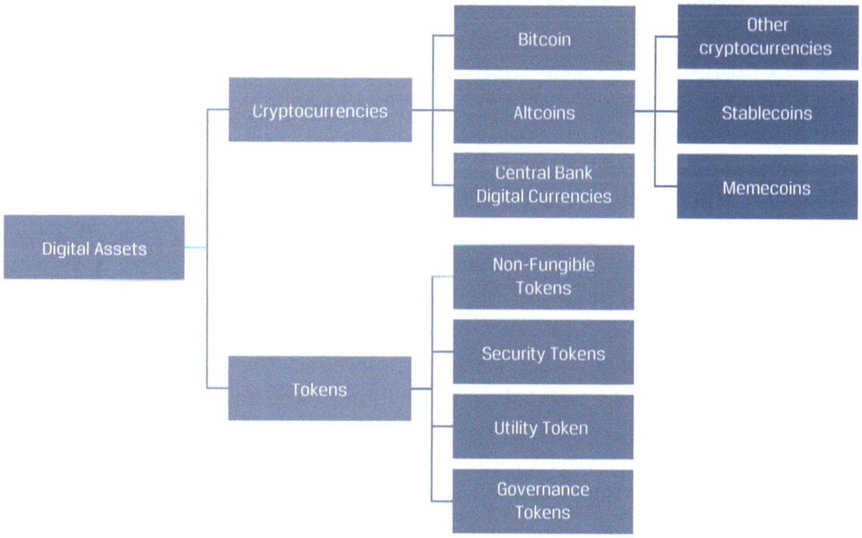

Cryptocurrencies

Digital assets are assets that exist only as an electronic record with rights to use, buy, or sell. They can be securities, currencies, properties, or commodities. The most common digital assets are units used to transfer or store value, referred to as **cryptocurrency** and digital currency, which allow near-real-time transactions between parties without the need for an intermediary.

As electronic mediums of exchange, cryptocurrencies lack physical form and are issued privately by individuals, companies, and other organizations. Hence, they do not benefit from the backing of a central bank or a monetary authority. Most issued cryptocurrencies utilize open DLT systems in which a decentralized distributed ledger is used to record and verify all digital currency transactions. Several different types of cryptocurrency exist, such as altcoins and stablecoins.

Many cryptocurrencies have a self-imposed limit on the total amount of currency they may issue. Although such limits could help maintain their store of value, it is important to note that many cryptocurrencies have experienced high levels of price volatility. There is no consensus on how to value cryptocurrencies, and the apparent lack of clear fundamentals underlying these currencies has contributed to their volatility.

Cryptocurrencies are not government backed or regulated. Central banks around the world, however, are recognizing potential benefits and examining use cases for their own cryptocurrency versions as an alternative to physical currency. Such **central bank digital currencies (CBDCs)** are typically designed as a tokenized version of the currency issued by the central bank ("fiat currency")—essentially a digital bank note or coin.

Tokens

Transactions involving physical assets, such as real estate, luxury goods, and commodities, often require substantial efforts in ownership verification and examination each time a transfer in ownership takes place. Through **tokenization**, the process of representing ownership rights to physical assets on a blockchain or distributed ledger, DLT has the potential to streamline this process by creating a single, digital record of ownership with which to verify ownership title and authenticity, including all historical activity.

Another form of digital assets is the **non-fungible token (NFT)**. An NFT links digital assets to certificates of authenticity using blockchain technology. NFTs differ from "fungible" tokens, such as cryptocurrencies, because each token and the authenticated object it represents is unique. As such, they uniquely "stamp" assets and can represent digital assets in a virtual world. The most common use for NFTs is trading in digital artwork.

Security tokens digitize the ownership rights associated with publicly traded securities. The custody of these security tokens can be stored on a blockchain, which increases the efficiency of post-trade processing, settlement, record keeping, and custody. Such a single ledger solution would eliminate the need for reconciliation and validation of transactions and allow participants to perform various transactions more easily and with greater transparency.

An example of security tokens is **initial coin offering** (ICO), an unregulated process whereby companies sell their crypto-tokens to investors in exchange for money or for another agreed upon cryptocurrency. An ICO is typically structured to issue digital tokens to investors that can be used to purchase future products or services being developed by the issuer. ICOs provide an alternative to traditional, regulated capital-raising processes, such as IPOs. Compared to the regulated IPO market, ICOs might have lower associated issuance costs and shorter capital-raising time frames. However, most ICOs do not typically have attached voting rights. Regulation for ICOs is under consideration in several jurisdictions, and numerous instances of investor loss have resulted from fraudulent schemes.

There are also **utility tokens** that provide services within a network, such as pay for services and network fees. While security tokens may pay out dividends, utility tokens only compensate for activities on the network.

Governance tokens are important in permissionless networks. They serve as votes to determine how particular networks are run. For instance, when there is a technical problem on a permissionless blockchain network, it is the owners of governance tokens who can vote on a solution or any major changes to maintain the stability and integrity of the network.

QUESTION SET

1. Which of the following is *not* a potential benefit of distributed ledger technology?

   A. Facilitation of smart contracts

   B. Energy-efficient way of record keeping

   C. Immutable and secure transaction records

   Solution:

   The correct answer is B. Distributed ledger technology provides greater accuracy, transparency, and security in record keeping; enables faster transfer of ownership; and enables peer-to-peer interactions. A DLT network relies on certain consensus mechanisms in which all nodes that are connected on the network agree on new transactions and ledger updates. Once verified by all the nodes of the network, the transaction ledger is immutable and is kept by each of the nodes. However, the transaction validation process requires material computational power of all the miners on the network, especially in the case of proof-of-work consensus protocol.

2. Identify the following statement as true or false: Prices of cryptocurrencies can be volatile because there are finite limits on the total amount of currencies that may be issued.

   Solution:

   False. Prices of cryptocurrencies have been volatile because there is no consensus on how to value cryptocurrencies. The apparent lack of clear fundamentals underlying these currencies has contributed to their volatility.

3. The process where a node on a blockchain network pledges its digital asset to verify a new block's validity is called:

   A. tokenization.

   B. proof of work.

   C. proof of stake.

   Solution:

   The correct answer is C. This proof-of-stake protocol requires selected participants on a blockchain network, the validators, to pledge digital assets to vouch for the block's validity. This stake signals to the network that a validator is available to verify the veracity of a transaction and propose a block. Other validators who stake a digital asset to the network must then attest to the validity of proposed block. Validators benefit from both proposing and attesting to the validity of blocks that have been proposed by other participants in a similar staking process in the form of new digital assets.

4. Identify the various types of digital assets according to their general classifications:

A. Cryptocurrencies	1. ICO
B. Tokens	2. NFT
	3. CBDC
	4. Ether
	5. Stablecoin
	6. Utility token

Solution:

A. Cryptocurrencies	3. CBDC
	4. Ether
	5. Stablecoin
B. Tokens	1. ICO
	2. NFT
	6. Utility token

3 DIGITAL ASSET INVESTMENT FEATURES

☐ explain investment features of digital assets and contrast them with other asset classes

Digital assets have a growing presence in the financial services industry and have become a more prevalent asset class for investors. Most digital assets are cryptocurrencies, and their growth has been spectacular. While there were around 70 cryptocurrencies recorded in 2013, by early 2022, there were close to 10,000 different cryptocurrencies issued by corporations, organizations, and in many cases, individuals.

Cryptocurrency investment is typically viewed as an alternative asset. As digital assets increase in prominence, some institutional investors selectively seek exposure to these assets for their potential higher returns and possible diversification benefits. When institutional investors become more comfortable with investing in digital assets, it may be a very early indication that the market may be close to reaching a tipping point. As more institutional investors are becoming comfortable with the idea of owning digital assets outright, various financial service providers, such as digital exchanges and custodians, have expanded their infrastructure in anticipation to support potential investment in these digital assets.

Distinguishing Characteristics of Digital Assets

There are notable differences between digital assets and traditional financial assets. The main similarity between these asset types is the emergence of indirect investment vehicles such as exchange-traded funds and hedge funds that invest both in traditional financial assets and in digital assets. The main differences between these asset types are as follows:

- *Differences in inherent value.* Unlike financial assets, most digital assets do not have an inherent value based on underlying assets or on the potential cash flow—interest and dividends—they can or are expected to generate. With no expected earnings to inform today's value and indicate the likely direction for tomorrow's prices, digital assets do not have a fundamental value. They derive their price solely from an anticipated asset appreciation from a perceived scarcity value (due to limitations on the total supply of currency) and the potential ability to transfer value in the future (due to unique features in the underlying algorithms that may facilitate certain types of financial transactions).
- *Differences in validating transactions.* One key difference between digital assets and traditional financial instruments is that traditional assets are generally recorded in private ledgers maintained by central intermediaries. The ownership and exchange of digital assets are generally recorded on a decentralized digital ledger using cryptography and enhanced algorithms. Whether a digital asset transaction is validated in a permissionless or permissioned network using either a PoS or PoW standard impacts its perceived value.
- *Differences in the uses as a medium of exchange.* Financial assets are traditionally priced and traded in widely accepted currencies; they can be readily transacted and exchanged into fiat currencies. Fiat currencies form the foundation of modern financial systems as the mediums of exchange in any country. In contrast, some digital assets—for example, cryptocurrencies, such as Bitcoins—are used as direct substitutes of real-world fiat currencies in certain circumstances—especially for online transactions in the emerging Web3 ecosystem. Web3 is a concept that refers to the third iteration of the internet built on blockchain technologies, decentralization, and token-based economies.
- While many digital assets, such as digital art and NFTs, are transacted and traded using cryptocurrencies, there is only a very limited acceptance of digital assets as a medium of exchange in the mainstream financial system to date. A reason has been the relative cost of the transactions, which can be prohibitively high to meaningfully process a large volume of transactions. While cryptocurrencies are being used to pay for certain goods and services and as investments, they are not legal tender in most jurisdictions and cannot usually be used to legally settle and extinguish debt in the same way as fiat currencies. Finally, the use of cryptocurrencies for payment and investment purposes is severely restricted in multiple countries; some countries have banned its usage outright and digital asset ownership may result in criminal conviction. Some governments are exploring the concept of CBDC as a tokenized version of fiat currencies, but the jury is still out how the idea will evolve.

EXAMPLE 1

Tesla's Acceptance of Bitcoin and Dogecoin

A high-profile supporter of cryptocurrencies and tokens has been Elon Musk, the CEO and major shareholder of Tesla Inc., the electric vehicle automaker. In February 2021, Tesla announced in a public filing that it has invested USD1.5 billion in Bitcoin to diversify its cash balance (of over USD19 billion at the end of 2020). It also indicated it would start accepting Bitcoin as a payment method for its vehicles subject to applicable laws and on a limited basis initially. But in May 2021, the company announced that it had suspended vehicle purchases using Bitcoin, citing concerns about increasing use of fossil fuels for Bitcoin mining and transactions. In July 2021, Musk indicated that Tesla would most likely restart accepting Bitcoin as payments once it had conducted due diligence on the amount of renewable energy used in Bitcoin mining. It resumed accepting Bitcoin; in January 2022, Musk announced that Tesla would start accepting Dogecoin as a payment method for selected brand merchandise. It is now the only cryptocurrency that Tesla accepts for online payment for certain Dogecoin-eligible products.

In July 2022, Tesla announced that it had sold off 75% of its Bitcoin holding as the price had plummeted, but none of its Dogecoin.

- *Differences in legal and regulatory protection.* The rules governing financial instruments and the trading of financial instruments are clear, predictable, and well defined across most jurisdictions. Legal and regulatory standards for traditional financial instruments and assets and trading in these are well developed and are often comparable across national borders; this is not the case with digital assets. Comprehensive rules that are specific to digital assets—their formation, trading, and legal standards—are still being developed. The unclear, ambiguous framework puts digital assets at a disadvantage. US regulators consider certain digital currencies as commodities, and other regulators consider them a non-financial asset. With no comprehensive and clear legal recognition—and protection—for digital assets, their value is highly speculative. Finally, the various exchanges at which digital currencies are traded are typically not regulated as a traditional financial exchange. Therefore, certain market behaviors, such as price manipulation and outright fraud, that are considered to be illegal activities on traditional financial transactions are not necessarily prohibited on a digital exchange. Exhibit 5 shows differences between digital and traditional financial assets.

Exhibit 5: Digital Assets vs. Traditional Financial Assets

	Digital Assets	Traditional Financial Assets
Inherent value	▪ No fundamental value or future cash flow generation ▪ Price driven by certain features on the blockchain	▪ Value determined by future cash flow generated from the assets
Transaction validation	▪ Usually recorded on decentralized digital ledgers using cryptography and algorithms for permissionless blockchain networks	▪ Recorded in private ledgers maintained by central intermediaries

	Digital Assets	Traditional Financial Assets
Uses as a medium of exchange	▪ Very few digital assets are used as a direct medium of exchange, mainly targeting large-scale commercially viable acceptance	▪ Not used directly as a medium of exchange but can be readily transacted and exchanged into traditional fiat currencies that are widely used in the real world
Legal and regulatory protection	▪ Ambiguous, often contradictory, evolving framework; generally unregulated, with minimal legal protections ▪ Use can be illegal or criminal in some countries	▪ Well-established, tested, and proven legal, regulatory, and commercial standards that are clear, predictable, and well defined across all jurisdictions

Investible Digital Assets

The rapid growth of digital assets has been remarkable. That several digital assets and cryptocurrencies exist reflects that their underlying blockchains are designed and optimized for different purposes. The most popular cryptocurrencies are Bitcoin and Ether. Bitcoin and Ether together make up over 80% of total cryptocurrency market value as of July 2022.

Bitcoin (BTC or XBT) and was launched to secure payments in a P2P network. It was designed as an alternative to traditional currencies: as a medium of exchange and store of value. It is the best-known and most widely traded cryptocurrency and its fundamental design continues to influence the development of new types of digital assets. Thousands of other cryptocurrencies exist based on technology similar to Bitcoin: These are called **altcoins**.

Altcoins

The most prominent altcoin is **Ether**, launched in 2015 on its own Ethereum network. Ether involves the added feature of a programmable blockchain that allows users to construct applications using the blockchain to validate or secure transactions or payments for markets or other uses. Ether and other programmable coins therefore have the possibility to be more widely used than simply as a store of value. Such programmable altcoins are also called smart coins or smart contracts, a self-executing contract with the salient terms of the contract directly written into the lines of code, which allows for execution of the contract using the blockchain network. That execution provides a trackable and irreversible record, subject to immutable verification by the nodes of the network. Other altcoins include stablecoins and meme coins.

Stablecoins

Stablecoins are designed to maintain a stable value by linking their value to another asset and are collateralized by a basket of assets, typically legal tender, precious metals, or other cryptocurrencies. The reserve basket protects the holders from price volatility and minimizes the risk to the holders of the stablecoin should the cryptocurrency face transaction problems, including failure. Some stablecoins—smart stablecoins or algorithmic stablecoins—are designed to use algorithms to control the available supply of the asset, such as minting additional assets when there is increased demand for the coin. It is important to note that stablecoins cannot be exchanged for fiat money and do not have any legal or regulatory backing.

Stablecoins may potentially facilitate settlement and streamline cross-border trading, investing, and payments. In recent years, several competing solutions have been developed to facilitate transactions across various physical and tokenized financial assets and instruments using the stablecoin concept. A special example is the **asset-backed token**, which maintains price parity with some target asset (the

US dollar or gold) through tokenization and will be covered later in this module. For an investor holding assets in in a cryptographic wallet, asset-backed tokens provide exposure both to assets that are on the chain (cryptocurrencies and digital assets) and off the chain (financial instruments).

EXAMPLE 2

Market Shakeout of Stablecoins

Stablecoins are designed to track the value of real-world conventional fiat currencies and to provide immediate access to liquidity for traders to redeem their digital stablecoins at par with the value of fiat currencies. Some of these stablecoins are collateralized by financial assets, such as a basket of fiat currencies, gold, Treasuries, and other liquid or illiquid assets. Two of the largest stablecoins in terms of collateral, Tether and USD Coins, use this approach and can either be traded freely on the open market or be redeemed for their dollar value from the issuers.

Another popular stablecoin, Terra, was often called an "algorithmic stablecoin." It was backed not by collateral of financial and physical assets but through an algorithm that sought to keep its value stable.

For instance, TerraUSD was Terra's stablecoin pegged to the US dollar "algorithmically" instead of the value of the underlying collateral in US dollar reserves. The computer algorithm developed by the issuer of Terra, Terraform Labs, used Luna, a governance token also issued by Terraform Labs, to maintain the stability of Terra's value. The relationship between Terra and Luna was designed so that the holders of Terra could always redeem it for a stable value of newly minted Luna coins. If the pricing relationship between Terra and Luna was not in equilibrium, new Luna coins could be issued or existing Luna coins would be destroyed to maintain the value relationship and this algorithmic peg between Terra and Luna. Through financial arbitrage, the stability of Terra's value by trading between Terra and Luna would be held. Effectively, Terra was simply backed by Luna, both bearing a US dollar value.

In May 2022, this relationship was tested. On 9 May, the price of Luna first began to slide, putting pressure on the Terra's peg. Many Terra owners rushed to redeem their coins, leading to a sudden surge in supply of newly issued Luna: In just one week, the number of Luna increased from 350 million coins to 6.5 trillion. Consequently, the price of Luna collapsed, as did that of Terra.

TerraUSD was finally depegged from the US dollar on 9 May 2022. Though Terra's co-founder tried to revive Terra in a reincarnated form of TerraClassicUSD, the stablecoin had since lost its credibility. With its appeal diminished, the coin was practically defunct.

The collapse of Terra sparked serious concern over the collateral backing of its largest stablecoin counterparts, Tether and USD Coins, because of the limited transparency of their reserves. A massive run and redemption by nervous holders of these stablecoins soon followed.

While the "securitized" stablecoins, such as Tether, may have survived market turbulence, other "algorithmic" stablecoins may not when their technical flaws are exploited. Likewise, the value of asset-backed tokens depends on both the underlying assets and the prices of the relevant tokens. An example of Tether is shown in Exhibit 6.

Exhibit 6: Market Price of Tether

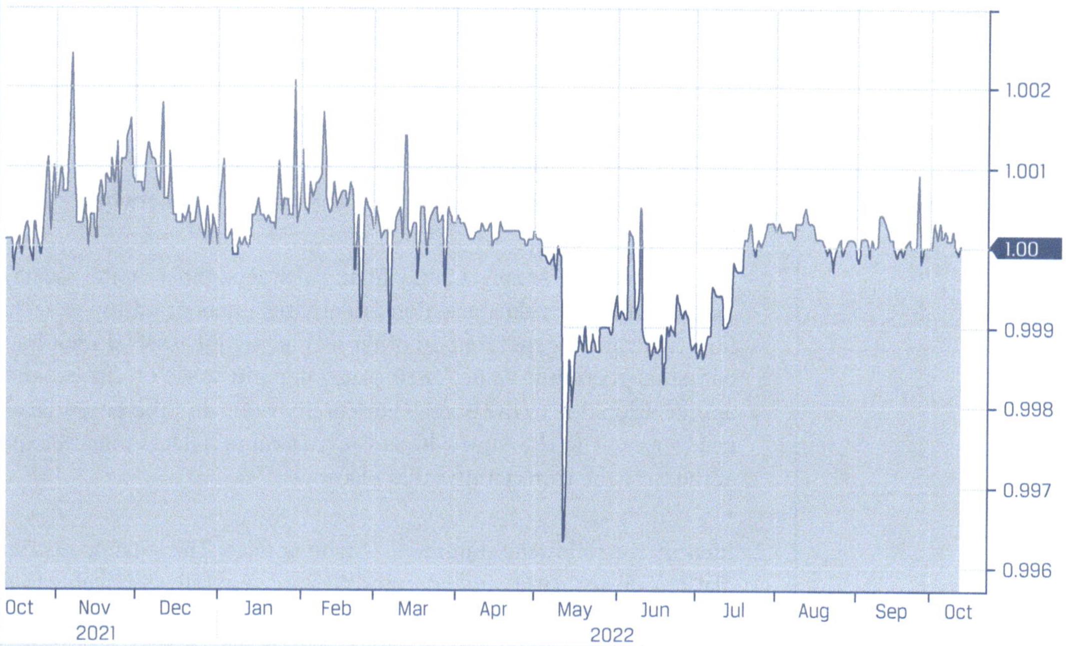

Source: Bloomberg

Meme Coins

Meme coins are cryptocurrencies often inspired by a joke and are generally launched for entertainment purposes as they gain popularity in a short period of time, which allows early purchasers to sell their holdings at an often considerable profit.

EXAMPLE 3

Meme Coins—The History of Dogecoin

The original and probably most popular meme coin is Dogecoin, which is based on the popular "doge" internet meme. Dogecoin, featuring a Shiba Inu dog on its logo, was originally founded in 2013 as a mockery of the popularity of cryptocurrencies, mainly Bitcoin. Even the name "dog" was misspelled as "doge" as part of a light-hearted parody.

While some cryptocurrencies are scarce by design, Dogecoins were intentionally designed to have no limit in supply. But what started as a joke soon gained popularity among fervent followers as a cult symbol, especially after social media endorsements by some high-profile business figures. At its peak in May 2021, Dogecoin's market value had jumped to over USD80 billion. However, the price and market cap of Dogecoins plummeted as investors and speculators dumped these coins because their value seemed hardly justifiable. By May 2022, its market dropped to USD11 billion.

QUESTION SET

1. The market value of a digital asset is primarily driven by:

   A. the future price expectation of speculators.

   B. the future earnings generated from the digital assets.

   C. the cryptographic algorithm of the blockchain network.

   Solution:

   The correct answer is A. Unlike financial assets, most digital assets do not have an inherent value based on underlying assets or on the expected cash flow that can be generated. In other words, digital assets do not have a fundamental economic value. Their prices depend solely on the expected asset appreciation due to the perceived scarcity value and the potential ability to transfer value in the future; however, that value reflects market expectations at the time the transaction takes place.

2. Identify the following statement as true or false: The legal protection regulations on securities and commodities are generally applicable to digital assets.

   Solution:

   False. Whereas legal and regulatory standards for traditional financial instruments are well developed, legally tested, and proven; widely and uniformly enforceable; and often comparable across different jurisdictions and legal systems, comprehensive rules that are specific to digital assets—their formation, trading, and legal standards—are being developed. Additionally, the various digital exchanges on which digital currencies are traded are typically not as heavily regulated as traditional financial markets. Consequently, certain irregular market behaviors, such as price manipulation and outright fraud, are not always prohibited on a digital exchange.

3. The ownership and exchange of digital assets on permissionless networks are usually recorded on a:

   A. centralized ledger maintained by a central intermediary.

   B. decentralized ledger maintained by a central intermediary.

   C. decentralized ledger without any central intermediary.

   Solution:

   The correct answer is C. The ownership and exchange of digital assets on permissionless networks are generally recorded on a distributed (i.e., decentralized) digital ledger using cryptography and enhanced algorithms without the use of any central intermediary.

4. Compare and contrast the main types of stablecoins.

   Solution:

   The traditional type of stablecoin, or "securitized stablecoin," is backed by physical collateral of fiat currencies, precious metals, or other financial assets as reserves for every stablecoin issued. Each coin can be traded freely on the open market or redeemed for its dollar value from the issuer by liquidating the collateral. A special example of the stablecoin is the asset-backed token, which maintains price parity with some target asset—for example, the US dollar or gold—through tokenization.

Another unique type of stablecoin is called a "smart stablecoin" or an "algorithmic stablecoin," because there is no backing of physical assets for the cryptocurrency. Rather, its value is backed by another cryptocurrency or token and is linked to the US dollar "algorithmically" instead of using actual dollar reserves.

DIGITAL ASSET INVESTMENT FORMS

4

☐ describe investment forms and vehicles used in digital asset investments

Investment in digital assets can take the form of direct investment on the blockchain or indirect investments in exchange-traded products and hedge funds. Direct ownership of Bitcoin and other cryptocurrencies involves the use of a **cryptocurrency wallet**, which stores the (public and private) digital codes required to access the asset on a computer website or mobile device application. Two different types of cryptocurrency exchanges exist.

- *Centralized exchanges* are the most popular type of exchange. These privately held exchanges provide trading platforms for cryptocurrencies and offer volume, liquidity, and price transparency. Although the concept of centralized exchanges is incompatible with Bitcoin's decentralized ideology, they are very popular. Trading is electronic and direct, without any intermediating broker or dealer, and is hosted on private servers, exposing the centralized exchanges and their clients to security vulnerabilities. Should the exchange's servers become compromised, the entire system may become paralyzed, halting trade, and leaking vital user information—such as cryptographic keys accessing the custodial wallets leaked. Some exchanges are regulated, and depending on jurisdiction, these exchanges may be regulated as financial exchanges or other types of financial intermediaries.
- *Decentralized exchanges* emulate blockchain's decentralized protocol and operate similarly to how Bitcoin operates. Decentralized exchanges lack a centralized control mechanism and operate on a distributed platform without central coordination or control. This comes with the benefit that should one of the computers on the network be attacked, the exchange remains operational since there are numerous other computers that continue to operate on the network. That is why attacking decentralized exchanges is substantially more difficult, rendering such attacks almost certain to fail. Decentralized exchanges are difficult to regulate because no single individual, organization, or group controls the system. This means that those trading on decentralized exchanges are generally free to transact without any regulatory scrutiny, allowing for potentially illegal activity.

Both centralized and decentralized exchanges may face problems with fraud and manipulation and raise investor-protection concerns because they are not subject to rigorous oversight. Unlike the exchanges for more traditional assets, such as equity securities and futures contracts, cryptocurrency and cryptocurrency trading venues are largely unregulated, and individuals or groups may engage in fraud or market manipulation (including using social media to promote cryptocurrencies in a way that artificially increases the price of a cryptocurrency).

EXAMPLE 4

Pump and Dump Schemes of Cryptocurrencies

In a typical pump and dump scheme, earlier investors of an asset talk it up to encourage others to buy, pushing the price up. When the price is high enough, the scheme orchestrators quickly realize profits and dump the asset in the market, leaving unknowing investors with often steep trading losses. Given the hype around cryptocurrencies and the unregulated nature of the digital assets, pump and dump schemes are widespread.

EthereumMax (EMAX) is a digital token created on the Ethereum blockchain in May 2021, but it has no other connection to Ethereum. Touted as a "culture coin" that "bridges the gap between community-driven coins and foundational coins," it was endorsed and heavily promoted by pop celebrities and famous sports stars just a month after it came into being. The price of EMAX rose sharply, with frenzied buying likely fueled by receiving heavy social media exposure. Its ascent was rapid, but its descent was faster: After one month, it had lost almost all its value and the interest in trading in it disappeared. It was then alleged that EMAX was a classic example of the typical pump and dump scheme. Subsequent legal action against the celebrities endorsing and "pumping" EMAX with false and misleading statements alleged that this scheme allowed EMAX executives to dump their holdings of EMAX for substantial profit while leaving other investors with worthless tokens.

EXAMPLE 5

FTX Bankruptcy

FTX, a Bahamas-based cryptocurrency exchange that also owns FTX.US (available to US investors), grew rapidly after its founding in 2019.

As a centralized exchange for spot cryptocurrency and stablecoins, as well as futures, FTX became one of the largest such exchanges. It also provided custodial and transaction services. In 2021, it had 1.2 million users and generated over USD 1 billion in revenue. Like many digital currency exchanges, FTX issues an exchange token (FTT), a form of utility token used on its platform by market participants. As FTT may be borrowed or lent—and grants holders a discount on FTX trading fees—it represents some value (shown in Exhibit 7).

FTX has been funded by several successive rounds of venture capital (VC) investments, raising USD 400 million from VC firms and a major pension fund. In January 2022, FTX was valued at USD 31.6 billion.

FTX was considered to be a relatively stable and trusted alternative among digital currency exchanges. In 2022, declining cryptocurrency prices and rising interest rates created liquidity pressures for FTX and other cryptocurrency market participants.

This growing liquidity stress was compounded by reports that FTX and Alameda Research, a quantitative trading firm controlled by FTX's founder, held significant collateral assets in illiquid investments, including FTX-related assets. On 2 November 2022, a *Coindesk* article cited close ties between FTX and Alameda Research and noted that Alameda Research held over a third of its

USD 14.6 billion balance sheet either directly in FTT or as FTT-based collateral. This revelation prompted an FTT selloff by investors and customer withdrawals, with the FTT price falling from over USD 25 to around USD 1 in just over a week, as Exhibit 7 shows. On 11 November 2022, FTX filed for bankruptcy.

Exhibit 7: FTT Digital Token Price (USD), January–November 2022

Source: Bloomberg.

In its bankruptcy filing, FTX listed USD 9 billion in liabilities, with liquid investments comprising just USD 900 million of total assets. The number of creditors exceeds 100,000.

EXAMPLE 6

Ponzi Scheme Allegation over Forsage

A Ponzi scheme is an investment scam that typically involves the distribution of high returns to existing investors not from any real investment but from funds contributed by new investors. A variant of the Ponzi scheme is the pyramid Ponzi scheme, in which each level of schemers lures new investors in by promising high returns from investment opportunities that are usually fabricated. The new funds then go in to pay back the "returns" one level up. In effect, the "returns" earned by the earlier investors at the top are paid for by the cash contribution from the different levels of new investors.

Launched in January 2020, Forsage ran a decentralized blockchain platform that purportedly enabled online businesses to transact through smart contracts based on Ethereum, Tron, and Binance networks. But in August 2022, the US Securities and Exchange Commission (SEC) laid charges against 11 individuals, including the four founders based in Russia, Georgia, and Indonesia and certain US promoters, for investment fraud. The SEC alleged that Forsage operated a typical fraudulent crypto pyramid and Ponzi scheme that raised more than USD300 million from retail investors worldwide, helped by heavy endorsement and marketing by promoters on social media.

Direct Digital Asset Investment Forms

Direct investments in digital assets are made on various digital exchanges where the transaction is recorded on the blockchain. Once such a transaction is entered between the parties, it becomes validated on the blockchain and a permanent record of the transaction is created. Most cryptocurrency exchanges are open and available 24/7, which allows for continuous trading.

There are several risks with direct investment in cryptocurrencies. First, there is the risk for fraud, which has increased with the popularity of cryptocurrencies. Such fraud comes in many forms and includes scam ICOs, various pump and dump schemes, market manipulation, theft, and schemes that seek to gain access to credentials needed to access cryptocurrency wallet information. Second, since cryptocurrencies are usually held in a wallet that is accessible only using a unique passkey, losing access to the passkey makes the holdings in the wallet irretrievable. Around 20% of all Bitcoins are reportedly in lost or deserted wallets that their owners cannot access.

Moreover, many of the smaller cryptocurrencies may be held primarily by a small number of holders, sometimes referred to as "whales." "Whales" is jargon used by the cryptocurrency community to mean individuals or entities that hold an amount of a cryptocurrency large enough to have the ability to manipulate the price.

EXAMPLE 7

Cryptocurrency Whales

It was reported in mid-2022 that big investors on the Ethereum blockchain were accumulating the newly created meme coin, Shiba Inu (SHIB), a close competitor to Dogecoin. According to Whalestats, the crypto whale-watching platform, by August 2022, 41% of SHIB were "burned" (sent to "dead wallets" and effectively taken out of circulation). However, the next top 10 SHIB holders were estimated to be holding around 21%–23% of the total tokens (or 36%–39% of total coins in circulation). This might have allowed those "whales" to easily influence the price of SHIB. A glimpse into the trading volume might offer a hint about the effect on price action in a thin trading market environment, when the average daily trading volume was less than 10% of the total SHIB tokens. Exhibit 8 shows data on SHIB's price and trading volume.

Exhibit 8: Price Action and Trading Volume in Shiba Inu

Indirect Digital Asset Investment Forms

Several alternatives exist to gain indirect exposure to digital assets, including the following:

- *Cryptocurrency coin trusts* allow investors to trade shares in trusts holding large pools of a cryptocurrency and that trade over the counter (OTC) and behave like closed-end funds. For an investor in a coin trust, there is no need to create a digital wallet and use encryption keys to invest in cryptocurrencies. Additionally, the trusts may provide additional transparency into trading. The trusts charge substantial fees and expenses, in some cases in excess of 2%, and may trade at a premium or discount to their net asset values.
- *Cryptocurrency futures* contracts are agreements to buy or sell a specific quantity of Bitcoin or other cryptocurrency at a specified price on a particular future date. For instance, trading in Bitcoin futures on the Chicago Mercantile Exchange (CME) is based on the CME CF Bitcoin Reference Rate, which tracks the price of spot Bitcoin trading on cryptocurrency exchanges. Unlike physical commodities, these contracts are typically cash settled, with no actual cryptocurrency changing hands. Trading in futures is inherently leveraged. The market for cryptocurrency futures may be less developed and potentially less liquid and more volatile than more established futures markets.

- *Cryptocurrency exchange-traded funds:* An increasing number of exchange-traded products, such as ETFs, seek to replicate digital asset investment returns. These ETFs typically do not directly invest in cryptocurrencies and gain exposure to the value of cryptocurrencies using cash and cryptocurrency derivatives.

Baywhite Financial Cryptocurrency ETF (Fund) Term Sheet

Fund description	The Fund is designed to provide investment results that generally correspond to the performance of major traded cryptocurrencies. It offers investors a convenient way to incorporate a rapidly growing digital asset into their portfolios as an alternative to traditional investments. The Fund does not invest directly in Bitcoin or other cryptocurrencies.
Fund investment strategy	The Fund seeks to provide capital appreciation primarily through managed exposure to cryptocurrency futures contracts. The Fund does not invest directly in cryptocurrencies. The value of cryptocurrencies is not backed by any government, corporation, or other identified body authorized to legally issue currency. Instead, its value is determined in part by the supply and demand in markets created to facilitate trading of cryptocurrencies. Ownership and transaction records for cryptocurrencies are protected through public-key cryptography. The supply of cryptocurrencies is typically determined by protocols that are unique to each specific cryptocurrency. The Fund may also invest in *Cryptocurrency futures contracts*, standardized, cash-settled cryptocurrency futures contracts traded on exchanges *Money market instruments*, such as short-term cash instruments with high-quality credit profiles, including short-term government debt and repurchase agreements
Fund trading	The Fund is bought and sold through a brokerage account, eliminating the need for a cryptocurrency exchange account or wallet.
Fund expenses	Annual Fund operating expenses are 1.50% of NAV.
Additional considerations	The Fund is non-diversified, with the ability to invest a relatively high percentage of its assets in financial instruments with a single counterparty or a few counterparties. Cryptocurrencies and cryptocurrency futures are relatively new investments. They are subject to unique and substantial risks and historically have been subject to significant price volatility. The value of an investment in the Fund could decline significantly and without warning, including to zero.

- *Cryptocurrency stocks* provide indirect exposure due to their activity and relationship to digital assets. Examples include equity in publicly traded digital exchanges; payment providers accepting cryptocurrencies; corporations accepting cryptocurrencies as payments, investing in cryptocurrencies, or mining cryptocurrencies; and corporations developing and/or manufacturing products or services that are used for running blockchain networks, such as specialized computers used for mining.
- *Hedge funds investing in cryptocurrencies*, such as discretionary long, long/short, quantitative, and multi-strategy, have emerged as a major source of indirect digital asset investing. Several hedge funds actively mine for Bitcoin to generate further returns.

Sequester Capital LLC Crypto Hedge Fund ("Fund") Term Sheet

Fund description	The Fund is designed to provide investment results that generally correspond to the performance of major traded cryptocurrencies. The Fund invests directly in multiple cryptocurrencies.
Fund investment strategy	The Fund uses a combination of common hedge fund strategies, including quantitatively driven trading strategies, discretionary long/short positions, and discretionary long-only positions in cryptocurrencies and other digital assets. The Fund invests in multiple cryptocurrencies, including Bitcoin, Ether, Litecoin, Cardano, Solana, and Polkadot. Additionally, the Fund trades in cryptocurrency derivatives and may from time to time take speculative short positions in certain cryptocurrencies that it believes to be overvalued. The Fund may engage in lending and borrowing cryptocurrencies.

Digital Forms of Investment for Non-Digital Assets

These represent similar digital forms of investment with an underlying *non-digital* asset from which the investment derives its value.

A recent development is asset-backed tokens, digital claims on physical assets, financial assets, or financial instruments that are collateralized by the underlying asset and derive their value directly from the underlying asset. Asset-backed tokens are a digital representation of the ownership. Tokenized assets include gold, crude oil, real estate, and equities.

Asset-backed tokens could increase liquidity by allowing for fractional ownership of high-priced assets, such as houses, art, precious metals, and precious stones, which allows multiple investors to possess a fractional interest of the same asset. The digital representation of the ownership allows for an immutable record of ownership information and ownership transfer, which increases the transparency of these transactions and reduces transaction, intermediation, and record-keeping costs.

Financial regulators typically classify asset-backed tokens as securities, as the ownership of the token entitles the holder to an ownership interest in the underlying asset.

Asset-backed tokens are often issued on the Ethereum network or other smart contract platforms that allow for peer-to-peer interaction using interoperable, transparent smart contracts that persist for the duration of the chain. These decentralized applications, or dApps, allow for transactions to take place—and to be recorded on the blockchain—without a central coordinating mechanism.

The push for financial decentralized applications grew into a movement known as decentralized finance, or DeFi. DeFi seeks to design, combine, and develop various open-source financial applications as building blocks for sophisticated financial products and services. Effectively, DeFi is a marketplace of dApps that are designed to perform various core financial functions, including potentially acting as a medium of exchange, storage of value, tokenization of underlying assets, and immutable record keeping of ownership and transfer of ownership. Effectively, all kinds of smart contracts can be embedded in dApps to handle nearly all aspects of the traditional financial system, such as lending, trading, investment, settlement, payment, and transfer in a decentralized, authenticated and instantaneous manner. Some advocates of DeFi argue that the modern blockchain ecosystem may have more technical advantages over the traditional finance system—for example, time saving and risk reduction in settlement and asset transfer. However, the nascent idea of DeFi is yet to be fully developed. To date, most dApps have centered around extending leverage to investment and speculation in digital assets.

QUESTION SET

1. Compare and contrast centralized cryptocurrency exchanges and decentralized cryptocurrency exchanges.

Solution:

- *Centralized exchanges* are privately held. They provide trading platforms for cryptocurrencies and offer volume, liquidity, and price transparency. Trading is electronic and direct, without any intermediating broker or dealer, and is hosted on private servers, exposing the centralized exchanges and their clients to security vulnerabilities. Should the exchange's servers be attacked, the entire system may be compromised, halting trade, and leaking vital user information. Depending on jurisdiction, some centralized exchanges are regulated as financial exchanges or other types of financial intermediaries.
- *Decentralized exchanges* emulate blockchain's decentralized protocol. Decentralized exchanges lack a centralized control mechanism and operate on a distributed platform without central coordination or control. The benefit is that should one of the computers on the network be attacked, the exchange remains operational since there are numerous other computers that continue to operate on the network. That is why decentralized exchanges are substantially less susceptible to computer hacks. Decentralized exchanges are difficult to regulate because no single individual, organization, or group controls the system. Therefore those trading on decentralized exchanges are generally free of any regulatory scrutiny, allowing for potentially illegal activity.

2. Identify the direct and indirect forms of investment in digital assets:

A. Direct investment	1. Cryptocurrency ETF
B. Indirect investment	2. Cryptocurrency coin trust
	3. Initial coin offering
	4. Hedge fund investing in digital tokens
	5. Buying a digital art NFT
	6. Trading cryptocurrency stocks
	7. Trading tokens on a cryptocurrency exchange
	8. Buying Bitcoin futures on a futures exchange

Solution:

A. Direct investment	3. Initial coin offering
	5. Buying a digital art NFT
	7. Trading tokens on a cryptocurrency exchange
B. Indirect investment	1. Cryptocurrency ETF
	2. Cryptocurrency coin trust
	4. Hedge fund investing in digital tokens
	6. Trading cryptocurrency stocks,
	8. Buying Bitcoin futures on a futures exchange.

3. Which of the following is *not* a risk in direct investment in digital assets?

   A. Market manipulation

   B. Pump and dump schemes

   C. Failure to validate asset transfers

   Solution:

   The correct answer is C. There are several risks with direct investment in cryptocurrencies, including the risk for fraud, such as scam ICOs, pump and dump schemes, market manipulation, theft, and schemes that seek to gain access to credentials needed to access cryptocurrency wallet information. However, transactions in digital assets such as cryptocurrencies and tokens are verified and authenticated by cryptographical algorithms and consensus protocols. Once a transaction is entered between the parties, it becomes validated on the blockchain and creates a permanent record of the transaction. Therefore, the DLT technology makes it very unlikely to fail validating asset transfers.

4. Determine the correct answers to fill in the blanks: DeFi is loosely defined as a marketplace for ________________ that allows for financial transactions to take place and to be recorded on the ________________ without a central coordinating mechanism. DeFi seeks to design, combine, and develop various ____________________ as building blocks for sophisticated financial products and services.

   Solution:

   DeFi is loosely defined as a marketplace for *dApps (or decentralized applications)* that allow for financial transactions to take place and to be recorded on the *blockchain* without a central coordinating mechanism. DeFi seeks to design, combine, and develop various *open-source financial applications* as building blocks for sophisticated financial products and services.

DIGITAL ASSET INVESTMENT RISK, RETURN, AND DIVERSIFICATION 5

☐ analyze sources of risk, return, and diversification among digital asset investments

Value appreciation of digital assets, such as Bitcoin and Ethereum, has been rapid since inception, most recently fueled by the introduction of more traditional indirect forms of investment. Because cryptocurrencies are a relatively new innovation, their market is subject to rapid price swings, changes, and uncertainty, with most investors considering them alternative investments.

Digital Asset Investment Risks and Returns

Bitcoin and other cryptocurrency values are based solely on asset appreciation, with no underlying cash flows. The market demand for the limited supply of cryptocurrencies is a significant driver of prices. For instance, the supply of Bitcoin is limited to 21 million Bitcoins, by design. For this reason, Bitcoins are sometimes viewed by some investors as the digital version of gold.

Since its launch in 2009, Bitcoin's performance has been characterized by high return, high volatility, and low correlations with traditional asset classes, as seen in Exhibit 9 and Exhibit 10.

Exhibit 9: Monthly Log-Returns for Bitcoin and Asset Class Benchmarks between January 2011 and January 2022

	Bitcoin in USD	S&P 500 Index Total Return	MSCI World Index Return	Bloomberg Global Aggregate Index
Average	8.84%	1.13%	0.66%	0.16%
Standard deviation	0.32	0.04	0.04	0.01
Coefficient of variation	3.66	3.43	6.09	8.16

Notes: Bitcoin price in US dollars, S&P 500 Total Return, MSCI World Index, and Bloomberg Global Aggregate Bond Index are log-returns for January 2011 to December 2022. All series are in US dollars.

From mid-2010, when publicly available market prices were available, Bitcoin price has risen from USD0.05 at inception to the historical peak of USD68,789 on 10 November 2021, before a subsequent crash took it down to around USD17,709 on 18 June 2022. Early investors in Bitcoins were hugely rewarded with phenomenal price appreciation.

Investing in cryptocurrencies therefore comes with material risks unique to digital assets. Cryptocurrencies have a relatively brief track record, yet their volatility has remained high, as Exhibit 10 shows. Although the volatility of Bitcoin has declined, it is still much higher than the volatility of traditional financial assets, such as the S&P 500 Index.

Exhibit 10: Distribution of Monthly Log-Returns for Bitcoin and Asset Class Benchmarks between January 2011 and January 2022

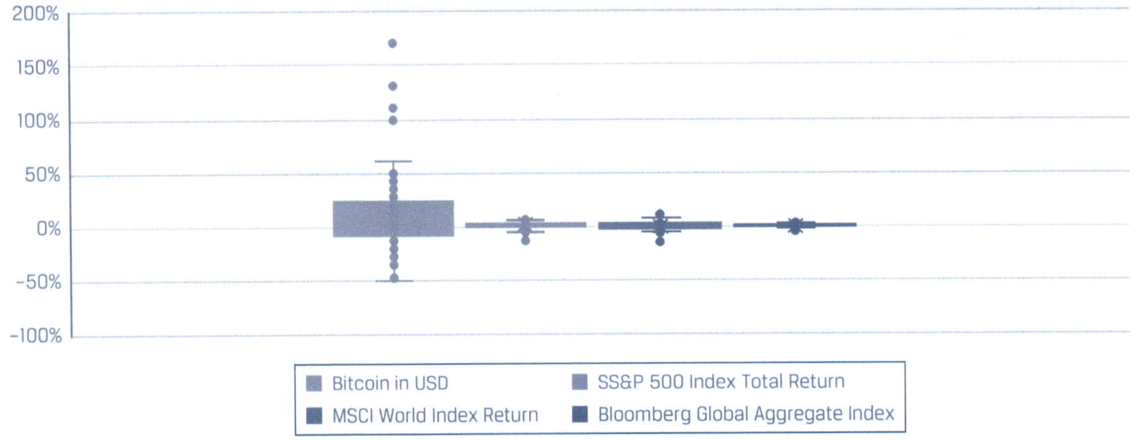

Notes: Bitcoin price in US dollars, S&P 500 Total Return, MSCI World Index, and Bloomberg Global Aggregate Bond Index are log-returns for January 2011 to January 2022. All series are in US dollars.

Bitcoin-like price and return patterns are often observed in other cryptocurrencies and may reflect a great deal of uncertainty about cryptocurrencies as an investable asset class. Given that regulation of cryptocurrencies is evolving, there still is no clear legal protection for using them as a medium of exchange. While they are regulated as a digital commodity in the United States and comprehensive rules in the EU remain pending, there is a great deal of uncertainty from an investor perspective about the quality of legal protection an investor can enjoy when investing in these assets. Considering that fraud and criminal activities are rampant among buyers, sellers, issuers, and marketers of digital assets, the continued legal and regulatory uncertainty is non-trivial. Multiple countries have placed extensive restrictions on trading and owning cryptocurrencies, such as China, which banned the asset in 2021.

Diversification Benefits of Digital Asset Investments

Although purely speculative in nature, considered by some to have value drivers distinct from common equity and debt markets, cryptocurrencies have exhibited low correlations with traditional asset class returns. This may provide a hint that the long-term determinants of cryptocurrency prices differ from those of traditional investment assets. In practice, prices (or returns) of cryptocurrencies are driven more by market adoption, network effects, technological advancement, regulatory development, speculation, and general market risk appetite. Some of these factors are unique to this asset class. Exhibit 11 shows the monthly correlation of Bitcoin with some benchmarks.

Exhibit 11: Correlations between Monthly Log-Returns for Cryptocurrencies and Selected Asset Classes (January 2011 to January 2022)

	Bitcoin in US Dollars	S&P 500 Index Total Return	MSCI World Index Return	Bloomberg Global Aggregate Index
Bitcoin in US dollars	1			
S&P 500 Index Total Return	0.21	1		
MSCI World Index Return	0.22	0.97	1	
Bloomberg Global Aggregate Index	0.14	0.25	0.33	1

Notes: Bitcoin price in US dollars, S&P 500 Total Return, MSCI World Index, and Bloomberg Global Aggregate Bond Index are log-returns for January 2011 to January 2022. All series are in US dollars.

In this way, cryptocurrencies are potential portfolio diversifiers. The correlation of cryptocurrencies with traditional assets appears to increase, and the correlation and diversification benefits of cryptocurrencies remain to be seen.

QUESTION SET

1. More institutional investors are allocating capital to cryptocurrencies because of their:

   A. low price volatility.

   B. high expected cash flow.

   C. low correlation with other traditional asset classes.

   Solution:

   The correct answer is C. The value of Bitcoin and other cryptocurrencies is based solely on asset appreciation, with no underlying cash flows. Historically, their price volatility has been extremely high. As such, cryptocurrencies are often considered a high-risk investment. Nevertheless, more institutional investors allocate their investment into cryptocurrencies because of the low historical correlation with other traditional asset classes, providing potential diversification benefits to a portfolio.

2. Explain the historical characteristics of cryptocurrencies' correlation with other traditional investments.

   Solution:

   Cryptocurrencies have historically exhibited low long-term correlations with traditional asset class returns. Prices of cryptocurrencies are driven more by market adoption, network effects, technological advancement, regulatory development, and general market risk appetite. Some of these factors are unique to this asset class. But as institutional participation increases in digital assets, the correlations with traditional assets have risen.

3. Identify the following statement as true or false: Regulatory uncertainty is a non-trivial risk for investors in cryptocurrencies.

   Solution:

   True. Regulatory uncertainty is a non-trivial risk for investors in cryptocurrencies because there is considerable risk of fraud and criminal activity among participants, and legal protection over these assets remains uncertain. Regulation of cryptocurrencies is evolving; some countries have adopted them, while some have banned them altogether.

PRACTICE PROBLEMS

1. A benefit of distributed ledger technology (DLT) that increases its use by the investment industry is its:

   A. scalability of underlying systems.

   B. ease of integration with existing systems.

   C. streamlining of current post-trade processes.

2. What is a DLT application suited for physical assets?

   A. Tokenization

   B. Cryptocurrencies

   C. Permissioned networks

3. A cryptocurrency miner can earn new digital assets by:

   A. solving complex algorithm puzzles to validate blocks of transactions onto a blockchain network based on a PoS protocol.

   B. staking his own cryptocurrencies to validate blocks of transactions onto a blockchain network based on a PoW protocol.

   C. validating and locking transactions onto a blockchain irrespective of the consensus protocol adopted by the particular network.

4. The perceived value of a cryptocurrency depends on the following factors *except*:

   A. the maximum supply of the cryptocurrencies.

   B. the underlying cash flow of the cryptocurrencies.

   C. whether the relevant blockchain operates on a permissionless or permissioned network.

5. A key difference between digital assets and traditional financial assets is that:

   A. digital assets are usually subject to a well-defined set of regulations.

   B. transactions in digital assets are most likely kept on private centralized ledgers.

   C. digital assets are valued not on their earnings but on the expected price appreciation given supply limitation.

6. Asset-backed tokens have the potential of improving the liquidity of the underlying assets because:

   A. they allow for fractional ownership of high-value assets.

   B. costs of validating the transactions are reduced on the blockchains.

   C. they make it easier to trade the underlying assets on centralized exchanges.

7. Which of the following is the least vulnerable to a computer security hack?
   - **A.** Cryptocurrency wallets
   - **B.** Centralized cryptocurrency exchanges
   - **C.** Decentralized cryptocurrency exchanges

8. An investor who wants to replicate the return on Bitcoins without the use of a digital wallet can *best* do so by:
   - **A.** investing in a cryptocurrency coin trust that holds Bitcoins.
   - **B.** investing in a listed cryptocurrency exchange stock.
   - **C.** buying Bitcoins from a centralized cryptocurrency exchange.

9. Which of the following is a key building block of dApps?
   - **A.** Bitcoins
   - **B.** Smart contracts
   - **C.** Centralized exchanges

10. Compared to traditional equity investment, the historical return distribution of Bitcoins shows:
    - **A.** negative skewness.
    - **B.** high mean returns.
    - **C.** low standard deviation.

11. Despite higher volatility, cryptocurrencies may offer diversification benefits to an investment portfolio due to their:
    - **A.** scarcity value.
    - **B.** expected higher return.
    - **C.** lower correlation with other traditional investments.

12. Price volatility of cryptocurrencies is high most likely because they are:
    - **A.** subject to self-imposed limit on supply.
    - **B.** correlated with traditional risky asset classes.
    - **C.** highly speculative with no fundamental value or cash flow.

SOLUTIONS

1. The correct answer is C. DLT has the potential to streamline the existing, often complex and labor-intensive post-trade processes in securities markets by providing close to real-time trade verification, reconciliation, and settlement, thereby reducing related complexity, time, and costs.

2. The correct answer is A. Through tokenization—the process of representing ownership rights to physical assets on a blockchain or distributed ledger—DLT has the potential to streamline this rights process by creating a single digital record of ownership with which to verify ownership title and authenticity, including all historical activity.

3. The correct answer is C. Under both PoW and PoS consensus protocols, the validation of the transactions, or "mining," always comes with rewards. A successful miner that validates the transactions obtains new digital assets—either a cryptocurrency or a token. For blockchain networks based on the PoW protocol, the miner earns his digital assets by solving complex algorithm puzzles to validate blocks of transactions onto a blockchain network. For blockchain networks based on the PoS protocol, the miner earns his digital assets by staking his own to validate and attest to the new blocks of transactions.

4. The correct answer is B. A cryptocurrency derives its price solely from an anticipated asset appreciation given the perceived scarcity value arising from a self-imposed limit of supply. Whether a cryptocurrency transaction is validated in a permissionless or permissioned network using either PoS or PoW standard also impacts its perceived value. But most digital assets do not have an inherent value based on underlying assets or on the potential cash flow.

5. The correct answer is C. Unlike traditional financial assets, most digital assets do not have an inherent value based on underlying assets or the potential cash flow or earnings they are expected to generate. Digital asset transactions are usually kept on decentralized digital ledgers using cryptography and algorithms without any central intermediaries. Regulations around digital assets are also ambiguous and evolving, unlike most traditional financial assets, which are subject to a well-defined set of regulations.

6. The correct answer is A. Asset-backed tokens can increase liquidity by allowing for fractional ownership of high-priced assets, such as houses, art, precious metals, and precious stones, which allows multiple investors to possess a fractional interest of the same asset. B is incorrect because the validation of transactions on the blockchains takes up a substantial amount of computing power, which can be expensive.

7. The correct answer is C. Decentralized exchanges operate on a distributed platform without central coordination or control. The benefit is that should one of the computers on the network be attacked, the exchange remains operational since there are numerous other computers that continue to operate on the network. For this reason, decentralized exchanges are substantially more difficult to hack, rendering such attacks almost certain to fail. However, transactions on centralized cryptocurrency exchanges are hosted on private servers, exposing the centralized exchanges and their clients to security vulnerabilities. Should the exchange's servers become compromised, the entire system may become paralyzed, halting trade and leaking vital user information, such as cryptographic keys stored in the cryptocurrency wallets.

8. The correct answer is A. Investing in a cryptocurrency coin trust that holds Bitcoins is the best way to replicate the return on Bitcoins. Investing in a listed cryptocurrency exchange stock provides very indirect exposure that may not necessarily replicate the performance of Bitcoins because of a variety of company-specific factors, as well as the sensitivity to the general stock market environment. Buying Bitcoins from a centralized cryptocurrency exchange provides a direct exposure, but it would require a digital wallet.

9. The correct answer is B. Smart contracts are the building block of dApps. dApps are usually developed on the Ethereum blockchain network or other smart contract platforms that allow for peer-to-peer interaction using interoperable, transparent smart contracts that persist for the duration of the chain. These decentralized applications, or dApps, allow for transactions to take place—and to be recorded on the blockchain—without a central coordinating mechanism or centralized exchange.

10. The correct answer is B. Historical Bitcoin returns are characterized by high mean returns and high standard deviation. Despite the high volatility, the return distribution is positively skewed.

11. The correct answer is C. Although purely speculative in nature, cryptocurrencies have historically exhibited low correlations with traditional asset class returns and are considered to have value drivers distinct from common equity and debt markets. Therefore, cryptocurrencies are potential diversifiers of an investment portfolio.

12. The correct answer is C. Cryptocurrencies are purely speculative, with no fundamental value or future cash flow. There is no consensus on how to value them. Their markets are therefore subject to rapid price swings, changes, and uncertainty. But historically, their performance has relatively low correlations with traditional asset classes.

Glossary

Abandonment option The option to terminate an investment at some future time if the financial results are disappointing.

Abnormal return The amount by which a security's actual return differs from its expected return, given the security's risk and the market's return.

Absolute dispersion The amount of variability present without comparison to any reference point or benchmark.

Accelerated book build An offering of securities by an investment bank acting as principal that is accomplished in only one or two days.

Accounting profit Income as reported on the income statement, in accordance with prevailing accounting standards, before the provisions for income tax expense. Also called *income before taxes* or *pretax income*.

Accredited investors Investors that meet certain minimum regulatory net worth or other requirements in order to invest in certain types of alternative assets.

Accrued interest The amount of interest in currency or par value terms of a fixed-income instrument that accumulates from the last coupon payment until the trade settlement date. The amount is paid by the buyer to the seller.

Action lag Delay from policy decisions to implementation.

Active investment An approach to investing in which the investor seeks to outperform a given benchmark.

Active return The return on a portfolio minus the return on the portfolio's benchmark.

Activist Short for "activist shareholder." Managers secure sufficient equity holdings to allow them to seek a position in a company's board and influence corporate policies or direction.

Activity ratios Ratios that measure how well a company is managing key current assets and working capital over time.

Ad hoc committee A small group of lenders or bondholders who negotiate with an issuer on debt restructuring and refinancing before the issuer submits a final proposal to the wider group of all lenders and bondholders.

Add-on pricing A pricing approach based on high-margin optional features, customizations, and additional content.

Add-on rate A yield or pricing convention for money market instrument quotations. It is the interest earned on an instrument, derived from the difference between the price and face value, expressed as a percentage of the price and multiplied by the periodicity of the annual rate.

Agency costs Direct and indirect costs borne by the principal in a principal-agent relationship owing primarily to information asymmetries. Agency costs include the costs of monitoring and assessing the agent as well as missed opportunities.

Agency RMBS Securities created by the pooling of residential mortgage-backed securities in the United States by either the Federal National Mortgage Association (Fannie Mae) or the Federal Home Loan Mortgage Corporation (Freddie Mac). These RMBS carry the full faith and credit of the government, essentially a guarantee with respect to timely payment of interest and repayment of principal.

All-or-nothing (AON) orders An order that includes the instruction to trade only if the trade fills the entire quantity (size) specified.

Allocationally efficient A characteristic of a market, a financial system, or an economy that promotes the allocation of resources to their highest value uses.

Altcoin A cryptocurrency other than Bitcoin.

Alternative data Data that are generated from non-traditional sources, such as social media and sensor networks.

Alternative hypothesis The hypothesis that is accepted if the null hypothesis is rejected.

Alternative investment markets Market for investments other than traditional securities investments (i.e., traditional common and preferred shares and traditional fixed income instruments). The term usually encompasses direct and indirect investment in real estate (including timberland and farmland) and commodities (including precious metals); hedge funds, private equity, and other investments requiring specialized due diligence.

Alternative trading systems Trading venues that function like exchanges but that do not exercise regulatory authority over their subscribers except with respect to the conduct of the subscribers' trading in their trading systems. Also called *electronic communications networks* or *multilateral trading facilities*.

American depository receipt A US dollar-denominated security that trades like a common share on US exchanges.

American depository share The underlying shares on which American depository receipts are based. They trade in the issuing company's domestic market.

American options Options that may be exercised at any time from contract inception until maturity.

American-style Type of option contract that can be exercised at any time up to the option's expiration date.

Amortization The process of allocating the cost of intangible long-term assets having a finite useful life to accounting periods; the allocation of the amount of a bond premium or discount to the periods remaining until bond maturity.

Amortizing debt A loan or bond with a payment schedule that calls for the complete repayment of principal over the instrument's time to maturity.

Analysis of variance (ANOVA) A table that presents the sums of squares, degrees of freedom, mean squares, and F-statistic for a regression model.

Analytical duration Estimates of duration using mathematical formulas. Estimates of the impact of yield changes on bond prices using analytical duration implicitly assume that benchmark yields and spreads are independent variables and are uncorrelated.

Anchoring and adjustment bias An information-processing bias in which the use of a psychological heuristic influences the way people estimate probabilities.

Annual general meeting (AGM) A yearly meeting of the corporate board of directors and shareholders, typically held in person and digitally, during which votes on directors, compensation plans, shareholder resolutions, and any other matters properly brought forward at the meeting are held. Issuer management may also make presentations and hold events.

Anomalies Apparent deviations from market efficiency.

Antidilutive With reference to a transaction or a security, one that would increase earnings per share (EPS) or result in EPS higher than the company's basic EPS—antidilutive securities are not included in the calculation of diluted EPS.

Arbitrage (1) The simultaneous purchase of an undervalued asset or portfolio and sale of an overvalued but equivalent asset or portfolio in order to obtain a riskless profit on the price differential. Taking advantage of a market inefficiency in a risk-free manner. (2) The condition in a financial market in which equivalent assets or combinations of assets sell for two different prices, creating an opportunity to profit at no risk with no commitment of money. In a well-functioning financial market, few arbitrage opportunities are possible. (3) A risk-free operation that earns an expected positive net profit but requires no net investment of money.

Arbitrageurs Traders who engage in arbitrage. See *arbitrage*.

Arithmetic mean The sum of the observations divided by the number of observations.

Artificial intelligence (AI) Computer systems that are capable of performing tasks that previously required human intelligence. AI methods are sometimes better suited to identify complex, non-linear relationships than are traditional quantitative and statistical methods.

Ask The price at which a dealer or trader is willing to sell an asset, typically qualified by a maximum quantity (ask size). See *offer*.

Ask size The maximum quantity of an asset that pertains to a specific ask price from a trader. For example, if the ask for a share issue is $30 for a size of 1,000 shares, the trader is offering to sell at $30 up to 1,000 shares.

Asset allocation The process of determining how investment funds should be distributed among asset classes.

Asset class A group of assets that have similar characteristics, attributes, and risk–return relationships.

Asset utilization ratios Ratios that measure how efficiently a company performs day-to-day tasks, such as the collection of receivables and management of inventory.

Asset-backed commercial paper Secured form of commercial paper issuance. Loans or receivables are sold to a special purpose entity that issues the ABCP and makes interest and principal payments to investors from asset cash flows.

Asset-backed securities (ABS) A type of bond issued by a legal entity called a special purpose entity created solely to own assets such as loans, receivables, and mortgages and to distribute cash flows to ABS investors. Generally, ABS backed by mortgages are known as mortgage-backed securities (MBS) while ABS refer to non-mortgage ABS.

Asset-backed token A token that represents the ownership of a physical asset that does not exist on the blockchain and whose value is based on the underlying asset.

Asset-based valuation models Valuation based on estimates of the market value of a company's assets.

Asymmetric information Also known as *information asymmetry*; the differential of information between corporate insiders and outsiders regarding the company's performance and prospects. Managers typically have more information about the company's performance and prospects than owners and creditors.

At-the-money Describes a unique situation in which the price of the underlying is equal to an option's exercise price. Like an out-of-the-money option, the intrinsic value is zero.

Auction/reverse auction models Pricing models that establish prices through bidding (by sellers in the case of reverse auctions).

Autarky Countries seeking political self-sufficiency with little or no external trade or finance. State-owned enterprises control strategic domestic industries.

Automatic stabilizer A countercyclical factor that automatically comes into play as an economy slows and unemployment rises.

Availability bias An information-processing bias in which people take a heuristic approach to estimating the probability of an outcome based on how easily the outcome comes to mind.

Available-for-sale Under US GAAP, debt securities not classified as either held-to-maturity or held-for-trading securities. The investor is willing to sell but not actively planning to sell. In general, available-for-sale debt securities are reported at fair value on the balance sheet, with unrealized gains included as a component of other comprehensive income.

Average revenue (AR) Total revenue divided by quantity sold.

Backfill Bias A problem whereby certain surviving hedge funds may be added to databases and various hedge fund indexes only after they are initially successful and start to report their returns. Also see *survivorship bias*.

Backup line of credit A type of credit enhancement provided by a bank to an issuer of commercial paper to ensure that the issuer will have access to sufficient liquidity to repay maturing commercial paper if issuing new paper is not a viable option.

Backwardation A downward-sloping, or inverted, forward curve in a futures market.

Balance sheet ratios Financial ratios involving balance sheet items only.

Balanced With respect to a government budget, one in which spending and revenues (taxes) are equal.

Balloon payment A large payment required at maturity to retire a bond's outstanding principal amount.

Base rates The reference rate on which a bank bases lending rates to all other customers.

Base-rate neglect A type of representativeness bias in which the base rate or probability of the categorization is not adequately considered.

Basic EPS Net earnings available to common shareholders (i.e., net income minus preferred dividends) divided by the weighted average number of common shares outstanding.

Basis risk The possibility that the expected value of a derivative differs unexpectedly from that of the underlying.

Basket of listed depository receipts (BLDR) An exchange-traded fund (ETF) that represents a portfolio of depository receipts.

Bayes' formula The rule for updating the probability of an event of interest—given a set of prior probabilities for the event, information, and information given the event—if you receive new information.

Bearer bonds Bonds for which ownership is not recorded; only the clearing system knows who the bond owner is.

Behavioral finance A field of finance that examines the psychological variables that affect and often distort the investment decision making of investors, analysts, and portfolio managers.

Behind the market Said of prices specified in orders that are worse than the best current price; e.g., for a limit buy order, a limit price below the best bid.

Benchmark A bond used to compare against another bond to discern attributes, often a government bond with the same or similar time-to-maturity as the bond under analysis.

Benchmark spread The difference in yield-to-maturity between a bond and that of a benchmark bond.

Best bid The highest bid in the market.

Best effort offering An offering of a security using an investment bank in which the investment bank, as agent for the issuer, promises to use its best efforts to sell the offering but does not guarantee that a specific amount will be sold.

Best offer The lowest offer (ask price) in the market.

Best-in-class An ESG implementation approach that seeks to identify the most favorable companies and sectors based on ESG considerations. Also called *positive screening*.

Beta A measure of the sensitivity of a given investment or portfolio to movements in the overall market.

Bid The price at which a dealer or trader is willing to buy an asset, typically qualified by a maximum quantity.

Bid size The maximum quantity of an asset that pertains to a specific bid price from a trader.

Big data The vast amount of information being generated by both traditional sources—for example, stock exchanges, companies, governments—and non-traditional sources—for example, electronic devices, social media, sensor networks, and company exhaust.

Bilateralism The conduct of political, economic, financial, or cultural cooperation between two countries. Countries engaging in bilateralism may have relations with many different countries but in one-at-a-time agreements without multiple partners. Typically, countries exist on a spectrum between bilateralism and multilateralism.

Bimodal A distribution that has two most frequently occurring values.

Bitcoin A cryptocurrency using blockchain technology that was created in 2009.

Bivariate correlation Also known as Pearson correlation. A parametric measure of the relationship between two variables.

Black swan risk An event that is rare and difficult to predict but has an important impact.

Block brokers A broker (agent) that provides brokerage services for large-size trades.

Blockchain A type of digital ledger in which information is recorded sequentially and then linked together and secured using cryptographic methods.

Blue chip Widely held large market capitalization companies that are considered financially sound and are leaders in their respective industry or local stock market.

Board of directors A body or individual selected by a limited company's member(s) or shareholder(s), in a manner determined by the company's charter, that manages the company. Typically, for larger companies, boards of directors appoint and oversee executive management.

Bond equivalent yield A money market interest rate quoted on a 365-day add-on rate basis.

Bond indenture A legal document between a bond issuer and investors that governs each party's rights and responsibilities.

Bond market vigilantes Bond market participants who might reduce their demand for long-term bonds, thus pushing up their yields.

Bondholders Investors in an entity's securitized debt claims, such as commercial paper, notes, and bonds. Common types of bondholders include investment funds and institutional investors.

Bonds Contractual agreements between an issuer and bondholders.

Bonus issue of shares A type of dividend in which a company distributes additional shares of its common stock to shareholders instead of cash.

Book building Investment bankers' process of compiling a "book" or list of indications of interest to buy part of an offering.

Book value Shareholders' equity (total assets minus total liabilities) minus the value of preferred stock; common shareholders' equity.

Boom An expansionary phase characterized by economic growth "testing the limits" of the economy.

Bootstrap A resampling method that repeatedly draws samples with replacement of the selected elements from the original observed sample. Bootstrap is usually conducted by using computer simulation and is often used to find standard error or construct confidence intervals of population parameters.

Bottom-up analysis An investment selection approach that focuses on company-specific circumstances rather than emphasizing economic cycles or industry analysis.

Box and whisker plot A graphic for visualizing the dispersion of data across quartiles. It consists of a box with "whiskers" connected to the box.

Breakeven point Represents the price of the underlying in a derivative contract in which the profit to both counterparties would be zero.

Bridge financing Interim financing that provides funds until permanent financing can be arranged.

Broker An agent who executes orders to buy or sell securities on behalf of a client in exchange for a commission.

Brokered market A market in which brokers arrange trades among their clients.

Broker–dealer A financial intermediary (often a company) that may function as a principal (dealer) or as an agent (broker) depending on the type of trade.

Brownfield investments The third stage of development of an infrastructure asset. Brownfield investments involve expanding existing facilities and may involve privatization of public assets or a sale leaseback of completed greenfield projects. They are characterized by a shorter investment period with immediate cash flows and an operating history.

Budget surplus/deficit The difference between government revenue and expenditure for a stated fixed period of time.

Bullet bond A bond whose principal repayment is made entirely at maturity.

Bundling A pricing approach that refers to combining multiple products or services so that customers are incentivized or required to buy them together.

Business cycles Are recurrent expansions and contractions in economic activity affecting broad segments of the economy.

Business model A concise description of how a business works and makes revenues and profits, including its customers, products or services, channels for reaching customers, and pricing.

Businesses Organization entities formed and managed for the purpose of providing a return or economic benefits to its investors and owners.

Buy-side firm An investment management company or other investor that uses the services of brokers or dealers (i.e., the client of the sell side firms).

Buyback A transaction in which a company buys back its own shares. Unlike stock dividends and stock splits, share repurchases use corporate cash.

Cabotage The right to transport passengers or goods within a country by a foreign firm. Many countries—including those with multilateral trade agreements—impose restrictions on cabotage across transportation subsectors, meaning that shippers, airlines, and truck drivers are not allowed to transport goods and services within another country's borders.

Call market A market in which trades occur only at a particular time and place (i.e., when the market is called).

Call money rate The interest rate that buyers pay for their margin loan.

Call option The right to buy an underlying.

Call period The time during which the issuer of a callable bond can exercise the call option.

Call price The price at which the issuer of a callable bond has the right to purchase the bond from investors.

Call protection period The time during which the issuer of a callable bond is not allowed to exercise the call option.

Call risk The uncertain maturity and limited price appreciation associated with callable bonds.

Callable bond A bond containing an embedded call option that gives the issuer the right to buy the bond back from the investor at specified prices on predetermined dates.

Cannibalization A transfer of sales or market share from one product to another product owned by the same company. It tends to occur when the two products are actual or perceived substitutes.

Capacity The ability of the borrower to make its debt payments on time.

Capital Other company resources available that reduce reliance on debt.

Capital allocation The process that companies use for decision making on capital investments—those projects with a life of one year or longer.

Capital allocation line (CAL) A graph line that describes the combinations of expected return and standard deviation of return available to an investor from combining the optimal portfolio of risky assets with the risk-free asset.

Capital asset pricing model (CAPM) An equation describing the expected return on any asset (or portfolio) as a linear function of its beta relative to the market portfolio.

Capital expenditure Expenditure on physical capital (fixed assets).

Capital investments An expenditure for an asset or resource with a useful life of more than one year.

Capital market expectations (CME) Expectations concerning the risk and return prospects of asset classes.

Capital market line (CML) The line with an intercept point equal to the risk-free rate that is tangent to the efficient frontier of risky assets; represents the efficient frontier when a risk-free asset is available for investment.

Capital market securities Fixed-income securities with original maturities greater than one year.

Capital markets Financial markets that trade securities of longer duration, such as bonds and equities.

Capital restrictions Controls placed on foreigners' ability to own domestic assets and/or domestic residents' ability to own foreign assets.

Capital structure The mix of debt and equity that a company uses to finance its business; a company's specific mix of long-term financing.

Capital-indexed bond A type of index-linked bond for which changes in the index are captured with adjustments to the principal. A common example is Treasury Inflation Protected Securities (TIPS) issued by the United States government.

Capital-intensive businesses Companies or business activities that are characterized by a relatively low fixed asset turnover, a high percentage of capital expenditures to sales, or a high net-working-capital-to-sales ratio.

Capital-light businesses Also known as *asset light businesses*, companies or business activities characterized by relatively high fixed asset turnover, a low percentage of capital expenditures to sales, or a low net-working-capital-to-sales ratio.

Carried interest A performance fee (also referred to as an incentive fee, or carry) that is applied based on excess returns above a hurdle rate.

Carrying Investing and holding an asset for a period of time.

Carrying amount The amount at which an asset or liability is valued according to accounting principles.

Carrying value Of a fixed-income instrument is the purchase price plus (minus) the amortized amount of the discount (premium) if the bond is purchased at a price below (above) par value.

Cartel Participants in collusive agreements that are made openly and formally.

Cash conversion cycle The amount of time between an issuer paying its suppliers in cash and receiving cash from its customers.

Cash flow additivity principle The principle that dollar amounts indexed at the same point in time are additive.

Cash flow from operations A cash profit measure over a period for an issuer's primary business activities. It includes cash from customers as well as interest and dividends received from financial investments, less cash paid to employees and suppliers as well as taxes paid to governments and interest paid to lenders.

Cash flow hedge Refers to a specific **hedge accounting** classification in which a derivative is designated as absorbing the variable cash flow of a floating-rate asset or liability, such as foreign exchange, interest rates, or commodities.

Cash markets Markets in which specific assets are exchanged at current prices. Cash markets are often referred to as **spot markets**.

Cash prices The current prices prevailing in **cash markets**.

Cash ratio A measure of liquidity that is the ratio of cash and marketable securities to current liabilities.

Catch-up clause A clause in an agreement that favors the GP. For a GP who earns a 20% performance fee, a catch-up clause allows the GP to receive 100% of the distributions above the hurdle rate *until* she receives 20% of the profits generated, and then every excess dollar is split 80/20 between the LPs and GP.

CDS credit spread Reflects the credit spread of a credit default swap (CDS) derivative contract. As with cash bonds, CDS credit spreads depend on the probability of default (POD) and the loss given default (LGD).

Central bank digital currencies (CBDCs) A tokenized version of the currency issued by the central bank, such as a digital bank note or coin, and a digital liability of the central bank.

Central bank funds market The market in which deposit-taking banks that have an excess reserve with their national central bank can lend money to banks that need funds for maturities ranging from overnight to one year. Called the federal or fed funds market in the United States.

Central bank funds rate The interest rate at which central bank funds are bought (borrowed) and sold (lent) for maturities ranging from overnight to one year. Called federal or fed funds rate in the United States.

Central clearing mandate A requirement instituted by global regulatory authorities following the 2008 global financial crisis that most **over-the-counter (OTC)** derivatives be **cleared** by a **central counterparty (CCP)**.

Central counterparty (CCP) An economic entity that assumes the **counterparty credit risk** between derivative **counterparties**, one of which is typically a financial intermediary. CCPs provide **clearing** and **settlement** for most **derivative contracts**.

Central limit theorem The theorem that states the sum (and the mean) of a set of independent, identically distributed random variables with finite variances is normally distributed, whatever distribution the random variables follow.

Certificate of deposit (CD) An instrument that represents a specified amount of funds on deposit with a bank for a specified maturity and interest rate. CDs are issued in various denominations and can be negotiable or non-negotiable.

Channels Venues where a company markets and/or delivers its products and services.

Character The quality of a debt issuer's management.

Checking accounts Bank deposits with no stated maturity available for transactional purposes that pay little or no interest. Also known as a *demand deposit*.

Circuit breaker A pause in intraday trading for a brief period if a price limit is reached.

Classical cycle Refers to fluctuations in the level of economic activity when measured by GDP in volume terms.

Clawback A requirement that the general partner return any funds distributed as incentive fees until the limited partners have received their initial investment and a percentage of the total profit.

Clearing An exchange's process of verifying the execution of a transaction, exchange of payments, and recording of participants.

Clearing instructions Instructions that indicate how to arrange the final settlement ("clearing") of a trade.

Clearinghouse An entity associated with a futures market that acts as middleman between the contracting parties and guarantees to each party the performance of the other.

Closed-end fund A mutual fund in which no new investment money is accepted. New investors invest by buying existing shares, and investors in the fund liquidate by selling their shares to other investors.

Cluster sampling A procedure that divides a population into subpopulation groups (clusters) representative of the population and then randomly draws certain clusters to form a sample.

Co-investing In co-investing, the investor invests in assets *indirectly* through the fund but also possesses rights (known as co-investment rights) to invest *directly* in the same assets. Through co-investing, an investor is able to make an investment *alongside* a fund when the fund identifies deals.

Code of ethics An established guide that communicates an organization's values and overall expectations regarding member behavior. A code of ethics serves as a general guide for how community members should act.

Coefficient of determination (R^2) The percentage of the variation of the dependent variable that is explained by the independent variable. It is a measure of goodness of fit of a regression model.

Coefficient of variation The ratio of a set of observations' standard deviation to the observations' mean value.

Cognitive cost The effort involved in processing new information and updating beliefs.

Cognitive dissonance The mental discomfort that occurs when new information conflicts with previously held beliefs or cognitions.

Cognitive errors Behavioral biases resulting from faulty reasoning; cognitive errors stem from basic statistical, information-processing, or memory errors.

Coincident economic indicators Turning points that are usually close to those of the overall economy; they are believed to have value for identifying the economy's present state.

Collateral Assets or financial guarantees underlying a debt obligation that are above and beyond the issuer's promise to pay.

Collateral manager Buys and sells debt obligations for and from the CDO's collateral pool to generate sufficient cash flows to meet the obligations to the CDO bondholders.

Collateralized bond obligations (CBOs) CDOs backed by high-yield corporate and emerging market bonds.

Collateralized debt obligations (CDOs) Securities backed by a diversified pool of one or more debt obligations. CDOs can be backed by a broad range of debt.

Collateralized loan obligations (CLOs) Investment vehicle with exposure to a portfolio of leveraged loans separated into tranches with different cash flow claims and exposure to losses based on a waterfall.

Collateralized mortgage obligations Securitize mortgage pass-through securities or multiple pools of loans. CMOs are structured to redistribute the cash flows to different bond classes or tranches and create securities that have different exposures to prepayment risk.

Commercial paper (CP) Short-term, negotiable, unsecured promissory note that represents a debt obligation of the issuer.

Committed (regular) lines of credit Bank commitments to extend credit; the commitment is considered a short-term liability and is usually in effect for 364 days (one day short of a full year).

Committed capital The amount that the limited partners have agreed to provide to the private equity fund.

Commodities A product or service from a firm that is indistinguishable from products or services of competing firms, usually conforming to a common standard or grade imposed by convention or regulation.

Commoditization A process by which competing products become less differentiated over time and become interchangeable "commodities" in the eyes of customers. This process is typically associated with declining profitability for the selling firms.

Commodity producers A firm that makes and/or sells commodities.

Commodity swap A type of swap involving the exchange of payments over multiple dates as determined by specified reference prices or indexes relating to commodities.

Common market Level of economic integration that incorporates all aspects of the customs union and extends it by allowing free movement of factors of production among members.

Common shares A type of security that represents an ownership interest in a company. Also called *common stock*.

Common stock A type of security that represents an ownership interest in a company. Also called *common shares*.

Common-size analysis The restatement of financial statement items using a common denominator or reference item that allows one to identify trends and major differences; an example is an income statement in which all items are expressed as a percent of revenue.

Companies Organization entities formed and managed for the purpose of providing a return or economic benefits to its investors and owners.

Company research report A document that presents an analyst's investment recommendation on an issuer and its securities, supported by financial modeling, industry overviews and competitive analyses, valuation scenarios, ESG considerations, and investment risks.

Complete markets Informally, markets in which the variety of distinct securities traded is so broad that any desired payoff in a future state-of-the-world is achievable.

Concession agreement A contractual arrangement under which an entity (also known as a grantor) establishes terms and conditions with a developer or operator (referred to as a concessionaire) to plan, build, operate, finance, and maintain an infrastructure asset for a specific period.

Conditional expected value The expected value of a stated event given that another event has occurred.

Conditional pass-through covered bonds Convert to pass-through securities after the original maturity date if all bond payments have not yet been made.

Conditional variances The variance of one variable, given the outcome of another.

Conditions The general economic, competitive, and business environment faced by all borrowers that may affect their ability to service or refinance debt.

Confidence level The complement of the level of significance.

Confirmation bias A type of cognitive bias that makes individuals view information that confirms beliefs they already hold as more salient.

Consensus protocol A set of rules governing how blocks can join the blockchain that is designed to resist attempts at malicious manipulation up to a certain level of security; it can be either a proof of work or a proof of stake.

Conservatism bias A belief perseverance bias in which people maintain their prior views or forecasts by inadequately incorporating new information.

Constant yield-price trajectory A graphical depiction of the relationship between time to maturity and a bond price, assuming no default, that shows that a bond price approaches par as time passes.

Constituent securities With respect to an index, the individual securities within an index.

Contango Refers to spot price below forward price in a futures market.

Contingency provision Clause in a legal document that allows for some action if a specific event or circumstance occurs.

Contingency table A table of the frequency distribution of observations classified on the basis of two discrete variables.

Contingent claim A type of derivative in which one of the *counterparties* determines whether and when the trade will settle. An *option* is a common type of contingent claim.

Contingent convertible bonds Bonds that automatically convert to equity if a specific event or circumstance occurs, such as the issuer's equity capital falling below the minimum requirement set by regulators.

Continuous trading market A market in which trades can be arranged and executed any time the market is open.

Continuously compounded return The natural logarithm of 1 plus the holding period return, or equivalently, the natural logarithm of the ending price over the beginning price.

Contract manufacturers Companies that make products for other companies that meet specific terms and specifications.

Contract size Amount(s) used for calculation to price and value the derivative. The contract size is often referred to as "notional amount or notional principal."

Contraction The period of a business cycle after the peak and before the trough; often called a *recession* or, if exceptionally severe, called a *depression*.

Contraction risk The risk of earlier repayment of a mortgage-backed security than expected.

Contractionary Tending to cause the real economy to contract.

Contractionary fiscal policy A fiscal policy that has the objective to make the real economy contract.

Contribution margin A profitability measure using variable costs: unit price less unit variable cost. It can also be expressed as a percentage of price or sales.

Controlling shareholder An individual or entity that owns a majority of the voting rights in a corporation.

Convenience sampling A procedure of selecting an element from a population on the basis of whether or not it is accessible to a researcher or how easy it is for a researcher to access the element.

Convenience yield A non-cash benefit of holding a physical commodity versus a derivative.

Conversion price Predetermined share price at which convertible debt may be fully exchanged for common shares during the conversion period.

Conversion ratio The number of common shares a convertible bond or noteholder may receive in exchange for a specific bond par value.

Conversion value The current contingency feature value derived by comparing a convertible bond's price with its value if a bondholder were to exchange bonds for shares.

Convertible bond A bond that gives the bondholder the right to exchange the bond for a specified number of common shares in the issuing company.

Convertible debt A fixed-income instrument which combines the features of debt with equity via a contingent feature, allowing debtholders to exchange their claim for common shares at a predetermined fixed price in the future.

Convertible preference shares A type of equity security that entitles shareholders to convert their shares into a specified number of common shares.

Convexity The second order, usually a positive change in the price of a bond for a given change in yield, which can be negative for a callable bond such as a high-yield bond.

Convexity adjustment A measure that is used to complement modified duration to capture the second-order effect of yield changes on a bond's price. It is equal to the annual convexity statistic times one-half times the given change in the yield-to-maturity squared.

Convexity bias Refers to the difference in price changes for a given change in yield between interest rate futures and interest rate forward contracts. That is, interest rate forwards exhibit a non-linear or convex relationship between price and yield, while the price–yield relationship is linear for interest rate futures.

Cooperation The process by which countries work together toward some shared goal or purpose. These goals may, and often do, vary widely—from strategic or military concerns, to economic influence, to cultural preferences.

Cooperative country A country that engages and reciprocates in rules standardization; harmonization of tariffs; international agreements on trade, immigration, or regulation; and allowing the free flow of information, including technology transfer.

Core real estate strategies Strategies with exposure to well-leased, high-quality commercial and residential real estate in the best markets, generally offered by open-end funds. Investors expect core real estate to deliver stable returns, primarily from income from the property.

Core-plus real estate strategies Value-add investments that require modest redevelopment or upgrades to lease any vacant space together with possible alternative use of the underlying properties. Compared to core real estate strategies, these may be appealing for investors seeking higher returns and willing to accept additional risks from development, redevelopment, repositioning, and leasing.

Corporate issuers Limited companies or corporations that seek financing in financial markets by, for example, issuing debt or equity securities.

Corporations Another term for limited companies, though often used to refer to public limited companies. See *limited company*, *private limited company*, and *public limited company*.

Correlation A measure of the linear relationship between two random variables.

Correlation coefficient A number between −1 and +1 that measures the consistency or tendency for two investments to act in a similar way. It is used to determine the effect on portfolio risk when two assets are combined.

Cost averaging The periodic investment of a fixed amount of money.

Cost of capital The cost of financing for a company; the rate of return that suppliers of capital require as compensation for their contribution of capital (also called *opportunity cost of funds*).

Cost of carry The net of the costs and benefits related to owning an underlying asset for a specific period.

Cost of debt The required return on debt financing for a company, such as when it issues a bond, takes out a bank loan, or leases an asset through a finance lease.

Cost of equity The return required by equity investors to compensate for both the time value of money and the risk. Also referred to as the required rate of return on common stock or the required return on equity.

Counterparty Legal entities entering a **derivative contract**.

Counterparty credit risk The likelihood that a **counterparty** is unable to meet its financial obligations under the contract.

Counterparty risk The risk that the other party to a contract will fail to honor the terms of the contract.

Country The geopolitical environment as well as the legal and political system faced by all issuers in a jurisdiction that may affect debt payment.

Coupon Periodic interest payments paid by a bond issuer to investors, typically expressed as a percentage of par on an annual basis.

Cournot assumption Assumption in which each firm determines its profit-maximizing production level assuming that the other firms' output will not change.

Covariance A measure of the co-movement (linear association) between two random variables.

Covenants The terms and conditions of lending agreements that the issuer must comply with; they specify the actions that an issuer is obligated to perform (affirmative covenant) or prohibited from performing (negative covenant).

Credit default swap (CDS) A type of credit derivative in which one party, the credit protection buyer who is seeking credit protection against a third party, makes a series of regularly scheduled payments to the other party, the credit protection seller. The seller makes no payments until a credit event occurs.

Credit enhancements Provisions or methods that allow a borrower improve their creditworthiness in a structured transaction.

Credit event An occurrence that triggers the settlement of a CDS contract, including failure to make a debt payment, debt restructuring, or a bankruptcy filing.

Credit facilities Loan agreements with pre-specified terms and limits but with fluctuating balances based on borrower-specific needs at different points in time, analogous to a credit card.

Credit migration risk The risk that a bond issuer's creditworthiness deteriorates, or migrates lower, leading investors to believe the risk of default is higher. Also called **downgrade risk**.

Credit rating Letter-grade, qualitative measures of an issuer's ability to meet its debt obligations based on both the probability of default and the expected loss under a default scenario.

Credit rating agencies Institutions that issue and maintain credit ratings. The three largest are Standard & Poor's, Moody's, and Fitch Ratings.

Credit risk The expected economic loss under a potential borrower default over the life of the contract.

Credit spread The compensation for the risk of default in a debt security, typically measured by the yield-to-maturity difference between a bond and a comparable government benchmark security.

Credit spread risk The risk of greater expected loss due to changes in credit conditions as a result of macroeconomic, market, and/or issuer-related factors.

Credit tranching Internal credit enhancement where cash flows into a senior/subordinate structure.

Credit-linked notes Bonds whose coupon changes when the bonds' credit rating changes.

Critical values Values of the test statistic at which the decision changes from fail to reject the null hypothesis to reject the null hypothesis.

Cross-default clause Covenant or contract clause that specifies borrowers are considered in default if they default on another debt obligation.

Cross-sectional analysis Analysis over a group as of a given time.

Crossing networks Trading systems that match buyers and sellers who are willing to trade at prices obtained from other markets.

Crowdsourcing A business model that enables users to contribute directly to a product, service, or online content.

Cryptocurrency An electronic medium of exchange that lacks physical form.

Cryptocurrency wallet A storage unit for public and/or private keys for cryptocurrency transactions. These wallets may be a physical device, program, or service.

Cryptography An algorithmic process to encrypt data, making the data unusable if received by unauthorized parties.

Cumulative preference shares Preference shares for which any dividends that are not paid accrue and must be paid in full before dividends on common shares can be paid.

Cumulative voting A voting process whereby shareholders can accumulate and vote all their shares for a single candidate in an election, as opposed to having to allocate their voting rights evenly among all candidates.

Currencies Monies issued by national monetary authorities.

Currency Money issued by national monetary authorities.

Currency swap A swap in which each party makes interest payments to the other in different currencies.

Current government spending With respect to government expenditures, spending on goods and services that are provided on a regular, recurring basis including health, education, and defense.

Current ratio A measure of liquidity that is the ratio of current assets to current liabilities.

Current yield The sum of the coupon payments received over the year divided by the flat price. Also called the income, interest yield, or running yield.

Customs union Extends the free trade area (FTA) by not only allowing free movement of goods and services among members, but also creating a common trade policy against nonmembers.

CVaR Conditional VaR, a tail loss measure. The weighted average of all loss outcomes in the statistical distribution that exceed the VaR loss.

Daily settlement A specific process of *mark-to-market* by a central clearing party in which the profits and losses of all counterparties to derivatives contracts are determined using settlement prices for each contract.

Dark pools Alternative trading systems that do not display the orders that their clients send to them.

Data mining The practice of determining a model by extensive searching through a dataset for statistically significant patterns. Also called *data snooping.*

Data science An interdisciplinary field that harnesses advances in computer science, statistics, and other disciplines for the purpose of extracting information from big data (or data in general).

Data snooping The subconscious or conscious manipulation of data in a way that produces a statistically significant result (i.e., the p-value is sufficiently small or the t-statistic sufficiently large to indicate statistical significance), such as by running multiple simulations and naively accepting the best result. Also known as p-hacking.

Day order An order that is good for the day on which it is submitted. If it has not been filled by the close of business, the order expires unfilled.

Days of inventory on hand (DOH) The average number of days it would take to sell the amount of inventory on hand. It is calculated as either the ending or average balance of inventories divided by (cost of goods sold/days in the period).

Days payable outstanding (DPO) The average number of days it takes a company to pay its suppliers. It is calculated as either the ending or average balance of accounts payable divided by (cost of goods sold/days in the period).

Days sales outstanding (DSO) The average number of days it takes for a company to receive payment from customers who purchase goods or services on credit. It is calculated as either the ending or average balance of accounts receivable divided by (revenues/days in the period).

Dealers Financial intermediaries, such as commercial banks or investment banks, who transact as **counterparties** with derivative end users.

Debt A claim against an entity to receive cash, stock, or other assets at a future date. From the perspective of the debtor or borrower, an obligation to pay cash, stock, or other assets at a future date. Generally, debt claims are unconditional and are senior to equity claims.

Debt service coverage ratio A key indicator of credit performance equal to the ratio of net operating income to debt service.

Debt tax shield The tax benefit from interest paid on debt being tax deductible from income, equal to the marginal tax rate multiplied by the value of the debt.

Debt-to-assets ratio A solvency ratio calculated as total debt divided by total assets.

Debt-to-capital ratio A solvency ratio calculated as total debt divided by total debt plus total shareholders' equity.

Debt-to-equity ratio A solvency ratio calculated as total debt divided by total shareholders' equity.

Debt-to-income ratio (DTI) Residential lending metric that compares an individual's monthly debt payments to their monthly pre-tax, gross income.

Debut issuer An issuer approaching the bond market for the first time.

Deciles Values that divide a distribution ranked smallest to largest into 10 equal parts.

Declaration date The day that the corporation issues a statement declaring a specific dividend.

Decreasing returns to scale When a production process leads to increases in output that are proportionately smaller than the increase in inputs.

Deductible temporary differences Temporary differences that result in a reduction of or deduction from taxable income in a future period when the balance sheet item is recovered or settled.

Deep learning An area of artificial intelligence in which a system uses neural networks to perform multistage, non-linear data processing to identify patterns. Also called *deep learning nets.*

Deep learning nets See *Deep learning.*

Deep-in-the-money option An option that is highly likely to be exercised.

Deep-out-of-the-money option An option that is highly unlikely to be exercised.

Default When a borrower on a mortgage loan fails to meet the obligations of the loan.

Default risk premium An extra return that compensates investors for the possibility that the borrower will fail to make a promised payment at the contracted time and in the contracted amount.

Defeasance Mechanism that allows prepayment on mortgage, but the borrower must purchase a portfolio of government securities that fully replicates the cash flows of the remaining scheduled principal and interest payments, including the balloon loan balance, on the loan.

Defensive interval ratio A liquidity ratio that estimates the number of days that an entity could meet cash needs from liquid assets; calculated as (cash + short-term marketable investments + receivables) divided by daily cash expenditures.

Deferred coupon bonds Bonds that pay no coupons for their first few years but then pay a higher coupon than they otherwise normally would for the remainder of their life. Also called *split coupon bonds.*

Deferred tax assets A balance sheet asset that arises when an excess amount is paid for income taxes relative to accounting profit. The taxable income is higher than accounting profit and income tax payable exceeds tax expense. The company expects to recover the difference during the course of future operations when tax expense exceeds income tax payable.

Deferred tax liabilities A balance sheet liability that arises when a deficit amount is paid for income taxes relative to accounting profit. The taxable income is less than the accounting profit and income tax payable is less than tax expense. The company expects to eliminate the liability over the course of future operations when income tax payable exceeds tax expense.

Defined benefit pension plans (DB plans) Plans in which the company promises to pay a certain annual amount (defined benefit) to the employee after retirement. The company bears the investment risk of the plan assets.

Defined contribution pension plans Individual accounts to which an employee and typically the employer makes contributions during their working years and expect to draw on the accumulated funds at retirement. The employee bears the investment and inflation risk of the plan assets.

Deflation Negative inflation.

Degree of financial leverage The ratio of percentage change in net income to percentage change in operating income over a period. It is a measure of how sensitive net income is to changes in operating income, driven by the firm's use of debt in its capital structure.

Degree of operating leverage The ratio of percentage change in operating income to percentage change in sales over a period. It is a measure of how sensitive operating income is to changes in sales, driven by the fixed and variable cost composition of operating expenses.

Delta The sensitivity of the derivative price to a small change in the value of the underlying asset.

Demand shock A typically unexpected disturbance to demand, such as an unexpected interruption in trade or transportation.

Dependent variable The variable that is explained by a regression model.

Depository bank A bank that raises funds from depositors and other investors and lends it to borrowers.

Depository institutions Commercial banks, savings and loan banks, credit unions, and similar institutions that raise funds from depositors and other investors and lend it to borrowers.

Depository receipt A security that trades like an ordinary share on a local exchange and represents an economic interest in a foreign company.

Depreciation The process of systematically allocating the cost of long-lived (tangible) assets to the periods during which the assets are expected to provide economic benefits.

Derivative A financial instrument that derives its value from the performance of an underlying asset or factor (e.g., stock price, interest rate, or exchange rate).

Derivative contract A legal agreement between counterparties with a specific **maturity**, or length of time, until the closing of the transaction, or **settlement**.

Derivative pricing rule A pricing rule used by crossing networks in which a price is taken (derived) from the price that is current in the asset's primary market.

Differentiated products A product or service from a firm that is distinguishable or distinct from those of competing firms. It is customers who determine and value whether a product is differentiated.

Diffuse prior The assumption of equal prior probabilities.

Diffusion index Reflects the proportion of the index's components that are moving in a pattern consistent with the overall index.

Digital assets The umbrella term covering assets that can be created, stored, and transmitted electronically and have associated ownership or use rights. Digital assets include a variety of assets, such as cryptocurrencies, tokens (security and utility), and digital collectables.

Diluted EPS The EPS that would result if all dilutive securities were converted into common shares.

Dilution An increase in the number of shares outstanding from share issuance that decreases the percentage of shares owned by existing shareholders.

Direct investing Occurs when an investor makes a direct investment in an asset without the use of an intermediary.

Direct lending Providing capital directly from private debt investors.

Direct listing Where the equity of a security is floated on the public markets directly, without underwriters, reducing the complexity and cost of the transaction.

Direct sales Marketing and/or delivering products and services to customers without an intermediary or third party between the customer and seller.

Direct taxes Taxes levied directly on income, wealth, and corporate profits.

Discount factor The price equivalent of a zero rate. Also may be stated as the present value of a currency unit on a future date.

Discount rate A yield or pricing convention for money market instrument quotations. It is the interest earned on an instrument, derived from the difference between the price and face value, expressed as a percentage of the face value and multiplied by the periodicity of the annual rate.

Discounted cash flow models Valuation models that estimate the intrinsic value of a security as the present value of the future benefits expected to be received from the security.

Discriminatory pricing rule A pricing rule used in continuous markets in which the limit price of the order or quote that first arrived determines the trade price.

Diseconomies of scale Increase in cost per unit resulting from increased production.

Dispersion The variability of a population or sample of observations around the central tendency.

Display size The size of an order displayed to public view.

Disposition effect A type of cognitive bias that makes individuals unwilling to sell their possessions at a loss.

Distressed debt Debt of mature companies in financial difficulty, in bankruptcy, or likely to default on debt.

Distressed/restructuring These strategies focus on securities of companies either in or perceived to be near bankruptcy. In one approach, hedge funds simply purchase fixed-income securities trading at a significant discount to par but that are still senior enough to be backed by sufficient corporate assets.

Distributed ledger A type of database that can be shared among entities in a network.

Distributed ledger technology (DLT) Technology based on a distributed ledger.

Diversification ratio The ratio of the standard deviation of an equally weighted portfolio to the standard deviation of a randomly selected security.

Dividend discount model (DDM) The model of the value of stock that is the present value of all future dividends, discounted at the required return on equity.

Dividend payout ratio The ratio of cash dividends paid to earnings for a period.

Dividends Distributions of profits and/or net assets from a corporation to its shareholders. While often in cash, dividends can be also be paid in stock or assets, such as property.

Divisor A number (denominator) used to determine the value of a price return index. It is initially chosen at the inception of an index and subsequently adjusted by the index provider, as necessary, to avoid changes in the index value that are unrelated to changes in the prices of its constituent securities.

Domestic bonds A type of bond for which the issuer's domicile and jurisdiction of issuance are the same.

Domestic content provisions Stipulate that some percentage of the value added or components used in production should be of domestic origin.

Double taxation Income is taxed twice.

Downside risk The potential for loss.

Drag on liquidity An action or event that reduces available funds or delays cash inflows.

Drivers Causative factors that explain the level of and changes in an output variable.

DSC ratio A property's annual net operating income (NOI) divided by the debt service.

Dual-class structure A capital structure that includes at least two classes of equity shares with unequal voting rights.

Dupont analysis An approach to decomposing return on investment, e.g., return on equity, as the product of other financial ratios.

Duration The first-order, linear change in a bond's price for a given yield change in yield, which is a negative or inverse relationship.

Duration gap the difference between a bond's Macaulay duration and its investor's investment horizon.

Dynamic pricing A pricing approach that charges different prices at different times. Specific examples include off-peak pricing, "surge" pricing, and "congestion" pricing.

Early repayment option May entitle the borrower to prepay all or part of the outstanding mortgage principal prior to maturity. This creates a risk from the lender's or investor's viewpoint because the cash flow amounts and timing cannot be known with certainty.

Earnings surprise The difference between reported EPS and expected EPS. Also referred to as *unexpected earnings.*

Economic indicators Economic statistics provided by government and established private organizations that contain information on an economy's recent past activity or its current or future position in the business cycle.

Economic infrastructure investments A category of infrastructure investments that support economic activity through transportation assets, information and communication technology assets, and utility and energy assets.

Economic stabilization Reduction of the magnitude of economic fluctuations.

Economic union Incorporates all aspects of a common market and in addition requires common economic institutions and coordination of economic policies among members.

Economies of scale A decline in costs per unit as output grows, generally resulting from having fixed costs in the cost structure that are spread over more units of output.

Economies of scope A decline in costs per unit as the number of product or business lines increases, generally resulting from having shared costs between the product lines.

Effective annual rate An interest rate with a periodicity of one.

Effective convexity An interest rate risk statistic that measures the non-linear/second-order effect of changes in the benchmark yield curve on a bond's price.

Effective duration The sensitivity of the bond's price to an instantaneous parallel shift in a benchmark yield curve—for example, the government par curve.

Efficient market A market in which asset prices reflect new information quickly and rationally. See also, *informationally efficient market.*

Either/or fee A custom fee arrangement whereby major investors are offered a structure where managers agree to charge *either* a lower management fee *or* a higher incentive fee, whichever is greater.

Electronic communications networks (ECNs) See *alternative trading systems* and *multilateral trading facilities.*

Embedded derivative A derivative within an underlying, such as a callable, putable, or convertible bond.

Embedded options Contingency provisions found in a bond's indenture representing rights that enable their holders to take advantage of interest rate movements. They can be exercised by the issuer, by the bondholder, or automatically depending on the course of interest rates.

Emotional biases Behavioral biases resulting from reasoning influenced by feelings; emotional biases stem from impulse or intuition.

Empirical duration Estimation of the price–yield relationship using historical bond market data in statistical models.

Employee stock ownership plan (ESOP) A type of employee benefit plan in which a company sets up a trust fund to receive contributions of newly issued shares or cash to buy existing shares. Contributions are tax deductible up to certain limits. Shares in the trust fund are allocated to individual employees based on relative pay or a formula.

Endowment bias An emotional bias in which people value an asset more when they hold rights to it than when they do not.

Enterprise risk management An overall assessment of a company's risk position. A centralized approach to risk management sometimes called firmwide risk management.

Enterprise value A measure of a company's total market value from which the value of cash and short-term investments have been subtracted.

Equal weighting An index weighting method in which an equal weight is assigned to each constituent security at inception.

Equity Ownership interest in an entity. A residual claim on the assets of an entity after more senior claims, such as debt, have been satisfied. Also known as *net assets*.

Equity swap A swap transaction in which at least one cash flow is tied to the return to an equity portfolio position, often an equity index.

Error term Represents the difference between the observed value of the independent variable and that expected from the true underlying population relation between the dependent and independent variable.

Estimated parameters In a simple linear regression, the estimated parameters are the intercept and slope of the fitted line.

Ether A programmable cryptocurrency created on the Ethereum blockchain in 2015 that allows for the execution of smart contracts.

Ethical principles Beliefs regarding what is good, acceptable, or obligatory behavior and what is bad, unacceptable, or forbidden behavior.

Ethics The study of moral principles or of making good choices. Ethics encompasses a set of moral principles and rules of conduct that provide guidance for our behavior.

Eurobonds A type of bond issued internationally, outside the jurisdiction of the country in whose currency the bond is denominated.

European options Options that may be exercised only at contract maturity.

European-style Said of an option contract that can only be exercised on the option's expiration date.

Event risk Risk that evolves around set dates, such as elections, new legislation, or other date-driven milestones, such as holidays or political anniversaries, known in advance. Example: Brexit referendum.

Ex-dividend date The first date that a share trades without (i.e., "ex") the right to receive the declared dividend for the period.

Excess kurtosis Degree of kurtosis (fatness of tails) relative to the kurtosis of the normal distribution.

Excess spread Surplus difference of yield remaining after payments to bondholders are made after expenses are made and losses are covered.

Exchange A rules-based, open access market venue where financial instruments are traded, with price and volume transparency accessible by issuers, investors, and their intermediaries.

Exchange-traded derivative (ETD) Futures, options, and other financial contracts available on exchanges.

Execution instructions Instructions that indicate how to fill an order.

Exercise The decision to transact the underlying by an option holder.

Exercise date The day that an option is exercised by its holder. For a call option, the day the strike price is paid and underlying is purchased. For a put option, when the strike price is received and the underlying is sold.

Exercise price The pre-agreed execution price specified in an option contract. Sometimes, this price is referred to as the strike price.

Exogenous risk A sudden or unanticipated risk that impacts either a country's cooperative stance, the ability of non-state actors to globalize, or both. Examples include sudden uprisings, invasions, or the aftermath of natural disasters.

Expansion The period of a business cycle after its lowest point and before its highest point.

Expansionary Tending to cause the real economy to grow.

Expansionary fiscal policy Fiscal policy aimed at achieving real economic growth.

Expected exposure (EE) The size of the investor's claim at the time of default.

Expected loss (EL) Default probability times loss severity given default.

Expected return on the portfolio Denoted as ($E(R_p)$). The weighted average of the expected returns (R_1 to R_n) on the component securities using their respective weights (w_1 to w_n).

Expected value of a random variable The probability-weighted average of the possible outcomes of a random variable.

Expert system A type of computer programming, often based on "if–then" rules, that attempts to simulate the knowledge base and analytical abilities of human experts in specific problem-solving contexts.

Export subsidy Paid by the government to the firm when it exports a unit of a good that is being subsidized.

Exposure at default (EAD) The size of the investor's claim at the time of default.

Extension risk The risk of later repayment of a mortgage-backed security than expected.

External credit enhancements Provisions or methods from a third party that allow a borrower improve their creditworthiness in a structured transaction.

External debt Sovereign debt owed to foreign creditors.

Extra dividend A dividend paid by a company that does not pay dividends on a regular schedule, or a dividend that supplements regular cash dividends with an extra payment.

Extraordinary general meetings (EGMs) Meetings besides an AGM of the corporate board and shareholders, typically held to deliberate and vote on urgent matters. Corporate charters and bylaws specify who can call an EGM and under what conditions.

Extreme value theory A branch of statistics that focuses primarily on extreme outcomes.

Face value The amount of principal on a bond, also known as par value.

Factoring arrangement When a company sells its accounts receivable to a lender (known as a factor) that assumes responsibility for the credit-granting and collection process.

Fair value A market-based measure of an investment based on observable or derived assumptions to determine a price that market participants would use to exchange an asset or liability in an orderly transaction at a specific time.

Fair value hedge Refers to a specific **hedge accounting** designation that applies when a derivative is deemed to offset the fluctuation in fair value of an asset or liability.

Fallen angels Formerly investment-grade-rated issuers whose bonds are downgraded to high yield due to credit deterioration.

Fat-Tailed Describes a distribution that has fatter tails than a normal distribution (also called leptokurtic).

Fed funds rate The US interbank lending rate on overnight borrowings of reserves.

Federal funds rate The US interbank lending rate on overnight borrowings of reserves. Also known as *Fed Funds rate.*

Fiat money Money that is not convertible into any other commodity.

Fiduciary call A combination of a purchased call option and investment in a risk-free bond with face value of the option's exercise price.

Fill or kill See *immediate or cancel order.*

Finance lease A type of lease which is more akin to the purchase or sale of the underlying asset.

Financial leverage The use of debt in the capital structure. Measured using ratios such as operating income to operating income less interest expense, total assets to total equity, or debt to equity.

Financial leverage ratio A measure of financial leverage calculated as average total assets divided by average total equity.

Financial risk The risk arising from a company's capital structure and, specifically, from the level of debt and debt-like obligations.

Fintech Technological innovation in the financial services industry, specifically with the design and delivery of financial services and products. It may also refer more broadly to companies involved in developing the new technologies and their applications, as well as the business sector that includes such companies.

Firm commitment A pre-determined amount (price and quantity) is agreed to be exchanged at settlement. Examples of firm commitments include forward contracts, futures contracts, and swaps.

First lien Also known as a priority lien, this investor protection grants a lender the right to take possession of property from a borrower which fails to repay debt.

First lien debt Debt secured by a pledge of certain assets that could include buildings, but it may also include property and equipment, licenses, patents, brands, etc.

First mortgage debt Debt secured by a pledge of a specific property.

Fiscal multiplier The ratio of a change in national income to a change in government spending.

Fiscal policy The use of taxes and government spending to affect the level of aggregate expenditures.

Fixed charge coverage A solvency ratio measuring the number of times interest and lease payments are covered by operating income, calculated as (EBIT + lease payments) divided by (interest payments + lease payments).

Fixed charge coverage ratio A measure of how well a company's earnings covers its fixed expenses, which may include debt payments, interest expense, and lease costs.

Fixed-income instruments Debt instruments such as loans or bonds.

Fixed-income securities Fixed-income instruments designed to be more easily tradeable than a loan, such as a bond.

Fixed-price call A contingency provision that grants an issuer the right to buy back a bond at a predetermined price in the future.

Fixed-rate payer The counterparty paying fixed cash flows in a swap contract. May also be referred to as the floating-rate receiver.

Flat price The full price of a bond minus accrued interest. Flat prices are usually quoted by bond dealers.

Float-adjusted market-capitalization weighting An index weighting method in which the weight assigned to each constituent security is determined by adjusting its market capitalization for its market float.

Floating-rate notes Notes on which interest payments are not fixed but instead vary from period to period depending on the current level of a reference interest rate. Also known as *floaters*.

Floating-rate payer The counterparty paying the variable cash flows in a swap contract. May also be referred to as the fixed-rate receiver.

Forecast object A variable on or related to an issuer's financial statements that an analyst makes a projection for. Examples include drivers of financial statements, financial statement lines, and summary measures like EBITDA.

Foreclosure Allows a lender to take possession of the property and ultimately sell the property to recover funds toward satisfying the outstanding debt obligation.

Foreign bonds A type of bond for which the issuer's domicile and jurisdiction of issuance are different.

Foreign currency reserves Holding by the central bank of non-domestic currency deposits and non-domestic bonds.

Foreign direct investments (FDI) Long-term investments in the productive capacity of a foreign country.

Foreign exchange gains (or losses) Gains (or losses) that occur when the exchange rate changes between the investor's currency and the currency that foreign securities are denominated in.

Forward contract A **derivative contract** for the future exchange of an **underlying** at a fixed price set at contract signing.

Forward price Represents the price agreed upon in a forward contract to be exchanged at the contract's maturity date, T. This price is shown in equations as $F_0(T)$.

Forward price-to-earnings ratio A P/E calculated on the basis of a forecast of EPS; a stock's current price divided by next year's expected earnings.

Forward rate agreement (FRA) An OTC derivatives contract in which counterparties agree to apply a specific interest rate to a future time period.

Founders class shares A way to entice early participation in startup funds whereby managers offer incentives that entitle investors to a lower fee structure and/or other favorable terms.

Framing bias An information-processing bias in which a person answers a question differently based on the way in which it is asked (framed).

Franchising A situation where an owner of an asset and associated intellectual property divests the asset and licenses intellectual property to a third-party operator (franchisee) in exchange for royalties. Franchisees operate under the constraints of a franchise agreement.

Free cash flow The actual cash that would be available to the company's investors after making all investments necessary to maintain the company as an ongoing enterprise (also referred to as free cash flow to the firm); the internally generated funds that can be distributed to the company's investors (e.g., shareholders and bondholders) without impairing the value of the company.

Free cash flow hypothesis The hypothesis that higher debt levels discipline managers by forcing them to make fixed debt service payments and by reducing the company's free cash flow.

Free float The portion of a listed company's equity securities that are not held by insiders, strategic investors, sponsors, founders, and so on, that are more freely available for trading.

Free trade areas One of the most prevalent forms of regional integration, in which all barriers to the flow of goods and services among members have been eliminated.

Free-cash-flow-to-equity models Valuation models based on discounting expected future free cash flow to equity.

Freemium business model A pricing approach that allows customers a certain level of usage or functionality at no charge. Those who wish to use more must pay.

Frequency table A representation of the frequency of occurrence of two discrete variables.

Full price The price of a bond including any accrued interest owed to the seller. It is the flat price plus accrued interest.

Fully amortizing loan A loan or bond with a payment schedule that calls for the complete repayment of principal over the instrument's time to maturity.

Fund investing In fund investing, the investor invests in assets indirectly by contributing capital to a fund as part of a group of investors. Fund investing is available for all major alternative investment types.

Fund of funds Funds that hold a portfolio of hedge funds; also called *funds of hedge funds*.

Fundamental analysis The examination of publicly available information and the formulation of forecasts to estimate the intrinsic value of assets.

Fundamental growth These strategies use fundamental analysis to identify companies expected to exhibit high growth and capital appreciation.

Fundamental long/short In this strategy, the hedge fund takes a long position in companies that are trading at inexpensive levels compared to their potential intrinsic value and shorts those that trade in the other direction, with the intention of reversing this trade to obtain alpha.

Fundamental value These strategies use fundamental analysis to identify undervalued and unloved companies for which there is a possibility that a corporate turnaround, with future revenue and cash flow growth, will result in higher valuations.

Fundamental weighting An index weighting method in which the weight assigned to each constituent security is based on its underlying company's size. It attempts to address the disadvantages of market-capitalization weighting by using measures that are independent of the constituent security's price.

Fungible Freely exchangeable, interchangeable, or substitutable with other things of the same type. Money and commodities are the most common examples.

Futures contract A variation of a forward contract that has essentially the same basic definition but with some additional features, such as a clearinghouse guarantee against credit losses, a daily settlement of gains and losses, and an organized electronic or floor trading facility.

Futures contract basis point value (BPV) The change in price of a futures contract given a 1 basis point (0.01%) change in yield.

Futures margin account An account held by an exchange clearinghouse for each derivatives counterparty. The funds in such an account are used to ensure that counterparties do not default on their contract obligation.

Futures price The pre-agreed price at which a futures contract buyer (seller) agrees to pay (receive) for the underlying at the maturity date of the futures contract.

FX swap The combination of a spot and a forward FX transaction.

G-spread Yield spread in basis points between a bond's yield-to-maturity and that of an actual or interpolated government bond. It represents the return for bearing risks relative to the government bond.

Game theory The set of tools decision makers use to incorporate responses by rival decision makers into their strategies.

Gamma A numerical measure of how sensitive an option's delta (the sensitivity of the derivative's price) is to a change in the value of the underlying.

Gate A provision that when implemented limits or restricts redemptions for a period of time.

General collateral repo Rather than involving a specific security, a repo that instead references a specific group of securities as eligible collateral (such as government bonds of a specific maturity).

General collateral repo rate The interest rate on a general collateral repo.

General obligation (GO) bonds Unsecured bonds issued by a non-sovereign government which are backed by the taxing authority of the issuer.

General obligation bonds Also known as GO bonds. Bonds issued by non-sovereign governments for general purposes and repaid from tax cash flows.

General partners (GPs) Private fund managers responsible for sourcing and deploying capital from limited partner investors over an investment life cycle and distributing returns to those investors over a finite investment holding period.

General partnership A business organizational form owned entirely by general partners.

Geophysical resource endowment Includes such factors as livable geography and climate as well as access to food and water, which are necessary for sustainable growth. Geophysical resource endowment is highly unequal among countries.

Geopolitics The study of how geography affects politics and international relations. These relations matter for investments because they contribute to important drivers of investment performance, including economic growth, business performance, market volatility, and transaction costs.

Gilts Bonds issued by the UK government.

Global depository receipt (GDR) A depository receipt that is issued outside of the company's home country and outside of the United States.

Global minimum-variance portfolio The portfolio on the minimum-variance frontier with the smallest variance of return.

Global registered share (GRS) A common share that is traded on different stock exchanges around the world in different currencies.

Globalization The process of interaction and integration among people, companies, and governments worldwide. It is marked by the spread of products, information, jobs, and culture across borders.

Gold standard With respect to a currency, if a currency is on the gold standard a given amount can be converted into a prespecified amount of gold.

Good-on-close An execution instruction specifying that an order can only be filled at the close of trading. Also called *market-on-close*.

Good-on-open An execution instruction specifying that an order can only be filled at the opening of trading.

Good-till-cancelled order An order specifying that it is valid until the entity placing the order has cancelled it (or, commonly, until some specified amount of time such as 60 days has elapsed, whichever comes sooner).

Goodwill An intangible asset that represents the excess of the purchase price of an acquired company over the value of the net identifiable assets acquired.

Governance tokens In permissionless networks, governance tokens serve as votes to determine how the particular network is run.

Government debt management Government policies that relate to the issuance of debt securities, typically handled by a treasurer or finance ministry.

Government equivalent yield Measures quoted using actual/actual day counts.

Grant date The day that terms of compensation are communicated by an issuer and accepted by an employee recipient.

Green bonds Bonds used to specifically finance environmental-related projects.

Greenfield investments New, "to-be-built" infrastructure projects and assets created to provide a specific essential service or to supply a public good.

Gross profit margin The ratio of gross profit to revenues.

Groupthink A behavioral bias that occurs when a team minimizes conflict and dissent in reaching and maintaining a consensus.

Growth cycle Refers to fluctuations in economic activity around the long-term potential trend growth level, focusing on how much actual economic activity is below or above trend growth in economic activity.

Growth option The option to make additional investments in a project at some future time if the financial results are strong. Also called an *expansion option.*

Growth rate cycle Refers to fluctuations in the growth rate of economic activity.

Haircut The difference between the market value of the security used as collateral and the value of the loan. Also called *repo margin.*

Halo effect An emotional bias that extends a favorable evaluation of some characteristics to other characteristics.

Hard commodities Traded natural resources, such as crude oil and metals, with markets often involving the physical delivery of the underlying upon settlement.

Hard hurdle rate Hurdle ratewhere the manager earns fees on annual returns in excess of the hurdle rate

Hard-bullet covered bonds Type of security where if payments do not occur according to the original schedule of a covered bond, a bond default is triggered and bond payments are accelerated.

Harmonic mean A type of weighted mean computed as the reciprocal of the arithmetic average of the reciprocals.

Hedge The **derivative contract** used in **hedging** an exposure.

Hedge accounting Accounting standard(s) that allow an issuer to offset a hedging instrument (usually a derivative) against a hedged transaction or balance sheet item to reduce financial statement volatility.

Hedge funds Private investment vehicles that may invest in public equities or publicly traded fixed-income assets, private capital, and/or real assets, but they are distinguished by their investment *approach* rather than by the investments themselves.

Hedge ratio The proportion of an underlying that will offset the risk associated with a derivative position.

Hedging The use of a derivative contract to offset or neutralize existing or anticipated exposure to an **underlying**.

Hegemony Countries that are regional or even global leaders and use their political or economic influence of others to control resources.

Held-to-maturity Debt (fixed-income) securities that a company intends to hold to maturity; these are presented at their original cost, updated for any amortisation of discounts or premiums.

Herding Clustered trading that may or may not be based on information.

Herfindahl-Hirschman Index (HHI) A measure of market concentration, calculated as the sum of the squares of competitor market shares. Antitrust regulators in some countries consider markets with an HHI between 1,500 and 2,500 moderately concentrated and consider markets with an HHI over 2,500 highly concentrated.

Heteroskedasticity Non-constant variance across all observations.

Hidden order An order that is exposed not to the public but only to the brokers or exchanges that receive it.

Hidden revenue business model Business models that provide services to users at no charge and generate revenues elsewhere.

High yield Bond issuers and issues rated BB+ (Ba1 on Moody's scale) or lower. Also known as speculative grade and junk.

High-water mark The highest value, net of fees, that a fund has reached in history. It reflects the highest cumulative return used to calculate an incentive fee.

Hindsight bias A type of cognitive bias that makes individuals misremember the past in ways that make them appear to have made better and more well-informed choices.

Holder-of-record date The date that a shareholder listed on the corporation's books will be deemed to have ownership of the shares for purposes of receiving an upcoming dividend.

Holding period return The single-period internal rate of return for a real estate property that includes property income and the change in property value over the period.

Home bias A preference for securities listed on the exchanges of one's home country.

Homogeneity of expectations The assumption that all investors have the same economic expectations and thus have the same expectations of prices, cash flows, and other investment characteristics.

Homoskedasticity Constant variance across all observations.

Horizon yield An investor's total rate of return on a fixed income instrument over their holding period, including reinvested coupon payments. It is an internal rate of return expressed as an annualized rate.

Hostile takeover When a potential acquirer seeks to acquire a company (the target) against the wishes of the target's board of directors. Typically, a tender offer is used to carry out the hostile takeover, against which a board might use a poison pill in its defense.

Household A person or a group of people living in the same residence, taken as a basic unit in economic analysis.

Human capital The present value of an individual's future expected labor income.

Hurdle rate Also called "preferred return." The minimum rate of return on investment that a fund must reach before a GP receives carried interest.

Hypothesis A proposed explanation or theory that can be tested.

Hypothesis testing The process of testing of hypotheses about one or more populations using statistical inference.

I-spread also known as interpolated spread, it is the yield spread for a bond over the standard swap rate in that currency of the same tenor.

Iceberg order An order in which the display size is less than the order's full size.

If-converted method A method for accounting for the effect of convertible securities on earnings per share (EPS) that specifies what EPS would have been if the convertible securities had been converted at the beginning of the period, taking account of the effects of conversion on net income and the weighted average number of shares outstanding.

Illusion of control bias A bias in which people tend to believe that they can control or influence outcomes when, in fact, they cannot.

Immediate or cancel order An order that is valid only upon receipt by the broker or exchange. If such an order cannot be filled in part or in whole upon receipt, it cancels immediately. Also called *fill or kill*.

Impact lag The lag associated with the result of actions affecting the economy with delay.

Implied forward rate An interest rate or yield over a future period implied by the current term structure of interest rates.

Import license Specifies the quantity of a good that can be imported into a country.

In-the-money Describes an option with a positive intrinsic value.

Income tax paid The actual amount paid for income taxes in the period; not a provision, but the actual cash outflow.

Income tax payable The income tax owed by the company on the basis of taxable income.

Increasing returns to scale When a production process leads to increases in output that are proportionately larger than the increase in inputs.

Incurrence test A financial ratio or other measurement taken prior to an action such as debt issuance, usually on a pro forma basis taking the action into account. Satisfaction of the test (e.g., leverage ratio below a certain value) is linked to covenants between the issuer and investors.

Indenture A written contract between a lender and borrower that specifies the terms of the loan, such as interest rate, interest payment schedule, or maturity.

Independent With reference to events, the property that the occurrence of one event does not affect the probability of another event occurring. With reference to two random variables X and Y, they are independent if and only if $P(X,Y) = P(X)P(Y)$.

Independent directors Members of a corporation's board of directors who do not have an employment or familial relationship with the company, nor do they have a relationship that would impair their independence such as an economic interest in a vendor or competitor of the company.

Independent variable An explanatory variable in a regression model.

Independently and identically distributed With respect to random variables, the property of random variables that are independent of each other but follow the identical probability distribution.

Index-linked bonds A bond whose coupon payments or principal repayment is linked to a specified index.

Indexing An investment strategy in which an investor constructs a portfolio to mirror the performance of a specified index.

Indicator variable A variable that takes on only one of two values, 0 or 1, based on a condition. In simple linear regression, the slope is the difference in the dependent variable for the two conditions. Also referred to as a *dummy variable*.

Indifference curve A curve representing all the combinations of two goods or attributes such that the consumer is entirely indifferent among them.

Indirect taxes Taxes such as taxes on spending, as opposed to direct taxes.

Inflation premium An extra return that compensates investors for expected inflation.

Inflation reports A type of economic publication put out by many central banks.

Inflation-linked bonds Debt instruments that link the principal and interest to inflation.

Information cascade The transmission of information from those participants who act first and whose decisions influence the decisions of others.

Information-motivated traders Traders that trade to profit from information that they believe allows them to predict future prices.

Informationally efficient market A market in which asset prices reflect new information quickly and rationally.

Infrastructure A type of real asset that is intended for public use and provides essential services. These assets are typically long-lived fixed assets, such as bridges and toll roads.

Initial coin offering (ICO) An unregulated process whereby companies raise capital by selling crypto-tokens to investors in exchange for fiat money or another agreed-upon cryptocurrency.

Initial margin The ratio of the price of collateral to the value of cash exchanged in a repo; a value over 1.0 or 100% indicates overcollateralization.

Initial margin requirement The margin requirement on the first day of a transaction as well as on any day in which additional margin funds must be deposited.

Initial public offering (IPO) The first issuance of common shares to the public by a formerly private corporation.

Inside directors Members of a corporation's board of directors who are not independent. Typically, inside directors are employees or founders (and their family) of the company.

Insolvency A situation in which an issuer's total liabilities exceed the market value of its assets.

Institution An established organization or practice in a society or culture. An institution can be a formal structure, such as a university, organization, or process backed by law; or it can be informal, such as a custom or behavioral pattern important to society. Institutions can, but need not be, formed by national governments. Examples of institutions include non-governmental organizations, charities, religious customs, family units, the media, political parties, and educational practice.

Intangible assets Assets without a physical form, such as patents and trademarks.

Interbank market The market of loans and deposits between banks for maturities ranging from overnight to one year.

Intercept The estimated value of the dependent variable when the independent variable is zero.

Interest coverage A solvency ratio calculated as EBIT divided by interest payments.

Interest coverage ratio A measure of an issuer's ability to service its debt, typically the ratio of operating income or EBIT to interest expense.

Interest rate A rate of return that reflects the relationship between differently dated cash flows; a discount rate.

Interest rate swap A swap in which the underlying is an interest rate. Can be viewed as a currency swap in which both currencies are the same and can be created as a combination of currency swaps.

Interest-indexed bond A type of index-linked bond for which changes in the index are captured with adjustments to interest payments.

Internal credit enhancements Provisions or methods a borrower initiates to improve their creditworthiness in a structured transaction, such as overcollateralization or excess spread.

internal rate of return The discount rate that makes net present value equal 0; the discount rate that makes the present value of an investment's costs (outflows) equal to the present value of the investment's benefits (inflows).

Internal rate of return (IRR) The uniform discount rate for a series of cash flows over *n* periods that returns a net present value of zero.

Internet of things The vast array of physical devices, home appliances, smart buildings, vehicles, and other items that are embedded with electronics, sensors, software, and network connections that enable the objects in the system to interact and share information.

Interquartile range The difference between the third and first quartiles of a dataset.

Intrinsic value The amount gained (per unit) by an option buyer if an option is exercised at any given point in time. May be referred to as the exercise value of the option.

Investment banks Financial intermediaries that provide advice to their mostly corporate clients and help them arrange transactions such as initial and seasoned securities offerings.

Investment grade Bond issuers and issues rated BBB- (Baa3 on Moody's scale).

Investment policy statement (IPS) A written planning document that describes a client's investment objectives and risk tolerance over a relevant time horizon, along with constraints that apply to the client's portfolio.

Issue rating A rating which seeks to capture the probability of default or expected loss of the issuer's senior unsecured bonds.

Issuer rating A rating which seeks to capture the credit risk of a specific financial obligation of an issuer which takes such factors as seniority into account.

J-curve effect Net income over a multiyear private investment holding period characterized by negative returns in an initial phase, followed by cash flow and income growth toward the end of the holding period.

Jackknife A resampling method that repeatedly draws samples by taking the original observed data sample and leaving out one observation at a time (without replacement) from the set.

January effect Calendar anomaly that stock market returns in January are significantly higher compared to the rest of the months of the year, with most of the abnormal returns reported during the first five trading days in January. Also called *turn-of-the-year effect.*

Joint probability function A function giving the probability of joint occurrences of values of stated random variables.

Judgmental sampling A procedure of selectively handpicking elements from the population based on a researcher's knowledge and professional judgment.

Junior debt Debt obligation with lower priority of payment than senior debt obligations.

Key rate duration Also known as partial duration, is a measure of a bond's sensitivity to a change in the benchmark yield at a specific maturity.

Keynesians Economists who believe that fiscal policy can have powerful effects on aggregate demand, output, and employment when there is substantial spare capacity in an economy.

Kurtosis The statistical measure that indicates the combined weight of the tails of a distribution relative to the rest of the distribution.

Lagging economic indicators Turning points that take place later than those of the overall economy; they are believed to have value in identifying the economy's past condition.

Law of one price A principle that states that if two investments have the same or equivalent future cash flows regardless of what will happen in the future, then these two investments should have the same current price.

Lead underwriter The lead investment bank in a syndicate of investment banks and broker–dealers involved in a securities underwriting.

Leading economic indicators Turning points that usually precede those of the overall economy; they are believed to have value for predicting the economy's future state, usually near-term.

Legal tender Something that must be accepted when offered in exchange for goods and services.

Lender of last resort An entity willing to lend money when no other entity is ready to do so.

Leptokurtic Describes a distribution that has fatter tails than a normal distribution (also called fat-tailed).

Lessee Tenant or property user that enters a lease with a property owner or lessor.

Lessor Property owner or manager that leases a property to a tenant or property user.

Level of significance The probability of a Type I error in testing a hypothesis.

Leverage A measure for identifying a potentially influential high-leverage point.

Leveraged buyout (LBO) A transaction in which a private acquiror uses equity and a high proportion of debt to acquire a public or private company in order to make changes to increase value over an investment period.

Leveraged loan Where private debt investor firms borrow money to make a direct loan to a borrower.

Leveraged loans Loans made to a borrower or issuer with relatively lower credit quality and/or higher leverage.

Liability-driven investing An investment industry term that generally encompasses asset allocation that is focused on funding an investor's liabilities in institutional contexts.

Licensing arrangements Rights to produce a product or have access to intangible assets using someone else's brand name in return for a royalty (often a percentage of revenues).

Lien A legal right or claim to property by a creditor.

Likelihood The probability of an observation, given a particular set of conditions.

Limit order Instructions to a broker or exchange to obtain the best price immediately available when filling an order, but in no event accept a price higher than a specified (limit) price when buying or accept a price lower than a specified (limit) price when selling.

Limit order book The book or list of limit orders to buy and sell that pertains to a security.

Limited company A business organizational form owned by shareholders or members with limited liability who elect a board of directors to appoint management. Generally, limited companies have indefinite life and easier transfer of ownership interests than limited partnerships.

Limited liability partnership (LLP) A business organizational form available in some jurisdictions owned entirely by limited partners with limited liability.

Limited partners (LPs) Outside investors in a private market fund who own a fractional interest in a limited, closed-end partnership managed by a general partner based on the investment commitment and other terms set out in a limited partner agreement.

Limited partnership Closed-end form of ownership frequently used in private market funds in which private market fund investors, or limited partners, commit capital that is invested, managed, and distributed by a private market fund manager, or general partner, over an investment holding period.

Limited partnership agreement (LPA) A legal document that outlines the rules of the partnership and establishes the framework that ultimately guides the fund's operations throughout its life.

lin-log model A functional form for transforming regression model data in which the dependent variable is linear but the independent variable is logarithmic.

Linear derivatives Firm commitment derivative contracts in which the contract's payoff/profit function is linear with respect to the price of the underlying.

Liquid market Said of a market in which traders can buy or sell with low total transaction costs when they want to trade.

Liquidity The extent to which a company is able to meet its short-term obligations using cash flows and those assets that can be readily transformed into cash.

Liquidity premium The compensation for liquidity risk that increases in proportion to the investment's illiquidity.

Liquidity ratios Financial ratios measuring the company's ability to meet its short-term obligations to creditors as they come due.

Liquidity risk The risk that an investment may not be readily sold at its true value.

Liquidity trap A condition in which the demand for money becomes infinitely elastic (horizontal demand curve) so that injections of money into the economy will not lower interest rates or affect real activity.

Load fund A mutual fund in which, in addition to the annual fee, a percentage fee is charged to invest in the fund and/or for redemptions from the fund.

Loan-to-value ratio (LTV) Ratio of the amount of the mortgage to the property's value. The lower the LTV, the higher the borrower's equity. From the lender's perspective, the higher the borrower's equity, the less likely the borrower is to default.

Loans Debt instruments agreed to between a borrower and lender, typically a bank.

Lockout or revolving period For an ABS with a non-amortizing collateral pool, such as credit card debt, is the period in which the cash proceeds from principal repayments are reinvested in additional loans with a principal equal to the principal repaid. During this period, there is no prepayment risk and potential default risk is generally limited. When the lockout period is over, principal repayments are used to pay off the outstanding principal on the ABS. Lockout period and revolving period are interchangeable.

Lockup period The minimum holding period before investors are allowed to make withdrawals or redeem shares from a fund. Its purpose is to allow the hedge fund manager the required time to implement and potentially realize a strategy's expected results.

log-lin model A functional form for transforming regression model data in which the dependent variable is logarithmic but the independent variable is linear.

log-log model A functional form for transforming regression model data in which both the dependent and independent variables are in logarithmic form.

Long A trading position in a **derivative contract** that gains value as the price of the **underlying** moves higher.

Long position A position in an asset or contract in which one owns the asset or has an exercisable right under the contract.

Long-run average total cost The curve describing average total cost when no costs are considered fixed.

Loss aversion The tendency of people to dislike losses more than they like comparable gains.

Loss given default (LGD) The amount a debtholder fails to recover if a default occurs, usually expressed as a percentage of par value.

Loss severity Portion of a bond's value (including unpaid interest) an investor loses in the event of default.

Loss-aversion bias A bias in which people tend to strongly prefer avoiding losses as opposed to achieving gains.

Low-cost producer A firm with lower production costs than its industry competitors.

M^2 A measure of what a portfolio would have returned if it had taken on the same total risk as the market index.

M^2 alpha Difference between the risk-adjusted performance of the portfolio and the performance of the benchmark.

Macaulay duration the present-value weighted average time to receipt of cash flows for fixed-income instrument, also the holding period needed to balance coupon reinvestment risk and price risk for a one-time instantaneous "parallel" shift in the yield curve once the bond purchase is settled. It is named after Frederick Macaulay, the Canadian economist who introduced the concept in 1938.

Machine learning (ML) Involves computer-based techniques that seek to extract knowledge from large amounts of data without making any assumptions about the data's underlying probability distribution. The goal of ML algorithms is to automate decision-making processes by generalizing, or "learning," from known examples to determine an underlying structure in the data.

Maintenance capital expenditures Investments in assets to keep them in operation or increase their efficiency without extending their useful lives.

Maintenance margin Minimum balance set below the initial margin that each contract buyer and seller must hold in the futures margin account from trade initiation until final settlement at maturity.

Maintenance margin requirement The margin requirement on any day other than the first day of a transaction.

Management buy-in A type of leveraged buyout where the current management team is replaced with the acquiring team involved in managing the company.

Management buyout A private sale to a strategic buyer that includes a company's existing management. The management team commits their own equity capital along with other investors as an incentive to grow the firm's cash flows and value.

Management guidance Management of public companies may publicly provide targets for earnings, revenues, and other measures (e.g., capital expenditures) for the next quarter, year, or longer term. Guidance can be detailed or rather directional and is often updated throughout the year. Initial guidance for next fiscal year might be provided during the fourth-quarter earnings call and updated for completed quarters, and new information provided at the first-, second-, and third-quarter earnings calls. Also known simply as *guidance*.

Margin call Request to a derivatives contract counterparty to immediately deposit funds to return the futures margin account balance to the initial margin.

Margin financing A financing arrangement whereby the prime broker lends shares, bonds, or derivatives and the hedge fund (or investment manager) deposits cash or other collateral into a margin account at the prime broker based on certain fractions of the investment positions.

Margin loan Money borrowed from a broker to purchase securities.

Marginal propensity to consume The proportion of an additional unit of disposable income that is consumed or spent; the change in consumption for a small change in income.

Marginal propensity to save The proportion of an additional unit of disposable income that is saved (not spent).

Mark to market (MTM) The practice in which a central clearing party assigns profits and losses to counterparties to derivative contracts. In exchange-traded markets, this practice takes place daily and is often referred to as daily settlement.

Market anomaly Change in the price or return of a security that cannot directly be linked to current relevant information known in the market or to the release of new information into the market.

Market bid–ask spread The difference between the best bid and the best offer.

Market discount rate The rate of return required by investors given the risk of the bond investment, also known as the required yield or required rate of return.

Market float The number of shares that are available to the investing public.

Market makers **Over-the-counter (OTC) dealers** who typically enter into offsetting bilateral transactions with one another to transfer risk to other parties.

Market model A regression model with the return on a stock as the dependent variable and the returns on a market index as the independent variable.

Market multiple models Valuation models based on share price multiples or enterprise value multiples.

Market neutral These strategies use quantitative, fundamental, and technical analysis to identify under- and overvalued equity securities. The hedge fund takes long positions in undervalued securities and short positions in overvalued securities, while seeking to maintain a market-neutral net position.

Market order Instructions to a broker or exchange to obtain the best price immediately available when filling an order.

Market reference rate (MRR) The interest rate underlying used in interest rate swaps. These rates typically match those of loans or other short-term obligations. Survey-based Libor rates used as reference rates in the past have been replaced by rates based on a daily average of observed market transaction rates. For example, the Secured Overnight Financing Rate (SOFR) is an overnight cash borrowing rate collateralized by US Treasuries. Other MRRs include the euro short-term rate (€STR) and the Sterling Overnight Index Average (SONIA).

Market risk Risk related to market movements, e.g., unexpected changes in share prices, interest rates, currency exchange rates, and commodity prices.

Market share A company's or product's revenue expressed as a percentage of its market size.

Market size Total sales for a good or service, which can be calculated on a global or more regional basis.

Market value The price at which an asset or security can currently be bought or sold in an open market.

Market-capitalization weighting An index weighting method in which the weight assigned to each constituent security is determined by dividing its market capitalization by the total market capitalization (sum of the market capitalization) of all securities in the index. Also called *value weighting*.

Market-on-close An execution instruction specifying that an order can only be filled at the close of trading.

Marketable limit order A buy limit order in which the limit price is placed above the best offer, or a sell limit order in which the limit price is placed below the best bid. Such orders generally will partially or completely fill right away.

Markowitz efficient frontier The graph of the set of portfolios offering the maximum expected return for their level of risk (standard deviation of return).

Master limited partnership (MLP) Has similar features to limited partnerships but is usually a more liquid investment that is often publicly traded.

Master repurchase agreement A legal document governing all repo trades between two parties.

Match funding Financing an asset with a source, such as a loan or bond, that is aligned with certain attributes of the asset, such as duration and the respective streams of income and financing costs.

Material (materiality) Refers to information that is decision-useful for a reasonable investor.

Matrix pricing An estimation process for financial instruments based on the prices of comparable instruments.

Maturity The date of a fixed-income instrument's final payment to investors.

Maturity premium An extra return that compensates investors for the increased sensitivity of the market value of debt to a change in market interest rates as maturity is extended.

Maturity structure of interest rates Also known as the term structure of interest rates, refers to the difference in interest rates or benchmark yields by time-to-maturity.

Mean absolute deviation With reference to a sample, the mean of the absolute values of deviations from the sample mean.

Mean square error (MSE) Calculated as the sum of squares error (SSE) divided by the degrees of freedom, which are the number of observations minus the number of independent variables minus one. Since simple linear regression has just one independent variable, the degrees of freedom calculation is the number of observations minus 2.

Mean square regression (MSR) Calculated as the sum of squares regression (SSR) divided by the number of independent variables in the regression model. In simple linear regression, there is only one independent variable, so MSR equals SSR.

Mean–variance analysis An approach to portfolio analysis using expected means, variances, and covariances of asset returns.

Measure of central tendency A quantitative measure that specifies where data are centered.

Measures of location Quantitative measures that describe the location or distribution of data. They include not only measures of central tendency but also other measures, such as percentiles.

Median The "middlemost" observation; i.e., in a set of observations that has been ranked from highest to lowest, the median will lie in the middle.

Meme coin A type of altcoin that is often inspired by a joke.

Mental accounting bias An information-processing bias in which people treat one sum of money differently from another equal-sized sum based on which mental account the money is assigned to.

Merger arbitrage Special situations investments related to business combinations in which investors seek to capitalize on price discrepancies of securities issued by the target company.

Mesokurtic Describes a distribution with kurtosis equal to that of the normal distribution, namely, kurtosis equal to three.

Mezzanine debt Refers to private credit subordinated to senior secured debt but senior to equity in the borrower's capital structure.

Mezzanine-stage financing Mezzanine venture capital that prepares a company to go public as it continues to expand capacity and enhance its growth trajectory. It represents the bridge financing needed to fund a private firm until it can execute an IPO or be sold.

Miner A validator of transactions on the blockchain that locks blocks of transactions into the blockchain and receives compensation for this process in the form of a digital asset.

Minimum efficient scale The smallest output that a firm can produce such that its long-run average total cost is minimized.

Minimum-variance portfolio The portfolio with the minimum variance for each given level of expected return.

Minority shareholder An individual or entity that owns less than a majority of the voting rights in a corporation.

Mode The most frequently occurring value in a distribution.

Modern portfolio theory (MPT) The analysis of rational portfolio choices based on the efficient use of risk.

Modified duration The first derivative of a bond's price with respect to its yield, this statistic is a measure of interest rate risk used to estimate the percentage price change for a given change in yield-to-maturity.

Monetarists Economists who believe that the rate of growth of the money supply is the primary determinant of the rate of inflation.

Monetary policy Actions taken by a nation's central bank to affect aggregate output and prices through changes in bank reserves, reserve requirements, or its target interest rate.

Monetary transmission mechanism The process whereby a central bank's interest rate gets transmitted through the economy and ultimately affects the rate of increase of prices.

Monetary union An economic union in which the members adopt a common currency.

Money convexity A measure that is used to complement modified duration to capture the second-order effect of yield changes on a bond's price, expressed in currency terms.

Money duration A measure of the price change of a fixed-income instrument in currency units from a change in yield-to-maturity. The money duration can be stated per 100 of par value or in terms of the actual position size. In the United States, money duration is commonly called "dollar duration."

Money market The market for short-term debt instruments (one-year maturity or less).

Money market securities Fixed-income securities with original maturities of one year or less.

Money-weighted return The internal rate of return on a portfolio, taking account of all cash flows.

Moneyness Expresses the relationship between an option's value and its exercise price across the full range of possible underlying prices.

Monopolistic competition Highly competitive form of imperfect competition; the competitive characteristic is a notably large number of firms, while the monopoly aspect is the result of product differentiation.

Monopoly In pure monopoly markets, there are no substitutes for the given product or service. There is a single seller, which exercises considerable power over pricing and output decisions.

Monte Carlo simulation A technique that uses the inverse transformation method for converting a randomly generated uniformly distributed number into a simulated value of a random variable of a desired distribution. Each key decision variable in a Monte Carlo simulation requires an assumed statistical distribution; this assumption facilitates incorporating non-normality, fat tails, and tail dependence as well as solving high-dimensionality problems.

Moral principles Beliefs regarding what is good, acceptable, or obligatory behavior and what is bad, unacceptable, or forbidden behavior.

Mortgage loan Agreement to finance real estate by the collateral of a specified property that obliges the borrower to make a predetermined series of payments to the lender.

Mortgage pass-through security Security created when mortgage lenders pool mortgages together and sell securities to investors. The cash flow from the mortgage pool––monthly payments of principal, interest, and prepayments––are "passed through" to the security holders.

Mortgage-backed securities (MBS) Debt obligations that represent claims to the cash flows from pools of mortgage loans, most commonly on residential property.

Multi-factor model A model that explains a variable in terms of the values of a set of factors.

Multi-market indexes Comprised of indexes from different countries, designed to represent multiple security markets.

Multilateral trading facilities See *alternative trading systems*.

Multilateralism The conduct of countries who participate in mutually beneficial trade relationships and extensive rules harmonization. Private firms are fully integrated into global supply chains with multiple trade partners. Examples of multilateral countries include Germany and Singapore.

Multiple of invested capital (MOIC) Also referred to as the multiple of money or total value to paid-in, this private market performance measure incorporates both the cumulative distributions received and the net asset value of a fund as a proportion of invested capital.

Multiple-price auction A debt securities auction in which bidders receive distinct prices based on their bids.

Multiplier models Valuation models based on share price multiples or enterprise value multiples.

Mutual fund A comingled investment pool in which investors in the fund each have a pro-rata claim on the income and value of the fund.

Nash equilibrium When two or more participants in a non-coop-erative game have no incentive to deviate from their respective equilibrium strategies given their opponent's strategies.

Nationalism The promotion of a country's own economic interests to the exclusion or detriment of the interests of other nations. Nationalism is marked by limited economic and financial cooperation. These actors may focus on national production and sales, limited cross-border investment and capital flows, and restricted currency exchange.

Natural language processing (NLP) A field of research within the field of text analytics and at the intersection of computer science, AI, and linguistics that focuses on developing computer programs to analyze and interpret human language.

Natural resources These include commodities (hard and soft), agricultural land (farmland), and timberland.

Negative externalities A cost to a third party because of the production or consumption of a good or service.

Negative pledge clause Limitations on investments, the disposal of assets, or issuance of debt senior to existing obligations. Negative covenants seek to ensure that an issuer maintains the ability to make interest and principal payments.

Net cash An issuer's total debt less cash and marketable securities. When the balance is negative it is referred to as net cash.

Net debt An issuer's total debt less cash and marketable securities. When the balance is positive it is referred to as net debt.

Net investment hedge Refers to a specific **hedge accounting** designation that applies when either a foreign currency bond or a derivative, such as an FX swap or forward, is used to offset the exchange rate risk of the equity of a foreign operation.

Net present value (NPV) The present value of an investment's cash inflows (benefits) minus the present value of its cash outflows (costs).

Net profit margin An indicator of profitability, calculated as net income divided by revenue; indicates how much of each dollar of revenues is left after all costs and expenses. Also called *profit margin* or *return on sales*.

Net tax rate The tax rate net of transfer payments.

Net working capital Working capital excluding short-term items unrelated to business operations, such as cash, marketable securities, and short-term debt.

Network effects A business model that enables users to contribute directly to a product, service, or online content.

Neural networks A type of computer program design based on how the human brain learns and processes information.

Neutral rate of interest The rate of interest that neither spurs on nor slows down the underlying economy.

No-load fund A mutual fund in which there is no fee for investing in the fund or for redeeming fund shares, although there is an annual fee based on a percentage of the fund's net asset value.

Node Each value on a binomial tree from which successive moves or outcomes branch.

Non-agency RMBS MBS backed by residential mortgages that are issued by private entities and not guaranteed by a federal agency or a GSE.

Non-amortizing loans Type of debt where there are no scheduled principal repayments.

Non-cooperative country A country with inconsistent and even arbitrary rules; restricted movement of goods, services, people, and capital across borders; retaliation; and limited technology exchange.

Non-cumulative preference shares Preference shares for which dividends that are not paid in the current or subsequent periods are forfeited permanently (instead of being accrued and paid at a later date).

Non-financial risks Risks that arise from sources other than changes in the external financial markets, such as changes in accounting rules, legal environment, or tax rates.

Non-fungible token (NFT) A unique cryptographic token on the blockchain that cannot be replicated and is used to represent ownership of physical assets, such as artwork, real estate, or other assets.

Non-linear derivatives Derivatives, such as options or other contingent claims, with payoff/profit profiles that are non-linear (asymmetric) with respect to the price of the underlying.

Non-participating preference shares Preference shares that do not entitle shareholders to share in the profits of the company. Instead, shareholders are only entitled to receive a fixed dividend payment and the par value of the shares in the event of liquidation.

Non-probability sampling A sampling plan dependent on factors other than probability considerations, such as a sampler's judgment or the convenience to access data.

Non-recourse loan Loan in which the lender does not have a claim against the borrower and thus can look only to the property to recover the outstanding mortgage balance.

Non-state actors Those that participate in global political, economic, or financial affairs but do not directly control national security or country resources. Examples of non-state actors are non-governmental organizations (NGOs), multinational companies, charities, and even influential individuals, such as business leaders or cultural icons.

Nonparametric test A test that is not concerned with a parameter or that makes minimal assumptions about the population from which a sample comes.

Nonsystematic risk Unique risk that is local or limited to a particular asset or industry that need not affect assets outside of that asset class.

Normal distribution A continuous, symmetric probability distribution that is completely described by its mean and its variance.

Normalized earnings The expected level of mid-cycle earnings for a company in the absence of any unusual or temporary factors that affect profitability (either positively or negatively).

Notching Ratings adjustment methodology where specific issues from the same borrower may be assigned different credit ratings.

Notice period The length of time (typically 30–90 days) in advance that investors may be required to notify a fund of their intent to redeem some or all of their investment. This allows a fund manager to liquidate a position in an orderly fashion without magnifying losses.

Novation process A process that substitutes the initial **swap execution facility (SEF)** contract with identical trades facing the **central counterparty (CCP)**. The CCP serves as **counterparty** for both financial intermediaries, eliminating bilateral **counterparty credit risk** and providing **clearing** and **settlement** services.

Null hypothesis The hypothesis that is tested.

Off-the-run Seasoned government bonds that are often less liquid.

Off-the-run securities Sovereign debt securities outstanding other than on-the-sun securities. Off-the-run securities are less liquid than on-the-run securities.

Offer The price at which a dealer or trader is willing to sell an asset, typically qualified by a maximum quantity (ask size).

Official interest rate An interest rate that a central bank sets and announces publicly; normally the rate at which it is willing to lend money to the commercial banks. Also called *official policy rate* or *policy rate.*

Official policy rate An interest rate that a central bank sets and announces publicly; normally the rate at which it is willing to lend money to the commercial banks.

Oligopoly Market structure with a relatively small number of firms supplying the market.

Omnichannel Refers to a company selling its products or services in multiple channels, such as in store and online.

On-the-run Most recently issued, and liquid, government bonds.

On-the-run securities The most recently issued and liquid sovereign debt securities.

Open interest The number of outstanding contracts.

Open market operations The purchase or sale of bonds by the national central bank to implement monetary policy. The bonds traded are usually sovereign bonds issued by the national government.

Open-end fund A mutual fund that accepts new investment money and issues additional shares at a value equal to the net asset value of the fund at the time of investment.

Operating cycle The length of time between a company's acquisition of goods or raw materials and the collection of cash from sales to customers.

Operating efficiency ratios Ratios that measure how efficiently a company performs day-to-day tasks, such as the collection of receivables and management of inventory.

Operating leases A type of lease which is more akin to the rental of the underlying asset.

Operating leverage The sensitivity of a firm's operating profit to a change in revenues, determined by the composition of fixed and variable operating costs.

Operating profit margin A profitability ratio calculated as operating income (i.e., income before interest and taxes) divided by revenue. Also called *operating margin.*

Operational deposits Bank deposits generated by clearing, custody, and cash management activities.

Operational independence A bank's ability to execute monetary policy and set interest rates in the way it thought would best meet the inflation target.

Operational risk The risk that arises from inadequate or failed people, systems, and internal policies, procedures, and processes, as well as from external events that are beyond the control of the organization but that affect its operations.

Operationally efficient Said of a market, a financial system, or an economy that has relatively low transaction costs.

Opportunistic real estate strategies Include major redevelopment, repurposing of assets, taking on large vacancies, or speculating on significant improvement in market conditions. These may be appealing for investors seeking higher returns and willing to accept additional risks from development, redevelopment, repositioning, and leasing.

Opportunity cost Reflects the foregone opportunity of investing in a different asset. It is typically denoted by the risk-free rate of interest, r.

Optimal capital structure The capital structure at which the value of the company is maximized.

Option A primary example of a **contingent claim**. A **derivative contract** that provides the buyer the right, but not the obligation, to buy or sell an **underlying**.

Option contract See *option.*

Option premium An amount that is paid upfront from the option buyer to the option seller. Reflects the value of the option buyer's right to exercise in the future.

Option-adjusted price The sum of a bond's flat price and value of an embedded option.

Option-adjusted spread or OAS for a bond is its Z-spread adjusted for the value of an embedded option.

Option-adjusted yield A yield measure for a bond adjusted for embedded options.

Order A specification of what instrument to trade, how much to trade, and whether to buy or sell.

Order precedence hierarchy With respect to the execution of orders to trade, a set of rules that determines which orders execute before other orders.

Order-driven markets A market (generally an auction market) that uses rules to arrange trades based on the orders that traders submit; in their pure form, such markets do not make use of dealers.

Ordinary shares Equity shares that are subordinate to all other types of equity (e.g., preferred equity). Also called *common stock* or *common shares.*

Organizational form A legal and tax classification of a business, specific to a jurisdiction, that determines the organization's legal identity, owner–manager relationship, owner liability, taxation, and access to financing.

Out-of-the-money Describes an option with zero intrinsic value because the option buyer would not rationally exercise the option. An example of such would be the case in which the price of the underlying is less than the option's exercise price for a call option.

Over-the-counter (OTC) Refers to derivative markets in which **derivative contracts** are created and traded between derivatives end users and **dealers**, or financial intermediaries, such as commercial banks or investment banks.

Overcollateralization Credit enhancement technique where collateral underlying the transaction exceeds the face value of the issued bonds.

Overconfidence bias A bias in which people demonstrate unwarranted faith in their own intuitive reasoning, judgments, and/or cognitive abilities.

Overfitting When a machine learning model learns the input and target dataset too precisely, making the system more likely to discover false relationships or unsubstantiated patterns that will lead to prediction errors.

P-value The smallest level of significance at which the null hypothesis can be rejected.

Par rate A yield-to-maturity that makes the present value of a bond's cash flows equal to par.

Par swap rate The fixed swap rate that equates the present value of all future expected floating cash flows to the present value of fixed cash flows.

Par value The amount of principal on a bond, also known as face value.

Parallel shift When all maturities along a yield curve increase or decrease in yield in the same direction by the same magnitude. A parallel shift in the yield curve is implicitly assumed in analytical duration and convexity.

Parameter A descriptive measure computed from or used to describe a population of data, conventionally represented by Greek letters.

Parametric test Any test (or procedure) concerned with parameters or whose validity depends on assumptions concerning the population generating the sample.

Pari passu clause A covenant or contract clause that ensures a debt obligation is treated the same as the borrower's other senior debt instruments and is not subordinated to similar obligations.

Partially amortizing bond A loan or bond with a payment schedule that calls for partial repayment of principle over the life of the bond, with the remaining principal paid at maturity.

Participating preference shares Preference shares that entitle shareholders to receive the standard preferred dividend plus the opportunity to receive an additional dividend if the company's profits exceed a pre-specified level.

Pass-through businesses Businesses that, by virtue of their organizational form and/or other legal and regulatory attributes, do not pay entity-level taxes on income or loss; income or loss is passed through to owners, who pay personal taxes.

Pass-through rate The coupon rate of a mortgage pass-through security that is received by the investor after administrative charges. It is lower than the weighted average mortgage rate earned on the underlying pool of mortgages because of administrative charges. The pass-through rate that the investor receives is said to be "net interest" or "net coupon."

Passive investment A buy-and-hold approach in which an investor does not make portfolio changes based on short-term expectations of changing market or security performance.

Payable date The day that the company actually mails out (or electronically transfers) a dividend payment.

Payment date The day that the company actually mails out (or electronically transfers) a dividend payment.

Payment-in-kind A bond feature whereby coupon payments can be fully or partially paid in the form of additional issuance or added to the principal amount.

Payments system The system for the transfer of money.

Pearson correlation A parametric measure of the relationship between two variables.

Pecking order theory The theory that managers consider how their actions might be interpreted by outsiders and thereby order their preferences for various forms of corporate financing. Forms of financing that are least visible to outsiders (e.g., internally generated funds) are most preferable to managers, and those that are most visible (e.g., equity issuance) are least preferable.

Penetration pricing A discount pricing approach used when a firm willingly sacrifices margins in order to build scale and market share.

Percentiles Values that divide a distribution into 100 equal parts.

Perfect competition A market structure in which the individual firm has virtually no impact on market price, because it is assumed to be a very small seller among a very large number of firms selling essentially identical products.

Performance evaluation The measurement and assessment of the outcomes of investment management decisions.

Performance fee Fee paid to the general partner from the limited partner(s) based on realized net profits.

Period costs Costs (e.g., executives' salaries) that cannot be directly matched with the timing of revenues and which are thus expensed immediately.

Periodicity Number of periods in a year, used for compound interest. The periodicity of a fixed-income instrument usually matches the frequency of its coupon payments.

Permanent differences Differences between tax and financial reporting of revenue (expenses) that will not be reversed at some future date. These result in a difference between the company's effective tax rate and statutory tax rate and do not result in a deferred tax item.

Permissioned networks Networks that are fully open only to select participants on a DLT network.

Permissionless networks Networks that are fully open to any user on a DLT network.

Perpetual bonds Bonds with no stated maturity date.

Perpetuity A perpetual annuity, or a set of never-ending level sequential cash flows, with the first cash flow occurring one period from now.

PESTLE analysis A framework for analyzing factors that influence an industry's economic outcomes.

Pet projects A capital investment that is pursued by management but is not economically justifiable by a disinterested party. Motivations for pet projects include self-dealing and vanity.

Physical risks Economic and financial losses from the increase in the severity and frequency of extreme weather due to climate change—for example, the loss of coastal real estate from a storm.

PIPE (private investment in public equity) A private offering to select investors with fewer disclosures and lower transaction costs that allows the issuer to raise capital more quickly and cost effectively.

Platykurtic Describes a distribution that has relatively less weight in the tails than the normal distribution (also called thin-tailed).

Pledge A legal right or claim to property by a creditor. Also called a lien.

Poison pill Officially known as a shareholder rights plan, a poison pill is a hostile-takeover defense adopted by boards of directors according to rules specified in the corporate charter. There are several types of poison pills. Generally, they allow shareholders, *excluding* the shareholder making the hostile bid and their affiliates, to buy newly issued shares at a discounted price. The share issuance would dilute the bidder's ownership percentage, rendering it impossible for the bidder to attain control.

Policy rate An interest rate that a central bank sets and announces publicly; normally the rate at which it is willing to lend money to the commercial banks.

Portfolio companies The individual companies owned by a private equity firm.

Portfolio investment flows Short-term investments in foreign assets, such as stocks or bonds.

Portfolio planning The process of creating a plan for building a portfolio that is expected to satisfy a client's investment objectives.

Position The quantity of an asset that an entity owns or owes.

Posterior probability An updated probability that reflects or comes after new information.

Power of a test The probability of correctly rejecting the null—that is, rejecting the null hypothesis when it is false.

Pre-funding period Allows the trust to acquire during a certain period of time after the close of the transaction.

Preference shares A type of equity interest which ranks above common shares with respect to the payment of dividends and the distribution of the company's net assets upon liquidation. They have characteristics of both debt and equity securities. Also called *preferred stock*.

Preferred stock See *preference shares*.

Premium In the case of bonds, premium refers to the amount by which a bond is priced above its face (par) value. In the case of an option, the amount paid for the option contract.

Prepayment option May entitle the borrower to prepay all or part of the outstanding mortgage principal prior to maturity. This creates a risk from the lender's or investor's viewpoint because the cash flow amounts and timing cannot be known with certainty.

Prepayment risk The risk that the some or all of a mortgage-backed security's principal is repaid at a different speed than expected, either in the form of contraction risk (or earlier repayment than expected) or extension risk (later repayment).

Present value models Valuation models that estimate the intrinsic value of a security as the present value of the future benefits expected to be received from the security. Also called *discounted cash flow models.*

Pretax margin A profitability ratio calculated as earnings before taxes divided by revenue.

Price discrimination A pricing approach that charges different prices to different customers based on their willingness to pay.

Price index Represents the average prices of a basket of goods and services.

Price limits Establish a band relative to the previous day's settlement price within which all trades must occur.

Price multiple A ratio that compares the share price with some sort of monetary flow or value to allow evaluation of the relative worth of a company's stock.

Price priority The principle that the highest priced buy orders and the lowest priced sell orders execute first.

Price return Measures *only* the price appreciation or percentage change in price of the securities in an index or portfolio.

Price return index An index that reflects *only* the price appreciation or percentage change in price of the constituent securities. Also called *price index.*

Price stability In economics, refers to an inflation rate that is low on average and not subject to wide fluctuation.

Price takers Producers that must accept whatever price the market dictates.

Price value of a basis point (PVBP) An estimate of the change in the full price of a bond given a 1 bp change in its yield-to-maturity. The PVBP is also called the "PV01," standing for the "price value of an 01" or "present value of an 01," where "01" means 1 bp. In the United States, it is commonly called the "DV01" for the "dollar value" of 1 bp.

Price weighting An index weighting method in which the weight assigned to each constituent security is determined by dividing its price by the sum of all the prices of the constituent securities.

Price-setting option The option to adjust prices when demand or supply varies from what is forecast.

Price-to-earnings ratio (P/E) The ratio of share price to earnings per share.

Pricing power A company's ability to set prices and other economic terms with customers without affecting its sales volumes.

Primary bond markets Fixed-income markets comprised of issuers issuing bonds to investors to raise capital, often intermediated by a third-party such as an investment bank.

Primary capital markets (primary markets) The market where securities are first sold and the issuers receive the proceeds.

Primary dealer Financial institution that is authorized to deal in new issues of sovereign bonds and that serves primarily as a trading counterparty of the office responsible for issuing sovereign bonds.

Primary market The market where securities are first sold and the issuers receive the proceeds.

Prime broker A broker that provides services that commonly include custody, administration, lending, short borrowing, and trading.

Prime loans Lending made to borrowers of high credit quality with strong employment and credit histories, a low DTI, substantial equity in the underlying property, and a first lien on the mortgaged property serving as the collateral for the loan.

Principal The amount that an issuer agrees to repay the debtholders on the maturity date.

Principal-agent relationship An arrangement in which one party (the agent) has authority to act for or on behalf of another party (the principal). Such an arrangement imposes a duty on the agent to act in the principal's best interest.

Prior probabilities Probabilities reflecting beliefs prior to the arrival of new information.

Priority of claims Priority of payment, with the most senior or highest ranking debt having the first claim on the cash flows and assets of the issuer.

Private capital Funding provided to companies that is not sourced from the public markets.

Private company A company, typically a limited company, that does not list its equity securities on an exchange.

Private debt Capital extended to companies through a loan or other form of debt.

Private debtholders Investors in an entity's non-securitized debt claims, such as a loan or lease. The most common type of private debtholder is a bank.

Private equity Equity investment capital raised from sources other than public markets and traditional institutions.

Private equity fund A hedge fund that seeks to buy, optimize, and ultimately sell portfolio companies to generate profits. See *venture capital fund.*

Private equity securities Securities that are not listed on public exchanges and have no active secondary market. They are issued primarily to institutional investors via non-public offerings, such as private placements.

Private investment in public equity (PIPE) An investment in the equity of a publicly traded firm that is made at a discount to the market value of the firm's shares.

Private limited company A type of limited company in many jurisdictions with pass-through taxation but restrictions on the number of shareholders or members and on the transfer of ownership interest.

Private placement A sale of debt or equity securities to a small group of investors on an unregulated basis. The terms of the offering are negotiated by the issuer and investors.

Probability of default (POD) The likelihood that a borrower fails to make full and timely payments of principal and interest according to debt terms, usually expressed in annual percentage terms.

Probability sampling A sampling plan that allows every member of the population to have an equal chance of being selected.

Probability tree diagram A diagram with branches emanating from nodes representing either mutually exclusive chance events or mutually exclusive decisions.

Production flexibility option The option to alter production when demand varies from what is forecast.

Profession An occupational group that has specific education, expert knowledge, and a framework of practice and behavior that underpins community trust, respect, and recognition.

Profit margin An indicator of profitability, calculated as net income divided by revenue; indicates how much of each dollar of revenues is left after all costs and expenses.

Profitability ratios Ratios that measure a company's ability to generate profitable sales from its resources (assets).

Prospectus Legal document in securitization that describes the structure of the transaction, including the priority and amount of payments to be made to the servicer, administrators, and the ABS holders, as well as the credit enhancements used in the securitization.

Protective put A strategy of purchasing an underlying asset and purchasing a put on the same asset.

Proxy contest When a shareholder or group of shareholders campaigns for certain matters they have submitted to a shareholder vote, often a slate of directors who oppose the incumbent board and management. The incumbent board and management simultaneously campaign for their side.

Proxy voting A form of casting a ballot in an election in which a voter authorizes a representative to vote on their behalf according to instructions. In corporate elections, proxy ballots are cast by shareholders that direct a representative, typically the corporate secretary, to enter their votes as instructed.

Public (listed) company A company with its equity securities traded on an exchange.

Public limited companies A type of limited company in many jurisdictions with entity-level taxation but no restrictions on the number of shareholders or transferability of ownership interest; the most suitable organizational form for a company that seeks to go public.

Public–private partnership A long-term contractual relationship between the public and private sectors for the purpose of having the private sector deliver a project or service traditionally provided by the public sector. Infrastructure is increasingly being financed privately through public–private partnerships by local, regional, and national governments.

Public–private partnership (PPP) An agreement between the public sector and the private sector to finance, build, and operate public infrastructure, such as hospitals and toll roads.

Pull on liquidity An action or event that accelerates cash outflows.

Purchase agreement Legal document in a securitization transaction that outlines the representations and warranties that the seller makes about the assets sold.

Pure discount bonds Bonds that do not pay interest during their life. They are issued at a discount to par value and redeemed at par. Also called zero-coupon bonds.

Put An option that gives the holder the right to sell an underlying asset to another party at a fixed price over a specific period of time.

Put option The right to sell an underlying.

Putable bonds Bonds that give the bondholder the right to sell the bond back to the issuer at a predetermined price on specified dates.

Put–call forward parity Describes the no-arbitrage condition in which at $t = 0$ the present value of the price of a long forward commitment plus the price of the long put must equal the price of the long call plus the price of the risk-free asset (with face value of the exercise price of both the call and the put).

Put–call parity Describes the no-arbitrage condition in which at $t = 0$ the price of the long underlying asset plus the price of the long put must equal the price of the long call plus the price of the risk-free asset (with face value of the exercise price of both the call and the put).

Quantile A value at or below which a stated fraction of the data lies. Also referred to as a fractile.

Quantitative easing An expansionary monetary policy based on aggressive open market purchase operations.

Quartiles Quantiles that divide a distribution into four equal parts.

Quick ratio A measure of liquidity that is the ratio of cash, marketable securities, and receivables to current liabilities.

Quintiles Quantiles that divide a distribution into five equal parts.

Quota rents Profits that foreign producers can earn by raising the price of their goods higher than they would without a quota.

Quotas Government policies that restrict the quantity of a good that can be imported into a country, generally for a specified period of time.

Quote-driven market A market in which dealers acting as principals facilitate trading.

Quoted margin Specified spread of a floating rate instrument over a market reference rate or benchmark.

Range The difference between the maximum and minimum values in a dataset.

Rapid amortization provisions Provisions in receivable ABS that may require early principal amortization if specific events occur. Such provisions are referred to as early amortization and are included to safeguard the credit quality of the issue, particularly during the revolving period.

Razor, razorblade pricing A pricing approach that combines a low price on a piece of equipment and high-margin pricing on repeat-purchase consumables.

Real assets Generally, these are tangible physical assets, such as real estate, infrastructure, and natural resources, but they also include such intangibles as patents, intellectual property, and goodwill. Real assets generate current or expected future cash flows and/or are considered a store of value.

Real estate Includes borrowed or ownership capital in buildings or land. Developed land includes commercial and industrial real estate, residential real estate, and infrastructure.

Real option A right, but not an obligation, for management to make a decision with respect to a capital investment that alters future cash flows from the original forecasted scenario.

Real risk-free interest rate The single-period interest rate for a completely risk-free security if no inflation were expected.

Rebalancing Adjusting the weights of the constituent securities in an index.

Rebalancing policy The set of rules that guide the process of restoring a portfolio's asset class weights to those specified in the strategic asset allocation.

Recapitalization Recapitalization via private equity describes the steps a firm takes to increase or introduce leverage to its portfolio company and pay itself a dividend out of the new capital structure.

Recognition lag The lag in government response to an economic problem resulting from the delay in confirming a change in the state of the economy.

Recourse loan Loan in which the lender has a claim against the borrower for the shortfall (deficiency) between the amount of the outstanding mortgage balance and the proceeds received from the sale of the property.

Recovery rate (RR) The percentage of an outstanding debt claim recovered when an issuer defaults

Redemption fee A fee charged to discourage redemptions and to offset the transaction costs for remaining investors in the fund.

Refinancing rate A type of central bank policy rate.

Regionalism In between the two extremes of bilateralism and multilateralism. In regionalism, a group of countries cooperate with one another. Both bilateralism and regionalism can be conducted at the exclusion of other groups. For example, regional blocs may agree to provide trade benefits to one another and increase barriers for those outside of that group.

Registered bonds Bonds for which ownership is recorded by either name or serial number.

Regression analysis Allows us to test hypotheses about the relationship between two variables, by quantifying the strength of the relationship between the two variables, and to use one variable to make predictions about the other variable.

Regression coefficients The collective term for the intercept and slope coefficients in the regression model.

Regret The feeling that an opportunity has been missed; typically, an expression of *hindsight bias.*

Regret-aversion bias An emotional bias in which people tend to avoid making decisions that will result in action out of fear that the decision will turn out poorly.

Relative dispersion The amount of dispersion relative to a reference value or benchmark.

Reopening Issuing bonds by increasing the size of an existing bond issue with a price significantly different from par.

Replication A strategy in which a derivative's cash flow stream may be recreated using a combination of long or short positions in an underlying asset and borrowing or lending cash.

Repo rate The interest rate on a repurchase agreement.

Representativeness bias A belief perseverance bias in which people tend to classify new information based on past experiences and classifications.

Repurchase agreement (Repo) A form of collateralized loan involving the sale of a security with a simultaneous agreement by the seller to buy back the same security from the purchaser at an agreed-on price and future date. The party who sells the security at the inception of the repurchase agreement and buys it back at maturity is borrowing money from the other party, and the security sold and subsequently repurchased represents the collateral.

Repurchase date The date when the party who sold the security at the inception of a repurchase agreement buys back the security from the cash lending counterparty.

Repurchase price The price at which the party who sold the security at the inception of the repurchase agreement buys back the security from the cash lending counterparty.

Required margin Also known as discount margin. The market-determined yield spread over or under the market reference rate such that a floating-rate loan is priced at par on a rate reset date following issuance.

Required rate of return The rate of return required by investors given the risk of the bond investment, also known as the market discount rate or required yield.

Required yield The rate of return required by investors given the risk of the bond investment, also known as the market discount rate of required rate of return.

Required yield spread The difference in yield-to-maturity between a bond and that of a government benchmark bond with the same or similar time-to-maturity.

Resampling A statistical method that repeatedly draws samples from the original observed data sample for the statistical inference of population parameters.

Reserve currency A currency held by global central banks in significant quantities and widely used to conduct international trade and financial transactions.

Reserve requirement The requirement for banks to hold reserves in proportion to the size of deposits.

Residual The amount of deviation of an observed value of the dependent variable from its estimated value based on the fitted regression line.

Restricted domestic currency A currency with limited convertibility into other currencies due to illiquidity.

Return on assets (ROA) A profitability ratio calculated as net income divided by average total assets; indicates a company's net profit generated per dollar invested in total assets.

Return on equity (ROE) A profitability ratio calculated as net income divided by average shareholders' equity.

Return on invested capital (ROIC) A measure of the profitability of a company relative to the amount of capital invested by the equityholders and debtholders.

Return on sales An indicator of profitability, calculated as net income divided by revenue; indicates how much of each dollar of revenues is left after all costs and expenses. Also referred to as *net profit margin.*

Return-generating model A model that can provide an estimate of the expected return of a security given certain parameters and estimates of the values of the independent variables in the model.

Revenue bonds Bonds issued by non-sovereign governments related to a government sponsored project expected to generate future cash flow as a primary source of repayment.

Reverse repurchase agreement A repurchase agreement viewed from the perspective of the cash lending counterparty.

Reverse stock split A reduction in the number of shares outstanding with a corresponding increase in share price but no change to the company's underlying fundamentals.

Revolving credit agreements The most reliable form of short-term bank borrowing facilities; they are in effect for multiple years (e.g., three to five years) and can have optional medium-term loan features. Also known as *revolvers.*

Rho The change in a given derivative instrument for a given small change in the risk-free interest rate, holding everything else constant. Rho measures the sensitivity of the option to the risk-free interest rate.

Ricardian equivalence An economic theory that implies that it makes no difference whether a government finances a deficit by increasing taxes or issuing debt.

Risk Exposure to uncertainty. The chance of a loss or adverse outcome as a result of an action, inaction, or external event.

Risk averse The assumption that an investor will choose the least risky alternative.

Risk aversion The dislike for risk such that compensation is required in terms of higher expected returns for assuming higher risk.

Risk budgeting The establishment of objectives for individuals, groups, or divisions of an organization that takes into account the allocation of an acceptable level of risk.

Risk exposure The state of being exposed or vulnerable to a risk. The extent to which an organization is sensitive to underlying risks.

Risk governance The top-down process and guidance that directs risk management activities to align with and support the overall enterprise.

Risk management The process of identifying the level of risk an organization wants, measuring the level of risk the organization currently has, taking actions that bring the actual level of risk to the desired level of risk, and monitoring the new actual level of risk so that it continues to be aligned with the desired level of risk.

Risk management framework The infrastructure, process, and analytics needed to support effective risk management in an organization.

Risk premium An extra return expected by investors for bearing some specified risk.

Risk shifting Actions to change the distribution of risk outcomes.

Risk tolerance The level of risk an investor is willing and able to bear.

Risk transfer Strategies implemented to mitigate the impact of specific risks by transferring them to an insurance company.

Risk-neutral pricing A no-arbitrage derivative value established separately from investor views on risk that uses underlying asset volatility and the risk-free rate to calculate the present value of future cash flows.

Risk-neutral probability The computed probability used in binomial option pricing by which the discounted weighted sum of expected values of the underlying equal the current option price. Specifically, this probability is computed using the risk-free rate and assumed up gross return and down gross return of the underlying.

Rollover risk The likelihood that a property owner will lose an existing tenant and forgo income until a new one is found.

Safety-first rules Rules for portfolio selection that focus on the risk that portfolio value or portfolio return will fall below some minimum acceptable level over some time horizon.

Sample correlation coefficient A standardized measure of how two variables in a sample move together. It is the ratio of the sample covariance to the product of the two variables' standard deviations.

Sample covariance A measure of how two variables in a sample move together.

Sample excess kurtosis A sample measure of the degree of a distribution's kurtosis in excess of the normal distribution's kurtosis.

Sample mean The sum of the sample observations divided by the sample size.

Sample skewness A sample measure of the degree of asymmetry of a distribution.

Sample standard deviation The positive square root of the sample variance.

Sample variance The sum of squared deviations around the mean divided by the degrees of freedom.

Sample-size neglect A type of representativeness bias in which financial market participants incorrectly assume that small sample sizes are representative of populations (or "real" data).

Sampling distribution The distribution of all distinct possible values that a statistic can assume when computed from samples of the same size randomly drawn from the same population.

Sampling error The difference between the observed value of a statistic and the estimate resulting from using subsets of the population.

Sampling plan The set of rules used to select a sample.

Saving deposits Bank deposits typically held for non-transactional purposes that often have a stated term.

Scatter plot A two-dimensional graphical plot of paired observations of values for the independent and dependent variables in a simple linear regression.

Scenario analysis A variation of the valuation process combining a base case with alternative outcomes, allowing the incorporation of more favorable or adverse scenarios in the valuation process.

Scraping An automated, large-scale, algorithm-driven approach that retrieves otherwise unstructured data available on websites and creates data in a more structured format.

Seasoned offering An offering in which an issuer sells additional units of a previously issued security.

Secondary bond markets Fixed-income markets comprised of investors trading existing bonds amongst themselves.

Secondary market The market where securities are traded among investors.

Secondary precedence rules Rules that determine how to rank orders placed at the same time.

Secondary sale Sale of a private company stake to another private equity firm or group of financial buyers.

Secondary-stage investments The second stage of development of an infrastructure asset. Secondary-stage investments involve existing infrastructure facilities or fully operational assets that do not require further investment or development over the investment horizon. These assets generate immediate cash flow and returns expected over the investment period.

Sector indexes Indexes that represent and track different economic sectors—such as consumer goods, energy, finance, health care, and technology—on either a national, regional, or global basis.

Secured With collateral; secured debt is backed by the cash flows of the issuer and the collateral as a secondary source of repayment.

Secured loans Loans collateralized by an asset of the borrower.

Security Evidence of equity or debt interest or in an entity or a related right, such as a derivative. Often standardized to conform to security exchange requirements.

Security characteristic line A plot of the excess return of a security on the excess return of the market.

Security market index A portfolio of securities representing a given security market, market segment, or asset class.

Security market line The graphical representation of the CAPM formula, showing the relationship between expected return and beta.

Security selection The process of selecting individual securities; typically, security selection has the objective of generating superior risk-adjusted returns relative to a portfolio's benchmark.

Security tokens Digitizes the ownership rights associated with publicly traded securities.

Segmenting A process of identifying and grouping customers by decision-useful attributes.

Self-attribution bias A bias in which people take too much credit for successes (*self-enhancing*) and assign responsibility to others for failures (*self-protecting*).

Self-control bias A bias in which people fail to act in pursuit of their long-term, overarching goals because of a lack of self-discipline.

Self-investment limits With respect to investment limitations applying to pension plans, restrictions on the percentage of assets that can be invested in securities issued by the pension plan sponsor.

Sell-side firm A broker/dealer that sells securities and provides independent investment research and recommendations to their clients (i.e., buy-side firms).

Semi-strong-form efficient market A market in which security prices reflect all publicly known and available information.

Semiannual bond basis yield Also known as a semiannual bond equivalent yield, it is an annualized interest rate with a periodicity of two.

Semiannual bond equivalent yield Also known as a semiannual bond basis yield, it is an annualized interest rate with a periodicity of two.

Senior debt A debt obligation with higher priority of payment than junior debt obligations.

Senior unsecured debt The highest-ranked debt in an issuer's capital structure which is a general obligation of the borrower.

Seniority Priority of payment of various debt obligations.

Sensitivity analysis A form of analysis used to determine the impact of a change in one or more key variables affecting investment returns or valuation.

Separately managed account (SMA) An investment portfolio managed exclusively for the benefit of an individual or institution.

Service period The time between the grant and vesting dates for an employee share-based award, usually measured in years.

Settlement The closing date at which the counterparties of a derivative contract exchange payment for the underlying as required by the contract.

Settlement price The price determined by an exchange's clearinghouse in the daily settlement of the mark-to-market process. The price reflects an average of the final futures trades of the day.

Share class Types of equity securities that have different voting rights—for example, an issuer may issue Class A shares that carry one vote per share and Class B shares that carry ten votes per share.

Share repurchase A transaction in which a company buys back its own shares. Unlike stock dividends and stock splits, share repurchases use corporate cash.

Shareholder activism A range of actions by a corporation's shareholders that are intended to result in some change in the corporation, typically a change in the board of directors, management, or business strategy.

Shareholder derivative lawsuit A legal action by a shareholder on behalf of a company, not the shareholder personally, against a third party. Often, the third party is a director or manager who the shareholder believes has harmed the company.

Shareholder engagement Shareholder engagement reflects active ownership by investors in which the investor seeks to influence a corporation's decisions on ESG matters, either through dialogue with corporate officers or votes at a shareholder assembly (in the case of equity).

Shareholder theory of corporate governance Espoused by Milton Friedman in his famous 1970 essay, the shareholder theory holds that the objective of a business is to increase profits and shareholder value.

Shareholders Hold a direct equity position in a firm, and both individual persons and financial institutions can be shareholders. The term comes from the individual or investment firm literally having a share of the company. It is most commonly used when talking about the rights and responsibilities that come with being an "owner" of a company, such as stewardship, voting, and engagement. This differentiates it from a situation where an individual or an investment firm lends money or invests in a bond (in other words, they are not an equityholder of a company). Because bond investors do not have a share and are not owners of a company, they cannot vote. Nonetheless, expectations around engagement are increasing for those who invest in loans and bonds as well, making the difference between the two terms more subtle.

Shares Units of ownership interest in a limited company.

Sharpe ratio The ratio of mean excess return to standard deviation (excess return).

Shelf registration A type of public offering that allows the issuer to file a single, all-encompassing offering circular that covers a series of bond issues.

Short A trading position in a **derivative contract** that gains value as the price of the **underlying** moves lower.

Short biased These strategies use quantitative, technical, and fundamental analysis to short overvalued equity securities with limited or no long-side exposures.

Short position A position in an asset or contract in which one has sold an asset one does not own, or in which a right under a contract can be exercised against oneself.

Short selling A transaction in which borrowed securities are sold with the intention to repurchase them at a lower price at a later date and return them to the lender.

Short-run average total cost The curve describing average total cost when some costs are considered fixed.

Shortfall risk The risk that portfolio value or portfolio return will fall below some minimum acceptable level over some time horizon.

Shutdown point The point at which average revenue is equal to the firm's average variable cost.

Side letter A side agreement created between the GP and specific LPs. These agreements exist *outside* the LPA. These agreements provide additional terms and conditions related to the investment agreement.

Signpost An indicator, market level, data piece, or event that signals a risk is becoming more or less likely. An analyst can think of signposts like a traffic light.

Simple linear regression (SLR) An approach for estimating the linear relationship between a dependent variable and a single independent variable by minimizing the sum of the squared deviations between the fitted line and the observed values.

Simple random sample A subset of a larger population created in such a way that each element of the population has an equal probability of being selected to the subset.

Simple random sampling The procedure of drawing a sample to satisfy the definition of a simple random sample.

Simple yield The sum of the coupon payments plus the straight-line amortized share of the gain or loss divided by the bond's flat price. Simple yields are used mostly to quote JGBs.

Simulation A technique for exploring how a target variable (e.g. portfolio returns) would perform in a hypothetical environment specified by the user, rather than a historical setting.

Simulation trial A complete pass through the steps of a simulation.

Single-price auction A debt securities auction in which all bidders pay the same price.

Sinking fund Provisions that reduce the credit risk of a bond issue by requiring the issuer to retire a portion of the bond's principal outstanding each year.

Situational influences External factors, such as environmental or cultural elements, that shape our behavior.

Skewed Not symmetrical.

Skewness A quantitative measure of skew (lack of symmetry); a synonym of skew. It is computed as the average cubed deviation from the mean standardized by dividing by the standard deviation cubed.

Slope coefficient The change in the estimated value of the dependent variable for a one-unit change in the value of the independent variable.

Small country A country that is a price taker in the world market for a product and cannot influence the world market price.

Smart beta Involves the use of simple, transparent, rules-based strategies as a basis for investment decisions.

Smart contracts Computer programs that are designed to self-execute on the basis of pre-specified terms and conditions agreed to by parties to a contract.

Social infrastructure investments A category of infrastructure investments that are directed toward human activities and include such assets as educational, health care, social housing, and correctional facilities, with the focus on providing, operating, and maintaining the asset infrastructure.

Soft commodities Standardized agricultural products, such as cattle and corn, with markets often involving the physical delivery of the underlying upon settlement.

Soft hurdle rate Hurdle rate where the fee is calculated on the entire return when the hurdle is exceeded. With a soft hurdle, GPs are able to catch up performance fees once the hurdle threshold is exceeded.

Soft power A means of influencing another country's decisions without force or coercion. Soft power can be built over time through actions, such as cultural programs, advertisement, travel grants, and university exchange.

Soft-bullet covered bonds Delay the bond default and payment acceleration of bond cash flows until a new final maturity date, which is usually up to a year after the original maturity date.

Solvency Refers to the condition in which firm value exceeds the face value of debt used to finance the firm's assets.

Solvency ratios Ratios that measure a company's ability to meet its long-term obligations.

Solvency risk The risk that an organization does not survive or succeed because it runs out of cash, even though it might otherwise be solvent.

Sophisticated investors Individuals or entities that are permitted in a jurisdiction to trade unregistered or, generally, less regulated securities, including shares of privately held companies; also called *accredited investors*.

Sovereign immunity A principle that limits legal recourse of lenders from forcing a sovereign borrower to declare bankruptcy or liquidate its assets to settle debt claims.

Spearman rank correlation coefficient A measure of correlation applied to ranked data.

Special dividend A dividend paid by a company that does not pay dividends on a regular schedule, or a dividend that supplements regular cash dividends with an extra payment.

Special purpose acquisition company A "blank check" company that exists solely for the purpose of acquiring an unspecified private company within a predetermined period or return capital to investors.

Special purpose entity (SPE) Also referred to as a special purpose vehicle (SPV), this legal entity is created for a specific economic purpose. In the case of a project SPV, the entity's sole purpose is to facilitate the construction, operation, and financing of an infrastructure asset over its contractual life.

Special purpose vehicle See *special purpose entity*.

Special situations An area of private capital investment which targets return by investing in stressed, distressed, or event-driven opportunities.

Split ratings Complex risks viewed very differently by rating agencies

Sponsored A type of depository receipt in which the foreign company whose shares are held by the depository has a direct involvement in the issuance of the receipts.

Spot curve Yields-to-maturity on a series of default-risk-free zero-coupon bonds.

Spot markets Markets in which specific assets are exchanged at current prices. Spot markets are often referred to as **cash markets.**

Spot prices The current prices prevailing in **spot markets**.

Spot rates Yields-to-maturity on default-risk-free zero-coupon bonds.

Spread The difference in yield-to-maturity between a bond and that of a another bond.

Spread risk Bond price risk arising from changes in the yield spread on credit-risky bonds; reflects changes in the market's assessment and/or pricing of credit migration (or downgrade) risk and market liquidity risk.

Spurious correlation Refers to: 1) correlation between two variables that reflects chance relationships in a particular dataset; 2) correlation induced by a calculation that mixes each of two variables with a third variable; and 3) correlation between two variables arising not from a direct relation between them but from their relation to a third variable.

Stablecoin A cryptocurrency that aims to maintain a stable value relative to a specified asset or to a pool or basket of assets.

Stackelberg model A prominent model of strategic decision making in which firms are assumed to make their decisions sequentially.

Staggered board A structure of board elections in which only part of the board is elected simultaneously—for example, only one-third of the board may be up for election each year, so the board can be replaced over three years, not in one year if all seats were elected annually. This structure fosters greater continuity of board members but is an obstacle for shareholders seeking to effect change.

Stakeholder theory of corporate governance An expansion of the shareholder theory of corporate governance under which the objective of a business is to maximize value for, and balance the interests of, a broad group of stakeholders, including shareholders, employees, society, and the non-human environment.

Stakeholders Any party with an interest, financial or non-financial, in an entity or its actions.

Standard deviation The positive square root of the variance; a measure of dispersion in the same units as the original data.

Standard error of the estimate A measure of the distance between the observed values of the dependent variable and those predicted from the estimated regression. The smaller this value, the better the fit of the model. Also known as the standard error of the regression and the root mean square error.

Standard error of the forecast Used to provide an interval estimate around the estimated regression line. It is necessary because the regression line does not describe the relationship between the dependent and independent variables perfectly.

Standard error of the slope coefficient Calculated for simple linear regression by dividing the standard error of the estimate by the square root of the variation of the independent variable.

Standardization The process of creating protocols for the production, sale, transport, or use of a product or service. Standardization occurs when relevant parties agree to follow these protocols together. It helps support expanded economic and financial activities, such as trade and capital flows that support higher economic growth and standards of living, across borders.

Standards of conduct Behaviors required by a group; established benchmarks that clarify or enhance a group's code of ethics.

Standing limit orders A limit order at a price below market and which therefore is waiting to trade.

State actors Typically national governments, political organizations, or country leaders that exert authority over a country's national security and resources. The South African President, Sultan of Brunei, Malaysia's Parliament, and the British Prime Minister are all examples of state actors.

Statement of cash flows A financial statement that details the movement of cash over a period. The statement is classified into operating, investing, and financing activities.

Static trade-off theory of capital structure A theory pertaining to a company's optimal capital structure; the optimal level of debt is found at the point where additional debt would cause the costs of financial distress to increase by a greater amount than the benefit of the additional tax shield.

Statistically significant A result indicating that the null hypothesis can be rejected; with reference to an estimated regression coefficient, frequently understood to mean a result indicating that the corresponding population regression coefficient is different from zero.

Status quo bias An emotional bias in which people do nothing (i.e., maintain the status quo) instead of making a change.

Statutory voting A common method of voting where each share represents one vote.

Step-up bonds Bonds for which the coupon, be it fixed or floating, increases by specified margins at specified dates.

Stock dividend A type of dividend in which a company distributes additional shares of its common stock to shareholders instead of cash.

Stock exchange An exchange in which equity securities are traded. See *exchanges*.

Stock split An increase in the number of shares outstanding with a consequent decrease in share price, but no change to the company's underlying fundamentals.

Stockholder overhang The downward pressure on the share price of stock as large blocks of shares are being sold on the open market.

Stop order An order in which a trader has specified a stop price condition. Also called *stop-loss order*.

Stop-loss order See *stop order*.

Stranded assets A resource that is no longer economically valuable owing to changes in demand, regulations, or availability of substitutes—for example, a newly discovered oil well that will not be brought into production.

Strategic asset allocation A long-term strategy that establishes target allocations for various asset classes and aims to optimize the balance between risk and reward by diversifying investments.

Stratified random sampling A procedure that first divides a population into subpopulations (strata) based on classification criteria and then randomly draws samples from each stratum in sizes proportional to that of each stratum in the population.

Street convention For yield measures on fixed-income instruments that assume payments are made on scheduled dates and ignore weekends and holidays.

Stress testing A specific type of scenario analysis that estimates losses in rare and extremely unfavorable combinations of events or scenarios.

Strong-form efficient market A market in which security prices reflect all public and private information.

Structural budget deficit Also known as the cyclically adjusted budget deficit. The deficit that would exist if the economy was at full employment (or full potential output).

Structural subordination Refers to the positioning of debt, which is issued by a legal entity, typically a holding company, which is separate and therefore one step removed from an operating company, which holds assets pledged under a security agreement to senior secured debtholders.

Structured notes A broad category of securities that incorporate the features of debt instruments and one or more embedded derivatives designed to achieve a particular issuer or investor objective.

Subordinated debt A class of unsecured debt that ranks below a firm's senior unsecured obligations.

Subordination A form of internal credit enhancement that relies on creating more than one bond tranche and ordering the claim priorities for ownership or interest in an asset between the tranches. The ordering of the claim priorities is called a senior/subordinated structure, where the tranches of highest seniority are called senior, followed by subordinated or junior tranches. Also called **credit tranching**.

Subprime loans Lending to borrowers with lower credit quality, high DTI, and/or are loans with higher LTV, and include loans that are secured by second liens otherwise subordinated to other loans.

Sum of squares error (SSE) A measure of the total deviation between observed and estimated values of the dependent variable. It is calculated by subtracting each estimated value $\hat{Y}_i$ from its corresponding observed value Y_i, squaring each of these differences, and then summing all of these squared differences.

Sum of squares regression (SSR) A measure of the explained variation in the dependent variable, calculated as the sum of the squared differences between the predicted value of the dependent variable, Y ^_i, based on the estimated regression line, and the mean of the dependent variable, $\bar{Y}$.

Sum of squares total (SST) A measure of the total variation in the dependent variable in a simple linear regression. It is calculated by subtracting the mean of the observed values $\bar{Y}$ from each of the observed values Y_i, squaring each of these differences, and then summing all of these squared differences.

Sunk costs A cost that has already been incurred.

Supervised learning A type of machine learning in which the system attempts to learn to model relationships based on labeled training data.

Supervisory board In some jurisdictions, a corporation's board of directors is formally composed of a supervisory board and a management board. The supervisory board appoints and oversees the management board and often includes representatives of employees and other non-shareholder stakeholders.

Supply chain The sequence of processes involved in the creation and delivery of a physical product to the end customer, both within and external to a firm, regardless of whether those steps are performed by a single firm.

Supply shock A typically unexpected disturbance to supply.

Survivorship bias Relates to the inclusion of only current investment funds in a database. As such, the returns of funds that are no longer available in the marketplace (have been liquidated) are excluded from the database. Also see *backfill bias*.

Swap A firm commitment involving a periodic exchange of cash flows.

Swap contract An agreement between two parties to exchange a series of future cash flows.

Swap execution facility (SEF) A swap trading platform accessed by multiple **dealers**.

Swap rate The fixed rate to be paid by the fixed-rate payer specified in a swap contract.

Syndicate A group of lenders, typically made up of banks.

Synthetic protective put The combination of a synthetic long underlying position (i.e., a long forward and risk-free borrowing) and a purchased put on the underlying.

Systematic risk Risk that affects the entire market or economy; it cannot be avoided and is inherent in the overall market. Systematic risk is also known as *non-diversifiable* or *market risk*.

Systematic sampling A procedure of selecting every *k*th member until reaching a sample of the desired size. The sample that results from this procedure should be approximately random.

Systemic risk Refers to risks supervisory authorities believe are likely to have broad impact across the financial market infrastructure and affect a wide swath of market participants.

Tactical asset allocation A proactive strategy that adjusts asset class allocations within a portfolio based on short-term market trends, economic conditions, or valuation changes to capitalize on temporary market inefficiencies or opportunities to improve returns or manage risk more effectively.

Target capital structure Management's desired proportions of debt and equity financing, usually stated on a book value basis or indirectly using a financial leverage metric, such as net or gross debt to EBITDA or credit rating.

Target independent A bank's ability to determine the definition of inflation that they target, the rate of inflation that they target, and the horizon over which the target is to be achieved.

Target semideviation A measure of downside risk, calculated as the square root of the average of the squared deviations of observations below the target (also called *target downside deviation*).

Tariffs Taxes that a government levies on imported goods.

Tax base The amount at which an asset or liability is valued for tax purposes.

Tax expense An aggregate of an entity's income tax payable (or recoverable in the case of a tax benefit) and any changes in deferred tax assets and liabilities. It is essentially the income tax payable or recoverable if these had been determined based on accounting profit rather than taxable income.

Taxable income The portion of an entity's income that is subject to income taxes under the tax laws of its jurisdiction.

Taxable temporary differences Temporary differences that result in a taxable amount in a future period when determining the taxable profit as the balance sheet item is recovered or settled.

Technical analysis A form of security analysis that uses price and volume data, often displayed graphically, in decision making.

Tender offer A solicitation by a current or prospective shareholder to other shareholders to acquire a substantial percentage, including 100%, of shares at a specified price. This action is usually undertaken by a potential acquirer whose bid was rejected by the issuer's board of directors, prompting the potential acquirer to appeal directly to shareholders.

Tenor Remaining time-to-maturity for a fixed-income instrument.

Term repos Repos with a maturity longer than one day.

Term structure of interest rates Also known as the maturity structure of interest rates, refers to the difference in interest rates or benchmark yields by time-to-maturity.

Terminal stock value The expected value of a share at the end of the investment horizon—in effect, the expected selling price. Also called *terminal value*.

Terminal value The expected value of a share at the end of the investment horizon—in effect, the expected selling price.

Test of the mean of the differences A statistical test for differences based on paired observations drawn from samples that are dependent on each other.

Text analytics Involves the use of computer programs to analyze and derive meaning typically from large, unstructured text- or voice-based datasets, such as company filings, written reports, quarterly earnings calls, social media, email, internet postings, and surveys.

Thematic risks Known risks that evolve and expand over a period of time. Climate change, pattern migration, the rise of populist forces, and the ongoing threat of terrorism fall into this category.

Thin-tailed Describes a distribution that has relatively less weight in the tails than the normal distribution (also called platykurtic).

Tiered pricing A pricing approach that charges different prices to different buyers, commonly based on volume purchased.

Timberland investment management organizations Entities that support institutional investors by managing their investments in timberland by analyzing and acquiring suitable timberland holdings.

Time tranching Structure of a securitization that allows for the redistribution of "prepayment risk" among bond classes by creating bond classes of different expected maturities.

Time value The difference between an option's premium and its intrinsic value.

Time value decay The process by which the time value of an option declines toward zero as the option's expiration date is approached.

Time-weighted rate of return The compound rate of growth of one unit of currency invested in a portfolio during a stated measurement period; a measure of investment performance that is not sensitive to the timing and amount of withdrawals or additions to the portfolio.

Tokenization The process of representing ownership rights to physical assets on a blockchain or distributed ledger.

Top-down analysis An investment selection approach that begins with consideration of macroeconomic conditions and then evaluates markets and industries based upon such conditions.

Total probability rule for expected value A rule explaining the expected value of a random variable in terms of expected values of the random variable conditional on mutually exclusive and exhaustive scenarios.

Total return Measures the price appreciation, or percentage change in price of the securities in an index or portfolio, plus any income received over the period.

Total return index An index that reflects the price appreciation or percentage change in price of the constituent securities plus any income received since inception.

Total working capital The difference between current assets and current liabilities.

Tracking error The standard deviation of the differences between a portfolio's returns and its benchmark's returns; a synonym of active risk.

Tracking risk The standard deviation of the differences between a portfolio's returns and its benchmarks returns. Also called *tracking error.*

Trade creation When regional integration results in the replacement of higher cost domestic production by lower cost imports from other members.

Trade diversion When regional integration results in lower-cost imports from non-member countries being replaced with higher-cost imports from members.

Trade sale A portion or division of a private company sold via either direct sale or auction to a strategic buyer interested in increasing the scale and scope of an existing business.

Trade settlement date The date when the buyer and seller transfer consideration and securities.

Traditional investment markets Markets for traditional investments, which include all publicly traded debts and equities and shares in pooled investment vehicles that hold publicly traded debts and/or equities.

Tranches A grouping of securities within an issue with characteristics that vary from other tranches, such as different credit quality and seniority.

Transfer payments Welfare payments made through the social security system that exist to provide a basic minimum level of income for low-income households.

Transition risks Economic and financial losses from the transition to a lower-carbon economy in response to climate change—for example, the abandonment of an oil well that is no longer economical.

Treasury Inflation-Protected Securities (TIPS) US Treasury bonds with a principal that is adjusted for changes in the Consumer Price Index. TIPS are issued in 5-, 10-, and 30-year maturities.

Treynor ratio A measure of risk-adjusted performance that relates a portfolio's returns in excess of the risk-free rate to a portfolio's beta.

Trimmed mean A mean computed after excluding a stated small percentage of the lowest and highest observations.

Triparty repo A repurchase agreement in which the transacting parties agree to use a third-party agent that provides access to a larger collateral pool and multiple counterparties, as well as valuation and safekeeping of assets.

True yield Measures on fixed-income instruments use actual payment dates, accounting for weekends and holidays. The true yield on an instrument is always lower than the street convention yield.

Turn-of-the-year effect Calendar anomaly that stock market returns in January are significantly higher compared to the rest of the months of the year, with most of the abnormal returns reported during the first five trading days in January.

Two-fund separation theorem The theory that all investors regardless of taste, risk preferences, and initial wealth will hold a combination of two portfolios or funds: a risk-free asset and an optimal portfolio of risky assets.

Two-way table A table of the frequency distribution of observations classified on the basis of two discrete variables. Also known as *Contingency table.*

Two-week repo rate The interest rate on a two-week repurchase agreement; may be used as a policy rate by a central bank.

Type I error The error of rejecting a true null hypothesis; a false positive.

Type II error The error of not rejecting a false null hypothesis; false negative.

Uncommitted lines of credit Sources of bank credit that a bank can refuse to honor. Uncommitted credit lines are made up to a certain principal amount for a pre-determined maximum maturity, charging a market reference rate plus an issuer-specific spread on only the principal outstanding for the period of use.

Underfitted When a machine learning model treats true parameters as if they are noise and is unable to recognize relationships in the training data, making the model more likely to fail to fully discover patterns that underlie the data.

Underlying The asset referred to in a **derivative contract**.

Underwritten offering A type of securities issue mechanism in which the investment bank guarantees the sale of the securities at an offering price that is negotiated with the issuer. Also known as *firm commitment offering.*

Unearned revenue A liability account for money that has been collected for goods or services that have not yet been delivered; payment received in advance of providing a good or service. Also called *deferred revenue* or *deferred income.*

Unimodal A distribution with a single value that is most frequently occurring.

Unit economics The expression of revenues and costs on a per-unit basis.

Unitranche debt A hybrid or blended loan structure combining different tranches of secured and unsecured debt into a single loan with a single, blended interest rate.

Unsecured Without collateral; unsecured debt is backed only by cash flows of the issuer.

Unsponsored A type of depository receipt in which the foreign company whose shares are held by the depository has no involvement in the issuance of the receipts.

Unsupervised learning A type of machine learning in which the system tries to learn the structure of unlabeled data.

Utility tokens Tokens that provide services within a network, such as paying for services and network fees.

Validity instructions Instructions which indicate when the order may be filled.

Value added resellers Businesses that distribute a product and also handle more complex aspects of product installation, customization, service, or support.

Value at risk A money measure of the minimum value of losses expected during a specified time period at a given level of probability.

Value chain The systems and processes in a firm that create value for its customers.

Value proposition The product or service attributes valued by a firm's target customer that lead those customers to prefer that firm's offering.

Value-add real estate strategies Strategies that involve larger-scale redevelopment and repositioning of existing assets and that may allow the investor to earn a higher return compared with core-plus real estate strategies.

Value-based pricing Pricing set primarily by reference to the value of the product or service to customers.

VaR See *value at risk*.

Variance The expected value (the probability-weighted average) of squared deviations from a random variable's expected value.

Variance of a random variable The expected value (the probability-weighted average) of squared deviations from a random variable's expected value.

Variation margin The difference between current margin required and the current collateral price in a repurchase agreement.

Vega A measure of the sensitivity of an option's price to changes in the underlying's volatility.

Velocity The pace at which geopolitical risk impacts an investor portfolio.

Venture capital Private equity investment in a startup or early-stage company involving high risk and a high rate of failure.

Venture capital fund A hedge fund that seeks to buy, optimize, and ultimately sell portfolio companies to generate profits. See *private equity fund*.

Venture debt Private debt funding that provides venture capital backing to start-up or early-stage companies that may be generating little or negative cash flow.

Vest To become unconditionally entitled to.

Vesting date The day that an employee becomes unconditionally entitled to compensation.

Vintage year The year in which a private capital fund makes its first investment.

Volatility The standard deviation of the continuously compounded returns on the underlying asset.

Vote by proxy A mechanism that allows a designated party—such as another shareholder, a shareholder representative, or management—to vote on the shareholder's behalf.

Voting rights The power of shareholders to cast votes in corporate elections for directors and other matters submitted to a shareholder vote.

Warrant Debt feature or security granting the right to purchase additional common equity shares issued by the company at a predetermined price for a given period.

Waterfall structures These represent the distribution order for cash flows and risk to different tranches in a financing structure.

Weak-form efficient market hypothesis The belief that security prices fully reflect all past market data, which refers to all historical price and volume trading information.

Weighted average coupon rate (WAC) Rate calculated for a mortgage pass-through security by weighting the mortgage rate of each mortgage in the pool by the percentage of the outstanding mortgage balance relative to the outstanding amount of all the mortgages in the pool.

Weighted average maturity (WAM) Calculated for a mortgage pass-through security by weighting the remaining number of months to maturity of each mortgage in the pool by the outstanding mortgage balance relative to the outstanding amount of all the mortgages in the pool.

Weighted-average cost of capital (WACC) A weighted average of the after-tax required rates of return on a company's equity, debt, preferred stock, and other long-term financing sources, where the weights are the fraction of each source of financing in the company's current market value or management's target capital structure.

Winsorized mean A mean computed after assigning a stated percentage of the lowest values equal to one specified low value and a stated percentage of the highest values equal to one specified high value.

Write-off/liquidation Refers to a transaction that has not gone well, and the investment is likely to lose value. The private equity firm revises the value of its investment downward or liquidates the portfolio company.

Yield curve A graphical depiction of yields-to-maturity of bonds from the same issuer across maturities.

Yield spread The difference in yield-to-maturity between a bond and that of a another bond.

Yield-to-call An internal rate of return on a fixed-income instrument's cash flows assuming cash flows are received on scheduled dates and the bond is called at a certain call price and date.

Yield-to-maturity Internal rate of return on a fixed-income instrument's cash flows assuming all cash flows are received on their scheduled dates.

Yield-to-worst The lowest among a fixed-income instrument's yields-to-call and yield-to-maturity. A commonly cited yield measure for fixed-rate callable bonds.

Z-spread or zero-volatility spread is a constant yield spread for a bond over a government or swap curve.

Zero-coupon bonds Bonds that do not pay interest during their life. They are issued at a discount to par value and redeemed at par. Also called pure discount bond.